Athletic Administration:
Successful Decision Making, Risk Taking And Problem Solving

Dr. William F. Stier, Jr.

Distinguished Service Professor
Graduate Director — Physical Education and Sport
Director of Sport Management & Athletic Administration
State University of New York — College at Brockport
Brockport, New York

american press
Boston, Massachusetts

Cover Photographs:

Crowd outside stadium. [Courtesy of Durham Bulls, photo by Brian Fleming]

A close play. [Photo by Geoff Anderson, Florida International University]

Red Wings fans lined up. [Courtesy of Rochester Red Wings (New York)]

A caring coach. [Courtesy of Central Michigan University Public Relations]

Injuries can occur. [Courtesy of Washington State University]

Thousands of fans at a basketball game. [Courtesy of Tennessee Sports Information Department]

Quality coaching by Coach Graham W. McNair. [Courtesy of Washington State University]

Dedication

This book is dedicated to my wife, Veronica Ann—for her loving encouragement and unselfish support—without which this book would not have been written. I also wish to dedicate this book to our five children, Mark, Missy, Michael, Patrick and Will III; and, our seven grandchildren, Sàmantha, Katie, Joshua, Mike, Jessica, Jackson, and Dalton.

A special dedication to Colonel (retired) Mark T. Martin, Jr., one of the editors of the Army's *Stars and Stripes* publication during the second world war and a successful businessman and entrepreneur, who was able to prevent, resolve and solve many problematic situations during his 45-year career in business and the armed services.

Acknowledgements

I wish to acknowledge and thank the numerous athletic administrators and coaches who have been most helpful in my own career as an athletic director on the high school, college and university levels. In addition, I wish to thank the numerous institutions, organizations and individuals who provided me with numerous photographs and figures that are used within this book. Without their unselfish and meaningful assistance this book would not have been written.

In addition, I need to acknowledge the significant contributions of my graduate and undergraduate students at the State University of New York, College at Brockport, with whom I field-tested portions of this book during the past three years. I have indeed been blessed with exceptional students in pursuit of their own professional careers within the world of sport management and athletic administration. From my association with these outstanding individuals, I have learned much as a result of their inquiring minds, challenging questions and insightful suggestions.

Finally, I wish to express my sincere appreciation to Ms. Marci Taylor, who served as the supervising editor for this book on behalf of the publisher, American Press, and who provided meaningful suggestions and input in terms of the final version of the book.

Contents

SECTION I
INTRODUCTION TO THE PRINCIPLES, PROCESSES AND STRATEGIES OF PROBLEM SOLVING — 1

1
Fundamental Principles of Problem Solving in Athletic Administration — 3

Chapter Objectives 3

Introduction to Problem Solving for Athletic Administrators 4

Addressing Problems and Meeting Challenges 4

An Overview of Problems and Problem Solving 5

The Process of Problem Solving—An Art and a Science 5

Being a Competent Problem Solver 6

The Abundance of Challenges and Problems within Athletic Circles 7

Problem Solving and the Element of Timeliness 8

Efficiency and Effectiveness in the Problem Solving Process 9

An Essential Element of Effective Problem Solving—
Quality Communication Skills 9

Personal and Professional Consequences of Problem Solving Efforts 12

Dealing with problems via the Crisis Mode 13

Problem Solving Risks Associated with Athletic Administration/Management 14

    Risk of Failure 14

    Operating in the Open—For All to See 14

    With Power Comes Responsibility 15

The Ultimate Power and Awesome Responsibility of Athletic Directors 15

Assumption of Risks and Reactions to Problems and Challenges 16

The Difficulty of Solving Problems 16

Preventing versus Solving Problems 17

A Question of Preventing Problems 17

The Matter of Control and Responsibility 18
    Responsibilities of Athletic Directors 19
    Effort versus Results 19
The Importance of Wise Decision Making 20
The Importance of Standard Operating Procedures,
Policies and Priorities (SOPPPs) 21
    Additional Advantages and Use of the 5P Handbook 21
Making Exceptions to Standard Operating Procedures, Policies and Priorities 22
Problem Solving—A Matter of Timeliness 22
    Efficient Problem Solving Required Effective Time Management 23
    One Example of an Inappropriate Response in Addressing a Potential Problem 24
    Another Example of Inappropriate Timing in Solving problems 24
Conclusion 26
Exercises for Chapter One 27
References 30

2

Problem Solving Processes in Athletic Administration — 33

Chapter Objectives 33
The process of Resolving and Solving Problems 34
    (1) Admitting the Existence of a Problem 34
    (2) Gathering of Information, Facts and Data 35
    (3) Developing the Strategic Action Play (SAP) 36
Problem Solving and Political Realities 39
    The Matter of Extenuating Circumstances 40
    (4) Implementing the Strategic Action Plan (SAP) 40
    (5) The Value of Hindsight—Assessing the Effectiveness
        of the Strategic Action Plan (SAP) 41
    (6) Taking Appropriate Corrective Action
        to Prevent a Reoccurrence of the Problem 42
The Process Versus End Results 42
    The Need to Educate Others in Terms of the Reality of the Situation(s) 43
Solving Problems and Dealing with People 44
Assigning Blame and the Problem Solving Process 46
The Legality of Problem Solving 47
    The Implications of Due Process 48
    Confidentiality and the Problem Solving Process 49
    The Shield of Confidentiality 50
    Confidentiality and the Potential for Embarrassment 50

Problems in Promising Confidentiality 51
Athletic Participation—A Privilege Rather than a Right! 52
The Need for Caring Problem Solvers 52
Being Unbiased and Remaining Objective as a Problem Solver 53
Problem Solving and Decision Making in Light of Ethical Considerations 58
Controversy and the problem Solving Process 60
Conclusion 60
Exercises for Chapter Two 61
References 65

3

Problem Solving Strategies and Tactics in Athletic Administration — 67

Chapter Objectives 67
Addressing the Challenges of problem Solving 68
Timing of One's Decisions and Actions 68
Planned and Anticipatory Management versus Crises Management 71
Reaction versus Proaction 71
Looking ahead to the Future 71
Act Wisely, Appropriately and Decisively—
Practice Effective Damage Control 72
Remaining Politically Astute as an Athletic Administrator and Problem Solver 73
Becoming personally Involved with the Problem Solving Process 75
One Gains Respect the Old Fashion Way—By Working at It 77
Receiving Data and/or Information from Others 78
Appropriate and Timely Decision Making 78
Conclusion 84
Exercises for Chapter Three 85
References 88

4

Strategies for Establishing and Maintaining
Productive Interpersonal Relationships — 91

Chapter Objectives 91
Developing Relationships with Athletes 92
Developing Relationships with Staff 93
Developing Relationships with Advisers 95
Developing Relationships with Family Members 97
Developing Relationships with Higher Administrators and Superiors 98

Developing Relationships with Others 102
Dealing with Adversity—And Surviving 104
    The problem with Blaming Others 106
    Three Strikes and You Are Out 107
The Necessity of Possessing Product Knowledge 108
How to Professional handle Criticism 108
Conclusion 109
Exercises for Chapter Four 110
References 113

SECTION II
THE CASE METHOD AND PROBLEM SOLVING — 115

5
Problem Solving via the Case Study Approach — 117

Chapter Objectives 117
Organization of Cases 118
    (1) Problems with Athletes 118
    (2) Problems with Athletic Coaches 119
    (3) Problems with other Individuals 120
    (4) Problems with Policies, Practices,
Procedures, Priorities and Philosophies 120
    (5) Problems with Controversial Issues 120
    (6) Problems with Special Situations 121
Suggestions for Reviewing Individual Case Studies 121
    Questions for Discussion 121
    The Value of a Strategic Action Plan (SAP) 122
    An Explanation of how the Case Studies are Presented 122
Case Studies are Fictional but Realistic Accounts
Depicting Possible Actual Events and Occurrences 123
    Reality-Based Cases 124
The Benefits of Utilizing the Case Study Method
In Studying Problem Solving in Athletic Administration 124
    The Use of Small Group Discussion in the Case Study Method ... 125
    The Use of the Case Study Method by Individuals 126

Concluding Statements on the Use of the Case Study Method 126
Conclusion 127
Exercises for Chapter Five 127
References 130

6

Problems with Athletes — 131

Chapter Objectives 131
Case #1: The Case of the Athlete Dismissed from the Team 133
Case # 2: The Case of Violence in Sports... 137
Case # 3: The Case of Code of Conduct 141
Case # 4: The Case of Drug Testing for Athletes 145
Case # 5: The Case of Poor Substituting during a Contest 149
Case # 6: The Case of the Athletic Team Boycott 153
Case # 7: The Case of Athletes Pushing for a New Sport 157
Case # 8: The Case of Athletes Demanding More Meal Money for Away Contests 161
Case # 9: The Case of Athletes Damaging Equipment and Facilities 165
Case #10: The Case of the Transportation Problems for Injured Athletes 169
Case #11: The Case of Athletes Dressing Like Slobs....................................... 173
Case #12: The Case of the Super Star's Recruitment for College........................ 177
Case #13: The Case of the Player's Eligibility 181
Case #14: The Case of the Questionable Conditioning of Athletes 186
Case #15: The Case of Athletes Demanding a Coach Be Fired 189

7

Problems with Athletic Coaches — 193

Chapter Objectives 193
Case #16: The Case of the Uninvolved Coach 195
Case #17: The Case of the Future of the Would-be Coach................................. 199
Case #18: The Case of the Two Coaches Who Worked Closely Together 203
Case #19: The Case of Remembering the Past 207
Case #20: The First-Time Losing Coach 211
Case #21: The Very Unhappy Coach 215
Case #22: The Case of Handling the Disorganized Coach 219
Case #23: The Case of the Coach's Inappropriate Appearance 223
Case #24: The Case of the Expectations of Coaches.. 227
Case #25: The Case of the Negative Motivation by the Coach 231

Case #26: The Case of Dealing with an Overly Conservative Coach 235
Case #27: The Case of the Coach Who Couldn't Follow Directions 239
Case #28: The Case of the Inconsiderate and Unthinking Coach 243
Case #29: The Case of the altered purchase Order 247
Case #30: The Case of the Person Who Quits Coaching but Remains as a Teacher 251

8

Problems with other Individuals — 255

Chapter Objectives 255
Case #31: The Case of the Athletic Directing
        Making Important Decisions too Quickly 257
Case #32: The Case of the Impolite Non-athletic Administrator 261
Case #33: The Case of the Would-Be head Coach 265
Case #34: The Case of Crisis Management 269
Case #35: The Case of the Athletic Director Faced with the Tough Decision 273
Case #36: The Case of the Broken-down Coach 277
Case #37: The Case of the Problem between the Coach and the Custodian 281
Case #38: The Case of Impressing the New Boss 285
Case #39: The Case of the Forgetful Athletic Director 289
Case #40: The Case of Influential Fundraising Contacts 293
Case #41: The Case of the Problem with the Media 297
Case #42: The Case of the Indispensable Athletic Director 301
Case #43: TheCase of the Athletic Director with the Difficult Superior/Boss 305
Case #44: The Case of the Sloppily Made newsletter 309
Case #45: The Case of the Improper Delegation 313

9

Problems with Controversial Issues — 317

Chapter Objectives 317
Case #46: The Case of the Mime Beautiful 319
Case #47: The Case of the promotion of the Would-be Big Time Program 323
Case #48: The Case of the Potential Rival and a new Boss 327
Case #49: The Case of the Impending Marriage 331
Case #50: The Case of the Rent-a-Coach Problem 335
Case #51: The Case of the Partying Coach 339
Case #52: The Case of the Unfair Treatment Charge 343
Case #53: The Case of the Reluctant Complainr 347
Case #54: The Case of Negative Atmosphere 351
Case #55: The Case of an Ad Administering by Walking Around (ABWA) 355

Case #56: The Case of the Secret Budget Process 359
Case #57: The Case of the Missing Equipment and Supplies 363
Case #58: The Case of the Sneaky Title IX Compliance 367
Case #59: The Case of the Inefficient Concession Stand 371
Case #60: The Case of Too Many Fundraising projects 375

10

Problems with Policies, Practices, Procedures, Priorities and Philosophies — 379

Chapter Objectives 379
Case #61: The Case of Having to Pass to Play 381
Case #62: The Case of the Problematic Vacation Policies 385
Case #63: The Case of the Questionable Travel Squad 389
Case #64: Applying for an Administrative Position 393
Case #65: The Case Involving the Coach's Little Kids 397
Case #66: The Case of Having to Pay to Play 401
Case #67: The Case of Accountability in Evaluating Coaches 405
Case #68: The Case of the Awards Ceremony 409
Case #69: The Case of the part-time Coach being Bumped by a Full-time Teacher 413
Case #70: The Case of the Athletic Shoe Purchase 417
Case #71: The Case of Inadequate Crowd Control 421
Case #72: The Case of the Problematic Departmental Handbook 425
Case #73: The Case of the Request for the Cheerleading Squad
    To Accompany the Basketball Team on the Team Bus 429
Case #74: The Case of Planning for the Athletic Banquet 433
Case #75: The Case of Creating Corporate Sponsorship 437

11

Problems with Special Situations — 441

Chapter Objectives 441
Case #76: The Case of the Lack of Goal Setting 443
Case #77: The Case of the New Publicity Director 447
Case #78: The Case of the Confused Would-be Athletic Coach 451
Case #79: The Case of the Glass Ceiling 455
Case #80: The Case of the Well-meaning Mentor 459
Case #81: The Case of the Coach being Told How to Do His Job 463
Case #82: The Case of the Athletic Director Hiding in His Office 467
Case #83: The Case of the Messy Athletic Director 471

Case #84: The Case of Problems Associated with Renting a Facility 475

Case #85: The Case of the Fiscal Irresponsibility 479

Case #86: The Case of the Unsafe practice Site 483

Case #87: The Case of the Upgrade to the Facility 487

Case #88: The Case of the Unkempt Facilities.. 491

Case #89: The Case of the Poorly Organized Inventory Process 495

Case #90: The Case of the Poorly Organized Game Promotion 499

Appendix A
A Partial List of Suggested Publications, Journals
and Magazines and Selected Journal Articles 503

Appendix B
Index 509

Preface

INTRODUCTION

This book, written by a former successful collegiate/university and high school athletic director, is designed to help current and future athletic administrators deal with the myriad of difficulties, challenges and problems that confront them in the performance of their jobs. This is a book about problems, specifically, how to recognize problems, how to avoid them, and how to resolve them, all within a school-based, competitive athletic setting. It is about having a global vision rather than tunnel vision. It is also about athletic administrators surviving problematic and stressful situations. Portions of the first five chapters have been adapted from an earlier work by the author, a book devoted to coaches and the problem solving challenges faced by mentors of amateur, competitive sports (Stier, 1999).

Everyone loves sports and competition.
[Courtesy of University of Southern California Sports Information]

This book was written specifically for use in collegiate courses dealing with the preparation of athletic administrators and sport managers. It is appropriate for future and current athletic directors, as well as other athletic/sport administrators, at all levels of amateur sport competition. The book can also be most helpful when used as an addendum in the "SPORT MANAGEMENT ADMINISTRATION" classes since this text deals specifically with teaching would-be athletic managers/administrators how to be successful as athletic administrators, especially in terms of solving the multitude of problems that face most administrators within the world of amateur, competitive sports.

Figure 1. Tunnel vision is a severe handicap in terms of problem solving

Most of the problem solving principles, strategies and tactics suggested within this book are applicable for all levels of amateur sport competition, i.e., youth sports, junior and senior high school levels, as well as the collegiate or university scene. It is up to the reader to apply and adapt the general principles and strategies that are presented throughout this book to one's own individual situation and circumstances (Stier, 1999, p. vii).

SOURCES OF PROBLEMS FOR ATHLETIC ADMINISTRATORS

Difficulties, challenges and problems in athletics seemingly occur in almost every program, almost on a daily basis. This is unfortunate but it is also reality. These challenges and problems can involve any number of different individuals, constituencies and groups including, but not limited to, coaches, spouses, athletic and central school administrators, athletes, teachers, staff, parents, volunteers, boosters, fans, news media, as well as members of the community (the general public). Successfully handling of such difficulties demands not only a significant amount of time and effort on behalf of athletic administrators, but also necessitates a great deal of patience, as well as appropriate and timely decision making.

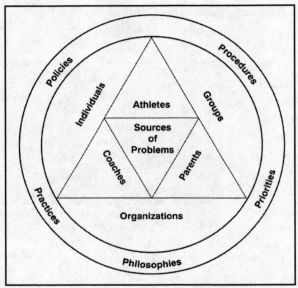

Figure 2. Sources of problems and challenges as well as opportunities

The sample problems and challenges presented within this book are unique and are taken from all aspects of individual and team competitive sports, both on and off the so-called practice and/or playing fields—within a school-based, competitive athletic program. Some problems are associated with actions (or inactions) by individuals. Some problems arise because of contrasting philosophies and priorities of organizations, individuals and/or groups. Other difficulties are team centered. And still others emanate from the policies, procedures, practices, priorities and philosophy(ies) of the school and/or athletic department and related entities, figure #2 (Stier, 1999, p. viii)

If athletic administrators are to enjoy success in this century, they must be able to appropriately handle a wide variety of problems and challenges, in a timely and appropriate manner, regardless of their source. Problems happen and only appropriated educated, competent, professional and skilled athletic administrators are going to find success in their roles as sport managers over the long haul.

UNIQUE ELEMENTS OF THIS BOOK

This book has *seven* separate but nevertheless related features or components that make it somewhat unique in terms of athletic administration and sport management books. The *first* component is the inclusion of **general information** relating to the process of problem solving per se as, including the tasks associated with strategic as well as long range planning for the prevention and resolution of problems and challenges.

Second, at the beginning of each chapter are listed the **chapter's objectives.** These are statements that summarize what you, the reader, should be able to do after reading that chapter. And, at the conclusion of each of the first five chapters are **exercises** that contain questions pertaining to each chapter, which can be answered in the spaces provided.

Third, **eighty-seven fundamental principles** are presented that speak specifically to the tasks and responsibilities generally associated with problem solving by athletic administrators, with various levels of responsibility. These fundamental principles are presented in chapters one and two as Problem Solving Principles (PSPs).

The *fourth* feature that makes this book unique is the inclusion, in chapters three and four, of **seventy–four specific survival strategies and tactics** relating to the problem solving process. These are specific survival strategies that are associated with sound managerial decisions, actions and practices. These survival strategies/tactics illustrate practical recommendations, suggestions and schemes based upon sound problem solving principles and concepts as well as the author's extensive experience as an athletic director on the junior high, high school and college/university levels. These survival strategies and tactics can also provide appropriate and timely guidance, counsel, cautions, and admonishments for the practitioner in terms real life decision-making and specific actions that should or should not be taken. All three of these unique features are presented within Section I.

Sports are a worldwide phenomenon
[Courtesy of Indiana University Athletics]

Section II contains three additional unique elements. In chapter five, the *fifth* distinctive feature of this book is presented and centers around **15 case study tenets**. Each tenet highlights an advantage of using the case study method to develop insight into the problem solving strategies and principles associated with administering athletic departments/programs. Note also that chapter five introduces the case study approach to gaining the knowledge and mastering the skills associated with successful problem solving by athletic administrators.

The *sixth* unique aspect of this book is the **inclusion of 90 unique case studies** (chapters six through eleven). Each case study is based upon a realistic problem or challenge prevalent in today's school-based athletic programs. Each of these case studies provides critical thinking opportunities for the reader in terms of athletic administration.

In addition, Section II includes the *seventh* and final special feature of this book, the inclusion of a series of questions (***Questions for Discussion***) that are included at the end of each case study. These series of questions are presented in an effort to assist the reader in assessing the specifics of each case and evaluating various courses of action (different scenarios) in light of the circumstances and situations presented. Answering these questions can also aid the reader in planning and creating an individual Strategic Action Plan (SAP) for each of the case studies. Such strategic action plans can be instrumental in providing for timely and appropriate resolutions for the sometimes perilous, contentious and litigious issues facing the athletic director.

BENEFITS FOR READERS

Current as well as would-be school-based athletic administrators, at all levels, will find the content and organization of this book helpful in their efforts to successfully meet the challenges and resolve many of the problems posed by the ever increasing complexity of amateur athletic competition in this country. *The specific benefits that can be derived from reading this book and working through the cases studies are threefold. First of all*, readers will be able to develop a better understanding of the principles and concepts behind the processes and tasks associated with problem solving (within the athletic department).

Women's sports participation has exploded since 1972.

Second, readers should be better able to make appropriate and timely decisions in terms of preventing and resolving a wide range of difficulties and challenges associated with the controversial, paradoxical and enigmatic world of school sports, both today and in the future. This is possible through the review of the various case studies. And, *finally*, readers will also be able to gain valuable experience and practice in establishing various strategic action plans (SAPs), under a variety of different scenarios, by means of working through the unique set of questions that accompany each case study.

Since school sports exist now and in the future as wholesome and productive learning environments for youngsters of all ages, it is imperative that there be available competent sport administrators, managers and leaders—skilled and experienced in preventing and resolving problems. Such administrators need to be intimately involved in the planning, implementation, management and evaluation of quality sports programs. Today, problem solving is a necessary part of the repertoire or arsenal of any successful athletic administrator. *Helping those given the responsibility for overseeing and managing athletic departments/ programs, at all levels of competitive school-based athletic programs, to develop competencies in the art and the science of problem solving, is what this book is all about* (Stier, 1999, p. xi).

REFERENCES

Stier, W.F., Jr. (1999). *Problem solving for coaches*. Boston: American Press.

SECTION I

Introduction to the Principles, Processes and Strategies of Problem Solving

Fundamental Principles of Problem Solving in Athletic Administration

CHAPTER OBJECTIVES

After reading this chapter you will be able to:

- Identify sources of problems facing athletic administrators
- Understand the use of problem solving principles in administering athletic programs
- Conceptualize problem solving as a *table with five legs*

- Differentiate between the "art" and "science" of problem solving
- Articulate that successful problem solvers are made rather than born
- Justify the need for attending professional conferences as an athletic administrator
- Be cognizant that problems will almost invariably happen within athletic programs

Joy of participation.
[Courtesy of Washington State University]

- Appreciate that problems can also be opportunities for athletic administrators
- Conceptualize the important elements of the communication process
- Outline various listening rules associated with communication
- Be familiar with the risks associated with problem solving
- Describe successful decision making strategies involved in problem solving
- Recognize the essential elements of the *5P handbook* in problem solving
- Provide examples of appropriate time management strategies
- Realize the importance of credibility when solving administrative problems

INTRODUCTION TO PROBLEM SOLVING
FOR ATHLETIC ADMINISTRATORS

Athletic administrators are often expected to assume a variety of very different roles in the performance of their duties. They are frequently expected to become authority figures for coaches, parents, athletes as well as a host of other individuals, both inside and outside of the school setting. Additionally, they frequently become risk takers, decision makers, facilitators, leaders, delegators, motivators, disciplinarians, counselors, substitute parents, teachers, recruiters, as well as mediators and arbitrators.

One of the most important and all encompassing role that any athletic administrator or sport manager can assume, at any level, is that of problem solver (Stier, 1993). Without the ability and willingness to solve, on a timely basis and in an appropriate manner, the multitude of problems, difficulties, and challenges that inevitably arise in any sport organization or entity—sport personnel fall far short of the minimum level of competency that is expected of them. Staffo (2001, p. 37) recommends that " . . . nothing be left to chance or taken for granted. Often it's the seemingly obvious tasks that are overlooked, and problems can result."

ADDRESSING PROBLEMS AND MEETING CHALLENGES

It is essential for those individuals who serve as administrators or managers within school-based athletic programs, at all levels, when dealing with problems facing the administration of competitive amateur sports, to develop insight and skills in recognizing and dealing appropriately and timely with potential as well as with actual problems. Problem solving involves dealing successfully with people, individually and in groups—both large and small. Wilson (2001, p. 22) states: "One of the first things an athletic director must do when a complaint arises is to understand his or her role in the process."

PROBLEM SOLVING PRINCIPLE #1:   *Problem solving involves dealing successfully with all types of people, individually and in groups, both large and small.*

There are five distinct tasks that are associated with the process of dealing with problems. *First*, to anticipate possible problems before they arise, as much as is humanly possible. *Second*, to prevent possible problems from occurring or at least reduce their impact upon the program and individuals. *Third*, to resolve difficulties and negative consequences within a reasonable amount of time and with a reasonable expenditure of resources before the so-called problem(s) becomes a significant nuisance or worse, a hindrance to one's sports program and activities. *Fourth*, to implement damage control in terms of negating or mitigating the negative consequences emanating from the problem itself. And, *lastly*, to preclude the reoccurrence of such (or similar) challenges or problems in the future.

It is possible to conceptualize the process of problem solving as a table with five legs, figure #1.1 (Stier, 1999a, p. 4). The tabletop itself represents the problem(s) or challenge(s) facing the sport organization or its programs and activities. Each of the five legs represent the five tasks involved in dealing with the problem. If any of the legs are inadequate in terms of supporting the tabletop or are missing—the table tilts, if not falls. Thus, the difficulty or problem itself becomes exacerbated and the situation is worse than before because of the inability (within an appropriate time frame) to adequately deal with and resolve the problem that has arisen.

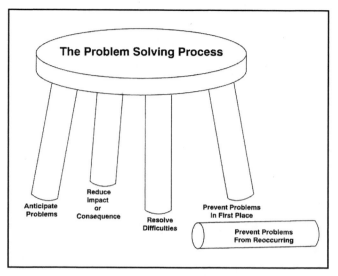

Figure 1.1. The conceptualization of problem solving.

AN OVERVIEW OF PROBLEMS AND PROBLEM SOLVING

Webster's dictionary (1973, p. 917) defines a problem as an intricate unsettled question, raised for inquiry, consideration or solution. Such questioning can often become a source of perplexity, distress, or vexation. A challenge can be thought of as a dispute, a taking exception to the status quo or a calling into question that which is thought to be unjust, invalid, or outmoded. In the real world, problems and challenges can frequently be viewed as threatening and intimidating as well as provocative, stimulating and inciting. Secondary and collegiate athletic directors and other athletic administrators can experience all of the above in the performance of their duties.

THE PROCESS OF PROBLEM SOLVING—AN ART AND A SCIENCE

In today's world of school-based sports programs, problem solving may be considered to be both an art and a science. It is an art because the strategies and tactics that any individual—male or female, athletic director or assistant AD, experienced or inexperienced—seeks to employ in dealing with problems "can be affected and enhanced through the creative and innovative utilization and application of these principles and concepts" (Stier, 1995, p. 38).

However, problem solving may also be considered to be a science. It is a science because there are generally accepted principles, concepts and a body of knowledge underlying and supporting the tasks and processes involved both in solving problems and addressing contentious issues in our society. These foundational principles and concepts hold true and are applicable regardless of the setting in which athletic administrators and sport managers find themselves. Chapters one and two include eighty-seven Problem Solving Principles.

BEING A COMPETENT PROBLEM SOLVER

The question is often asked: Are competent problem solvers made or born? Both antidotal information and scientific research suggest that problem solving can indeed be a learned skill. One way for athletic administrators to acquire the knowledge and to develop the necessary skills and competencies to be a successful problem solver is to combine both formal study with real-life experiences, on the so-called "firing line" of competitive sports (Stier, 1996).

> **PROBLEM SOLVING PRINCIPLE #2:** *Knowledgeable and competent problem solvers are made, not born.*

Problem solving is not easy. Rather, it takes concerted effort and concentrated work to become competent as a problem solver and to remain current with the times. An individual becomes more skilled in problem solving through experience, both successful and unsuccessful. Getting one's nose bloodied, if you will, by living through a problem or challenging situation can be a great learning and teaching experience. There is nothing more authentic than actually living through a confrontational situation—and surviving professionally.

> **PROBLEM SOLVING PRINCIPLE #3:** *One doesn't live long enough to learn only from one's own mistakes—therefore learn from others.*

No individual can learn merely from one's own experience. This would be far too limiting. Rather, one must learn from the experiences, both successes and failures, of others. None of us will live long enough to learn from only our own experiences. We must learn from the experiences (present and past) of others. One way to do this is to observe and learn how others have dealt with and are currently dealing with the challenges of problem solving, that is, how others attempt to prevent problems, resolve difficulties, reduce negative consequences and eliminate their reoccurrence.

> **PROBLEM SOLVING PRINCIPLE #4:** *One must remain current in one's professional reading and attend professional meetings if one is to be a competent problem solver.*

It is important, however, that one not assumes that practical experience is the only way to gain knowledge and develop competency in solving problems. Far from it. In addition to practical experience, it is also important for the would-be problem solver, for the athletic director or athletic administrator, to develop a conceptual understanding of the problem solving process itself, regardless of the competitive level, the setting or the circumstances involved.

This conceptual understanding, this knowledge base, can be obtained from formal study involving (1) actual college course work at the undergraduate and graduate levels, (2) keeping current with one's professional reading (such as this book as well as any number of professional journals and popular magazines and newspapers), and (3) through attendance at appropriate professional conferences and meetings. The ultimate goal for the athletic administrator is to become more enlightened about the whole problem solving (and prevention) process, that is, to develop an appropriate level of understanding, knowledge and skill necessary to be successful as a leader and problem solver within the athletic world. For in the final analysis, the mark of a truly successful leader/administrator is one who can adequately deal with and resolve, if not prevent, problems.

THE ABUNDANCE OF CHALLENGES AND PROBLEMS WITHIN ATHLETIC CIRCLES

> **PROBLEM SOLVING PRINCIPLE #5:** *Problems happen—that is the very nature of the athletic scene.*

Invariably, problems seem to be everywhere in today's complicated society. And the sports world is no exception. In reality, there is certainly no shortage of problems and challenges, both large and small; facing today's modern day sports programs. There is certainly no lack of problems facing school-based athletic programs and the individuals who are associated with them. And there is no end in sight.

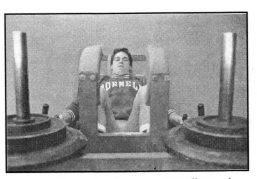
Athletic participation requires effort and dedication. [Courtesy of Cornell Athletics]

To the contrary, it seems that competitive sports, and those who are intimately associated with such activities and programs, will experience not only a greater number of problems but also more severe and complicated problems as time progresses. One of the consequences is that the process of preventing and solving problems and dealing with controversial and divisive issues within the sport matrix is going to be much more difficult, time consuming and taxing (Stier. 2003).

> **PROBLEM SOLVING PRINCIPLE #6:** *Problems and Challenges can also be viewed as professional opportunities.*

To some, the very existence of problems can be viewed as a great professional opportunity, an opportunity to demonstrate one's talents, skills and capabilities in reaction to and handling such problems, difficulties and challenges. The result, if one is successful in dealing with problems, can very well mean professional advancement of one's career.

The concept is simple. If there were not significant and numerous problems facing sports programs, facing schools, programs, athletes, parents, coaches and administrators, then there would be no need for skilled, highly trained athletic administrators and sport managers. However, since there are many difficult challenges facing sports programs and the people associated with them, it is necessary that there be highly trained and experienced problem solvers in leadership positions on the administrative/managerial staff. Not every Tom, Dick and Harry or Mary, Jane and Sue can be successful as a problem solving athletic administrator. It does take skill, it does take competency, it does take effort, and it does take experience to be a competent leader as an athletic administrator.

Thus, the very existence of problems or controversial situations can result in the enhancement of one's career—if these problems and situations can indeed be successfully resolved and/or serious consequences averted. Being recognized as a competent administrator, both in terms of the technical aspects of managing the sport activity, program and/or the department and the ability to prevent and resolve difficulties can do wonders for one's prestige, reputation and career. Solving difficulties in a professional manner can also be personally satisfying and invigorating, which is not an insignificant factor in and of itself.

PROBLEM SOLVING PRINCIPLE #7: *Keep in mind the ultimate goal of administering the athletic program when confronting problems.*

It is imperative that one not lose sight of the ultimate objective regardless of the extent of the problem(s) or the number of problems. Sometimes ADs become so immersed in the process of solving a particular difficulty that they forget about the ongoing or ultimate objective or goal. Yes, solving the problem is important. But so too is the proper operation of the athletic department, its programs and activities. Don't become distracted by the presence of a problem or challenge or the consequences or aftermath to such an extent that one's normal efforts at managing a quality athletic program suffers and the athletic activities are hampered.

PROBLEM SOLVING AND THE ELEMENT OF TIMELINESS

One of the challenges in dealing with controversial issues and problems is that athletic administrators need to understand the process and risks involved in dealing with people, individually and as members of different groups, constituencies and the general public. An important aspect of successful interpersonal relationships is patience.

PROBLEM SOLVING PRINCIPLE #8: *Effective problem solvers must exhibit patience combined with resolve.*

Problems are not solved overnight. Nor are they solved easily, without effort, work and time. Far too often inexperienced ADs act rashly in their attempt to solve problems. One must have patience. On the other hand, it is also necessary to be able to exhibit perseverance. This combination of patience and perseverance enables the athletic administrator to work toward the established objectives while still paying attention to the details, the crossing of the "T"s and the dotting of the "I"s.

EFFICIENCY AND EFFECTIVENESS IN THE PROBLEM SOLVING PROCESS

Frequently, it is not enough merely to be *effective* as a problem solver. In many instances, one must also be *efficient* in the process of resolving or solving the problem and limiting negative consequences. Of course, resolving a problematic situation is very important. But it is equally important to remain cognizant that must one also be capable of efficiently accomplishing the task at hand, that is, solving the problem.

PROBLEM SOLVING PRINCIPLE #9: *Successful problem solvers are both effective and efficient.*

Effectiveness is doing the right job or the correct tasks—whatever the job or tasks might be—that are necessary for the successful resolution of the difficulty or challenge that one faces. Efficiency pertains to how the job or task is done, that is, doing the job right or correctly.

One must always ask oneself (because others invariably will ask): "can the problem solving process be carried out in an efficient manner in terms of time spent as well energy expended and resources utilized?" Athletic directors and other administrators must be both effective and efficient in their efforts to recognize, confront, prevent and/or solve the various problems and challenges that will invariably crop up in the course of their professional and personal activities.

AN ESSENTIAL ELEMENT OF EFFECTIVE PROBLEM SOLVING— QUALITY COMMUNICATION SKILLS

Communication is one of the more important aspects of a well-run athletic department (Goldfine and Pastore, 1994). Since problems involve people (as well as inanimate objects, activities, procedures and policies), those who have the responsibility for resolving problems must be skilled in dealing with people, in recognizing and meeting needs of others, whenever possible. This involves dealing with individuals as well as groups, both large and small. Communication (verbal and non-verbal) skills are absolutely essential for an effective and efficient athletic administrator/problem solver.

PROBLEM SOLVING PRINCIPLE #10: *Effective problem solvers are skilled, effective and efficient communicators.*

It is extremely difficult, if not impossible, to address challenges and resolve problems if one is not adept in a wide range of communication skills, both verbal and non-verbal. Since so many problems involve people it behooves potential problem solvers to be able to relate to and interact with any number of individuals and groups. And, of course, the key to doing so is being able to successfully communicate with others.

Communication involves more than attempting to merely convey a message to another. In many instances it is equally important, if not more important, to be a willing and capable listener. Communication is a bi-modal, two-way process (Stier, 1994; Stier 2003). For communication to take place, there must be a sender of the message as well as a recipient of the message. In addition, there must be an actual message itself, either verbal or non-verbal, communicated through some type of medium. And, of course, the message that is sent, deliberately or accidentally, must be correctly interpreted and internalized by the recipient(s), figure #1.2.

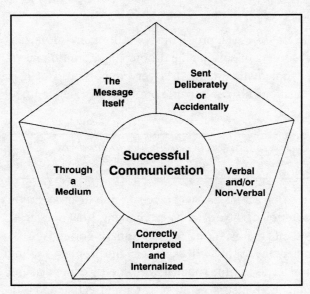

Figure 1.2. Successful communication.

Various listening rules have been suggested by Stier (1999b, August 13) as well as by Touhey (1999). Some of these rules or suggestions include:

1. Take time to stop talking and seek to actually hear what the other person is attempting to say.
2. Always allow the other person to be at ease. Let the person communicate at the person's own pace. Do everything you can to make them relax and feel at ease with you and themselves.
3. Show the individual you earnestly desire to listen to what the person has to say by being enthusiastic. Show a visible interest.
4. Use positive body language to facilitate communication. Let the person know that you understand what the person is attempting to communicate. That is, look at the person, move your head if you understand or agree with the person. If you don't understand, don't hesitate to ask the person for clarification or for more information.
5. Always be respectful to the person attempting to communicate with you. Show that you respect the individual as a person and what the person is attempting to convey by your verbal and body language.

6. Physically look the other person in the eyes when communicating—don't be constantly looking down or away during the conversation.

7. Pay full attention to the speaker and let the person know that you are giving undivided attention to what is being said. Don't be distracted from the communication process. To be able to listen one must focus on what is being communicating. *Stop what you are doing* and listen—and look like you are really listening. Don't do other tasks (multi-tasking) while attempting to listen. Empathize with the other person, especially if the person is telling you something painful, or something you intensely disagree with.

8. Ask questions, a lot of questions, or make comments to indicate that you understand the essence of what is being communicated. Ask the speaker to clarify, to say more, to give an example or explain further.

9. Take a moment to stand in the other person's shoes to look at the situation from that individual's point of view.

10. Remember that the good Lord gave humans two ears, two eyes and only one mouth— try and listen and observe at least twice as often as you speak.

There are numerous obstacles that can hinder or negate meaningful communication attempts (Horine, 1991). Some, but certainly not an exhaustive list of such obstacles include not paying attention or inattentive listening, poor choice of words, different interpretations of words, gestures and actions, different backgrounds of individuals (cultural, religious, social, economic), the existence of prejudices and biases, differences in age and sex, poor timing of the communication attempt, hidden meanings of words or words taken out of context, and interference by others.

> **PROBLEM SOLVING PRINCIPLE #11:** *To be an effective problem solver one must overcome obstacles to communication.*

There are several factors that must be present for accurate and successful communication to take place. *First*, the message must be accurate in its content. *Second*, the message must have clarity, i.e., the meaning must be clear to the sender and the recipient. *Third*, the message itself and the sender of the message must have credibility, it must be believable. *Fourth*, the message must be appropriate for the audience in content and form. *Fifth*, the content of the message must make sense, that is, there should be continuity from one idea or concept to another. *Sixth*, the medium of the message must be consistent, the thoughts and the words or actions must be consistent if the message is to be understood. And, *seventh*, there must be appropriate channels (medium) over which or through the message can be relayed (Jensen, 1988).

> **PROBLEM SOLVING PRINCIPLE #12:** *To be a successful communicator one must be persuasive.*

In today's world of school-based athletic programs, at all levels, there is much more to being a skilled communicator as well as a successful problem solver than merely being able to

*Quality coaching is the secret to
successful athletic programs.
[Courtesy of Washington State University]*

convey messages to others. It also entails being persuasive in convincing others of one's point of view. Thus, an essential element of problem solving is the persuading of others, individuals and groups, to accept a particular point of view and/or to act in a specific way.

To be influential and persuasive with others, in terms of their thinking, their behavior and their motivation, is highly desirable in any problematic situation. Being able to modify the attitude(s), perception(s), and action(s) of others is most helpful in being able to resolve differences of opinions and to motivate others to adopt a belief and to pursue a specific course of action. Such differences of opinions are frequently the basis of many problems.

As a result, successful problem solvers are usually excellent communicators skilled in persuading and convincing others that their best interests and needs will be met by acting in a certain way or by expressing a specific opinion or attitude. Competent problem solvers are adroit at influencing and motivating others.

> **PROBLEM SOLVING PRINCIPLE #13:** *Differences of opinions are frequently the basis of numerous problems.*

PERSONAL AND PROFESSIONAL CONSEQUENCES OF PROBLEM SOLVING EFFORTS

> **PROBLEM SOLVING PRINCIPLE #14:** *Problem solving is not for the lazy or the faint of heart—it can be physically exhausting and mentally draining, even debilitating in some instances.*

No one ever said that problem solving and the attendant activities and efforts are easy. To the contrary, being involved in the process of problem solving is difficult and can be very taxing and stressful—even for the stout of heart. In fact, it can be physically exhausting and mentally draining. And, it can be psychologically debilitating. It can take its toll on even the most stout hearted. It can wear down one's resistance and interfere with one's ability to do one's daily tasks, if one is not careful.

As a result, it is important for those facing problems and potential problems in their daily work, such as Athletic directors, Associate or Assistant ADs, Sport Information Directors (SIDs), Athletic Business Managers, Academic Compliance Officers, Senior Women Administrators (SWAs), Eligibility Coordinators, Athletic Academic Advisers, Home Event Directors, etc., to compensate for this onslaught against their physical, mental and psychological well-being. Part of the strategy of handling this type of pressure involves partaking in some type of *stress management* activity or therapy on a regular basis. Whether this involves proper eating, adequate exercise, meditation, or a portion of each day set aside for oneself ("time out"), the important point is that some method be used to relieve the stress that invariably accompanies problems and problematic situations in the world of sport management and athletic administration.

> **PROBLEM SOLVING PRINCIPLE # 15:**   *Athletic administrators should utilize any of the many methods to relieve the stress that invariably accompanies problems in the athletic scene.*

Problems can all too often become serious distractions and interfere with, and take valuable time from, one's primary responsibilities and tasks. This is one of the major negative consequences that athletic directors and their administrative associates must avoid, if at all possible, when faced with challenges and problems.

There are two perspectives from which to view these distractions. *First,* the problem or conflict itself can be a distraction and a source of concern to others in the organization. *Second,* the amount of time, effort and resources that all too often must be allocated and committed in an effort to deal with and resolve the problem can be devastating, both to individuals and to the organization or program. In fact, reallocation of resources in response or reaction to the problem (and the negative consequences resulting from such a move) can often be more harmful than the initial problem itself.

Since every organization has finite resources, the guarding and preserving of these resources becomes paramount. Thus, when resources (staff members' time and effort as well as actual expenditures of money and use of goods and services) are reallocated within an organization in an effort to meet the threat of a real or potential problem, there can be very real negative consequences. The result can be destructive and divisive not only to the staff but also to other programs within the organization and even to the entire organization itself.

> **PROBLEM SOLVING PRINCIPLE #16:**   *Problems and their consequences can frequently become serious distractions, interfering with one's primary responsibilities.*

DEALING WITH PROBLEMS VIA THE CRISIS MODE

That is why "problem solving by crisis" can become so insidious. When problems surface, especially those that are not anticipated, reaction to such problems frequently takes place in an atmosphere of crisis. And, solving "problems by crisis" invariably involves a waste of much needed resources, resources that could be put to much better use. Yet, unfortunately, in far too many situations, the mode of operation for handling problems is indeed that of crisis management.

PROBLEM SOLVING RISKS ASSOCIATED WITH ATHLETIC ADMINISTRATION/MANAGEMENT

No one ever said that directing an athletic program or managing a sports staff would be easy. No one believes that the life of an athletic administrator is uncomplicated. Rather, assuming the role of problem solver—whether as an athletic director or any type of athletic administrator—involves a high degree of personal and professional risk. Not only can an athletic administrator quite literally put one's present job, or even one's career, in jeopardy by assuming the role of problem solver, but the individual often can exert a truly significant impact, both positive or negative, on the lives of others, both inside and outside of the athletic entity.

> **PROBLEM SOLVING PRINCIPLE #17:** *In problem solving—risks are inherent both in terms of processes and outcomes.*

Problem solvers are, by definition, risk takers. Usually one cannot make real progress or achieve real success unless and until one is willing to stick one's neck out and take calculated risks. The danger of assuming risk(s) is often exacerbated by the fact that athletic administrators usually do not solve problems, address controversial issues or resolve difficulties in a vacuum. There are usually other individuals, or even groups of individuals, involved in the problematic situation. In addition, the process of problem solving is all too frequently undertaken in the public eye, for all to see. This is especially true in terms of the actual outcome or aftermath of the problem solving effort or process.

Risk of Failure

When acting as a problem solver, one always runs the risk of failure in that effort—either by not being able to do anything or by doing something that ends in failure. This is significant because many times such failure becomes a public failure, that is, the failure on behalf of the athletic administrator is viewed by many other individuals, the general public as well as one's peers and supervisors. One has to be both willing and able to "stand the heat or else get out of the kitchen" as former President Harry Truman was quoted as saying. In terms of problem solving, athletic directors and their fellow athletic administrators need to be able to withstand the public and professional scrutiny when faced with the prospect of dealing with problems and challenges—or else choose another profession.

Operating in the Open—For All to See

> **PROBLEM SOLVING PRINCIPLE #18:** *All athletic directors operate under a magnifying glass—in front of the public.*

Since the outcome or results emanating from the attempt to resolve a problem is often visible to the public, there is the potential for greater impact upon both the problem solver and others involved with the situation. This visibility aspect sometimes makes the process itself more difficult and cumbersome because of the additional challenge of operating under the proverbial magnifying glass, that is, in the public eye. Public scrutiny places more pressure on the problem solver and that individual's superiors. Anytime an individual operates within the full view of the public there is a great deal of exposure and risk, both in one's efforts to address the problem and in the actual outcome of one's decisions. For one thing, if one is successful or unsuccessful, others, including superiors, are all too often aware of that fact.

With Power Comes Responsibility

Another aspect of risk associated with an attempt to solve a problem or address a controversial situation is making a mistake, committing an error in judgment or an inappropriate decision—resulting in negative consequences for others. It is this very possibility of harming other individuals (or the program itself) that discourages some individuals from assuming the role of problem solver. It is indeed important for one to possess sufficiently broad shoulders to make the difficult decisions often associated with solving problems or resolving difficulties.

THE ULTIMATE POWER AND AWESOME RESPONSIBILITY OF ATHLETIC DIRECTORS

Athletic directors, by the very nature of their positions, as chief operating officers, have great power and equally significant responsibilities. It is important that one remembers that decisions made in an effort to solve problems or resolve controversial issues have the potential for grave and far reaching consequences for a whole host of others (individuals and groups, adults and children/minors) as well as for oneself.

> **PROBLEM SOLVING PRINCIPLE #19:** *Problem solvers can wield great power over other people's lives—Use it judiciously.*

By dealing with problems and resolving controversial issues, athletic administrators exercise a tremendous amount of power over total athletic programs as well as individuals, especially young, impressionable athletes. Part of the role of any athletic director involves being able to handle and resolve problems—necessitating making decisions, decisions that can significantly affect the lives of others. However, there is a risk in assuming this power lest such authority and accompanying responsibility be misused or abused.

ASSUMPTION OF RISKS AND REACTIONS TO PROBLEMS AND CHALLENGES

Generally, there are several courses of action an individual can take when faced with problems. *First,* one can simply ignore the problem. This tactic sometimes takes the form of avoiding the problem by simply not addressing it. This is done with the expectation that others will accept or assume the responsibility for dealing with the problem. Or, that the problem will simply go away, vanish. *Second,* an individual can always make the conscious decision to leave, that is, to remove oneself from the problem situation.

This tactic can involve actually quitting one's position and moving on to another job, perhaps in another organization. Or, one can attempt to simply move to another area of responsibility within the same organization, where one would not be faced with such problematic situations. And, of course, a *third* course of action when faced with problems is to meet such challenges head-on, deliberately addressing each problem in an effort to honestly, fairly and expeditiously address the difficulties for the good of the organization or program and for the good of those individuals involved.

THE DIFFICULTY OF SOLVING PROBLEMS

> **PROBLEM SOLVING PRINCIPLE #20:** *If it was easy—anyone could do it.*

The fact is, problem solving is usually not an easy task—that is why it is referred to as *problem solving*. To the contrary, it is a difficult process. Not everyone can be an effective problem solver. If it was easy, if anyone could do the job of preventing and resolving problems within the athletic arena, then there would be no need for highly trained, experienced and dedicated professionals serving as problem solvers (athletic administrators). This is true in the world of athletic organizations and sports programs/activities as it is for any other organization or program.

> **PROBLEM SOLVING PRINCIPLE #21:** *Many people believe they know more than the athletic director and that they can do a better job in administering the sports program and activities.*

As an athletic director, it sometimes seems like everyone believes that they know more about how to run or manage an athletic program than the person who holds the official title of athletic director. This in itself is not an insignificant problem. When the general public as well as many individuals closely associated with a sports program (athletes, parents, fans, boosters, coaches etc.) feel that they are as knowledgeable or more knowledgeable (competent or more competent) than the individual officially assigned to be the official leader and manager of the organization/program, the potential problems are innumerable and often frequent.

Thus, it is imperative that those who are athletic administrators clearly and consistently demonstrate an atmosphere of competency and proficiency as leaders, managers/administrators, decision makers and problem solvers. Failure to do so, failure to act as a knowledgeable and confident school-based athletic administrator only invites a multitude of problems instigated by others who sense a weakness or deficiency in the individual given the responsibility and authority of athletic leader (athletic administrator).

PREVENTING VERSUS SOLVING PROBLEMS

> **PROBLEM SOLVING PRINCIPLE #22:** *It is far better to prevent problems than having to attempt to solve them.*

If a problem can be prevented then there is no need to react within a crisis mode. *It is always better to prevent a problem* than to have to react and then attempt to address and ultimately resolve a problem. And, if a challenge, problem or difficulty can be anticipated, then there is often sufficient time to adequately address the issue in a timely manner, often to such an extent that the problem never materializes (at least to the degree that it might have if foresight had not intervened). In this event, there is an opportunity to set aside or allocate adequate resources to deal with the anticipated problem, if and when it occurs. Frequently, anticipation of a problem or difficulty enables the competent athletic administrator to nip the situation "in the bud" and prevent its occurrence. This anticipation of problems and ability to plan well in advance are marks of a competent professional.

A QUESTION OF PREVENTING PROBLEMS

Of course, it would indeed be great if most or all of an athletic director's problems could be prevented. However, we don't happen to live in a utopia. Rather, we live in the real world, one in which problems become part of our very existence. Whenever we have to deal with people, individually or in groups, there is the very real possibility of difficulties. That is just human nature. Throw in the controversial, aggressive and sometimes dog-eat-dog nature of competitive sports and competitive people (coaches, parents, athletes, media, fans, boosters, general public, etc.) and it is no wonder that problems seem to permeate the world of sports. Not every problem can be foreseen, much less prevented, even with great effort and anticipation. Such is the nature of sports.

> **PROBLEM SOLVING PRINCIPLE #23:** *Unfortunately, not every problem can be prevented.*

For example, the athletic director might have done all the things humanly possible regarding educating one's staff in terms of student-athletes' ethical and proper behavior, on and off the proverbial playing field. The athletic director might have overseen the implementation of any number of specific programs and strategies (supported by coaches and parents) designed to help the players understand the need and advisability of correct action(s). The athletic administrators and coaches could have provided an exemplary example for the youngsters to follow. The athletic director could have seen to it that individual coaches would spend a significant amount of quality time, individually and with the athletes as a group, so that they would have the benefit of appropriate and professional guidance and reinforcement. Yet, there could still be problems.

Within the world of sports athletic administrators are quite literally forced to rely upon, communicate and cooperate with others, e.g. athletes, coaches, parents, boosters, news media, other athletic administrators, central administrators, and the list could go on and on. Even with best-laid plans, not all problems can be prevented. Not all difficulties can be averted. Not all controversial issues can be skirted. Not all problems can be resolved, certainly not to everyone's satisfaction.

Sports are for everyone.
[Courtesy of Washington State University]

Thus, there is no guarantee that one or more of these same athletes might not go off the straight and narrow path of appropriate and proper behavior, either within the athletic (and/or school) setting or outside the confines of the sponsoring organization. Is there still a problem for the athletic director and/or athletic program that might emanate from such a situation? Of course! Can the athletic director be held responsible for such unacceptable behavior on behalf of the athletes, even in light of all that the AD has done in an effort to prevent such a problem from occurring in the first place? In far too many situations, the answer is, unfortunately, YES. That is the price of leadership and being in charge of an athletic program.

THE MATTER OF CONTROL AND RESPONSIBILITY

An athletic director should not feel inadequate or disheartened because there are problems that must be dealt with, almost on a daily basis. Some things are just out of one's control as an athletic administrator; regardless of how hard one might try to maintain control. Thus, the bottom line is how effective and efficient the individual is, under fire, when it comes to push or shove. How does the person react? Does the individual wilt under pressure?

Or, does the individual rise to the occasion and meet the challenge with appropriate decision-making and timely assertive action? Does the individual maintain one's composure and exhibit an air of confidence coupled with professional determination and demeanor? Is the person able to deal with the problem and its aftermath in a manner acceptable by those whose opinions count? How a person responds to the problem and the accompanying pressures and fallout is how that person will be judged, both as a professional administrator (leader) and as a problem solver.

Responsibilities of Athletic Directors in the Problem Solving Process

Although it may not be fair to do so, in today's society, athletic directors and other athletic administrators are all too frequently being held accountable for what their coaches as well as their athletes do or do not do—both in sport circles and outside of the sport scene. Such is the nature of the job, unfortunately. And, athletic administrators need to be ready and able to accept the challenge of dealing with such problems and challenges.

Of course, this doesn't imply that one should not attempt to prevent problems. What it does suggest is that one should not be surprised when problems and difficulties arise even in spite of one's best efforts. One must be prepared to address those problems that do occur in spite of best efforts to prevent or avoid them.

Sometimes Problems Happen—In Spite of the Best Laid Plans

> **PROBLEM SOLVING PRINCIPLE #25:** *There are no insignificant problems—at least for those who are affected.*

Since problems will occur in spite of our best efforts, it is obvious that athletic leaders/administrators must be capable of adequately handling the fallout arising from large as well as menial problems. In reality, there are no small or insignificant problems or difficulties to those individual(s) involved in or affected by the situation. Every problem is significant for those individuals and groups who are adversely affected by the problem and its aftermath.

Effort versus Results

> **PROBLEM SOLVING PRINCIPLE #26:** *Results are what counts—not talk or mere effort.*

Since athletic administrators live in the real world it is important to recognize that effort alone is simply not enough. True, effort is important in everything a human being does in our society. However, even more important than effort are the actual results. As stated previously, the athletic director might have put great effort and spent a significant amount of time in doing something, either attempting to prevent a problem or attempting to resolve a problem. However, if the problem is not solved, the end result is still failure.

This is because although one tries very hard and spends a great deal of time on a task, such as problem solving or problem prevention, it all doesn't mean very much unless there are meaningful and tangible results. Good intentions, regardless of how noble or meritorious, are often simply not enough. What counts are actual results. The outcome is often perceived, especially by the general public, as being far more important than the process involved or effort expended. Thus, actual production (spelled RESULTS) in our society is viewed as paramount, with effort and time spent on task being relegated to secondary importance, especially in the world of competitive sports.

For problem solvers, especially athletic directors, it is imperative that one does not rely on the crutch of merely attempting to do something (i.e., solve a problem) without being equally concerned with the results of one's efforts. Effort without results counts for naught.

THE IMPORTANCE OF WISE DECISION MAKING IN PROBLEM SOLVING AND PROBLEM PREVENTION

> **PROBLEM SOLVING PRINCIPLE #27:** *Results are the consequences of good decision making.*

Generally speaking, solving problems is significantly dependent upon one's decision-making ability. Usually, someone has to make an appropriate and well thought out decision, or series of decisions, in addressing a particular problem, challenge or difficulty.

For without timely and correct decisions, desired results are frequently neither feasible nor possible. However, before suitable decisions can be made, accurate facts and information must be obtained. But even with all available information, there is no guarantee of an easy or appropriate resolution of a problem. For the crux of solving any problem rests in the decision-making skill of the problem solver(s). Without quality (appropriate) decision making no problem can be adequately addressed.

> **PROBLEM SOLVING PRINCIPLE #28:** *Consistency and impartiality are two necessary elements for effective decision making.*

Problem solvers must be consistent in their actions, but especially so in terms of their decision-making. They cannot be seen as vacillating or wishy-washy types. An integral element of decision-making is the ability or capacity to be consistent in one's decisions.

In addition to the necessity for being consistent, there is an equally great need to be impartial and fair. Playing favorites or giving preferential treatment (decisions) to specific individuals while holding others to a different or higher (or lower) standard of behavior is a surefire way to gain a reputation for being unjust. "Consistency and the perception of being consistently fair are important. Survival suggests it. Justice necessitates it" (Stier, 1999a, p. 22).

THE IMPORTANCE OF STANDARD OPERATING PROCEDURES, POLICIES AND PRIORITIES (SOPPPs)

An essential element in the solving of problems is to take advantage of what is commonly referred to as the Standard Operating Procedures, Policies and Priorities (SOPPPs) within one's organization or program. These SOPPPs are typically contained in department handbooks typically referred to as the 5Ps—*Policies, Procedures, Practices, Priorities, and Philosophy(ies)* (Stier, 1999a).

A typical 5P handbook is generally utilized to facilitate the general operation of the sport program by stipulating, through advance planning, what the specific policies, procedures, practices, priorities and philosophy(ies) will be for any particular program. The contents in a department's or program's 5P handbook, various policies, procedures and practices, can go a long way in preventing problems as well as to guide decision making, and the handling and resolution of problems once they arise.

> **PROBLEM SOLVING PRINCIPLE #29:** *Take advantage of the existence of the standard operating procedures and policies to guide actions and decision making.*

In terms of dealing with problems, athletic administrators should operate in line with the contents of the 5P handbook. Since the various policies, procedures and priorities contained in such a handbook have been thought out well in advance, such they can go a long way in preventing problems from ever developing. When problems do arise, reference can be made to the contents of the 5P handbook and one can cite various policies, procedures, practices, priorities as well as a philosophy statement or mission statement as justification for various actions as well as for guidance in terms of what actions and decisions that might be appropriate.

Additional Advantages and Use of the 5P Handbook

The existence of such a document as the 5P handbook can have *additional advantages* other than helping in the general operation of the total athletic department and various sports programs and in the preventing and solving of problems. For example, the existence of such a handbook can also play a major role in making the athletic director look good (competent) in the eyes of superiors, supervisors and the central administration. In this sense, the existence of the 5P handbook becomes a positive public relations vehicle. And, finally, the existence of the 5P handbook can also go a long way to help indoctrinate and orient new athletic staff members and others (volunteers) associated with the sports program.

MAKING EXCEPTIONS TO STANDARD OPERATING PROCEDURES, POLICIES AND PRIORITIES

PROBLEM SOLVING PRINCIPLE #30: *Exceptions or deviations can always be made from standard operating procedures, policies and priorities (SOPPPs).*

Of course, this doesn't mean that every decision is made in a vacuum or that every policy or procedure is etched in stone. One need not be a robot when dealing with people, when confronted with problems. There should always be the possibility of making exceptions or deviating from the norm. Of course, if an exception is necessitated, and there indeed will be times when such will be the case, a clear explanation of why the exception was appropriate should be made clear to appropriate parties.

One of the reasons why there is a need for intelligent, caring and resourceful leaders of our athletic departments and sports programs is that in many instances there is a very real need for a unique decision to be made in light of extenuating circumstances. If there were to be no exceptions to the "rule" then all that would be required is to have anyone (with little or no training) merely follow the standard operating policies, procedures and priorities (SOPPPs) exactly, to the letter, without ever deviating the slightest.

Victory through cooperation [Courtesy of John Carroll Sports Information]

Of course, when dealing with human beings this is not always possible. That is why it is essential that the SOPPPs *be subject to change* and that athletic administrators be willing and capable of making exceptions to the standard operating procedures, policies and priorities when the situation and circumstances warrant it.

PROBLEM SOLVING—A MATTER OF TIMELINESS

It is important to remember that decisions not only have to be made correctly and in a consistent manner, but must be timely as well. The matter of timeliness is all-important. Decisions can be correct and the resulting actions can be efficient in terms of time spent and resources utilized, but if the decisions and the implementation of action plans are not timely, the results can be catastrophic.

PROBLEM SOLVING PRINCIPLE #31: *The matter of timeliness in addressing a problem is often critical to its final solution.*

There is a tightrope that must be walked by every problem solver in terms of being considered either (1) rash in one's decision-making and actions or (2) a procrastinator, a fence sitter. One must be capable of acting with due dispatch but not be viewed by others as rushing. One can just as easily be criticized for being too rash in one's decision making and actions as for being too timid or hesitant. The old saying, "you are damned if you do and damned if you don't," is most appropriate while acting as a problem solver.

A mark of a competent problem solver is being able to successfully maneuver this proverbial tightrope. An individual who is unable or unwilling to take a definitive position, to make a decision or decisions, and thus act in a timely fashion, is going to meet resistance from a whole host of individuals, groups and organizations.

A highly prized skill for any athletic director is being able to make decisions within an acceptable time frame. An equally important skill is the ability to implement on a timely basis the Strategic Action Plan (SAP) resulting from the analysis of the problem situation (problem solving analysis). It is important to be cognizant that determining an acceptable time frame for any course of action in light of any problem is dependent upon the individual situation itself, the accompanying circumstances, and the individuals who are involved. This is where experience comes into play.

Efficient Problem Solving Require Effective Time Management

Using time wisely is an important element of efficient problem solving. In many instances, time is of the essence (or it seems to be) when ADs are confronted with problems or challenges. Many decisions must be made in a timely manner lest opportunities become lost or mistakes made or compounded. This is especially true when dealing with the feelings of others. The wise use of the time available is essential in the problem solving process.

One must use time wisely when faced with the problem or challenge and it is important that others are aware that the athletic administrator is using time wisely and frugally. Perhaps nothing destroys the credibility of the problem solver as the perception of dragging one's feet, wasting valuable time and resources and/or being hesitant to address the problem itself. Proper time management implies that the individual is indeed addressing the problem itself in a timely and forthright fashion. It also implies that there will be a concerted effort to obtain the facts within a reasonable amount of time. And, lastly, proper time management implies that a just and appropriate decision (and course of action) will be initiated in a timely manner—as viewed by all parties involved.

Obviously, not every final decision and/or action taken by an athletic director in response to a particular problem will be agreeable or acceptable to everyone involved. However, a significant number of interested or involved parties should be generally satisfied with the *process of dealing with the problem itself*. This is especially true in respect to the time element in which the problem was recognized, evaluated and eventually resolved.

One Example of an Inappropriate Response in Addressing a Potential Problem

In 1990 the McDonald Corporation (of hamburger fame) got international positive publicity and advertising when it announced that it was planning on frying all of the French fries in "100% vegetable oil." This promotional campaign was especially well received in India and in Muslim countries. However, fast forward to 2001 and the McDonald's corporation was threatened not only with a public relations disaster but a $1B lawsuit to boot as a result of what commonly became known as the "French fry fiasco."

It seems that Harish Bharti filed a class-action lawsuit against the hamburger giant contending misrepresentation as to the contents of its French fries being meatless. In reality, the fries contained "a trace of beef flavoring in the potatoes, added at the processing plant" (Horovitz, 2001, p. 2-B.) Even though the company attempted to apologize by including a statement initially only on its web site, the attorney was unimpressed with such an effort and claimed that such a meager effort was just part of the overall deception by the company.

Had the company reacted quicker to this significant problem that affected millions of Hindus throughout the world it would not have found itself facing a billion dollar lawsuit as well as a million-dollar public relations nightmare. Reacting quickly and in an appropriate manner is an absolute must in today's world of instant communication and global commerce. Failure to do so can create a PR nightmare for the organization and its managers as well as a potential financial catastrophe.

Another Example of Inappropriate Timing in Solving Problems

> **PROBLEM SOLVING PRINCIPLE #32:** *Failure to tell the truth and to act expeditiously often results in disaster.*

One of the biggest snafus at the national level in recent memory involved the American Red Cross (ARC) following the infamous September 11, 2001 terrorists' attack on the World Trade Buildings. Shortly after this tragic attack on America, the ARC announced that it was establishing a separate fund [Liberty Fund] to accept donations and contributions to specifically benefit the victims of this attack. However, in reality, the American Red Cross was forced [as a result of national media exposure] to admit some weeks later *that it was not going to spend all of the money donated* – estimated to be $550 million at the time – *for those victims of the September 11th attack.*

Representatives of the American Red Cross were forced to admit that less than half of the money raised on behalf of the victims was to be spent for the victims—their families or rescue workers. It was acknowledged that the rest of the donated money was earmarked to be spent for an upgrade of its own organization as well as for other needy causes involving other disasters elsewhere in the country. This announcement outraged many, many people in this country as "donors expected their money to be helping now" (Tyrangiel, 2001, p. 77).

The consequence was a loud and consistent outcry and severe criticism from a wide range of constituencies, from individuals as well as the news media *throughout the country*. Those individuals who had donated money to this special fund only to find out that their donations were not being used for the purpose promised by the Red Cross were especially outraged and most vocal. Numerous radio shows roasted (criticized) the ARC because the organization had initially promised that all of the money in this special fund [Liberty Fund] would benefit the victims of September 11th while in reality the ARC simply lied about what was going to be done with the money. In reality the ARC decided to take a significant amount of the money donated for this purpose and chose to spend it for other purposes, some charitable (elsewhere, not for victims of the World Trade disaster) and some for a computer system upgrade for the organization itself.

> **PROBLEM SOLVING PRINCIPLE #33:** *"Credibility is everything."*

The *Chicago Tribune* published a searing editorial that appeared on October 31, 2001 (Red Cross squanders goodwill) that included the following quote that succinctly summed up the controversy.

> "Besieged by the controversy, the Red Cross announced Tuesday that it had stopped seeking donations for the Liberty Fund and that the money in the fund will be directed to victims of the Sept. 11 and future victims of terrorism. This is what is known as damage control. The Red Cross has some real work to do to restore its reputation. It can start by establishing a very simple idea as rule number one: Don't mislead your donors. . . . The fiasco at the Red Cross carries a reminder for everyone involved in philanthropy. Credibility is everything" (p. 14).

Finally, the American Red Cross relented and changed it public position, but not without severe negative consequences that damaged the reputation of the ARC and its personnel. In point of fact, on November 13, 2001, over national television, the ARC made an announcement that it was doing an abrupt turnaround and that contrary to its earlier position, the ARC would indeed spend 100% of the money ($543 million) that had been donated for the victims (Liberty Fund) of the Septem-

The pagentry of sports
[Courtesy of Washington State University]

ber 11th attack to the victims and their families (Nasser, 2001; Roy, 2001). But it was too late to curtail the severe damage to the organization, its programs, its fundraising capability and specific personnel. The eventual fallout even included the resignation of the president of the American Red Cross.

> **PROBLEM SOLVING PRINCIPLE #34**: *Admit when you have made a mistake—don't make an "ARC move."*

As a result of the ARC fiasco, it became clearly evident that the negative consequences had escalated beyond anything the organization had ever anticipated. The public outcry was important but it was the power of the press (news media), the national exposure of the media, which brought down the ARC and forced the organization to back track and change its untenable position. In short, it was the national outcry by the public coupled with the repeated attacks, commentary and exposure in the media, that literally forced the organization's change of heart (and policy). Unfortunately, it is too bad that it took a national outcry from the various publics and repeated criticism in the media to "force" such a decision.

> **PROBLEM SOLVING PRINCIPLE #35**: *Never understate the power, the influence and the wrath of the general public and/or the news media.*

In the end, the new leaders of the ARC reached the right decision and a strategic action plan (SAP) was subsequently and efficiently carried out. But, it was too late for optimal damage control. For the damage (to the reputation of the organization, its program, and selected personnel) had already taken place by the time the American Red Cross elected to do the right thing *and* do the thing right. And all because of the outcry from general public and the media.

The moral of this story is two-fold. *First*, there is a real need to act in a timely fashion, while the iron is hot, when faced with any problem. *Second*, never underestimate the power, anger or doggedness of either the general public or representatives of the news media.

CONCLUSION

> **PROBLEM SOLVING PRINCIPLE #36**: *Remain focused on the normal aspects of one's program while simultaneously handling the problem.*

It is necessary to be able to do two things at once when confronted with a problem. *First*, one must deal with the actual problem at hand and all that that entails. And *second*, one must maintain at least a minimum level of effort, energy and initiative in conducting the actual athletic program so that the program and activities don't suffer as a consequence of the problem. Being able to accomplish both tasks involves the proper determination of priorities and the appropriate allocation of resources. The concept is simple; one must remain focused on the normal sport operation as well as on solving the problem. Neither can be neglected, at least for very long.

EXERCISES FOR CHAPTER ONE

A.   Discuss why the process of problem solving is both an **art** and a **science**.

_____

_____

_____

_____

_____

_____

B.   Why are competent problem solvers not born, but are made?

_____

_____

_____

_____

_____

_____

C.   Under what circumstances can problems and challenges also be viewed as opportunities? Elaborate.

_____

_____

_____

_____

_____

_____

D. Provide an example of an athletic director who neglects the overall goal of the athletic program when facing problems.

_____

_____

_____

_____

_____

_____

E. Explain what is meant when one says that athletic administrators should be both efficient and effective in addressing problems facing the department and the programs.

_____

_____

_____

_____

_____

_____

F. Elaborate on the statement: *administrators should not operate via the crisis mode.*

_____

_____

_____

_____

_____

_____

G. If you are a competent problem solver you are "worth your weight in gold"—explain this statement.

_____

_____

_____

_____

_____

_____

H. What are two essential elements in effective decision making? Why?

_____

_____

_____

_____

_____

_____

I. How can the SOPPPs be helpful to the athletic administrator in dealing with problems? Explain in detail and provide an example.

_____

_____

_____

_____

_____

_____

J.   What should the athletic administrator do, generally speaking, when a mistake is made (within a problem solving situation)? And why? Provide an athletic example.

_____

_____

_____

_____

_____

REFERENCES

Goldfine, B., & Pastore, D.L. (1994). Upward feedback in athletic administration. *Scholastic Coach, 64*(1) 6-8.

Horine, L. (1991). *Administration of physical education and sport programs* (2nd ed.). Dubuque, Iowa: Wm. C. Brown Publishing.

Horovitz, B. (2001, May 25). Attorney hopes for 1B in McDonald's French fry suit, *USA Today*, p. 2-B.

Jensen, C.R. (1988). *Administrative management of physical education and athletic programs* (2nd ed.). Philadelphia: Lea Febiger.

Nasser, H.E. (2001, November 15). Sept. 11 Victims will receive all of Liberty Fund, *USA Today*, p. 5-A.

Roy, Y. (2001, November 15). Red Cross now says all monies to go to victims of 9-11 attacks, *Democrat and Chronicle*, p. 6-A.

Red Cross squanders goodwill. (2001, October 31). *Chicago Tribune*, p. 14.

Staffo, D. (2001). A First Down. *Athletic Management, XIII* (2), 37-41.

Stier, W.F., Jr. (1993, May). The ins and outs of evaluating coaches. *Athletic management, V*(3), 34-37, 39.

Stier, W.F., Jr. (1994). *Successful sport fund-raising*. Dubuque, Iowa; Wm. C. Brown & Benchmark, Publishers.

Stier, W.F., Jr. (1995). *Successful coaching*. Boston: American Press.

Stier, W.F., Jr. (1996, May). An overview of administering competitive sports programs through effective marketing, fundraising and promotion. *Applied research in coaching and athletic annual*, Volume 11, 116-128.

Stier, W.F., Jr. (1999a). *Problem solving for coaches*. Boston: American Press.

Stier, W.F., Jr. (1999b, August 13). *Success Stories in Fundraising, Promotions and Public Relations in the World of Sport/Fitness.* Presentation made at the 8th international convention of the National Sport Council of Taiwan (in Taipei City), Aerobic Fitness and Health Association of Taiwan.

Stier, W.F., Jr. (2003). *Marketing, fundraising and promotions—For sport, recreation and Fitness programs.* Boston: American Press.

Stier, W.F., Jr. (2003, April 4). *Problems Associated with Sport Hazing and Recommendations on how to Legally Protect Yourself.* Presentation made at the National Conference of the American Alliance for Health, Physical Education, Recreation and Dance, Philadelphia, Pennsylvania.

Webster's new collegiate dictionary. (1973). Springfield, MA: G. & C. Merriam Co.

Wilson, S. (2001). Keeping the peace. *Athletic Management, XIII* (2), 22—24, 26-29.

Touhey, K. (1999, September). A new-world mentoring program for athletic administrators. *Coach and athletic director, 69*(2), 60-62.

Tyrangierl, J. (2001, November 5). The Charity Olympics. *Time*, pp. 75, 77.

CHAPTER TWO

Problem Solving Processes
in Athletic Administration

CHAPTER OBJECTIVES

After reading this chapter you will be able to:

- Understand the multi-faceted process of resolving and solving problems
- Justify the need for practicing effective damage control
- List appropriate *fact finding questions*
- List the essential elements of a *strategic action plan (SAP)* and how to implement the *SAP*
- Recite questions that may be asked in establishing a *strategic action plan*
- Appreciate the political realities of athletic administration and problem solving
- Value the importance of extenuating circumstances when solving problems
- Realize that administrators can learn from *successes* as well as *mistakes*
- Be sensitive to the importance that perception plays in problem solving
- Recognize that problem solving is a people business
- Comprehend the difficulties involved in attempting to assign blame
- Be aware of the legal implications associated with problem solving
- Know the rules of due process relative to problem solving
- Appreciate the importance of maintaining confidentiality in the problem solving process
- Be cognizant of the importance of *Total Quality Management (TQM)* in dealing with problems

*A caring coach is essential
for successful athletic participation*
[Courtesy of Central Michigan University Public
Relations]

The process of dealing with and resolving problems is essentially the same wherever they are found. Just as administration is considered administration, regardless of the level at which the managing/administering takes place, problems are problems, regardless of where they exist. The ideal scenario is for athletic directors to be able to apply the principles of problem solving to their own particular situation in light of whatever situation or circumstances exist at the time.

THE PROCESS OF RESOLVING AND SOLVING PROBLEMS

> **PROBLEM SOLVING PRINCIPLE #37:** *The fundamental process of solving problems remains essentially the same—regardless of the type of problem.*

The fundamental process of resolving and solving problems once they have manifested themselves, is multi-faceted (Stier, 1999, p. 32). There are six tasks that are essential elements, that is, they must be present if one is to successfully deal with problems or adequately address challenges. These include:

(1) Recognizing the existence of a problem
(2) Gathering of information, facts and data
(3) Creating and developing a strategic action plan (SAP)
(4) Implementing the strategic action plan (SAP)
(5) Assessing, after the fact, the actual effectiveness of the strategic action plan (SAP)
(6) Taking appropriate corrective action to prevent a reoccurrence of the problem

Those who would be successful problem solvers should pay particular attention in mastering these components for ineptitude in any of these tasks or elements can lead to failure. And, failure as a problem solver leads to utter disaster for the school-based athletic administrator.

> **PROBLEM SOLVING PRINCIPLE #38:** *One must first recognize the existence of a problem before one can attempt to solve it.*

Figure 2.1. Sticking one's head in the sand just does not work (Stier, 1999, page 33).

(1) Admitting the Existence of a Problem

Being able to recognize that there is indeed a problem in the first place is an important element of problem solving. Witness the comedy of errors committed by the American Red Cross (ARC) (chapter one). Far too often there is a failure to recognize the existence of a problem only to find later that the problem itself, as well as its fallout, have been exacerbated beyond all expectations. Sticking one's head in the sand like an ostrich, hoping that the difficulty will go away, is not only foolish and foolhardy but can have catastrophic results, figure #2.1.

Practicing Effective Damage Control

Most major or serious problems just don't disappear of their own accord. However, many potentially serious problems, when addressed promptly and aggressively, can be successfully dealt with while they are yet small or minor difficulties. However, when problem situations are ignored, or worse yet stonewalled, they have a tendency to grow larger and more menacing. The consequences can be significantly more devastating when problems are neglected or when only half measures are exerted toward addressing the problem. The answer is simple: confront the problem head on!!!!

PROBLEM SOLVING PRINCIPLE #39: *Most problems just won't go away of their own accord.*

Recognizing the existence of a problem is the first step in effective problem solving. However, there are other equally important and essential tasks that face the athletic administrator if any given situation is to be adequately addressed. The next step in the process of problem solving rests upon a careful examination of the current situation, in light of the circumstances that currently exist. This involves a careful scrutiny of the problem itself in terms of all relevant factors, such as the possible causes of the difficulty, the people involved, and the possible consequences emanating from the problem if no action were taken.

(2) Gathering of Information, Facts and Data

The second step is concerned with the gathering of pertinent information, data and facts, so that the potential problem solver(s) will have the necessary background with which to make informed, timely and appropriate decisions. Figure #2.2 suggests various questions that might be asked in order to secure a clearer and accurate picture of the problem situation.

One of the challenges, of course, is being able to adequately and accurately ascertain the answers to the above questions *within a reasonable amount of time*. This task is all the more enigmatic when one considers that securing the answers to many of these questions involves dealing with people, that is, securing accurate and timely information from other individuals and/or groups. Anytime an athletic administrator is involved in communication with others, the process becomes more tedious and arduous due to the very nature of human beings and the all too often inadequacies and inaccuracies of communication efforts.

PROBLEM SOLVING PRINCIPLE #40: *One must possess adequate information to exercise insightful decision making.*

Appropriate Fact Finding Questions

1. What are the *key issues* of the case? What is *controversial?*
2. What are the *facts* of the case? What *events* are important? *What happened?*
3. How did such a situation *come to pass*? Through what means?
4. What were the direct and indirect *causes* of the problem?
5. What *people, groups or organizations are/were involved?*
6. What *extenuating circumstances or situations existed*, if any?
7. Why did people *act the way* the way that they did?
8. *When* did the problem occur? When did important events take place?
9. What *physical sites or facilities* were involved?
10. What are the *standard policies, procedures and practices* (the governing document) that affect this situation?
11. Could this situation have been *prevented* in the first place, and if so, how?
12. What are the possible *consequences and implications* of the problem?
13. What *political ramifications* exist, if any? Are pressure groups involved?
14. *Who should be involved* in the problem solving process? Who should serve as an *adviser or consultant?*
15. What is the *time frame* for addressing and resolving the difficulty?

Figure 2.2: Appropriate fact-finding questions (Stier, 1999, p. 34).

Once the athletic administrator has correctly ascertained the answers to the questions posed above, the individual has gone a long way to truly deciphering the puzzle facing the individual, group, program, activity or organization. However, if one doesn't know the correct or appropriate questions to ask, it is exceedingly difficult (if not impossible) to arrive at the appropriate and timely answers that are necessary for the creation and implementation of any strategic action plan (SAP), see below.

(3) Developing the Strategic Action Plan (SAP)

Before attempting to develop a plan or strategy to deal with any problem situation it is important to first secure and correctly interpret appropriate information regarding the existence and causes of the problem. *Even doing nothing or very little can involve a strategy.* Thus, an athletic administrator assuming the role of a problem solver needs to make a decision regarding the creation of a proper plan of attack. And an essential part of that plan is the defining and identifying what should be done, why it should be done, how it will be accomplished, when, by whom, and where.

The Conscious Decision to Do Nothing

In some instances, the decision may be to do nothing, absolutely nothing. This is decidedly different, however, from simply ignoring the problem or failing to even recognize its existence. Deliberately deciding (planning) to do nothing, means consciously taking no direct, specific action. In this eventuality, the strategic plan of action (SAP) is to indeed take no direct, overt action. It is not the same as sticking one's head in the ground like the proverbial ostrich.

PROBLEM SOLVING PRINCIPLE #41: *Sometimes doing nothing is an example of a deliberate act, an appropriate course of action.*

It is obvious that many problems cannot be dealt with by ignoring them and doing nothing. Frequently, problems are of such a nature that specific, direct action is warranted and necessary. When this is the case the athletic administrator involved in addressing the problem must take into consideration many factors when arriving at any decision, now and in the future.

It is imperative that all planning and decision making be done in light of the problem itself, the situation(s), and any extenuating circumstances that may or may not exist, now and in the foreseeable future. Part of this decision-making procedure involves presenting, evaluating and accepting, modifying or rejecting, different ideas and scenarios relative to steps that could or should be taken.

Successful basketball coaching at the elite level, University of Notre Dame. [Photo by Mike Bennett, Lighthouse Imaging]

Components of a Strategic Action Plan (SAP)

Essentially, a strategic action plan (SAP) consists of mapping out a strategy or course of action designed to resolve an existing or potential conflict or problem while controlling or minimizing any meaningful or significant damage. *The SAP answers the global question of what course(s) of action should or should not be undertaken.* Toward this end there are ten general categories of questions that will assist the problem solver in establishing an effective plan of action, figure #2.3 (Stier, 1999, p. 36).

**Questions That May Be Asked
in Creating A Strategic Action Plan(s) (SAPs)**

1. What could (should) now be done in this situation? That is, what immediate, mid-range and long-range steps should be taken?
2. What is possible in terms of damage control? That is, preventing even worse consequences from developing as a result of the initial problem(s)?
3. When would such action or steps be taken? What is the timetable for possible action(s)? What are the priorities of the various steps or actions?
4. Who would be involved? How should these individuals be involved and who should do what, and when?
5. Where would the action or activity take place?
6. Is there adequate justification (why?) for the proposed action(s)?
7. How would it be completed? What methods would be employed?
8. What are the possible consequences (risks) of your actions?
9. What general problem solving principles of management, administration or problem solving are involved in the recommended strategic action plan (SAP)?
10. What type of assessment process or system can be used in determining success or failure of the strategic action plan (SAP)? What specific evaluation techniques or techniques might be used?

Figure 2.3: Questions that maybe asked in creting a strategic action plan(s) (SAPs). [Stier, 1999, p. 34].

The strategic action plan (SAP), once established, becomes a blueprint guiding all actions and activities geared towards resolving the problem situation. A well-constructed and carefully thought out strategic action plan consists of a written outline of exactly what is to be done, when, where, how and by whom. It also includes a detailed timetable for the identification of needed resources and the implementation of the strategy. And, " . . . it is the athletic director's responsibility to put into place a system of checks and rechecks that will guarantee that all tasks, no matter how small, have been accomplished" (Staffo, 2001, p. 41).

PROBLEM SOLVING PRINCIPLE #42: *A strategic action plan is an outline or blueprint guiding one's problem solving decisions and actions.*

The challenge, for the would-be problem solver, is to select the most appropriate strategy that can be implemented within the limitations of the existing situation and available resources. Naturally, any plan of action may be modified as time goes on in light of new developments, changes in circumstances as well as the availability of additional information. Athletic administrators must remain cognizant that all too often there is no single course of action that would prove to be appropriate. Rather, there are many possible actions that might be suitable, again, depending upon the situation, and the people involved.

PROBLEM SOLVING AND POLITICAL REALITIES

> **PROBLEM SOLVING PRINCIPLE #43:** *Athletic administrators must operate within political climates.*

Athletic directors who are successful and experienced problem solvers recognize that the process of resolving difficulties must often be accomplished within a very real political atmosphere. There is nothing wrong with that—it is just reality. All human beings operate within a political climate, at least some of the time. However, this is especially true within a sport setting. To be successful in working with other individuals and with various groups and organizations, it always behooves an athletic administrator to remain cognizant of the political ramifications of all potential decisions and actions as well as non-decisions and inaction (non-action).

On a practical or pragmatic level it is necessary to have an understanding of the political processes within any social setting. This means being aware of political ramifications of one's actions and comments as well as one's inactions and lack of communication. It also means knowing when and where to choose to "go to the mat" or enter into battle.

It does little good to emerge victorious from a battle only to find out that one has lost the war. Recognizing when it would be foolish to continue to butt one's head against a stonewall is a great skill to possess in terms of survival within any political climate. In essence, the political survivor is one who recognizes which so-called battles are worth fighting for and which can actually be won. For those so-called battles that are not worth fighting for, and/or cannot be won, it is often wise to forego being involved in the confrontation. To become politically savvy is a highly desirable trait for any athletic administrator (problem solver) who is in "it" for the long haul.

> **PROBLEM SOLVING PRINCIPLE #44:** *Problem solving decisions should never be made in a vacuum—anticipate possible consequences.*

Being able to recognize the possible consequences that might result as fallout from the problem itself as well as from the solution or attempted solution is an integral part of recognizing the political realities of any problem solving situation. It is important to remember that any decision for an action or inaction must adequately address not only the problem itself but also take into account the processes involved in addressing the problem at hand *as well as* arriving at the proposed solution.

Very few decisions, if any, are made in a vacuum. The process(es) of attempting to resolve difficulties and solve problems is(are) likewise not undertaken in a vacuum. And, the eventual solution or plan of attack is not implemented in a vacuum. Other people are involved. Other organizations or groups are affected. Other considerations must be taken into account.

Therefore, it behooves the AD who is assuming the role of problem solver to anticipate the possible consequences that the problem solving process *and* the proposed solution might have on others, individually and within groups. Such impact must be anticipated if the political realities and consequences are to be adequately planned for, in advance, and subsequently dealt with at an appropriate time and place.

The Matter of Extenuating Circumstances

> **PROBLEM SOLVING PRINCIPLE #45:** *Assess problems in light of the specific situation and circumstances that exist at that time.*

Athletic directors must remain cognizant of the fact that no two athletic programs or situations are identical. There are differences, both severe and slight, within every athletic department and sports program. Different circumstances and varying situations will necessitate different solutions to what might otherwise appear to be very similar challenges and problems. Athletic administrators who take extenuating circumstances into consideration when evaluating or weighing various options are not only professionally prudent but also politically astute.

Naturally, there must always be the possibility of making exceptions or altering a possible decision in light of mitigating factors and extenuating circumstances. It is important to remember that this is not a sign of weakness, that is, making exceptions or taking into consideration other factors in arriving at a decision. Rather, this is a matter of fairness, justice, impartiality, responsibility and legitimacy.

(4) Implementing the Strategic Action Plan (SAP)

Of course no plan in and of itself is worth its salt unless it results in something, i.e., the elimination, solution or resolution of the problem. A plan is just that, an anticipated course of action. Until it is put into place, that is, actually implemented, it is something written on a piece of paper or is an idea in someone's mind. *And implementation of the plan is the next key step in problem solving.*

> **PROBLEM SOLVING PRINCIPLE #46:** *Talk is cheap—put one's money where one's mouth is.*

Once the athletic director and the administrative staff have successfully conceived and formulated the (detailed) strategic action plan (SAP), there remains the matter of its implementation. This simply entails carrying out the various elements of the PLAN according to the established timetable and in the manner prescribed by the SAP. Another element associated with implementation is that of *continual assessment* of how the PLAN is going, that is, whether or not it is successful. Continual evaluation of one's actions in response to the problem or "situation" is critical if the problem solving process is to be successful. Only with meaningful evaluation can one determine that alternate action or decisions are necessary or even advisable.

(5) The Value of Hindsight—Assessing the Effectiveness of the Strategic Action Plan (SAP)

The fifth element or task involved in the process of solving problems revolves around taking a detailed look, after the so-called "smoke" clears, at the entire problem solving effort just concluded. This final appraisal, taking place as it does after the difficulty has been resolved and the crisis has passed, enables individuals and the group itself to take an unbiased and critical glimpse into all phases of the efforts to solve or resolve the problem as well as the final result(s) (Stier, 1997).

> **PROBLEM SOLVING PRINCIPLE #47:** *Learn from the past how the problem might be prevented in the future—take advantage of hindsight.*

The AD's job is not over when the crisis is averted or has run its course. The wise athletic administrator looks to see how the situation could have been averted or prevented in the first place. This is an important and integral part of the evaluation process.

"How could this problem had been avoided or prevented?" is an important question that needs to be asked. Hindsight is a wonderful and productive tool, if used judiciously. The key is to learn through the use of hindsight so that the problem is not repeated, or a similar problem does not raise its ugly head. There is an old axiom that is most appropriate here. It states that a mistake doesn't become an error unless and until it is repeated. An essential element of problem solving is to prevent problems, once resolved, from reoccurring in the future.

Such assessment enables individuals to develop future strategic action plans (SAPs) that are appropriate to specific situations, SAPs that might not only aid in the addressing of future challenges and problems but in their prevention as well. This approach to assessing the success of one's efforts is critical to the overall problem solving process. The goal, as stated earlier, is to see to it that problems (and potential problems) are appropriately addressed; and hopefully, adequately resolved or prevented with as little negative consequences or fallout as possible.

> **PROBLEM SOLVING PRINCIPLE #48:** *Mistakes happen — a mistake doesn't become an error unless it is repeated — to err repeatedly is inexcusable.*

A key concept in terms of being involved in mistakes is that it is acceptable to make honest mistakes. However, this statement is applicable only as long as one learns from one's experience(s). And, learning from one's mistakes implies that mistakes should not be repeated. In reality, repeated mistakes are an indication that an individual is not only failing to learn from experience *but that the individual is not competent.*

> **PROBLEM SOLVING PRINCIPLE #49:** *One can learn from both negative experiences and positive experiences.*

Sports are big business at the major college level.
[Courtesy of Oklahoma State University Athletics]

One of the reasons why experienced athletic directors are usually more successful that inexperienced ADs in dealing with problems (both preventing and resolving them) is that the former enjoy the added advantage of hindsight. That is, they learn from experiences, *both their own and others*. They also learn from both positive and negative happenings. These individuals are able to learn from the past and thus use that knowledge and awareness to guide their future actions and decision making in different situations and under varying circumstances.

Of course, ADs who are successful problem solvers do not have to make mistakes themselves in order to learn from them and thereby develop and refine their problem solving skills. One can also take notice of and learn from the failures [as well as the successes] of others, both contemporaries as well as those who have preceded them. Doing so enables one to develop a reservoir of knowledge upon which to draw in making appropriate and timely decisions—knowledge that goes well beyond one's personal or professional experiences and activities.

(6) Taking Appropriate Corrective Action to Prevent a Reoccurrence of the Problem

The final step in solving the problem solving puzzle centers around taking corrective steps and measures to insure that the problem or similar problems (or problem situations) do not reoccur in the future. This may involve changing or creating new policies, procedures, practices and priorities. It might involve altering the organizational structure associated with the organization or the duties and responsibilities of the staff.

In essence, some changes in the way things are done might be warranted so as to prevent such problems and challenges from reasserting themselves sometime in the future. One does not want to report to a superior that the same (or similar) problem that occurred in the past has repeated itself once again. That is the job of the athletic administrator, to prevent problems from repeating themselves by taking corrective action.

THE PROCESS VERSUS END RESULTS

> **PROBLEM SOLVING PRINCIPLE #50:** *The process of solving a problem is sometimes as important as the solution itself.*

Of course, problems must be addressed and resolved. This is the reality in which we all live. However, it is important to remember that there is more to it than merely having a so-called problem solved or disappear. Yes, that is important, naturally. But so too is the *process* by which the problem is addressed and eventually resolved. Far too often a particular problem may be resolved, but in the process of dealing with that specific problem even greater difficulties or more severe negative consequences result.

This is because the manner in which the problem is approached or the process used to address the initial problem left much to be desired. Thus, *the concept that the process is frequently as important as the end result is certainly true in terms of problem solving.* Athletic administrators who forget or neglect this principle will find themselves in the inevitable position of creating more problems, more difficulties and bigger challenges than they solve.

> **PROBLEM SOLVING PRINCIPLE #51:** *The perception of how a problem is addressed and is solved is sometimes as important as the reality of the situation.*

Just as the process of problem solving is sometimes as important as the end result, so too is the perception of the solution and the problem solving process just as important as reality itself. How others perceive or view the problem solving process *and* the end result is as important as the actual process and the end result themselves. This is because if others view the process as improper, as unjust or unfair—for those individuals the process is indeed not proper, is not just and is not fair. This is especially important when those individuals happen to be the people who are adversely affected by the process (decision making) and/or the consequences of the problem.

What this means is that athletic directors, in their role as problem solvers, must be cognizant of the feelings and viewpoints of others because their perceptions, accurate or not, play a very big role in the overall scheme of dealing with problems. For it is the AD who bears the blunt of the reaction(s) as well as the perception(s) by others to the AD's final decision or response to the problem or challenge.

The Need to Educate Others in Terms of the Reality of the Situation(s)

The above statements should not be construed to mean that there is not a very real responsibility on behalf of others, both individuals and groups, to actively work to develop accurate perceptions, perceptions based on fact(s) and reality. Therefore, it behooves the problem solver, the athletic administrator, to help educate others in terms of the reality of the situation pertaining to both the process and the result(s) associated with any problem or problematic situation.

One cannot, must not, simply allow others to claim ignorance of reality and therefore use such a claim of ignorance as a crutch, all the while claiming that the process and/or the result(s) were improper, inappropriate, unjust and unfair to them. Therefore, athletic directors (as problem solvers) need to diligently work to see that the perceptions held by others are accurate, reliable and appropriate. This is an absolute must.

> **PROBLEM SOLVING PRINCIPLE #52:** *Dealing with problems necessitates the setting of priorities and following them.*

Dealing with problems frequently means that the athletic director must end up taking valuable resources (time, effort, money, etc.) from the overall athletic program or from individual sports, resources which today can scarcely be spared, to deal with the new challenge or problem. This diversion of much needed resources in reaction to the presence of a problem is one of the reasons why advance planning and preventative measures are so necessary by competent sport professionals.

SOLVING PROBLEMS AND DEALING WITH PEOPLE

In athletic departments and within athletic programs and activities there are problems everywhere and anywhere. There are problems revolving around facilities, money (or the lack thereof), equipment, supplies, policies, practices, procedures, computers, transportation, drugs and a whole host of other inanimate objects. *However, when all is done and said, most problems really involve people.*

> **PROBLEM SOLVING PRINCIPLE #53:** *Problem solving is a people business.*

If there were not people involved in and associated with athletic programs and activities there would be far fewer problems facing the modern day athletic director. Of course there would be no athletic programs or sporting activities in the schools either (Stier, 1995). Working with the tangible aspects of athletic administration, the so-called Xs and the Os of management and administration, is usually the easy part of being an athletic director (Stier and Schneider, 2001). It is dealing with and working with people, individually and in group settings, that is the real challenge. And this aspect of problem solving, relating and working with people, is absolutely vital.

> **PROBLEM SOLVING PRINCIPLE #54:** *Problem solving involves the management of human behavior and team building.*

All good athletic departments and successful athletic programs have excellent *teamwork* among the professional staff, led by the athletic director as the CEO of sport. "Team building among an athletic department staff is just as important as the teamwork on each individual squad" (Cardone, 2000, p. 44). Of course, team building is not really possible without superior leadership. And, superior leadership is expected of the athletic director, whether it is at the junior high, senior high or collegiate/university level.

As part of this overall approach toward *team building*, it is important, in the process of addressing or solving problems, for the athletic director to be able to get other people to do what the athletic administrator would like them to do, or to think what the AD wants them to think, within reason. This assumes that what the AD wants others to do and/or to think is appropriate and suitable or fair. This also assumes that the process by which the AD achieves this agreement or consensus is accomplished in an appropriate and professional fashion.

This does involve the manipulation of others, which is a negative process. Rather, *This is managing human behavior.* Managing human behavior is a matter of how persuasive and convincing one can be in terms of one's own position on a particular issue. It involves motivational skills on the person's behalf. And, it involves positive interpersonal interactions making other people feel good about themselves as well as about the athletic program(s) and the people associated with the athletic entity and its programs and activities.

Manipulation, on the other hand, is associated with control through dubious means. Manipulation is that negative action in which an individual, in a devious manner, attempts to inappropriately control, dominate and exploit another individual(s). Proper management, managing of human behavior, is associated with convincing others through one's own persuasiveness and a logical approach to information, facts and data.

> **PROBLEM SOLVING PRINCIPLE #55:** *Firing someone is the easy way out.*

Knowledgeable athletic directors are well aware of the fact that individuals involved in interscholastic and intercollegiate athletic departments and sports programs do not become less than competent or, worse yet, incompetent overnight. If part of a problem is with a particular individual or that individual's behavior, it is inappropriate to automatically assume that the person is simply incompetent and should be removed from the scene. That is the easy way out. Firing someone or releasing an individual from one's responsibility should be the last resort. Instead, the objective, the goal, should be to help the individual to want to do better, to want to perform in a capable and appropriate manner, whether the person is a full or part-time employee or even a volunteer.

> **PROBLEM SOLVING PRINCIPLE #56:** *People usually don't cause problems deliberately or out of spite.*

In the real world, most people simply don't cause problems deliberately, that is, on purpose. Most individuals don't intentionally go out and consciously decide to cause the athletic director or the athletic department or sports program grief. Nevertheless, problems happen. Difficulties arise. And, problems and difficulties happen sometimes because of people. Why?

The answer to that question is complicated and depends upon many factors. Sometimes problems develop because people just make a mistake or commit an oversight. Sometimes problems happen because people want to do things that they should not do; or they choose not to do things that they should do. Or, they want things they can't have. Or, they don't want to give up things that they are supposed to give up. Or, they disagree with procedures or policies, or with positions taken by other individuals. Or, they are forgetful, ignorant or negligent. Or, they misinterpret things.

And, in some instances, some individuals, especially those actively involved in competitive sports (coaches, athletes, parents, fans, boosters, etc.), can often have a very different or even biased perspective, especially as they relate to their own involvement in sports and their teams. Such people are competitive, they are aggressive and assertive, they are hard headed—and they can often be confrontational. It takes someone with great skill and savoir-faire to be able to successfully deal with such individuals.

> **PROBLEM SOLVING PRINCIPLE #57:** *The program's problem solver becomes the official spokesperson of the sports program whenever dealing with the public.*

Whenever an athletic director attempts to confront a potential or existing problem situation it is important to remember that the individual is the official representative of the sports program and the sponsoring organization. As a result, all decisions and actions (and inactions) by the athletic administrator may be viewed by others as "official acts" of the school, the athletic department and the individual sports program. Obviously, one needs to be careful how one is perceived and how one's words are interpreted by others.

> **PROBLEM SOLVING PRINCIPLE #58:** *What you are speaks so loudly it is difficult to hear what you are trying to say (Stier, 1999, p. 45).*

Example of effort, execution and effectiveness in sport
[Courtesy of Eastern Illinois University Sports Information]

In our society, individuals are judged in light of what they do and what they say as well as what they don't do and don't say. People are judged in terms of their behavior, that is, in light *of how their behavior is perceived by others*. They are judged especially in terms of how they deal with others. The cliché "what you are speaks so loudly that I cannot hear what you are attempting to say" has a great deal of truth within the problem-solving arena.

Individuals who "talk a great game" insofar as being honest, being forthright, having integrity—must back up such verbiage through actual performance. In other words, one must be able to *talk the talk and walk the walk*. Persons are deemed to possess such virtues as honesty and integrity if their behavior exemplifies and warrants such a reputation. However, "talk is indeed cheap" and it is one's behavior and actions that will determine whether or not others will hold the athletic administrator in high esteem as an individual of high moral character and integrity.

ASSIGNING BLAME AND THE PROBLEM SOLVING PROCESS

All too often, administrators are too concerned with assigning blame when confronted with a problem or a challenge. This is simply foolish. When faced with problems one of the worse reactions that can be initiated is attempting to place blame on someone for the disaster. Never immediately attempt to blame someone for the problem. Rather, fix the problem, the difficulty, and the challenge. Later, at an appropriate time and place, accountability, responsibility and culpability can be dealt with. When initially faced with the PROBLEM, the emphasis should be on addressing the situation, whatever it may be, and resolving the problem.

> **PROBLEM SOLVING PRINCIPLE #59:** *Rather than blaming someone—concentrate on solving the problem.*

In the real world, if people are afraid of being blamed and suffering severe consequences, there is too often the possibility of stonewalling taking place or attempts to hide one's involvement. As a result, too much time is wasted and effort expended by people trying to avoid blame, trying to get out of the line of fire. And, as a result, the process of solving the problem becomes all the more difficult and involved. Besides, blaming others doesn't do any real good except maybe to make one feel good for a few moments. But that doesn't always facilitate progress in solving the problem.

> **PROBLEM SOLVING PRINCIPLE #60:** *Don't always blame problems on the lack of resources.*

It is similarly unwise to always attempt to blame problems on the lack of resources. Competent administrators learn to work with what resources are available. *If there were always ample resources then anyone would be able to be successful.* It seems that whenever there is a problem, if one can't blame a particular person, then the culprit is often a lack of resources. This is both foolish and non-productive. Don't use excuses as a crutch as such behavior does nothing to enhance the status of the excuse maker.

As has been pointed out earlier, problems happen, period. There may be many causes and many contributing factors. But, attempting to fix blame on someone *or* something is often counterproductive. The primary responsibility for the athletic director, as the problem solver, is to fix the problem, not fix the blame on someone or something. Always blaming others is simply a cop out and is all too often simply seen as such by others.

ADs need to remember that if the job of being an athletic administrator was simplistic, almost anyone could successfully perform the tasks. And, there would be very few, if any, severe problems to even address. However, such is not the case. As pointed out in chapter one, there are numerous problems necessitating skilled and experienced athletic administrators, adept at handling the pressure and the fallout from such difficulties.

THE LEGALITY OF PROBLEM SOLVING

We live in a very litigious society. We also live in an era of ever increasing political correctness. As a result, it is absolutely essential that athletic directors, as problem solvers, be aware of the legal rights of individuals, groups and institutions as well as their own. This involves an awareness and recognition of legal and individual rights, including that of due process; legal liability; negligence; risk management; freedom of the press; appropriate behavior; justice; fairness; discrimination; harassment; as well as intimidation.

PROBLEM SOLVING PRINCIPLE #61: *Be aware of your legal rights as well as the legal rights of other individuals, of the school and the sponsoring organization.*

Athletic directors all too often get into a legal quagmire of even greater proportions when they attempt to solve a problem or resolve a controversial situation while being ignorant or semi-ignorant of the legal ramifications and implications of the situation or circumstances, or by ignoring same. ADs need to remain cognizant of the potential legal consequences that may involve any athletic problem or sports situation. Forewarned is forearmed. Nowhere is this more pertinent than in the problem-solving arena of school-based athletic sports.

The Implications of Due Process

Of course, not every controversial decision made by an athletic administrator will be accepted as fact by those who are adversely affected by the decision(s) policy or procedure. This is where due process comes into play. ADs must recognize and provide for appropriate due process for those individuals or groups adversely affected by their decision(s).

PROBLEM SOLVING PRINCIPLE #62: *Due process must be provided for all individuals involved in controversial situations.*

There are several elements or principles involved in due process. Lets look at the situation in which an athlete is to be punished or admonished. The *first* principle is the right to know what one is being accused of. An athlete has the right to know about rules and severe punishments prior to being disciplined by a coach or the athletic administration. For example, an athlete should not be hit with dismissal from the team for being 10 seconds late to practice unless the youngster had previously been informed by the coach of such a severe consequence for this particular infraction. The athlete must be made aware of the offense or infraction for which punishment is being administered. Due process gives to the individual the right to know what the person is being accused of and to be made aware of the "rules of the game" ahead of time.

Second, due process also gives the person the right to face one's accusers and to rebut the charges. That is, due process gives one the right to be heard, that is, to give a defense to known accusations or charges. In this case the athlete might have indicated that the English teacher had kept the entire class late because the instructor was not through handing out the previous quiz to the students. Such extenuating circumstances certainly might mitigate the punishment for being late to practice that would be deemed fair, just and appropriate.

And *finally,* due process provides the right to appeal a decision, under certain circumstances and within specific limitations, to a higher authority. In a high school, this higher authority might be to an assistant athletic director, the athletic director, the principal, the assistant superintendent or even the superintendent or school board. On the collegiate level, the appeal process might involve a committee of coaches, the AD, a dean, a vice president and eventually the president.

> **PROBLEM SOLVING PRINCIPLE #63:** *Due process provides protection against arbitrary and capricious action or inaction by another person.*

Due process, as cited in the above scenarios, provides protection to the athlete against arbitrary and capricious action or inaction by a coach or other authority figure, including an athletic administrator. It recognizes that an athlete, in this example, has certain inalienable rights that cannot be abrogated by an uncaring or unthinking authority figure.

In a school situation, the appeal process is typically invoked whenever a decision is made at a lower administrative level and the individual affected by the decision feels that said decision or the process by which the decision was arrived at was incorrect, inappropriate or unjust. As a consequence, the person who feels unjustly treated or maligned seeks an appeal to a higher authority. Exercising one's due process rights can involve one, two or even more appeals, each appeal made to a higher level of authority within the organization.

For example, a coach might make a decision regarding an athlete's behavior on the team and decree a punishment. The athlete (and/or parents) might appeal that decision to the athletic director. If an adverse decision is rendered by the athletic director, due process in some programs might provide for a further appeal to the principal in the high school or, if it was in a college setting, to a dean or vice president. A further appeal might even be possible to the superintendent of the school system (and/or school board) or to the president of the college or university.

At each level of the appeal process, the aggrieved party, in this case the athlete, has an opportunity to present that person's position and to point out any extenuating circumstances or situations supporting why the athlete believes that the punishment is unfair, unjust or inappropriate. The athletic department's policy handbook will clearly state the appeal process and specify at what level any appeal ends.

Confidentiality and the Problem Solving Process

> **PROBLEM SOLVING PRINCIPLE #64:** *Discretion and confidentiality are matters of great importance—both legally and morally.*

A factor that every athletic director and problem solver must remain cognizant of is the need for discretion, and especially confidentiality, in those instances where confidentiality and discretion is appropriate and necessary. And there are indeed numerous opportunities where confidentiality, in the legal sense, must be respected and strictly adhered to.

The Shield of Confidentiality

The issue of confidentiality is often a tricky one. All too frequently confidentiality is not a simple issue. Instead, there are judgment calls involved—depending upon the facts and extenuating circumstances surrounding the situation. Thus, it behooves the athletic director to approach situations in which confidentiality is a factor with great care and trepidation.

It must be remembered that not everyone has the right to know what transpires in every situation. There are some things that are best kept to oneself and should not be broadcast over the proverbial loud speaker. On the other hand, one doesn't want to be thought of as one who keeps inappropriate secrets or as someone who is attempting to (inappropriately) hide something. There is a big difference between inappropriately hiding something and a situation in which confidentiality must be respected. Athletic administrators need to recognize when it is warranted to invoke confidentiality and when it is inappropriate to do so—and then act accordingly and with confidence.

Confidentiality and the Potential for Embarrassment

An essential element of confidentiality is the matter of embarrassment. Athletic administrators should always go out of their way to prevent others from being embarrassed or humiliated. Embarrassment usually occurs when inappropriate information is shared with others and the hurtful information and/or the sharing act itself bring ill feelings such as humiliation or mortification to a third party.

PROBLEM SOLVING PRINCIPLE #65: *Don't embarrass others—allow individuals to save face.*

Parents, athletes as well as others have a right not to be embarrassed or humiliated by having private information concerning themselves shared openly with others or surreptitiously leaked to others. This is doubly true when the recipients have no right (morally, ethically or legally) to the information.

Concentration in athletic competition
[Courtesy of University of Wisconsin Sports Information]

Obviously, a student's grade point average or test scores are confidential and are not to be shared or distributed to other individuals or organizations unless there is a very real reason or need to do so. On the college level where the athlete is considered an adult, this includes the athlete's parents. A similar prohibition of the sharing of information can be seen when a high school or college-aged youngster is removed from a team or is not selected as a starter. The reason(s) why the student is removed or not selected is confidential between the coach and that youngster—such information should never be indiscriminately disseminated to others, such as the press or the booster club. To do so is to breach the confidentiality that should exist between the youngster and the representative of the athletic department.

In a similar manner, the posting of names of those youngsters who made the team or who didn't make the team by listing student's names or social security numbers in a public place is strongly discouraged—both from a legal standpoint as well as common sense perspective. There is no need to place anyone in a situation in which they are held up to ridicule. And, it is simply illegal today to publicly disclose the student's social security number.

Problems in Promising Confidentiality

> **PROBLEM SOLVING PRINCIPLE #66:** *Never promise confidentiality if it would not be appropriate to do so.*

One major area of concern for any athletic administrator in the role of problem solver or mediator is when one would like to promise confidentiality to an individual or individuals. The difficulty in this type of situation is that when an individual promises confidentiality then one is obligated to deliver on that promise. And, that is sometimes difficult to do, to the embarrassment and consternation of the one who makes the ill-advised promise as well as the individual(s) to whom the commitment was originally made.

Breaking the seal of confidentiality is like a priest breaking the seal of the confessional—it is simply not done. This in itself brings up another potential area of concern for the athletic director assuming the role of the would-be problem solver. Never promise confidentiality if you cannot follow through and retain confidentiality.

The concept is simple—an athletic administrator must never promise confidentiality carte blanche, especially before one knows what it is that is going to be shared in a confidential mode. This is because one might not know what the confidence to be shared might involve and it might be something that literally cannot be kept secret or confidential. Certainly an athletic director would not promise confidentiality in the instance where a serious violation of the law has occurred. Obviously, a warning signal should pop up whenever an athlete or other individual offers to share a confidence with the athletic director only on condition that the information is kept an absolute secret.

> **PROBLEM SOLVING PRINCIPLE #67:** *Beware of the potential dangers in promising confidentiality carte blanche when approached by an individual.*

Rather than making such a carte blanche commitment, the athletic administrator would do well to respond by indicating something like: "I am sincerely sorry. But I simply can't blindly promise not to tell someone—but I will keep your confidence (secret) if it is appropriate for me to do so." In this way the administrator offers to help the individual without committing to total silence in the event that the administrator is told something that one is morally or legally obligated to divulge.

Athletic Participation—A Privilege Rather than a Right!

Whether athletic participation is a right or privilege is frequently a problematic area or a matter of some confusion on behalf of athletes, parents and other members of the general public. Sometimes parents and athletes feel that such participation, in and of itself, is a God given right. If this would be the case, then many potential problem areas would have to be dealt with differently than if such athletic participation would be considered to be a privilege.

> **PROBLEM SOLVING PRINCIPLE #68:** *Athletic participation is a privilege—not a right!!!*

Fortunately, from both a historical perspective and as a result of court decisions, athletic participation in schools has been deemed to be a privilege rather than an absolute right. Being a privilege, participation in school-based amateur sports places far greater responsibility upon the would-be participant (and parents). Additionally, athletic administrators are able to manage and administer school athletic departments, programs and sports in a completely different fashion than if such athletic involvement were an absolute right. However, even with the concept as well as the legal interpretation that such participation is indeed a privilege the issue of athletic participation — that is, who participates on a team and who doesn't — is still ripe for a multitude of problems that can confront athletic administrators.

THE NEED FOR CARING PROBLEM SOLVERS

Being a competent athletic director is all about being able to deal with people in a variety of settings and circumstances. Administering and managing an athletic department in a school really is a people business. So too is problem solving. It is important that athletic administrators be caring, be tolerant of others' beliefs and opinions, empathetic of their situations, and sympathetic of their problems. Athletic administrators need to be humanistic and caring in their dealings with others.

> **PROBLEM SOLVING PRINCIPLE #69:** *Show that you care about people—be empathetic and sympathetic of others and their problems.*

Athletic directors who are successful over the long haul are those who are people oriented and who are recognized by others as being such. Successful problem solvers are able to demonstrate empathy and sympathy. They are able to honestly care about the plights and dilemmas of others and convey sincere feelings and attitudes to others. And, of course, making other individuals feel comfortable with the integrity of the problem solving process and the sincerity of the AD is half the battle.

Being Unbiased and Remaining Objective as a Problem Solver

Figure 2.4: Helping others in their time of consternation and unhappiness

It is not enough to merely be humanistic and caring when addressing problems. It is also necessary that one be unbiased and able to convey such neutrality to all interested parties. One should always strive to keep one's emotions and feelings to oneself and separate from the problem solving process itself. *Don't wear your heart on your sleeve.* The existence of emotions on behalf of an athletic administrator merely clouds the issue. Since most problem situations already are emotion packed it does little good for the AD to make it worse.

PROBLEM SOLVING PRINCIPLE #70: *In an effort to prevent a conflict of interest, remain objective and unbiased.*

The reason why it is important to keep one's personal biases and prejudices out of the problem situation is because it helps reduce both the reality and perception of any possibility of a conflict of interest. Lacking professional objectivity within the problem solving process — both in terms of fact finding and decision making — can create almost insurmountable obstacles. In the final analysis the athletic director must be completely objective and totally unbiased. *Professionalism suggests it and justice demands it.*

It is also imperative that one *conveys the impression of impartiality* when dealing with any problem or challenge. To do otherwise is courting disaster since others will have no real confidence or trust the AD as an honest and just mediator, problem solver and facilitator.

PROBLEM SOLVING PRINCIPLE #71: *TQM is a vital component of problem solving.*

The internationally famous Edward Deming initiated what has become known as Total Quality Management (TQM) some 50 years ago. Today, Total Quality Management is a well-used and recognized phrase in our society, especially in the world of business. In fact, *Total Quality Management* has become so-called buzzwords of modern day management.

In the world of business, TQM refers (among many other things) to the principled treatment of others. It is a strategy or approach that "involves employees working together as teams to identify ways to improve goods, services, or practices to increase customer satisfaction" (Nicklin, 1995, p. A-33). The concept of TQM also necessitates that employees and customers be dealt with *in a correct, respectful and caring manner.*

PROBLEM SOLVING PRINCIPLE #72: *TQM recognizes that the patron, the customer, the client, always come first.*

A common tenet of TQM has one leading through example. The TQM adherent always goes the extra step to insure that others are well treated and dealt with in an honest and appropriate fashion. It also implies that mutual respect; teamwork and consideration are watchwords governing all interpersonal relationships between the organization and the customers or employees. In the business world, TQM recognizes that the "customer" is of prime importance; that errors or mistakes within the organization should be kept to an absolute minimum; and, high ethical standards should be the rule of the day.

The TQM concept also has a role in athletics in that athletes, parents, boosters, media representatives, other coaches, etc., need to be treated with respect and honesty. In school-based athletic programs, student-athletes can be thought of as customers. As can parents. And, similarly, members of the general public. Thus, TQM suggests that these individuals receive the very best in professional care and attention so that the relationships that emerge will be fruitful rather than confrontational.

> **PROBLEM SOLVING PRINCIPLE #73:** *Problem solvers, to be truly effective, need "to walk in other people's footsteps."*

The author's classmate in graduate school was a Native American who displayed a sign on his desk that read: "Before you criticize another human being, walk a mile in that person's moccasins." That piece of advice is relevant today, tomorrow and always.

Athletic directors need to understand from whence other individuals are coming from, in terms of their attitudes, their beliefs, their experiences, their needs, their wants, their motivations, and their behavior. One should demonstrate empathy and sympathy while attempting to understand others and the positions that they are in and are coming from. Understanding others and why they behave the way they do enables the AD to be in a better position to relate to them, to communicate with them and to influence them.

There is a danger, however, in attempting to be sympathetic in one's problem solving efforts. It is important that one doesn't become so emotionally involved to such an extent that it is not possible to be impartial and fair—fair to yourself, to others and to the athletic department and individual sports programs. It is appropriate as well as necessary that athletic directors distance themselves to some extent from over involvement in the personal lives of others as they assume the role of administrator and problem solver.

> **PROBLEM SOLVING PRINCIPLE #74:** *It is literally impossible to please all the people all the time.*

It is just not possible to please all the people all the time. Nor, should anyone really try to do so. In the real world it is hard enough to please even some of the people, part of the time. Nowhere is this truer than in the secondary and collegiate athletic arena. For athletic directors, it is vital that they recognize this important facet of the problem solving challenge.

The athletic director, who wants (or needs) to be liked, or loved or appreciated by others, and who assumes the role of a problem solver, can be in for a rude awakening, if not an utter disaster. Problem solvers have to make decisions and initiate courses of action that might not be well accepted by any number of individuals, groups and/or organizations. The resulting antagonistic reaction by others need not frighten or discourage the competent problem solver who knows that the best decision was made in light of all available facts and in an unbiased manner.

> **PROBLEM SOLVING PRINCIPLE #75:** *Angry customers, clients or patrons infrequently complain—or come back.*

Believe it or not, school-based athletic departments and sports program are, in some very real respects, like a business with a variety of customers, patrons and clients. It is the responsibility of the leaders (athletic administrators) of such programs to attempt to satisfy these customers, patrons and clients, whether these individuals are athletes, parents, fans, media, boosters or people from the community. In a very real sense, many individuals have an aversion to officially complain to higher authorities unless the perceived injustice is severe and is personally affronting to the individual.

Promotion and publicity are two essential elements of athletic competition
[Couresy of Durham Bulls, photo by Brian Fleming]

Nevertheless, this doesn't mean that individuals who feel slighted, offended or affronted – and who choose not to officially complain or cause a ruckus – just quietly disappear. To the contrary, individuals who believe that they were mistreated or neglected often can cause devastating and immediate harm as well as long lasting negative consequences to the program, its coaches and the athletic administration by (1) not coming back to (not continuing to support) the program and/or (2) complaining and criticizing the department, the personnel and the programs/activities within the community. In fact, estimates have been given that as high as 90 percent of all dissatisfied or unhappy so-called "customers" don't ever make concrete, official complaints about their real or perceived grievances.

However, estimates as high as 66 percent have been made as to the number of aggrieved customers who continue to bad mouth and criticize, castigate and denounce the athletic administration, coaches, the program and the organization itself, figure #2.5. And this type of backbiting and criticism can often do irreparable harm to the to the department, programs, activities and personnel (Stier, 1999, p. 54).

Figure 2.5: Beware of those individuals who criticize you behind your back.

Athletic directors and their staffs should be alert to the need to satisfy their various constituencies—whether they are students, parents, fans, boosters or members of the community. If they fail in their effort to satisfy these various individuals and groups there is a very real danger that some of these individuals will remove themselves from their association or affiliation with the athletic administration, the athletic department or individual sports program. And, worse yet, there is the distinct possibility that these disassociated and dissatisfied customers, clients and patrons will continually bad-mouth the athletic leadership as well as the department, the programs/sports and athletic staff.

> **PROBLEM SOLVING PRINCIPLE #76:** *Athletic directors who are effective as problem solvers typically have the proverbial thick skin.*

The reason it is helpful for the athletic director to have thick skin is because it is impossible to impress everyone with one's problem solving prowess. The nature of school-based sports and the nature of problems that arise within competitive sports, at the secondary and collegiate levels, are such that there are adversarial positions taken by various individuals and groups, all too often powerful and influential individuals and groups. Since it is not possible to satisfy or please everyone, even when compromises are the order of the day, one must be prepared for both positive and negative reactions to one's efforts. One does not survive the management/administrative "game" by being overly sensitive to criticism leveled at oneself or one's closest associates.

> **PROBLEM SOLVING PRINCIPLE #77:** *Don't give up or take criticism personally— understand from whence it comes and react accordingly.*

In the athletic world criticism comes with the territory, period. Expect it. Understand from whence it comes, don't overreact, and don't become discouraged. Remember, the process of problem solving is hard work and time consuming. It is tiring and taxing. And it is frequently not even very rewarding or satisfying. Don't become discouraged either by the frequent or incessant criticism or by the barrage of seemingly unending problems demanding your time and attention.

If there were no significant problems for you, as an athletic administrator, to handle—then almost anyone could successfully manage your job. The reason that you are in the position that you are – as a school-based athletic administrator – *is because you have specific skills and competencies that are highly prized and that you are good at your job.* You are a professional. That is why you were hired or selected in the first place for your position as an athletic administrator or sport manager.

> **PROBLEM SOLVING PRINCIPLE #78:** *One earns respect the old fashioned way—by working at it, doing the right things and doing them correctly.*

Every human being wants to be liked, loved and respected by others. However, respect from others must actually be earned, it does not come automatically, it is not a gift. One does not gain respect through bribery, trickery or by attempting to please everyone all the time. Respect is earned by consistently demonstrating competency all the while being fair and honest in one's thinking, rationale and in one's dealings with others. Respect is neither purchased nor borrowed, but earned, the old fashioned way, by working at it.

PROBLEM SOLVING PRINCIPLE #79: *Competent administrators do not initiate nor perpetuate adversarial relationships—such involvement is counterproductive.*

In the real world in which we live, people all too often have long memories, really long memories, especially when they feel that they have been wronged or mistreated. If they feel thusly, there may be a tendency on behalf of some individuals to hold grudges, to remain embittered and to attempt to get even.

Athletic directors who are effective at solving problems and diminishing the negative consequences of such problems are able to successfully keep the entire process impersonal and impartial while eliminating any opportunity for an adversarial relationship to develop between themselves and others. One would not want future relationships or future actions to be negatively affected by past problems, past relationships, past confrontations, past decisions, or past actions.

PROBLEM SOLVING PRINCIPLE #80: *Don't attempt to be the Long Ranger as a problem solver.*

It is important that those who have administrative responsibilities in school-based athletic programs not attempt to "go it alone" when facing difficulties. Assuming the role of the legendary Lone Ranger is hardly the most effective method of addressing problems. In today's complicated society it is rare indeed that a single individual has sufficient skills, experience and resources to deal with significant problems by oneself.

This means that one should not be hesitant to ask for professional assistance and/or advice from others. Doing so is not a sign of weakness but rather an indication of maturity and responsibility. Asking for the opinions of those whom one trusts is simply a wise and prudent move. Asking for insight and information from others who are in a position to provide needed information and helpful assistance can prove to be of great benefit. It sometimes takes a strong and self-assured individual to admit that one needs help. But it is far easier to reach one's objective, especially when it involves solving a complicated problem, if one is able to work cooperatively and professionally with others.

PROBLEM SOLVING PRINCIPLE #81: *Utilize a collegial or team approach to problem solving.*

Thus, a team approach in addressing, preventing and solving problems can be a great asset, figure #2.6 (Stier, 1999, p. 57). Such a collegial strategy or teamwork effort enables one to take advantage of the skills, experiences and insight of others in evaluating the facts surrounding any specific problem situation as well as any number of possible options and decisions. Two heads are better than one, and three or more are better yet, especially when each is knowledgeable and professional. Development of collegial relationships with one's colleagues and peers, when dealing with problems, builds bridges and prevents barriers from being erected, thus facilitating progress towards a suitable solution.

PROBLEM SOLVING AND DECISION MAKING IN LIGHT OF ETHICAL CONSIDERATIONS

> **PROBLEM SOLVING PRINCIPLE #82:** *Don't just be expedient—do what is right, just and fair.*

Athletic directors (in their role as problem solvers) are subject to great scrutiny by a whole host of other individuals, groups and constituencies, including their immediate supervisors.

Figure 2.6: Solving problems through a collegial approach. [Courtesy of Diamond Baseball, Cypress, CA]

Consequently, it is wise to follow the practice of always being open about what one is doing and what one has done in the past. No, this does not imply that one has to volunteer everything that one is thinking or doing (or has done) to the whole town. But it does imply being open in what one is doing and what one shares with others (as long as such disclosure does not breach confidentiality).

Although athletic directors should not always be thinking in terms of pleasing or satisfying this group or that group, appeasing that individual or this individual. Instead, they nevertheless do need to do what is right. One must be honest. One must be unbiased. One must have integrity. One must act in an ethical fashion.

> **PROBLEM SOLVING PRINCIPLE #83:** *Do not hesitate to seek counsel from one's superior(s) when appropriate.*

To be actively involved in the problem solving business one cannot worry too much about having to please everyone. But, if there is one individual who should be satisfied with your efforts, it is one's boss or supervisor(s). For in reality, it is the superior(s) who will assess one's competency in any specific problem activity as well as the overall competency in the specific job held. Since athletic administrators should never keep their immediate boss or superior in the dark there are times when it is most appropriate to inform one's superior of the problem(s) that one if facing and how it is being treated. Additionally, there are times when it is appropriate for the athletic administrator to seek counsel and advice from one's superior.

With that said, it is also important that one does not always run for help or assistance, especially from one's superior, at the first sign of any difficulty or problem. One must not be viewed by others (especially one's superiors) as being unable, unwilling or incapable of handling difficulties or always being in the position of crying for help, advice or assistance. Athletic administrators always are faced with the dilemma of walking the tightrope between being seen as someone who constantly needs advice, reassurance, assistance and backup and an individual who consistently goes it alone, keeping everything close to the vest, like the Lone Ranger. Knowing when and if to approach a superior or other individual for advice and assistance is a judgment call. But, it is a judgment call that must be frequently made by athletic administrators.

> **PROBLEM SOLVING PRINCIPLE #84:** *One must not only be honest, trustworthy, believable and have integrity, but one must be viewed by others as such.*

For the athletic administrator to be viewed as being believable, as being trustworthy and possessing integrity, is an absolute necessity. There will be numerous instances in which the athletic administrator, as a problem solver, will be scrutinized in terms of the appropriateness of one's behavior. The successful problem solver must be able to pass the integrity test if one is to earn and retain the trust and confidence of others.

Every decision that an AD makes has the potential of having a significant impact on others, whether they are coaches, student-athletes, parents, fans, boosters, or groups within the community. This impact can be positive in some cases and very negative in others.

> **PROBLEM SOLVING PRINCIPLE #85:** *Almost all major decisions have potential ethical and moral implications.*

Many of the decisions pertaining to major problems have very real potential ethical implications. This is due to the severe and long lasting impact that such decisions can have on others. As a result, problem solvers are prone to ask such questions as: "Can I live with myself with this on my conscience? Have I made an impartial decision based upon the evidence? Have I been honest and forthright"?

Of course, it is hopeful that the answer to each question is a resounding YES. Hopefully, others will perceive that the answers to these same questions would also be YES. If that is the case, then the problem solver, the decision maker, should be able to sleep well.

Athletic support groups provide significant resources to major college athletic programs [Courtesy of Purdue University Sports Information]

CONTROVERSY AND THE PROBLEM SOLVING PROCESS

> **PROBLEM SOLVING PRINCIPLE #86:** *Determining whether or not actions and decisions are appropriate and/or controversial is crucial in the problem solving process.*

There is always the potential for controversy surrounding the actions and decisions of any athletic administrator. How does one go about determining whether one's actions or decisions would be appropriate or not, whether they would be ethical or not? What should ADs and other athletic administrators do in such potentially volatile or controversial situations?

Perhaps the litmus test for ethical decisionsand appropriate behavior is whether or not the individual would be comfortable in sharing the decision or making known the behavior to others, including one's superior(s) and the general public.

> **PROBLEM SOLVING PRINCIPLE #87:** *Overly secretive behavior invites closer scrutiny and suspicion.*

Effective problem solvers are up front in their dealings with people. This means being honorable and forthright in working with others, in communicating with individuals, both with those inside the school and the athletic program and with those outside. No, this doesn't mean that everyone knows your business or that you should not have appropriate professional confidences. What it does mean is that one should not be perceived as keeping deep, dark, inappropriate secrets, secrets that are viewed by others as a cover-up or a mask hiding all sorts of shenanigans. *Remember, the perception of impropriety is sometimes as bad as the actual act of impropriety.*

CONCLUSION

Since athletic departments are continually faced with a myriad of problems, both internal and external, it is important for leaders within the department to be able to deal with such problems in terms of preventing and resolving them. An important part of being prepared to deal with problems involves taking the time and effort to study problem solving. Yes, one can learn from experience but experience can often be a harsh teacher. It is far better for future and current athletic administrators to become professionally engaged in the study of problem identification, prevention and problem solving.

For, in reality, there is a body of knowledge associated with problem solving. And, there are recommended actions and decisions that one can learn to implement in an effort to deal with challenging situations facing the typical school-based athletic program. The strategic action plan (SAP) forms the foundation of an athletic administrator's arsenal when facing problems both from within and from outside of the school and athletic program. Additionally, the 87 problem solving principles presented within the first two chapters of this book offer practical and helpful suggestions in terms of dealing with problematic situations.

EXERCISES FOR CHAPTER TWO

A. Is the fundamental process of solving problems in varying situations different? Explain.

_____

_____

_____

_____

_____

_____

B. Explain what is meant by effective *damage control*. Provide an example.

_____

_____

_____

_____

_____

_____

C. Is it a proper tactic to just wait and see if a problem will go away? Explain your position.

_____

_____

_____

_____

_____

_____

D. What is a *strategic action plan (SAP)* and how can it help an athletic administrator in terms of problem solving?

_____

_____

_____

_____

_____

_____

_____

E. Explain why problem solving is almost always done within a political climate and provide an example appropriate for a school situation.

_____

_____

_____

_____

_____

_____

_____

F. Why should athletic administrators take extenuating circumstances into consideration when dealing with problematic situations? Provide an example.

_____

_____

_____

_____

_____

_____

G. Can one learn from negative as well as positive experiences, one's own and those of others? Explain and provide examples.

_____

_____

_____

_____

_____

_____

_____

H. Which is more important—the *process* or the *end result* of problem solving? Explain in detail your position.

_____

_____

_____

_____

_____

_____

_____

I. Explain your philosophy about assigning blame when mistakes or problems occur?

_____

_____

_____

_____

_____

_____

_____

J.   What is meant by *due process?*

_____

_____

_____

_____

_____

_____

_____

K.   Why is TQM important for the athletic administrator? What is TQM?

_____

_____

_____

_____

_____

_____

_____

L.   Why is it dangerous to create or to have unhappy or angry customers? Who are the customers of the athletic department?

_____

_____

_____

_____

_____

_____

REFERENCES

Cardone, D. (2000). Your best team. *Athletic Management XII,* 3, pp. 44-47.

Nicklin, J.L. (1995, January 27). Business buzzwords in academe. *The Chronicle of Higher Education. XLI* (20), A-33.

Staffo, D. (2001). A First Down. *Athletic Management, XIII* (2), 37-41.

Stier, W.F., Jr. (1995). *Successful Coaching—Strategies and Tactics.* Wm C. Brown. Iowa: Dubuque.

Stier, W.F. Jr. (1997). *More fantastic fundraisers for sport and recreation.* Human Kinetics. Illinois: Champaign.

Stier, W.F., Jr. (1999). *Problem solving for coaches.* Boston: American Press.

Stier, W.F., Jr. & Schneider, Robert C. (2001). Desirable Qualities, Attributes and Characteristics of High School Athletic Directors — As Viewed by Principals. *Applied Research in Coaching and Athletics Annual, 16,* 89-109.

CHAPTER THREE

Problem Solving Strategies and Tactics in Athletic Administration

CHAPTER OBJECTIVES

After reading this chapter you will be able to:

- Appreciate that an administrator is often judged in terms of how others views the person addressing problems and controversies
- Be aware of the importance of keeping one's emotions in check when solving problems and not overreacting to problems
- Provide examples of operating in a *crisis management mode*
- Acknowledge the importance of anticipating problems, difficulties and challenges
- Define the *worse case scenario* concept and provide examples
- Provide examples of being politically astute as an athletic administrator
- Realize the importance of compromise in the problem solving process
- Be familiar with the concept of *administering by walking around (ABWA)*
- Understand the *red queen syndrome (RQS)*
- Be familiar with the concept of *take everything that people tell you with a grain of salt*
- List some of the tools, resources and assets available to the problem solver
- Explain how the organization's policy manual (5P handbook) can be of assistance in solving and preventing problems
- Recognize the fallacy of instituting change for change sake
- Reveal why one should not rely exclusively upon precedents in solving problems
- Point out the value of maintaining exacting records in addressing problems

> **SURVIVAL STRATEGY/TACTIC #1:** *Athletic administrators must be prepared for problems or prepared to fail.*

Being an athletic director, by the very nature of the job, involves dealing with problems and problematic situations. Perhaps one of the most important skills or abilities that an athletic director can possess might well be the ability to *prevent, resolve or solve problems* (Stier, 1985). The time when the AD, at the secondary or the collegiate level, could look forward to professional involvement within the school-based athletic scene with little thought being given to dealing with severe and oftentimes demanding problems is long gone, if it ever existed. Today, and in the future, the mark of a competent athletic administrator is one who is adept in success-fully, i.e., effectively and efficiently, solving problems and handling challenges, and dealing with the resulting fallout.

ADDRESSING THE CHALLENGES OF PROBLEM SOLVING

The school-based athletic administrator in the 21st century, by the very nature of the job, must be able to deal with single as well as multiple problems, both large and small, almost on a daily basis. That is just the nature of the position. One must expect problems. Life is just like that. It may not be fair—but whoever said that life has to be fair.

> **SURVIVAL STRATEGY/TACTIC #2:** *How one deals with hurdles is the mark of an effective administrator.*

Excellence and execution in men's sports [Courtesy of Washington State University]

Excellence and effectiveness in women's sports [Courtesy of Washington State University]

How one deals with prob-lems, difficulties, challenges and hurdles associated with an athletic department is the mark of a truly effective manager and director, figure 3.1 (Stier, 2000). How one deals with problems and with the people involved in problematic situa-tions also determines the de-gree of success or failure of any athletic director in terms of the overall scheme of things, espe-cially in the eyes of the central administration. The person who is better skilled in dealing with potential and actual problems as well as with controversial issues will experience more success and enjoy greater longevity in one's role as an athletic administrator. Those who are less successful frequently do not stay in the profession as an administrator for a significant length of time.

Timing of One's Decisions and Actions

> **SURVIVAL STRATEGY/TACTIC #3:** *Don't make decisions when angry, in a hurry or under tremendous pressure.*

Athletic administrators must never make a decision when they are personally angry or upset. Likewise, ADs should never make a decision when they are in a hurry, when they are pressed for time. Instead, it is recommended that administrators be methodical, that they take their time while under "fire" or pressure (Wilson, 2001). A wrong decision is, all too frequently, much worse than no decision at all.

Before one makes a quick (rash) decision be sure you are playing with a full deck (in possession of all information and facts) *and* on a

Figure 3.1: Overcoming hurdles by going over, around, under or through.

level playing field. It is imperative that the decision making process not be impeded by outside or distracting factors. Decisions are hard enough to make, one should not make it doubly hard on oneself by working under adverse conditions.

SURVIVAL STRATEGY/TACTIC #4: *Don't be surprised by anything — expect the unexpected.*

Athletic directors and their fellow athletic administrators must be prepared for almost anything in the performance of their professional responsibilities. Don't be surprised by anything. Anticipate. Predict. Expect the unexpected.

Failing to anticipate is sometimes a sign of not being prepared. And, there can rarely be a legitimate excuse for a lack of preparation. Of course, no one can really accurately anticipate everything. However, experienced athletic administrators should nevertheless strive not to be surprised by almost anything. And, meaningful experience coupled with appropriate formal training can go a long way to helping the athletic administrator meet this challenge.

SURVIVAL STRATEGY/TACTIC #5: *Keep one's emotions under control—always maintain a proper professional demeanor.*

Everyone has feelings. Sports people have feelings. They are human. They can become excitable. They can be emotional. They can often become *really emotional*. And, they sometimes allow their emotions to affect their decision-making ability. This, however, for the athletic administrator engaging in the process of dealing with problems and challenges, is a big no-no. Never allow emotions to sway or affect the decision-making process when addressing a problem or controversial situation.

It is absolutely essential to keep one's activities and actions on a professional basis—at all times. Keep one's emotions and personal feelings separate and distinct from whatever decisions are made. It is important to remember that athletic administrators are always held to a higher level of behavior in terms of the expectations of others, especially their superior and the general public. This is because they are professionals, specifically trained and educated in the art and science of managing and administering athletic programs and dealing with a wide range of individuals, groups and organizations under all types of circumstances and situations (Stier, 2003).

One of the worse criticisms any athletic administrator can receive is to have one's integrity or impartiality called into question. This is especially true when the cause of such an accusation is one's own personal emotional involvement in the situation. The rule of thumb is simple: keep a proper, professional perspective when dealing with problems. Operate at arms length.

> **SURVIVAL STRATEGY/TACTIC #6:** *To overreact is never appropriate, especially in the face of controversy, the unusual or the unexpected.*

To overreact, by definition, involves a negative action. Whenever one is surprised or faced with controversy, it is imperative that one not overreact—visibly as well as internally. It is especially important not to be viewed by others as overreacting in terms of deed or action. Being ruffled and/or showing signs of being upset or disconcerted are poor examples for mature, experienced and knowledgeable athletic administrators to show to others. Additionally, overreacting often implies making hurried and inappropriate decisions, decisions not based on careful and rational reasoning.

It is important to *look confident* as a problem solver and decision maker. One should never lose one's composure as an athletic administrator. Others frequently see doing so as a sign of weakness. It calls into question the competency, the wisdom and the maturity of the athletic director. It is a deficiency that is not looked kindly upon by others, especially those who think that ADs should be the epitome of confidence and maturity. Making inappropriate decisions as a result of an overreaction to a problem or difficulty creates an additional difficulty/problem in addition to not resolving the problem—that of painting the AD as one who "shoots from the hip" rather than carefully weighing all options and then carefully choosing an appropriate course of action or inaction.

> **SURVIVAL STRATEGY/TACTIC #7:** *Deal with a problem when calm, cool, and collected.*

Figure 3.2 An Athletic Director should be like a duck—be cool, calm and collected on top while paddling like the dickens under the water.

An important tenet in problem solving is to deal with potential and actual problems while being *calm, cool and collected* (the three **Cs**). At least give the impression that you are calm, cool and collected even if on the inside you are not. Just don't run around like a chicken with its head cut off. Such action certainly doesn't inspire the greatest of confidence among coaches, other co-workers, athletes, their parents, or outsiders. And no one respects the department's or program's "chicken little" who constantly spouts doom and gloom whenever challenging problems crop up.

> **SURVIVAL STRATEGY/TACTIC #8:** *Problem solving is like a duck on water—present a picture of being calm, cool and collected while paddling like the dickens beneath (figure 3.2).*

Haste, in too many instances, does indeed make waste, especially when attempting to resolve a difficult or complicated situation. Decisions made under pressure, when there is stress and strain upon those individuals involved in decision making and problem solving, are too frequently poor decisions. Be like the duck on the pond — calm on top but working (paddling) like the dickens underneath — all the while allowing criticism (water) to run off your back.

PLANNED AND ANTICIPATORY MANAGEMENT VERSUS CRISES MANAGEMENT

Reaction Versus Proaction

> **SURVIVAL STRATEGY/TACTIC #9:** *Avoid the crisis management school of thought— be proactive, don't merely react.*

When confronting any major problem, successful problem solvers assume a proactive stance rather than merely a reactive stance. First of all, those who subscribe to the proactive model anticipate difficulties and problems and are prepared to deal with them well in advance of their actual occurrence. This involves advance planning, foresight and a willingness to anticipate possible happenings and consequences.

Looking Ahead to the Future

> **SURVIVAL STRATEGY/TACTIC #10:** *Anticipate problems, challenges and pitfalls as well as possible consequences.*

Obviously, It is better to take one's time to think through all of the possible consequences of one's potential options, prior to rushing headlong into a specific course of action only to find that the action has backfired. In such situations the consequences are sometimes worse than the original problem(s).

Whenever one is faced with problems, whenever one is faced with tough decisions, it is advisable to attempt to anticipate the consequences of *not only your decisions and actions but also the actions and decisions of others in reaction to your decision or your action(s)*. No, this is not double speak, it is anticipation. Act as if you are in a chess match and anticipate the consequences, two, three and even four moves in advance of your own actions and the reactions of others.

Being interviewed by the press—a necessary skill for today's collegiate athletes [Courtesy of University of Tennessee Sports Information Department]

In this way you are better able to foresee what the future might hold for you should you choose any one of several possible alternative courses of action. As the song goes, "only a fool rushes in where angels fear to tread." Only a fool or an incompetent would act or make a decision without taking into consideration the possible or probable reactions and responses of others, especially those who are intimately involved, or those who might be adversely affected, or those who might be in a position to evaluate (and reward/discipline) the athletic administrator. These individuals might be one's own superiors as well as the general public.

Act Wisely, Appropriately and Decisively—Practice Effective Damage Control

> **SURVIVAL STRATEGY/TACTIC #11:** *One must deal with problems before they become significant, possibly insurmountable embarrassments.*

Athletic administrators who fail to anticipate problems or challenges are seen as incompetent, it is as simple as that. Such failure is just unacceptable for a professional administrator of sports within a school setting. Procrastination can indeed be a Cardinal sin. Failure to deal with a problem in an appropriate and timely fashion when it arises is simply inexcusable. As indicted earlier in this book (chapter two), failure to address the possibility of problems arising is like an ostrich with its head stuck in the sand. However, for an administrator the consequences can be both immediate and quite negative, including the loss of the managerial position.

> **SURVIVAL STRATEGY/TACTIC #12:** *Be aware of the worst case scenario syndrome.*

The worst case scenario syndrome refers to being aware of what could possibly go wrong and then planning, in advance, what to do should a significant problem or catastrophe actually take place. In other words, planning for the worse case scenario means anticipating what could go wrong and then taking appropriate measures to either prevent it from going wrong or to correct or resolve the situation once the problem surfaces.

Planning for the worse case scenario assumes that Murphy's Law is operating at full force, that is, whatever can go wrong will go wrong at the worst possible time and place. Invoking the worse case scenario means that the negative consequences, if any, will be substantially reduced, if not fully negated.

> **SURVIVAL STRATEGY/TACTIC #13:** *Be cautious about making and implementing major changes when new to a position.*

Athletic directors, when new to a situation, often begin to immediately making major changes—in one or more areas. Here, a word of caution is due. Before embarking on a new particular course of action or deciding on and implementing truly major changes, it is wise for the administrator to first take time to assess the situation and circumstances in which one finds oneself. Rushing headlong into making changes without evaluating all aspects of the athletic situation is foolhardy indeed. *Change for change sake is imprudent, if not asinine.*

Granted, changes are often necessary when a new athletic director assumes responsibility for a school-based athletic program. Often, that is why a new AD is hired in the first place, i.e., to institute major changes.

Nevertheless, it is best to discern the political ramifications of any such major moves or changes prior to rushing headlong into what might well turn out to be a mistake. Thus, determining the past and present circumstances associated with the position, the personnel and the programs, and then determining — with input from other trusted colleagues, advisers and mentors — what changes might be suitable, appropriate and timely is the better course of action. Athletic directors new to a particular situation need to be quick learners in their new positions of responsibility and authority lest they fail to grasp the political ramifications of various actions and/or decisions.

REMAINING POLITICALLY ASTUTE AS AN ATHLETIC ADMINISTRATOR AND PROBLEM SOLVER

> **SURVIVAL STRATEGY/TACTIC #14:** *When solving problems never underestimate the political aspects.*

Every problematic situation facing an athletic director has significant potential political overtones and consequences. Failure to realize this fact of life can place an AD in great jeopardy. Being an AD involves power, power to make decisions, power to direct others, power to make demands, etc., of others.

Use of this power can have severe political ramifications and consequences in the athletic arena. Serving as an athletic administrator involves dealing with people, a whole host of individuals, groups and organizations. And when one deals with people there is always the possibility that others may exert power in a detrimental way towards the leader of the athletic program. Parents may have political power and influence over school boards and school administrators. Business people may have similar power and be able to influence those individuals who actually have formal power, authority and influence over the athletic administrator.

As a consequence, athletic directors (as well as all athletic administrators) must be political animals. An AD must be politically aware that specific decisions and actions might have fallout that could possibly result in power being exerted in a negative fashion against the AD—both from within the athletic organization and from without. Thus, it behooves the administrator to anticipate possible power moves and attempts by others to negatively influence the opinion held by the AD's superior(s) towards the AD.

> **SURVIVAL STRATEGY/TACTIC #15:** *Don't shoot oneself in the foot or stick a foot in one's mouth—don't make stupid mistakes.*

Think, think and then think some more. Being an athletic director is difficult enough without doing something stupid with the result that the AD's job is just that much more difficult. Don't commit moronic errors either through words or actions/inactions. Don't shoot oneself in the foot or stick one's foot in one's mouth as a result of truly inexcusable errors. There will be ample opportunities for any number of mistakes by the AD, both in and outside of school and the athletic scene. Don't compound the situation by committing foolish mistakes or errors that the typical, competent and prudent administrator would not make.

> **SURVIVAL STRATEGY/TACTIC #16:** *Have an open mind when facing problems and difficult situations.*

Many people often have preconceived ideas and beliefs about certain situations. These are sometimes expressed as biases and prejudices. Athletic directors don't have the luxury of acting in this manner. The problem with having preconceived ideas is that the individual is less open to new or different ideas, concepts, and ways of doing things. One shouldn't be stagnant—either in the way one thinks or in terms of how one acts. Doing so classifies the individual as a rigid, unbending and uncompromising ignoramus.

Instead, be open to new ideas. Be flexible. Listen to what others have to say, to suggest and to recommend. Be sensitive to the feelings of others by being receptive to their input and *then making up one's own mind in light of one's knowledge, experience and training.* Society is neither stagnant nor static and neither should the athletic administrator be when attempting to resolve difficult situations.

> **SURVIVAL STRATEGY/TACTIC #17:** *Be willing to compromise, to negotiate—don't always be a "hard person."*

Compromise is not a dirty word. Nor is it a sign of weakness. One should not be so proud as to be unwilling to entertain the possibility of making compromises. Of course, this does not imply that one can compromise one's ethics or morals. However, there are many situations that do not involve ethics or moral standards that can very well be suitable for wise negotiations and just compromises.

Yes, athletic directors need to be willing and capable of making tough decisions. But they also need to be just and fair in making these same decisions. Thus, it is not a mark of a competent AD or problem solver to be inflexible, unwilling to compromise. Rather, it is a mark of a competent administrator, a caring individual, to be able and willing to take extenuating circumstances into consideration while balancing a multitude of factors that might affecting a potential compromise.

In today's society, all of us live in a political world. In today's society, it is rarely "cut and dry" or "black and white"—there are many grades of gray. Athletic directors, both to be fair and to be able to survive as an administrator, out there on the "firing line" of sports, must be willing to remain flexible and to entertain appropriate compromises. In the end, such compromises do not cast aspersions upon the image of the AD or weaken the AD's position. Rather, willingness to remain flexible and adaptable only strengthens the position of the individual in question.

SURVIVAL STRATEGY/TACTIC #18: *Be wary of hidden agendas when dealing with people.*

Whenever you deal with others it is wise to ask yourself why these individuals are acting the way they are acting and why they are saying the things that they are saying. Attempt to determine the rationale behind the actions and words of other individuals. Attempt to determine the motivation behind what others do and say. But, also be wary of so-called hidden agendas.

Being alert to hidden agendas is a crucial element to the survival of any athletic administrator. People and groups of individuals do not always mean exactly what they say. People sometimes, many times, have alternative reasons for acting the way that they do. They frequently have hidden agendas, that is, their actions and communications do not adequately or honestly reflect their true attitudes, feelings, opinions or objectives. Some individuals say things and do things in order to reach objectives or accomplish tasks that are not clearly apparent to the casual observer. It sometimes takes concentrated effort to discern these hidden agendas, and even then there is no guarantee that one can truly ascertain such hidden agendas. Nevertheless, for the AD to be consistently successful and to enjoy longevity, being able to distinguish such hidden agendas is imperative.

BECOMING PERSONALLY INVOLVED
WITH THE PROBLEM SOLVING PROCESS

It is sound advice to never take things too personally as an AD. Don't become personally involved to the extent that when things happen you react as if you (or your family) were personally insulted or verbally abused or assaulted (even if you or they were). Athletic administrators have a job to do. Part of that job involves sometimes becoming a target for disparaging words and comments. Sometimes, people and organizations take opposite positions from the stance taken by the AD. Sometimes people are upset with the athletic department, its leadership, the sports programs and activities, with decisions that have been made or with decisions that have not been made.

SURVIVAL STRATEGY/TACTIC #19: *Never take things personally.*

It is important to remember that deep down people are usually not upset with the athletic director personally, that is, on a personal level. It is just that the AD is the ultimate authority figure, an individual who can easily become the target of others' exasperation, criticism, and yes, anger. It is the AD who personifies authority, the person who is in charge, the person who is responsible for seemingly any and all problems, challenges and difficulties. And, it is frequently the AD who makes decisions that not all individuals will either agree with or support.

Although there can be disagreements in any athletic situation. The key is to keep such disagreements on a professional level and not to allow the situation to gravitate into a personal confrontation. Ideally, even if people should feel uncomfortable or be upset with some aspect of the athletic department or program or with a decision of the AD, they are not usually personally angry at the AD, as an individual, as a person. From the AD's perspective, the objective is to keep any confrontation on an impersonal basis so that the resentment or anger vented by others does not become concentrated or focused solely upon the AD, thus making it personal.

SURVIVAL STRATEGY/TACTIC #20: *Don't think you know it all.*

No one appreciates a "know-it-all"—least of all those individuals who are involved in a controversial situation or problem and are fighting for what they believe to be right and just. Athletic administrators should never give the impression of being an arrogant nincompoop. Yet, sometimes that is just the image that others have of some administrators, that is, conceited, snobbish, and full of themselves.

A close play—a matter of microseconds
[Photo by Geof Anderson, Florida International University]

Instead of projecting an image of self–importance, ADs need to foster the image, both by their actions and their words, that they are down–to–earth, modest and unassuming. Part of this image creation and projection rests upon one's ability to know when to keep quiet and when to speak. Similarly, the manner in which one communicates — both verbally and non–verbally — can have a significant effect on how others perceive a person.

SURVIVAL STRATEGY/TACTIC #21: *Take a real personal interest in helping individuals with the problem or difficulty—don't be detached.*

It should be remembered that a key element in solving any problem relating to school-based athletic programs is for athletic administrators to take a personal/professional interest in the welfare of the youngsters participating in the athletic program. ADs need to really care about the athletes. They can demonstrate this caring by being willing to help youngsters help themselves, by staying close to the athletes and showing genuine interest in them and their activities not just because the individual might be an outstanding athlete but because the individual deserves such attention and consideration.

Caring is about having meaningful person-to-person relationships, professional relationships. Without such relationships existing between athletic directors and the school's athletes, it is much more difficult for ADs to be able to help athletes and to have a positive impact upon them.

SURVIVAL STRATEGY/TACTIC #22: *Practice good problem solving through ABWA— administering by walking around.*

Athletic directors need to be seen as actively working to solve problems and resolve difficulties. They need to be seen as working very hard at administering and managing the athletic department and all of the sports programs. They need to be seen as diligently working to help others (other managerial staff, coaches and athletes) develop skills and competencies.

In the world of athletic management such visibility is referred to as *Administering By Walking Around* or by the acronym ABWA (Stier, 1999, p. 106). Athletic administrators need to be seen by others as hard working and as caring individuals. They need to be recognized as competent mentors. They need to be seen by others as diligently working and competently discharging their responsibilities. Without such visibility it is more difficult for the individual administrator to do one's job and perform the myriad responsibilities that come with the title of athletic administrator, whether it is as athletic director or as an associate/assistant athletic director, or some other athletic administrator/sport manager.

SURVIVAL STRATEGY/TACTIC #23: *Be aware of the Red Queen Syndrome.*

Athletic directors must be aware of the Red Queen Syndrome, referring to the fairy tale *Alice in Wonderland* in which the Queen tells Alice to run as fast as she can just to stay where she is. Athletic directors need to be aware of this syndrome in which they perceive themselves as (or actually are) working ever harder and yet they seem to be making no real progress. To the contrary, athletic administrators must be perceived as hard working and also being productive in the sense of actually reaching meaningful and worthwhile objectives and goals.

One Gains Respect the Old Fashion Way—By Working At It

Respect must be earned. Respect cannot be merely demanded by the athletic director. Everything that an AD does and doesn't do has a direct effect upon what others think about that person. And, everything an AD does and doesn't do can affect the respect that others have of the person filling the shoes of the AD.

As a result, ADs need to be careful in their relationships with others lest they be viewed as overly demanding or expecting respect merely by means of the fact that they hold the title of athletic director. Nothing could be further from the truth. Respect does not automatically come with the title of athletic director or athletic administrator. Respect is earned. It is earned by what one does, by how one acts, by how one interacts with others. Similar to the television ad that was popular some years ago, one gains respect the old fashion way, by earning it.

Receiving Data and/or Information from Others

Experienced athletic administrators recognize that not everything they are told or shown should be accepted as gospel. It is not that people deliberately attempt to convey falsehoods or misrepresent facts. But, there is a tendency for some individuals to exaggerate information or embellish upon the truth. Others are simply biased in their perceptions and this colors the information they attempt to convey. And, of course, some people are just mistaken or misinformed in their attempts to communicate.

> **SURVIVAL STRATEGY/TACTIC #24:** *Take everything that people tell you with a "grain of salt."*

Whatever the cause of misinformation, it is imperative that ADs indeed take with a "grain of salt" that which they are told by others, whether they be coaches, athletes, parents, boosters, colleagues, etc. Always seek correct information and accurate facts. Always seek confirmation. Do not rely on hearsay or gossip or unsubstantiated information or data.

APPROPRIATE AND TIMELY DECISION MAKING

> **SURVIVAL STRATEGY/TACTIC #25:** *Make sure that others know that you are on top of the situation (problem).*

Whenever an athletic director deals with a problematic situation it is important that that individual convey to others, both internal and external to the sport organization, that the situation is under control and is being handled appropriately. Everyone, interested parties as well as bystanders, need to be reassured that everything is as it should be, that what is being done is being done by a trained, knowledgeable, experienced, caring, professional and competent administrator/manager.

As a consequence, it is simply good management to attempt to skillfully communicate in a timely fashion, via one's words, one's presence as well as actual activity, that one is on top of things, that pertinent information is being sought, appropriate decisions are being made and necessary actions are being considered. One of the goals of problem solving is to generate confidence among those individuals and groups involved that justice and fairness will prevail. Anything that will create an atmosphere of confidence in the athletic administrator as a problem solver is worth considering because of the importance that such confidence plays in the eventual acceptance of any final decision pertaining to the problem or challenge at hand.

> **SURVIVAL STRATEGY/TACTIC #26:** *Take stock of what has transpired previously when new on the job.*

When an athletic administrator is new to a particular job (position or responsibility) it is important to take time to learn what has taken place in the past within the new athletic scene. This is especially important when an individual assumes a new position *within a new organization*. New administrators need to understand what has happened in their new organization (and its programs and activities) in the past so that they can be in a better position to make informed decisions, both day-to-day managerial decisions as well as problem solving decisions.

> **SURVIVAL STRATEGY/TACTIC #27:** *Be cautious when making a major or important decision—always gather necessary and pertinent facts.*

One must have facts before making major decisions. Making a determination on a serious matter without adequate facts or data is akin to committing professional suicide. It is just irresponsible. It also is counterproductive in the world of problem solving. Yes, decisions must be made. However, they must be informed, intelligent and fair decisions. And without knowledge of all of the pertinent facts such decisions are few and far between.

Thus, it is important that administrators go the extra mile to become familiar and knowledgeable in terms of the facts and any extenuating factors surrounding any problem situation. Gathering, sorting and evaluating information, details and facts might be a time consuming task but the consequences are well worth the effort. This remains true even if the time it takes to gather and interpret such information seems to be inordinate.

> **SURVIVAL STRATEGY/TACTIC #28:** *Take advantage of all tools, resources and assets available.*

Of course it would be foolish indeed to attempt to resolve a difficulty or to meet a challenge without first having access to and taking advantage of all available resources, tools and assets, figure #3.3 (Stier, 1999, p. 92). This means being cognizant of all of the available resources in terms of individuals, their skills and their support. It also means being capable of utilizing numerous types of current technology and tangible assets when faced with solving problems or resolving difficulties.

Unfortunately, there are many athletic administrators who fail to take full advantage of the resources that may be available to them in their search for solutions to prob-

Figure 3.3: Taking advantage of all available tools, assets and resources when faced with problems and challenges

lems. Sometimes, these resources take the form of established policies, procedures and practices of the department or the school or organization. At other times the resources include personnel. And, in still other situations, resources are hard, tangible assets.

Regardless of the type of resources or tools, the important point to remember is that administrators must not be hesitant or neglectful in terms of taking advantage of such resources—whether these assets be (1) individuals (coaches, administrators, parents, boosters, etc.), (2) mechanical devices (computers, tape recorders, fax machines, phones, etc.), or (3) existing laws, rules, regulations, policies, procedures, practices or priorities.

> **SURVIVAL STRATEGY/TACTIC #29:** *Prior to making decisions in an effort to solve problems, one must have the authority to do so.*

It is important that one possess the appropriate authority, responsibility and power before attempting to make problem-solving decisions. One must not attempt to make decisions or to solve problems for which one has no responsibility or for which one does not have appropriate authority or the power to act.

To do so is worse than meddling, for such action usurps the responsibility of others and interferes with the normal operation of the organization. Athletic administrators should never be seen as interfering in situations in which one has no business (no direct responsibility or authority) as such action can lead to many more difficulties than the actual problem the administrator desires to revolve. To put it another way, the athletic administrator might do well not to put one's nose where it doesn't belong. One tends to get less bloodied that way.

> **SURVIVAL STRATEGY/TACTIC #30:** *Changing things for change sake is foolish and a waste of effort and resources.*

It is frequently claimed that change is inevitable. This may or may not be an accurate statement, but even if this were true, administrators should think twice before making significant changes in their department or any of their athletic programs just for the sake of making a change. In point of fact, athletic administrators should be sure that they have legitimate, reasonable and appropriate reasons for doing everything that they do, including instituting major changes or adjustments within the athletic domains.

To act in any other manner is not good managerial practice and just cannot be justified. To make changes on a whim is nonsense. To institute significant modifications in the department for less than a legitimate reason is a sign of a weak administrator. Such an action weakens the confidence that others should have in the administrator's judgment and decision-making. Simply put, significant changes should always be initiated only after suitable time has been spent appraising the appropriateness of such a change—including potential consequences, both negative and positive.

> **SURVIVAL STRATEGY/TACTIC #31:** *When addressing problems or considering possible decisions or actions—don't rely exclusively upon precedents.*

Just because something was done a specific way in the past does not necessarily mean that it has to continue to be done that way, now or in the future. There is a very real danger in relying upon precedents to such a degree that the athletic administrator loses sight of new, better, and perhaps unique ways available to address problematic situations or troublesome obstacles.

Different times necessitate looking for fresh and creative ways of handling challenges and difficulties. At least the athletic director needs to consider other courses of action rather than merely relying on past methods of handling troublesome situations.

Cheerleaders form a solid supportive base for today's competitive teams.
[Courtesy of Sports Information Office, University of Arkansas]

Problems solving tactics, techniques and methods that have proven to be successful in the past might or might not be equally effective and efficient in the present or in the future. There is nothing inherently wrong in looking for new ways to address challenges and solve or resolve problematic situations.

> **SURVIVAL STRATEGY/TACTIC #32:** *Maintaining excellent records facilitates effective decision making in problem-solving situations.*

Creating and maintaining excellent (accurate, complete, neat and organized) records is an absolute must for all athletic administrators. Both those who wish to prevent problems as well as those currently involved in the problem solving process must create and maintain excellent records. This means, in many instances, that an accurate historical record must be kept of one's actions prior to, during and following the actual problem solving effort.

Good record keeping is most important in the area of risk management, an area seemingly ripe for problems facing the athletic administrators. With the ever-present danger (and likelihood) of lawsuits being initiated against schools, athletic programs and athletic personnel, it behooves the athletic director to keep detailed and factual records and to insist that all athletic personnel do the same. The reason for this is simple; such records can help clarify what has and has not taken place as well as form a basis for future decision-making. The rule is simple—write it down, insure that it is accurate and understandable, make it easily accessible, and keep the documentation in a secure place.

> **SURVIVAL STRATEGY/TACTIC #33:** *Cross the T's and dot the I's when maintaining records.*

Record keeping is only as good as the content/quality of the records, both in terms of accuracy, legibility, completeness, impartiality and retrievability. When creating good records it is necessary to pay attention to detail—both in the prevention and the solving of problems. Yes, having a vision is all-important but one must not neglect the "nuts and bolts" that go to make up the bigger picture.

Athletic directors are all too often judged by others in terms of how much they pay attention to details. And managing a complex and complicated athletic program in a high school or college/university certainly involves a tremendous amount of details, details that cannot be overlooked without being negligent.

> **SURVIVAL STRATEGY/TACTIC #34:** *Be wary of someone who wishes you to act in a particular fashion.*

All problem solvers, including athletic administrators, are continually faced with the situation in which others, both inside and outside of the organization, are attempting to manipulate their decision-making and influence their actions. As a result, great caution must be exercised lest an administrator initiates a course of action as a result of undue influence of others, rather than because of a carefully thought out plan based upon careful consideration of all relevant facts and assessment of possible outcomes and consequences. ADs need and want input and suggestions from others, their staff as well as others. However, there is a difference between seeking and receiving counsel and input from others and being manipulated by others in one's decision making.

> **SURVIVAL STRATEGY/TACTIC #35:** *Do not allow others to unduly influence your thinking or decision making — your decisions must be your own.*

Just as athletic directors are often anxious to share their viewpoints and positions with new administrators or superiors, these same ADs will also have other individuals attempt to influence their thinking and actions as an administrator. This is not an infrequent situation insofar as managers/administrators are concerned. However, this situation is especially acute when a new athletic director comes into the picture. There are many individuals who might like to gain the ear of the new administrator in an effort to share their own viewpoints and beliefs, their own biases, and their own perspectives.

There is nothing inherently wrong in people attempting to communicate their positions, their viewpoints, with the athletic director. However, it is nevertheless crucial that the AD recognize that this process is taking place. It is also necessary to be capable and willing to adequately screen and accurately interpret and assess the numerous communications, opinions and suggestions one receives. ADs must be able to communicate effectively, they must be able to listen and decipher messages accurately and intelligently, but they also need to be in a position where they can sift through all of the various communications, ideas, concepts and suggestions and yet still arrive at their own decisions, based upon facts (data), their own experiences and their skills as an administrator, manager, motivator, and leader.

Every athletic director needs to be his or her own person. An AD should not be unduly influenced by others to the extent that one's decisions are not one's own but are the decisions of others, those who have influenced the administrator to think, act and/or speak in a certain way. Thus, every administrator must be a quick "learner" in his or her positions of authority. Every

AD also needs to be very perceptive in understanding what others are really attempting to communicate and still be able to make the so-called tough decision in a timely fashion.

> **SURVIVAL STRATEGY/TACTIC #36***: Be able and willing to go beyond the expected call of duty in terms of time expended and effort exerted.*

The nature of managing athletic programs within our nation's schools is such that those individuals who go into the sport management profession must recognize the need for putting in long hours as well as working very hard and very smart. However, in addition to this expectation of hard work and long hours, athletic administrators need to be willing to go beyond the expected call of duty and put in whatever energies are necessary to get the job done.

Of course, just trying hard is not the answer either. Every earnest and dedicated athletic administrator wants to try hard. The crux of the mater is being able to actually be successful in reaching objectives and goals, not just working hard or giving the impression of working diligently. Nevertheless, being seen as one who puts in the necessary time and who makes the appropriate effort (sacrifice) is necessary. One should be seen as one who goes beyond the normal expectations when the situation calls for it. But, there is still the matter of actually getting the job done.

> **SURVIVAL STRATEGY/TACTIC #37***: One of the most important tools in the arsenal of any athletic director is the organization's departmental policy manual (5P Handbook).*

A mark of a competent athletic director is the existence of a well thought out, thoroughly organized and updated, and concisely written departmental policy handbook (5P handbook). It is the duty of the athletic director not only to see to it that such a publication exists but that it is read, understood and followed by the appropriate staff (Problem Solving Principle # 29). Such a document is the Bible for the sports program. Such documents are often referred to as the 5P Handbooks or Documents—*Policies, Procedures, Practices, Priorities and Philosophies.* Such handbooks or manuals contain specific policies, procedures and practices governing the operation of the athletic department and hence it guides the actions of coaches, other staff members and athletes. They also include a statement of philosophy or a mission statement of the athletic department. And, the contents of the handbook or manual reveal the priorities of the sports program as well.

Failure to adhere to the stated policies, procedures and practices outlined in such a document is usually an invitation for trouble, unless there is a very good reason for deviating from the norm. Thus, generally speaking, following the guidelines and policies in the handbook is a key strategy in avoiding or preventing problems. Similarly, once problems occur, the policies, procedures and practices found in the handbook often times guide the athletic administrators to more effectively and efficiently deal with and handle those problems that do arise, whatever they might happen to be.

> **SURVIVAL STRATEGY/TACTIC #38:** *Encourage coaches to develop their own sport handbook or team playbook.*

There is another type of handbook that is very important for athletic departments in addition to the departmental handbook or manual (chapter one). There should also be various coaches' sport handbooks in existence. Each handbook (for each sport offered by the school) can either be shared with players or kept among the coaching staff. Such a handbook, depending upon its content and its purpose, may also be given to parents in an effort to communicate with them and to keep them informed as to what their youngsters will be doing and why.

If this handbook (created by individual coaches) is a players' handbook, it is referred to as a playbook. Such a playbook may contain information regarding team rules, physical and psychological conditioning plans, as well as actual strategies and tactics (plays) that the athletes are expected to master. However, some coaches feel that such a handbook is for the coaches' eyes only. In this eventuality, the coaching handbook might include even more detail in terms of strategies and tactics. It could include specific information relative to facts that coaches have a need to know and to have ready access to.

Some athletic directors encourage their coaches to share a type of handbook with parents. In this eventuality the publication should include informative and interesting tidbits particularly prepared for moms and dads. For example, a rationale for the individual coach's expectations of the youngsters, a detailed explanation of team rules and consequences for violations of such rules, an explanation of the conditioning programs that the youngsters are to be involved in, as well as information in terms of how parents might become appropriately involved with their youngster's athletic participation.

Naturally, although there is no single way that coaches' handbooks and players' playbooks have to be organized, there are some factors that are typically found in such publications prepared for athletes and/or parents. Nevertheless, since there are many different approaches in terms of what should or could comprise their content, it is up to the coaching staff (with assistance and input from the athletic administration) as to how to plan and organize such documents. The key concept, however, is that such devices (tools) should be used as teaching and/or reference documents. As such, these publications can serve as essential elements in the prevention and handling of problematic situations.

CONCLUSION

If athletic directors and other athletic administrators are to be consistently successful in addressing problematic situations within the school-based athletic environment, they must be capable of devising strategies and implementing tactics to prevent as well as resolve problems and challenges that they will inevitably confront. The key to surviving these troublesome situations rests in being able to take a proactive stance by anticipating their occurrence and the fallout from these difficulties. It is imperative that athletic administrators be capable and willing to preplan regarding how to avoid those situations that might develop into full-blown problems or challenges.

Nevertheless, since some problems and difficulties will always surface to plague athletic departments regardless of the amount of preplanning which takes place, it is vitally important that the leaders of athletic departments be extremely skilled and professionally prepared in handling these difficulties in such a manner that the fallout is minimized — for the sake of the athletic staff as well as for their athletic programs and teams. This necessitates that the individual athletic administrator be willing and has the ability and skill to make insightful and wise choices as well as to take decisive action when faced with adversity.

Successful athletic administrators are excellent (expedient, efficient and effective) problem solvers. They are also skillful in preventing many potential difficulties from ever becoming reality. They are resourceful in expeditiously and fairly resolving those problems that do manifest themselves. And, finally, successful athletic administrators (at both the secondary and the collegiate/university levels) learn from their own and others' experiences, both successes and failures.

EXERCISES FOR CHAPTER THREE

A.   Discuss: How one deals with problems is the mark of a competent athletic administrator.

_____

_____

_____

_____

_____

_____

B.   What is the so-called *crisis management school* of thought?

_____

_____

_____

_____

_____

_____

C. How can the *worse case scenario syndrome* be of assistance to the athletic administrator?

_____

_____

_____

_____

_____

_____

D. Provide an example of a *hidden agenda* situation in terms of addressing a potential or existing athletic problem.

_____

_____

_____

_____

_____

_____

E. Why would it be to the benefit of the athletic administrator to practice *ABWA?* Provide an example of a school athletic director subscribing to this practice?

_____

_____

_____

_____

_____

_____

F. How should athletic directors view information that others convey within a problematic situation? Why?

_____

_____

_____

_____

_____

_____

_____

G. How important is it that others (including one's superior[s]) be aware of the athletic director's effort and accomplishments in dealing with potential and real problems? Why?

_____

_____

_____

_____

_____

_____

_____

H. What role should precedents play in the athletic administrator's decision-making process in handling and preventing problems and difficulties?

_____

_____

_____

_____

_____

_____

I.   How can the athletic director maneuver the "land mine field" in terms of accepting the
     advice and/or influence of others, including subordinates?

     _____

     _____

     _____

     _____

     _____

     _____

     _____

J.   Outline the advantages of the athletic department's policy manual (5P handbook). What
     should be included in such a publication and who should be given a copy? Why?

     _____

     _____

     _____

     _____

     _____

     _____

REFERENCES

Stier, W.F., Jr. (1985). *Expectations of coaches toward athletic directors*. A paper presented at
     the New York State Athletic Administrators Association, Saratoga Springs, New York.

Stier, W.F., Jr. (1999). *Managing Sport, Fitness, and Recreation Programs: Concepts and Prac-
     tices*. Boston, MA: American Press.

Stier, W.F., Jr. (2000, August 26). *The Past, Present and Future of Sport Management*. The 2000
     International Sport Management Congress—*Current Situations and New Directions for Sport
     Management: From the Perspectives of Cultural Differences, Seoul Korea*.

Stier, W.F., Jr. (2003, April 5). *Challenges and Opportunities: International Multidisciplinary Organizations*. Presentation made at the National Conference of the American Alliance for Health, Physical Education, Recreation and Dance, Philadelphia, Pennsylvania.

Wilson, S. (2001). Keeping the peace. *Athletic Management, XIII* (2), 22–24, 26–29.

CHAPTER FOUR

Strategies for Establishing and Maintaining Productive Interpersonal Relationships

CHAPTER OBJECTIVES

After reading this chapter you will be able to:

- Understand strategies for developing and refining interpersonal relationships
- Cite reasons justifying why athletic administrators should treat each athlete as individuals
- Acknowledge the need to train one's staff in how to handle problems
- Describe appropriate delegation of responsibilities and authority
- Feel comfortable in seeking advice and assistance from advisers and experts
- Realize that the obtaining of facts is essential in the problem solving process
- Recognize that seeking guidance and assistance from others is not a sign of weakness
- Define the words *centers of influence* and understand their importance in problem solving
- Appreciate the importance of having loyal paid and loyal volunteer staff members
- Explain the rationale behind not jumping the chain of command
- List the possible consequences of a change in the administration of an athletic organization
- Illustrate the consequences of leaving a position under less than ideal circumstances
- Acknowledge the ineffectiveness of offering mere excuses for problems
- Recognize that administrators are held responsible for problems that occur *on their watch*
- Understand that effectively handling of adversity is the mark of a successful athletic administrator

Individual interaction between the coach and the athlete
[Courtesy of Larry Levanti, Rutgers Sports Media Relations]

There is always a need for athletic administrators to be able to relate well to others. In fact, being able to develop and foster positive interpersonal relationships with individuals and groups of individuals is one of the key factors in the survival rate of such administrators. This is true at all levels of school-based competition from junior high school through the collegiate/university level. Such positive relationships begin with one's administrative staff, coaches, athletes, with advisers, with family members, and with superiors (administrators) as well as with a variety of other individuals, both on and off the academic campus.

DEVELOPING RELATIONSHIPS WITH ATHLETES

Athletes are easily the most important category of individuals with whom an athletic director must develop sound interpersonal relationships. The relationships between the AD and individual athletes, and the various teams as a whole, are pivotal to the overall success of the athletic program as well as the success of the AD. Everything the AD says and doesn't say as well as everything the AD does and does not do will have an effect upon the relationships that will be created. Hence, ADs must be very careful in their actions and in their communication efforts with athletes. They need to be viewed by athletes as knowledgeable, supportive, fair, honest, and caring. To be viewed otherwise is inviting disaster.

> **SURVIVAL STRATEGY/TACTIC #39:** *Never embarrass or humiliate athletes.*

A major snafu among ADs is to cause embarrassment to others (Problem Solving Principle # 65). In terms of athletes, this can be done any number of ways—either deliberately or unintentionally, by word or deed, by omission or commission. Regardless, whenever an athlete is embarrassed or worse, humiliated, serious harm is done to the relationship between the athlete and the leadership of the athletic program. Not infrequently, such damage to this all important administrator-athlete relationship is irreparable.

The concept is simple. Athletic directors should never do anything that embarrasses or humiliates any athlete. ADs need to be very careful lest they inadvertently cause grief to athletes through thoughtless actions or statements. Similarly, it is essential that miscommunication does not play a role in causing ill feelings with athletes or other individuals within the athletic scene.

> **SURVIVAL STRATEGY/TACTIC #40:** *Treat all students and student-athletes as individuals—know their names.*

It is important that students and student-athletes feel as if they are individuals and not mere numbers or clogs in a large wheel. Students should feel as if they are recognized by the athletic leadership for whom they are and what they do, in school as well as outside of the school scene. This means that athletic directors need to really know who the students are. They need to know the student-athletes' names for a start. ADs also need to know the names of the parents of the youngsters. This show of personalization goes a long way to creating and nurturing a meaningful, professional relationship with athletes and their families.

> **SURVIVAL STRATEGY/TACTIC #41:** *When coaches encounter problems with dissident athletes, encourage the coaches to work with youngsters.*

One of the most common areas of problems has to do with the decision whether or not to keep an athlete on a team or to remove the youngster from the sports scene. Although this challenge faces coaches, almost on a daily basis, it also confronts ADs as the ultimate decision maker in the athletic department. Thus, it behooves the athletic director to assist coaches in handling problematic athletes so that any disciplinary action that is deemed necessary will not blow up in everyone's face. ADs and coaches always walk a thin line in terms of handling disruptive situations involving athletes.

DEVELOPING RELATIONSHIPS WITH STAFF

Athletic directors are only as successful (productive and competent) as their staff, both full and part-time, paid and volunteers. Therefore, it is absolutely essential that ADs possess excellent professional and personal relationships with their staff, especially in terms of the prevention and resolution of problems and conflicts.

> **SURVIVAL STRATEGY/TACTIC #42:** *Surround one self with competent staff and then listen to them while making the final decision oneself.*

If one is fortunate enough to have staff (volunteers and/or paid), one should not waste them by not taking the time to listen to them (always with a grain of salt). To not take advantage of one's staff and is a terrible waste of available talent. No athletic director is omnipotent. ADs should not act as if they are. The AD is only as strong as each staff member on the administrative team.

One's treatment of staff is an important element in the success of any administrator, especially in terms of preventing and resolving the multitude of problems faced in any athletic situation in terms of programs, activities and people. Treating staff members as gofers is not only wasteful but also alienating and counterproductive. Naturally, the final determination in every major decision making situation is that of the athletic director. But, failing to seek input from one's staff is inexcusable. Others can and do have good ideas, input and suggestions—take advantage of such.

> **SURVIVAL STRATEGY/TACTIC #43:** *Possessing qualified and motivated staff can often prevent problems as well as mitigate their negative consequences.*

One must have quality staff. It is often better to have no support staff than incompetent staff. But, it is often tedious and hard work to go through the process of seeking, evaluating and selecting appropriate athletic support staff, including assistant administrators, both paid and volunteer. In order to secure qualified personnel one must be involved in creating an accurate and adequate job description, advertising the vacancy, screening and interviewing potential employees; then hiring, orientating and training each new employee. Nevertheless, quality staff, competent staff, dedicated staff will more than compensate for all of the hard work and effort expended. With the presence of competent support personnel the task of administering the overall sports program is much easier.

When personnel problems do arise it is imperative that athletic directors attempt to *work their way through the difficulties*. All too frequently some ADs seem to think that the best and quickest way to resolve a personnel problem is to do away (fire) with the individual who is the apparent source of the difficulty. *Wrong. Dead wrong.* It is easy to fire. It is much more difficult to work with individuals to assist them with overcoming whatever difficulty or problem that they are experiencing.

> **SURVIVAL STRATEGY/TACTIC #44:**   *Athlete directors need to train their staff to adequately handle problems and pressures.*

Using one's staff to its fullest is a mark of a wise, prudent and intelligent administrator and manager. Part of the secret to taking advantage of the skills and talents of qualified staff is to train individuals to handle real and perceived problems associated with the athletic scene. Similarly, preparing staff to handle the accompanying pressures associated with such problems is likewise essential. Staff members who are able to adequately adjust to problematic situations can save a great deal of heartache and headache on behalf of the CEO of the athletic department.

> **SURVIVAL STRATEGY/TACTIC #45:**   *One must delegate appropriate responsibilities and authority to one's staff — ADs cannot do everything by themselves.*

A critical area where problems can frequently occur for athletic directors is associated with the process of delegation, specifically, delegation of authority, responsibilities *and* power. Athletic directors cannot and should not be expected to do everything themselves. They must, due to the very nature of their job and their responsibilities, be able and willing to delegate some significant tasks to others, their assistants, various volunteers and to coaches.

There are three key concepts concerning delegation whenever an athletic director delegates a task or tasks to another individual. *First*, the act of delegation does not free the athletic director from the ultimate responsibility for the task(s) in question. This necessitates that the AD must continue to supervise and check on the task(s) delegated to another person in an effort to insure that assignments are being carried out correctly, appropriately and in a timely fashion.

Second, whenever a job or chore is delegated it is imperative that appropriate authority is granted commensurate with the responsibility given to a person. The granting of responsibility without adequate authority (and support) is foolhardy, and yet it is done far too often. It all too frequently dooms the person, to whom the responsibility is delegated, to certain failure.

Third, along with responsibility and authority it is also necessary that the person being delegated a task or chore be given the power (resources) with which to complete the task or chore. Without the resources needed to do the job delegation is useless. Again, such failure all too frequently dooms the person, to whom the responsibility is delegated, to certain disaster.

SURVIVAL STRATEGY/TACTIC #46: *It is important to publicly support your staff (if at all possible)—privately, educate and reprimand the individual(s) if an error was made.*

Problems happen. Problems are often caused by people. Frequently, problems emanate from the actions or inactions of one's subordinates. When a staff member for whom an athletic director is responsible comes under fire or criticism for a possible error or poor judgment it is important for the athletic director to publicly support the besieged individual—if at all possible. Of course, this statement does not imply that all actions of a subordinate in all situations can or should be defended by the athletic director.

Obviously, there are times and situations in which specific conduct and judgment on behalf of a subordinate is simply wrong or inappropriate; and thus, is inexcusable, indefensible and unsupportable — regardless of the situation or circumstances. In such situations, swift and decisive action is warranted and indeed necessary on behalf of the athletic administrator (supervisor). This is especially true if the consequences of the subordinate's actions are significant in terms of causing harm to others or to the athletic program or activities.

However, in other situations, with different circumstances, it is indeed appropriate for the athletic director go to the proverbial wall to publicly support and defend one's staff, the staff's judgment and the staff's actions (or lack thereof). This is true even if an individual staff member is guilty of a mistake in judgment or incorrect action.

Thousands of fantastic and sometimes fanatical fans support their favorite team
[Courtesy of Tennessee Sports Information Department]

In some instances a staff member may make an honest mistake, may do something or say something that the athletic director would not have done or said—but the end result is not a matter of life and death. In such an event, it is suggested that the AD publicly support the individual staff member while privately consulting and advising that individual as to what might have been a better of course of action. The objective is to support the individual staff member while simultaneously educating the individual so that the person knows about the mistake as well as why it was wrong so that the faux pas is not repeated.

DEVELOPING RELATIONSHIPS WITH ADVISERS

SURVIVAL STRATEGY/TACTIC#47: *Solicit information from appropriate individuals and constituencies when addressing problematic situations.*

Obviously, it is very difficult, if not impossible, to adequately and fairly deal with all problems by oneself. Thus, it behooves the athletic director to solicit information from others, individuals and groups, who might possess knowledge and data that might prove helpful in the solution of the problem at hand. It is important to recognize that these individuals are not necessarily restricted to one's staff.

What one should never do is attempt to go it alone for fear of looking weak by asking for either assistance or for information. The key to seeking such testimony is to seek input and advice from those who are in a position to know things that are appropriate and pertinent to the current problematic situation. The manner in which one seeks such information, and the selection of the person from whom assistance is being sought, have a great deal to do with the quantity, the quality and the reliability of that information and data.

> **SURVIVAL STRATEGY/TACTIC #48:** *Don't hesitate to seek facts and information from others—seek additional information in order to understand the facts of the case.*

Athletic administrators are not expected to make decisions in complicated problem situations without taking time and expending the energy necessary to secure all of the facts. Without facts informed decisions are difficult, if not impossible. Information is vital. Knowledge is power. Yet, athletic directors, regardless of how many years they have been in the business, do not know everything—nor are they expected to.

When faced with problems or difficulties, it is imperative that ADs seek out information, facts and data from a variety of sources and individuals. And collecting and collating these facts and opinions involves asking or canvassing others for such knowledge. As a result, one should never be too proud to ask others for assistance or for additional facts pertaining to the problem. Besides, one of the greatest compliments any individual can give to another human being is to ask advice or suggestions of that person.

Asking for assistance or suggestions is not a sign of weakness. Rather, it is indicative of an individual who is sure of oneself, one who is unafraid to seek out the advice and counsel of others who might be able to shed light on a confusing or obscure situation. Athletic directors should not be so proud as to hesitate to ask for assistance in addressing a problematic situation.

> **SURVIVAL STRATEGY/TACTIC #49:** *Don't be too proud to seek help from others.*

Nowhere is it carved in stone that an athletic administrator must make the decision by oneself. Just as it is necessary to solicit facts, information, and opinions from others, it is also frequently necessary and appropriate to seek and obtain actual help in the decision making process itself.

All too often, other individuals, because of their position, their experience, and their training, possess skills and insight not held by the athletic administrator faced with the current difficulty. Consequently, asking these knowledgeable individuals for help in resolving conflicts or problems is not only a wise move but failing to do so is sometimes considered self-defeating.

Nowhere is it said that the athletic director cannot or should not ask for help from others in solving difficult situations [Problem Solving Principle #81] (Stier, 1997, p. 57).

SURVIVAL STRATEGY/TACTIC #50: *Take advantage of more experienced, knowledgeable and trusted advisors.*

Athletic directors need to cultivate individuals who can serve as trusted advisers and counselors. Such individuals are invaluable assets for the AD. ADs need to continually attempt to professionally cultivate and take advantage of such unselfish counselors and confidants throughout one's career. These intimate supporters should possess the loyalty, experience, wisdom and knowledge to truly be of significant help through their guidance and counsel.

These counselors and advisers, with no ax to grind or personal involvement, are frequently in an excellent position to provide both impartial and insightful guidance and direction. Athletic administrators, when facing big problems, are sometimes so close to the problem situation and are so intimately involved (both personally and professionally) with the situation and the people, that they have a much more difficult time remaining neutral and objective.

DEVELOPING RELATIONSHIPS WITH FAMILY MEMBERS

SURVIVAL STRATEGY/TACTIC #51: *Don't neglect one's family because of the* JOB.

Administering and managing a school-based athletic program is a very demanding and time consuming responsibility—at all levels. Many problems faced by athletic directors emanate from the relationships between themselves and their spouses (and children, if any). It is very important that the athletic directors neglect neither their spouses nor children in the quest for job excellence and professional success and advancement. It is just too high a price to pay.

An athletic director can be committed to being a successful administrator and manager *while still not neglecting the family scene.* One key is to have a spouse who understands the time commitments and sacrifices necessary in order for an athletic director to be competitive and successful within the profession. Having a supportive and understanding family is all important in the life of an AD because it allows the AD to spend the time and expend the energies required for survival and advancement in such a challenging and time consuming profession. However, an equally important key is for the AD to recognize the necessity of also spending *quality time* with one's family.

Lets face it, far too many times some athletic directors seem to make work for themselves and/or spend more time on sport related activities than is really necessity. When an AD has a spouse, it is important that the AD recognize *that one is married to that spouse and not to the job.* Failure to have this understanding and to prioritize one's efforts and time expenditures in an appropriate fashion can result in severe problems—both personally and professionally.

DEVELOPING RELATIONSHIPS WITH HIGHER ADMINISTRATORS AND SUPERIORS

> **SURVIVAL STRATEGY/TACTIC #52:** *Earn the confidence of influential people—both in and outside of one's organization.*

Every athletic director needs to be political, that is, professionally political, in a positive sense. This is necessary if one is to survive and thrive in the competitive business of athletic management. Part of being politically astute involves having the ear (earning the confidence) of individuals who are in influential and powerful positions. It is imperative that others who are able to wield significant power and/or are able to influence other centers of influence, both in and outside of the sport organization, hold the athletic director in high esteem.

Ease of access to such powerful individuals by athletic directors is very, very important. Being able to physically reach and communicate with people of influence empowers the individual AD. This is because the AD is able to obtain a personal audience where the administrator may be able to influence the powerful and influential and/or secure assistance as well as actual physical assets. Failure to have ready access to the successful and powerful within one's community and within the school itself places the athletic administrator at a decided disadvantage.

> **SURVIVAL STRATEGY/TACTIC #53:** *Don't keep your superior(s) in the dark.*

One of the worst things anyone can do when faced with problems or potential problems is to keep one's boss(es) in the dark. To the contrary, informing one's superior(s) that there is a potential or current problem and that you are on top of the situation is frequently a wise move. *First* of all, by informing your superior(s) of the situation you have an opportunity to not only keep others in the loop but also to solicit and actually receive advice.

Second, running by your superior(s) your tentative plans in terms of how you are thinking on handling the situation can effectively cover your backside should your action result in negative consequences. This is especially true when your boss(es) was(were) aware of your plans (and perhaps had even agreed to or given approval for that particular course of action). This is an example of having one's boss(es) climb out there on the proverbial limb with you — it is better to have company out there on that limb, especially those above you on the organizational ladder.

> **SURVIVAL STRATEGY/TACTIC #54:** *Don't by-pass your boss or jump the chain of command.*

It is a good rule of thumb in the world of business (and administering an athletic program is indeed a business) that says *if you are going to work for someone, then do it. If you work for an individual then do your job to the best of your ability. This includes being loyal to the individual who is your superior.* Jumping the chain of command, jumping over the so-called head of one's superior, is not only unprofessional but can easily prove to be a threat to one's very existence as an athletic administrator.

No one wants anyone on his or her staff who is not supportive, much less treacherous and disloyal. Supervisors of athletic administrators or managers look critically upon such staff who by-pass the so-called chain of command. This is true whether the person making the end-run is an assistant athletic director who complains directly to AD's boss or superior (without going through the athletic director) or an athletic director who attempts to by-pass one's boss or superior by heading straight to someone higher up on the ladder of authority (and power) with a complaint or grievance. If you work for a person, then work for that person and be honest. An appropriate poem dealing with loyalty between an employer and an employee is provided in figure #4.1. *[Note, in today's world of political correctness the term "man" would be replaced with "person"]* (Stier, 1999, p. 80)

Loyalty

If—you work for a man, in heavens name work for him:
speak well of him and stand by the institution he represents,
remember, an ounce of loyalty is worth a pound of cleverness
... if you must growl, condemn, and eternally find fault,
resign your position and when you are on the outside,
damn to your heart's content ... but as long as you are
a part of the institution do not condemn it ... if you do,
the first high wind that comes along will blow you away,
and probably you will never know why.

by Elbert Hubbard

Figure 4.1: Loyalty—A necessary ingredient when working with others

---

SURVIVAL STRATEGY/TACTIC #55:   *Take steps to insure one's superior agrees upon the major direction and goals of your program as well as your overall methods of operation.*

If athletic administrators would do one very simple thing—understand exactly what their superior(s) expect of them, and then work towards those objectives—many problems might be averted or at least diminished. It is truly foolish for an athletic administrator to act in a particular way or work towards a specific objective if one's superior does not feel that such actions are appropriate and/or the objective or goal is worthwhile and desirable.

And yet, that is exactly what some sports personnel do (Stier, 1995). That is, some individuals take it upon themselves to determine the priorities of a program or a given situation without conferring with higher-level administrators. This is simply a very bad idea. Severe problems can result in such situations with the end result being a strained relationship with the very person the athletic administrator is dependent upon, the very person with whom the AD should enjoy the very best of personal and professional relationships.

SURVIVAL STRATEGY/TACTIC #56: *When you don't agree with what is taking place, one must still always act professionally.*

Junior and Community Colleges offer a wide range of sports for students.
[Courtesy of the National Junior College Athletic Association—NJCAA]

No one ever said that athletic administrators have to agree with their superiors or other higher ups. However, they do have to always act professionally—especially when they find themselves *not in agreement* with a superior(s). Part of being professional in such instances is to remain supportive and loyal to the higher ups as well as the program and activities while keeping professionally confidential the disagreement between oneself and the superior(s) in question.

Under no circumstances should the athletic administrator take such disagreements public. Disagreements with what is being done within a program, that is, policies, procedures, practices, priorities and philosophies (5Ps), is to be expected whenever strong willed and assertive people are involved. Athletic administrators (as well as their superiors) are often strong willed and assertive, they must be if they are to survive in the often harsh world of competitive sports. However, any conflicts between athletic administrators and their superiors should be kept behind closed doors. Publicly, the athletic administrator should endorse the policies, procedures, practices, priorities and philosophies of the school within which the athletic program exists even if the individual does not agree with them.

SURVIVAL STRATEGY/TACTIC #57: *An athletic administrator must always publicly support the organization and adhere to its policies, procedures and practices.*

When athletic administrators (whether as athletic directors or other athletic managers) find themselves in disagreements with superiors in terms of decisions or with established policies, procedures, practices, priorities and philosophies, there are only three acceptable courses of action open. *First*, the person can stay in the position and merely accept things as they are—while continuing to work in a professional manner to change that which one finds disagreeable. *Second*, to stay in the position, accepting the situation, and concentrate on other matters at hand. And, *third*, to leave that particular athletic or administrative situation to seek another position more in tune with one's own philosophy and managerial style.

If any disagreement or conflict is so severe that the athletic administrator is professionally unable to publicly endorse or accept the disputed practice, decision or policy in question, then it behooves that person to leave that particular managerial position. It is better to depart and look for so-called greener pastures than to be caught in a situation in which one acts unprofessionally by being disloyal to one's organization and one's superiors and/or to compromise one's ethics and ideals.

SURVIVAL STRATEGY/TACTIC #58: *Change in the administration within a school (especially in personnel) usually brings about many changes—competent athletic administrators are adaptable and prepared for such change.*

Schools are always faced with a potential change in central administrators. It is important to realize that whenever one has a new boss or superior there is always a distinct possibility that other significant changes (5Ps) within the organization might also take place. Some of these changes might come early on in a new administrator's tenure. Other changes might take place later. But change will inevitably take place and the athletic administrator must be ready for any and all such changes.

While some of these changes might not bode well for the individual athletic administrator, other changes might very well benefit a particular person, program or activity. However, if such changes do create problems and challenges for the athletic administrator—such is life. It is important, nevertheless, to anticipate the possibility of such changes or impediments within the athletic arena, whenever new superiors come upon the scene. The objective at that point is to adapt and adjust to the new situation and circumstances and yet still reach appropriate objectives and goals.

SURVIVAL STRATEGY/TACTIC #59: *Insure that new administrators (superiors/supervisors) are aware of your strengths, competencies and contributions to the organization and program.*

A new arrival in the form of a superior and/or supervisor often necessitates a professional effort on behalf of the athletic administrator to see to it that the newcomer is appropriately made aware of one's areas of expertise, competencies and strengths as well as one's past and future contributions. Although this must be accomplished most discreetly and most professionally (lest one be viewed as a braggart, or worse), it is still advisable that the new person assuming the role of higher authority be made aware of the professional qualities and the value of the athletic administrator.

The tactics available to accomplish this task are many. They will vary in light of (1) the personality, experience, reputation and skills of the athletic administrator, (2) the individual situation in which the athletic administrator is employed, as well as (3) the circumstances currently existing within the school itself, including the athletic scene.

> **SURVIVAL STRATEGY/TACTIC #60:** *Be professionally assertive when dealing with superiors.*

An important element in the relationship between any athletic director and a superior, whether that person is a principal, assistant superintendent, superintendent, dean, vice president or president, is to remain professionally assertive. One does not have to be a mamsy pansy or milquetoast when dealing with superiors. Most quality supervisors don't want a mere yes person on their staff. However, one should not be overly aggressive either. There is a thin tightrope that athletic directors (as well as all athletic administrators) walk in their dealings with various superiors. Failure to manipulate this middle ground between being an over obnoxious prima donna and a wimp is a sure way to self-destruct.

> **SURVIVAL STRATEGY/TACTIC #61:** *One is remembered by how one leaves a professional position as much as by what one accomplished in the job.*

Sport administrators are frequently able to point to many accomplishments and achievements in their prior professional engagements or positions. And many others within the school and the community will also have memories of how individual athletic administrators were thought of while they were employed in the school, in their community.

However, athletic directors should remember that the perceptions that others hold of them (as administrators and as human beings) will be determined as much by the manner of their departure as by what they were or were not able to accomplish during their tenure within the institution and/or in the community. This is especially important when an athletic administrator has left under less than desirable conditions. If the manner of one's departure is negative, this can often leave a bad taste in people's mouths regardless of whatever positive accomplishments the administrator might otherwise have been able to achieve while on the job. It is wise to remember that people tend to have long, very long memories.

Leaving a post while taking pot shots at individuals, groups, the school or the community achieves nothing in the end except increasing animosity among others. There is little to gain, either personally or professionally, by leaving an athletic position while blasting or criticizing others. Many individuals who have utilized this tactic have found that it has backfired and has, in fact, hindered their professional efforts in the future. Hence, it is better, for the most part, to attempt to depart from one professional post for another under the most professional and cordial terms possible.

DEVELOPING RELATIONSHIPS WITH OTHERS

> **SURVIVAL STRATEGY/TACTIC #62:** *Always compliment others and say thanks—recognize the achievements of others.*

One of the great compliments a person can give to others is to *publicly* compliment and pay homage to those individuals for their accomplishments. Paying attention to achievements of others and then publicly recognizing such achievements and accomplishments is an appropriate course of action—both for motivational purposes as well as for political reasons.

> **SURVIVAL STRATEGY/TACTIC #63:** *Never display anger, annoyance or irritation with others who do not agree with you.*

It is also necessary that athletic director refrain from becoming acrimonious or hostile in their relationships with others. It simply does no good to actually become antagonistic toward another person or group. And it is certainly counterproductive to let such negative feelings affect one's own life, one's own decision-making processes. The adage: one gets more with sugar than vinegar is certainly appropriate in this instance.

Most individuals don't deliberately go around attempting to make life unbearable or difficult for others. People, for the most part, act and do things not out of malice but because they honestly believe that they are right or that their position is the correct or appropriate position. It just probably seems that way sometimes for some athletic administrators. However, in the long run, administrators would do well to refrain from becoming angry on a personal basis toward others because of the other person's actions or inactions. The resulting adversarial relationship that is sure to result can only hinder progress towards a reasonable settlement of the issue at hand.

> **SURVIVAL STRATEGY/TACTIC #64:** *Never burn one's bridges with people, organizations or programs.*

Burning so-called bridges only makes enemies and usually hurts the person doing the so-called burning. This is especially important when leaving an organization for a new job. It is always wiser to keep that professional lifeline intact between oneself and one's prior colleagues, superiors and employers.

From a very practical standpoint, one never knows when prior associates, contacts, friends, employers, etc., will be contacted in the future by potential employees as well as others. One never knows when one's prior contacts will prove to be an advantage or a hindrance in the future. And it does no good to burn one's bridges as the athletic administrator departs for seemingly greener pastures—regardless of how tempting it might be to tell someone off. Simply put, refrain from the temptation to lambaste or castigate someone—even if that individual deserves it.

> **SURVIVAL STRATEGY/TACTIC #65:** *Never criticize others behind their backs.*

There is a cliché that advises that *if you can't say anything nice about someone—then don't say anything.* This truism is something that all athletic administrators should adhere to in their normal performance of their managerial duties and administrative responsibilities. This is especially true when addressing problems and challenges in the workplace. Too often individuals criticize others—behind their backs. Such action is unacceptable, unprofessional and unethical. If one is to be critical then one should do it to the other person's face, not secretly behind that individual's back.

When one becomes known as a person who furtively criticizes others, that person earns a reputation as an individual who is not forthright, who is not honest, and who is not trustworthy. Such a reputation or characterization can, in itself, serve as an impediment when that individual attempts to develop trust within a problem-solving situation.

In the end, it is far better to say nothing than to castigate persons behind their back lest one become known as a person who is not forthright, that is, cannot be trusted. Problem solvers need such trust.

DEALING WITH ADVERSITY—AND SURVIVING

> **SURVIVAL STRATEGY/TACTIC #66:** *Don't hire a person for a job unless there is a good chance of that person being successful.*

All athletic directors need to adhere to this sound piece of advice. Since preventing problems is much easier than solving them, it is really important that individuals on one's staff have a reasonable chance of success in the performance of their duties and responsibilities. This necessitates that great care be taken in assessing all aspects of a potential job vacancy position – both internal and external – and then working very hard and diligently to create a good match between the job and the person filling the job.

> **SURVIVAL STRATEGY/TACTIC #67:** *There must be a good match between the job and the person filling that position.*

Finding, attracting and hiring the right person for the job prevents the often unnecessary job hoping found in many athletic departments and programs. Far too often staff job hop from one position to another, sometimes motivated because of the existence of numerous, inevitable and severe problems associated with the previous post.

Athletic directors should see to it that the candidates who apply for jobs on their staffs not fall in love with and accept an administrative or other type of managerial position unless there is a reasonable possibility that with hard work, dedication and skill, the potential employee will be successful, in a reasonable amount of time. If not, then it is best not to hire that person for if one fails as an athletic staff member the consequences can be disastrous for the staff member, the athletic program as well as the athletic director. Athletic directors should make would-be staff members aware that if they are unsuccessful in a job, regardless of the reasons, it sometimes becomes even more difficult to secure subsequent quality offers of employment as a coach or athletic staff member at a different school.

This is also an important concept for athletic directors to consider in terms of their own job placement and career planning. ADs need to accept professional positions where they will have a reasonable chance of being successful in the performance of their duties and the fulfillment of their responsibilities.

> **SURVIVAL STRATEGY/TACTIC #68:**   *Don't bite off more than you can chew.*

In the process of administering and managing an athletic program or department, and especially when attempting to resolve problems, it is very important that one does not take on more than can be handled in terms of time, effort and skill. Not infrequently, athletic administrators, especially young, inexperienced managers, assume that they can do everything—all the time. They fail to recognize the fact that there is a point of diminishing returns when an individual becomes less effective, less successful because that person is attempting to do too much, too soon and in too short a period of time, with inadequate resources and tools.

To the contrary, it is important for an athletic administrator, one who is held responsible for programs, activities and staff, to know what is possible, what can be accomplished in any given situation and under specific circumstances. In other words, *it is important to know what you can do well and don't attempt to do that which you cannot do well.* Don't try to be all things to all people—it doesn't work. Following this truism will enable athletic administrators to prevent many problems having to deal with their own level of competency and proficiency and their resulting image and reputation. One cannot do everything. Nor should one try. And it takes a confident, knowledgeable, skilled and competent administrator/manager to realize this and act accordingly.

Student/athletes must be successful in the classroom as well as on the proverbial playing field.
[Courtesy of University of Colorado Athletics]

> **SURVIVAL STRATEGY/TACTIC #69:**   *Know when to say "no" to people.*

Thus, knowing one's own capability and potential is a mark of a competent athletic administrator and adept problem solver. Sometimes, many times, administrators must simply say no when asked to assume duties and responsibilities. Individuals must feel free to decline further obligations on their behalf that might, in the end, reduce their overall effectiveness as a manager and as a problem solver. Frequently, failure to do so only places the person in a situation from which there is no escape and the negative consequences are even greater and there are more numerous problems than before.

SURVIVAL STRATEGY/TACTIC #70:   *Provide results—don't offer excuses.*

There will always be difficulties and problems encountered in running or supervising any athletic department, program or activity. People will make mistakes and commit errors—both of omission and commission. Even hard working, honest and forthright individuals goof, sometimes. In some instances, it might be coaches, parents, boosters, fans, or even athletes who will make mistakes and commit blunders. In others, it could be an athletic administrator, including the athletic director, who makes an error, who will be wrong, incorrect, mistaken. It is not the end of the world (usually) for a person, even the athletic director, to make a mistake. It is usually not the end of the world for the athletic administrator to admit to a mistake, one's own as well as a subordinate's or someone for whom the administrator is ultimately held responsible—and then go on, then to proceed with one's job.

The problem lies in those situations in which an individual, for whom the athletic director is ultimately responsible for, makes a mistake or there is a problem or difficulty within the athletic program and the athletic administrator attempts to offer excuses. Those to whom the athletic director report to don't want excuses, they want action, they desire results, positive results. In point of fact, nobody really likes excuses or excuse makers. Thus, it behooves athletic administrators to look beyond excuses and concentrate on resolving the difficulty or solving the problem—expediently, effectively and efficiently.

The Problem with Blaming Others

SURVIVAL STRATEGY/TACTIC #71:   *When problems arise don't waste time and effort attempting to blame others—work on resolving the difficulty.*

As stated earlier, problems will crop up within any athletic scene. It is part of the process of providing extensive athletic competitive opportunities (for participants and/or as spectators) for a wide range of individuals within the community. However, how one reacts to the existence of a problem is critical to the eventual success or failure that one experiences in attempting to solve it. When faced with a problem don't waste time attempting to immediately affix blame for the situation. It only wastes time and frequently impedes the problem solving process itself *(Problem Solving Principle #59).*

Instead of being overly concerned with who is at fault, concentrate on solving the difficulty. Start to evaluate the situation, collect data and determine the facts surrounding the difficulty or problem. Don't distract yourself and others by trying to find out who was at fault. There will be time enough for that after the problem has been dealt with in an appropriate and timely fashion.

There are two problems with attempting to blame others when a problem develops. *First*, it places others on the defensive and in some instances may encourage or force others to cover up details, data and information needed to solve the problem—lest these same details, data and information cast a negative light on them, their actions and their competency. *Second*, blaming others is akin to making excuses and does little to endear oneself to one's superior(s). It is too akin to making superfluous excuses.

Three Strikes and You Are Out (Stier, 1999, p. 88)

There is a well-known adage in athletic circles involving individuals who attempt to shift the blame and responsibilities or otherwise make excuses whenever there were problems. It seems a new athletic director, upon arriving at a new job site, found four sealed envelopes left by the previous AD, along with a personal handwritten note. The note indicated that should the new athletic director experience any difficulties or problems, that a possible solution could be found by merely opening, in order, one of the four envelopes marked #1, #2, #3 and #4—and following the directions provided within.

And, sure enough, shortly after taking over the new job, the athletic director encountered a significant problem. Sitting down at the desk, the AD cut open the envelope marked #1 and read the following message: "Give as an excuse the fact that you are new to the job." The AD did just that and, sure enough, this tactic worked.

Some weeks later another problem arose and the AD again was thankful for the legacy of the four envelopes left by the former administrator. Opening this second envelope revealed the following suggestion: "Blame me, your predecessor." And, as with the first excuse, this suggestion worked just as well—and the AD again survived a very difficult situation.

When a third problematic situation developed shortly thereafter, the athletic administrator went back to the office and sought out the third envelope. Opening the envelope, the following message was read: "Blame the problem on your subordinates." And, similar to the first two instances, this suggestion enabled the AD to survive this additional controversy.

Nevertheless, the inevitable happened and it wasn't too long before the athletic director was embroiled in yet a fourth challenging difficulty (read *problem situation*). Realizing that yet another envelope lay in his desk, the AD rushed to his office, sat down at his desk, and quickly opened the very last envelope. To the desperate AD's consternation there was only the following message: *"Prepare Four Envelopes."*

SURVIVAL STRATEGY/TACTIC #72: *One is ultimately held responsible for whatever happens on one's watch.*

The essence of this narrative is that one cannot continue to make excuses for problems or difficulties that one encounters by attempting to place the blame on other people or on the fact that one is new to that particular athletic situation. Making excuses is self-defeating. Attempting to place the blame on others for problems or for mistakes is shortsighted. Even if initially successful, blaming others and/or pleading inexperience or ignorance are only short-term solutions, very short-term solutions, indeed.

THE NECESSITY OF POSSESSING PRODUCT KNOWLEDGE

> **SURVIVAL STRATEGY/TACTIC #73:** *Know everything you can about your organization, program and staff—don't attempt to bluff your way through.*

Don't attempt to fly by the seat of your pants when confronted by problems. Athletes, parents and their peers usually quickly see through athletic directors who attempt to bluff their way past difficult situations. Bluffing one's way out of a tight situation is rarely effective. Be knowledgeable. It is vital that the athletic administrator possess what is commonly referred to as *product knowledge* about the athletic organization, its programs and activities as well as its personnel. ADs need to be knowledgeable not only in terms of the technical skills associated with the Xs and the Os of administering an athletic program, but also in terms of how to deal with individuals of all ages and from all walks of life.

Attempting to solve difficulties requires that the athletic administrator be conversant and informed about the particulars of that specific problem situation. Being confident, knowledgeable and skilled enables an individual to deal from a position of strength rather than ignorance (weakness). If an AD or other athletic administrator doesn't know the situation or isn't aware of the facts or is ignorant in some area—then that individual had better not attempt to fake it because others will usually see right through the charade.

HOW TO PROFESSIONALLY HANDLE CRITICISM

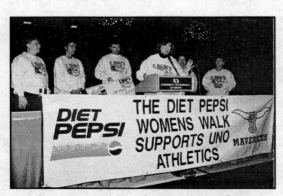

Corporate sponsors often provide significant financial support today.
[Photo by Tim Fitzgerald; Courtesy of University of Nebraska, Omaha, Athletics]

Athletic administrators will invariably be subject to criticism, sometimes from all sides. Administrators have to live with that aspect of being a manager of athletic programs. It just comes with the territory, period. Anyone with power and authority who makes decisions that can affect the lives of others is going to be criticized.

However, such decision makers must not wear their hearts on their sleeve and shouldn't be shocked when they are criticized. Being criticized, justly as well as unjustly, simply comes with the territory of being in a position of power as an athletic administrator. If an individual is unable or unwilling to be the target of such criticism, then being an athletic administrator becomes a significant challenge, if not an impossible task.

> **SURVIVAL STRATEGY/TACTIC #74:** *If one desires to be an athletic administrator, one must be prepared to accept criticism (just or unjust).*

Athletic directors who are able to accept criticism without letting such criticism severely interfere with their responsibilities and obligations will find themselves able to deal with the more important and pressing issues at hand. Conversely, those individuals who react to criticism by becoming easily upset and distracted by such criticism will find their administrative efforts significantly hampered and their overall effectiveness and efficiency severely diminished.

Theodore Roosevelt, former president of the United States created a brief poem that is most appropriate when one considers the topics of criticism and work. The poem is called The Battle of Life and is presented in figure #4.2. *[Note: In today's world of political correctness the term "man" would be replaced with "person."]*

The Battle of Life

In the battle of life it is not the critic who counts; not the man who points out how the strong man stumbled, or where the doer of a deed could have done better. The credit belongs to the man who is actually in the arena; whose face is marred by dust and sweat and blood; who strives valiantly; who errs and comes short again and again because there is no effort without error and shortcoming; who does actually strive to do the deeds; who knows the great enthusiasm, the great devotion, spends himself in a worthy cause; who at the best knows in the end the triumph of high achievement; and who at the worst, if he fails, at least fails while daring greatly, so that his place shall never be with those cold and timid souls who have tasted neither victory nor defeat.

Theodore Roosevelt

Figure 4.2: Handling adversity is the mark of a successful manager and administrator (Stier, 1999, p. 90)

CONCLUSION

Athletic administrators who conscientiously attempt to consistently develop positive relationships with others have a much better chance for a smooth running operation. It takes time, effort and skill to develop and maintain the kind of personal and professional relationships that facilitate the operation of the many aspects of any athletic department in a high school or college/university. Such relationships do not happen accidentally, they must be deliberately cultivated and maintained if they are to be meaningful.

However, regardless of how carefully an athletic administrator may work at developing meaningful relationships with others, there will be times when such efforts will be to no avail and there will be problems, and in many instances, the administrator will be severely criticized. One of the keys to sustained success as a manager or administrator is to be able to face such denigration without being angry or losing composure while at the same time continuing to do one's job as a decision maker and leader in the athletic arena.

EXERCISES FOR CHAPTER FOUR

A. What strategies might an athletic administrator follow to develop meaningful relationships with individual athletes?

_____

_____

_____

_____

_____

_____

B. How can an athletic director be sure to surround oneself with competent staff? Elaborate.

_____

_____

_____

_____

_____

_____

C. How far should an athletic director go to *protect* one's subordinates who make a mistake (including coaches)? Why? Provide an example.

_____

_____

_____

_____

_____

D. What strategies might an athletic director follow in an effort to not neglect one's spouse and family? Provide examples.

_____

_____

_____

_____

_____

_____

E. Should an athletic director be *political* within the problem-solving situation? Why or why not? Provide a positive example of an AD being political.

_____

_____

_____

_____

_____

_____

F. When addressing major problems, how might the athletic director protect oneself against the situation in which the AD is overruled upon appeal?

_____

_____

_____

_____

_____

_____

G. It doesn't really matter how the athletic director leaves a position because the athletic direc-
    tor is gone and onto another situation. React to this statement.

    _____

    _____

    _____

    _____

    _____

    _____

H. With whom might the athletic director confer in terms of seeking advice and counsel?

    _____

    _____

    _____

    _____

    _____

    _____

I. Provide some sound principles in hiring staff for the athletic department.

    _____

    _____

    _____

    _____

    _____

J. Why is it necessary for the athletic director to have *product knowledge*? Provide an example.

_____

_____

_____

_____

_____

_____

REFERENCES

Stier, Jr., W.F. (1995). *Successful Coaching—Strategies and Tactics*. Boston, MA.: American Press.

Stier, Jr., W.F. (1997). *More fantastic fundraisers for sport and recreation*. Illinois Champaign. Human Kinetics.

Stier, W.F., Jr. (1999). *Problem solving for coaches*. Boston: American Press.

SECTION II

The Case Method
and
Problem Solving

CHAPTER FIVE

Problem Solving Via the Case Study Approach

CHAPTER OBJECTIVES

After reading this chapter you will be able to:

- Be familiar with various case study tenets
- Understand that administrative skills can be learned through examination of case studies
- Be able to list the six categories of problematic situations that are provided within this book
- Illustrate how the absence of the 5P handbook can be a source of difficulty for the athletic administrator
- Appreciate how the use of case studies can aid in the creation of *strategic action plans*
- Be aware that the case studies presented are fictional accounts dealing with real world problems in competitive athletics
- List sources of information that might prove helpful in responding to the *questions for discussion*
- Understand that the case study method provides opportunities to develop a variety of appropriate courses of action to real world problems

Excellent facilities can be a boon for increased attendance.
[Courtesy of Rochester Red Wings (New York)]

- Ask pertinent questions in the examination of individual case studies
- Realize the benefits of small group discussion in dealing with case studies
- Justify the use of case studies in dealing with the topic of problem solving

This chapter provides an introduction to the problem solving process in athletic administration through the use of various case studies. Various **Case Study Tenets** are provided to help illustrate important information to be used in the examination of problem solving within the world of athletic administration. The case study approach has proven to be an appropriate method of improving skills appropriate for solving problems and meeting challenges within school-based sports programs.

> **CASE STUDY TENET #1:** *One can learn administrative skills through the examination of case studies.*

ORGANIZATION OF CASES

Chapters six through eleven are devoted to the presentation of actual case studies dealing with a wide variety of challenges and problems that can confront athletic directors and other athletic administrators in their day-to-day responsibilities. In all, 90 individual cases are provided. Each of the cases are realistic, pertinent and authentic in terms of presenting possible challenges that athletic administrators might face in the management of their school-based athletic programs. These cases, dealing with a variety of problematic situations, are equally divided within six general categories. These include:

(1) Problems with athletes—chapter six
(2) Problems with athletic coaches—chapter seven
(3) Problems with other individuals—chapter eight
(4) Problems with controversial issues—chapter nine
(5) Problems with policies, practices, procedures, priorities and philosophies —chapter ten
(6) Problems with special situations—chapter eleven

> **CASE STUDY TENET #2:** *Effective case studies are realistic, pertinent and authentic.*

These 90 cases are divided into six arbitrary classifications to help clarify the six major sources of difficulties, challenges and problems facing school-based athletic administrators at all levels of amateur competition. Although fictional, they are nevertheless realistic and pertinent in their content and their effect upon athletic programs. Being aware of these potential problematic areas can place the athletic director and/or the associate or assistant AD in a position of being able to anticipate, avoid, or minimize problems, difficulties and challenges that might have an adverse impact upon the athletic department, programs or activities.

(1) Problems with Athletes

Many sources of problems are associated with athletes themselves. These problems can arise because of what athletes do or fail to do, or say or fail to say, on or away from the proverbial playing field, court or pool. Such problems can arise because of how the athletes behave, speak as well as because of their appearance or attitude—both in and outside of school.

Today, both coaches and athletic administrators are being held accountable for the conduct of athletes both in and out of season as well as in and out of school. Being able to anticipate and to prevent as well as to resolve problems with athletes is essential for the survival of the athletic administrator.

> **CASE STUDY TENET #3:** *Most problems facing athletic directors are people related—athletes, coaches, parents, boosters, media, etc.*

(2) Problems with Athletic Coaches

Problems with coaches (head and assistants; full and part-time; paid and volunteer) usually arise because of actions and/or decisions of coaches themselves. In chapter seven, case studies are presented that deal with problems brought about because of the *failure* of coaches to act in a specific manner to make timely and appropriate decisions or because of *some overt act or decision* of a coach that might be considered improper or inappropriate.

> **CASE STUDY TENET #4:** *If athletic directors hire quality coaches, many problems would never arise.*

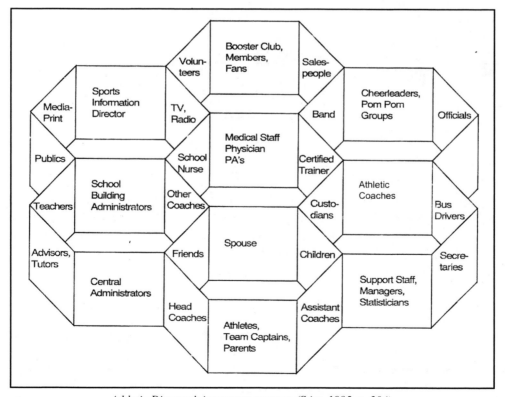

Athletic Director's important contacts (Stier, 1995, p. 204).

(3) Problems with Other Individuals

Other problems are explored through the third series of case studies that are organized around problems created by the actions (and inactions) and/or decisions of individuals *other than coaches and athletes*. These include, but are not limited to, parents, other athletic administrators, school and central administrators, teachers, opponents, business owners; tax payers; alumni/ae, fans, friends, boosters and booster clubs, news media, medical personnel, support staff, teachers, band and musical groups, cheerleaders, salespeople, custodians, volunteers, spouses, etc.

There is a myriad of individuals with whom the athletic director must be willing and capable of dealing with and relating to—in a professional manner. Figure #5.1 illustrates the large number of individuals, groups and organizations with whom most athletic administrators will have some interaction.

(4) Problems with Policies, Practices, Procedures, Priorities and Philosophies

The existence or lack of specific *policies, procedures, practices, priorities and philosophies* (5Ps) within the athletic department or program, the school as well as the school system itself, comprise the fourth category of case studies. How these *policies, procedures, practices, priorities and philosophies* are developed, publicized and implemented can frequently be a source of significant problems and challenges for the athletic administrator.

> **CASE STUDY TENET #5:**   *Every athletic department has standard operating procedures that guide the operation of the school's athletic program and activities—and can be sources of problems.*

Policies, practices and procedures are important not only for the athletic staff but for those athletes, parents, boosters and others, outside of the athletic department, who are intimately involved or associated with the department, various sports programs and individual activities. The value of departmental handbooks for coaches and other athletic personnel cannot be underestimated (Paling, 2000). Not only can such documents be an invaluable aid in the orientation of athletic staff but can also be of significant assistance in guiding the decisions and actions of athletic administrators in the pursuit of their daily activities.

(5) Problems with Controversial Issues

Controversial issues form the fifth source of potential problems and tribulations that may face the typical athletic director. These timely case studies are at the cutting edge in terms of addressing those troublesome difficulties that seem to plaque the current athletic scene at all levels of amateur competition, in spite of one's best efforts to avoid them.

> **CASE STUDY TENET #6:** *Case studies must be up-to-date in order to help athletic administrators deal with current, real life problems/situations.*

(6) Problems with Special Situations

The last category of challenges and difficulties faced by athletic administrators revolve around special situations that can arise within athletic departments. These are problems that are not easily or conveniently classified within any of the previous categories but, nevertheless, pose significant challenges to current day athletic administrators.

SUGGESTIONS FOR REVIEWING INDIVIDUAL CASE STUDIES

In today's athletic circles there seems to be an endless number of contentious or sticky issues that athletic administrators must be mindful of as they assume responsibility and exercise control over athletic programs and sports activities in schools, from the junior high level through the collegiate/university level. The reader should keep in mind, when reviewing each of the case studies, the fifteen *Appropriate Fact Finding Questions* (figure #2.2) revealed earlier in chapter two. These important questions should remain in the forefront of one's mind as each case study is read, reread and critically assessed. It is also important (see below) to be able to answer each of the questions poised at the end of each case study if one is to successfully resolve the conflicts, problems, dilemmas or controversial situations outlined in each of the case studies.

Questions for Discussion

At the conclusion of each case study is a list of interrogatories referred to as ***Questions for Discussion***. Each set of questions relates specifically to that particular case and are presented to assist the reader in the overall problem solving process. By actually writing down appropriate responses to these questions in the space provided at the end of each case, the reader will be establishing a foundation for devising a (strategic action) plan of attack (SAP) to resolve the stated problem. Although many of the questions are similar for various cases, the responses to these questions are often different, if not unique, depending upon the specific problem(s) or difficulty(ies) highlighted by the individual case in question.

Everyone cheers a victory!
[Courtesy of Washington State University]

> **CASE STUDY TENET #7:** *The use of case studies must include pertinent questions to guide the reader to make appropriate decisions based upon circumstances and the situation outlined in the case study.*

It may sometimes be helpful or necessary to gather information and data from other sources, such as scholarly journal articles, books, newspapers as well as popular magazines to be able to fully answer these questions at the end of a particular case study. For this reason, a partial list of suggested publications, journals and magazines is provided in appendix A.

The Value of a Strategic Action Plan (SAP)

Figure 5.2: Successful problem solvers must have a conceptual view of the world rather than operate as if one is wearing blinders.

An effective strategic action plan is, essentially, a blue-print outlining a course of action that will hopefully resolve a current crisis and/or eliminate a problem that threatens the athletic director or administrator, the athletic department, or a sport program. Refer to chapter two for *Components of a Strategic Action Plan (SAP),* specifically, figure #2.3*, Questions That May Be Asked in Creating a Strategic Action Plan(s) (SAPs).* The challenge is to be able to suggest ways and devise means by which the individual AD might be able to get out of, or otherwise address, a troublesome or embarrassing predicament as presented in a particular case study. This requires an individual with vision rather than one who operates as if one has blinders on.

> **CASE STUDY TENET #8:** *The use of case studies can help the reader develop better skills in creating strategic action plans.*

An Explanation of How the Case Studies Are Presented

Each of the 90 case studies presented within this section, chapters 6-11, involve a telling of a pertinent story involving one or more problems, challenges or difficulties that might be experienced by an athletic director or administrator. Each case is presented from a third person perspective.

Each narrative account, which describes a particular problem or series of problems, is presented so that the reader — either individually or as a member of a small or a large group — is challenged to creatively work through the difficulty(ies) presented. This may be accomplished by having the reader(s) examine the facts of the case and coming to some conclusion in terms of which actions might be appropriate to address, avoid and resolve the problem(s) (Boyce, 1992). Additionally, readers are also asked how such a problematic situation might have been prevented in the first place.

The Harvard Graduate School of Business Administration first introduced the case method of teaching/learning for its MBA students. The school initiated the MBA case study method in an effort to enable its graduates to have more practical knowledge and experience in solving business problems once they had earned the coveted MBA degree. Earlier, before the advent of the case method, their graduates were not always able to jump into the real world of business and experience success in making decisions and solving problems in the so-called real world of business (Pitts, 1998).

CASE STUDIES ARE FICTIONAL BUT REALISTIC ACCOUNTS DEPICTING POSSIBLE ACTUAL EVENTS AND OCCURRENCES

> **CASE STUDY TENET #9:** *Case studies are fictional accounts describing what can and does exist in the real world of competitive athletics in our schools today.*

Although the use of case studies have been utilized in many professional fields such as business and law, case studies have not been extensively included in the professional preparation of future athletic personnel. An earlier book by Stier (1999) dealing with case studies and problem solving challenges for coaches *was the first book based upon the case study approach for the professional preparation of athletic coaches.* **This book that you have in your hands is believed to be the first case study book designed specifically for the professional preparation of athletic administrators as general managers and administrators of school-based athletic programs.**

> **CASE STUDY TENET #10:** *There are no absolute, no single answer in terms of case studies and the problems they represent.*

Although one definition of the use of cases or the case method involves a "descriptive research document, often presented in a narrative form, that is based on a real-life situation or event" (Merseth, 1996, p. 1), *it is not necessary that the cases be based on actual or true life stories, situations or events.* They can also be based only partially on true-life events or can be developed from a combination of several or many actual situations that had taken place or might have occurred in the past.

The cases in this book might also be constructed on completely fictional (simulated) situations, situations that represent those real life situations that might very well exist, now or in the future, for those individuals involved in such a professional environment or working situation. The important point about the creation and use of case studies is that they represent and accurately reflect the world that they purport to represent or characterize (Stroot, 2000).

In terms of dealing with the case method (and the problems and challenges that they represent) there are any number of possible answers or courses of action that might be appropriate in dealing with a specific case study. There is not necessarily one single answer, one single decision, or one single approach to dealing with and solving the problems and challenges presented by a particular case study scenario.

> **CASE STUDY TENET #11:**   *The case method provides the reader with opportunities to suggest (develop) a variety of acceptable answers and appropriate courses of action.*

Reality-Based Cases

In this book, all of the 90 cases presented involve completely made-up scenarios (descriptive accounts) involving fictional characters in a make-believe (but nevertheless realistic) environment. All names of individuals, groups and organizations included in the various case studies are purely fictional. Any resemblance to individuals, living or deceased; or, to existing or past organizations or groups; or, to actual events, happenings or occurrences, is purely coincidental.

However, each case study is constructed to depict real life problematic situations that could confront athletic directors and other types of athletic administrators in a school-based setting (secondary schools as well as colleges and universities). These cases are presented in such a fashion as to convey an accurate representation of a variety of athletic situations that might very well face the school-based athletic administrator in the 21st century. Thus, these cases present to the reader realistic opportunities to confront a wide range of real life challenges and to attempt to resolve and/or prevent such problems or similar challenges.

THE BENEFITS OF UTILIZING THE CASE STUDY METHOD IN STUDYING PROBLEM SOLVING IN ATHLETIC ADMINISTRATION

The advantage of using case studies in improving one's skills and competencies as a future or current athletic administrator is that the realistic (real or simulated) cases involve situations that can be studied, discussed, interpreted, analyzed and evaluated. This is done in an attempt to understand and learn how to address, avoid and solve future problems facing athletic departments, programs, activities and personnel—from a variety of perspectives. Critically and correctly examining, understanding and reacting to problematic situations (whether based upon real facts or not) requires the ability to identify, analyze, and make decisions in light of available information and the possession of professional skills and experiences needed in the real world of athletic administration.

> **CASE STUDY TENET #12:** *One can learn how to address future problematic situations by examining case studies.*

The appropriate use of case studies provides opportunities for readers "to link the theoretical constructs developed in the classroom with the practical application in the workplace" (Wright, 1997, p. 190). Being able to bridge the gap between theory and practice in the real world is invaluable for the 21st century manager and administrator of school-based athletic programs. The use of case studies is an ideal method of facilitating the bridging of the gap between principles (theories) and real life situations (Shulman, L., 1992). Case methods enable the reader(s) to work in small or large clusters for team or group discussion of the elements of each case. It is also possible for a reader to work through each case individually in terms of written assessment, analysis and recommendation.

Stykes & Bird (1992) indicated that cases may be classified as *exemplars*, that is, emphasizing the theoretical aspect of a particular situation and to give priority to general, prepositional knowledge. Cases used as exemplars are used to point out correct, appropriate or effective decisions or actions as well as to enable effective and efficient athletic administration to engage in appropriate administrative practices and decisions making available for analysis, review and assessment..

The Use of Small Group Discussion in the Case Study Method

> **CASE STUDY TENET #13:** *Small group interaction, in conjunction with the case method, enhances the learning of all in the group.*

Ideally, group discussion is utilized to enhance the learning experience of the case study method and facilitate a dialogue between different participants (Silverman, Welty, & Lyon, 1992). The key to utilizing the case study method or approach is to encourage future athletic administrators to work independently of the instructor as they review and assess each case. Then, if working in a group setting, it is possible to continue to creatively analyze the specific case in question and provide recommendations and suggestions pertaining to solving or addressing the essential elements or problems presented by each case.

Each student must be capable and willing to dissect each case and to examine all of the ramifications and potential consequences presented therein. The role of the instructor is that of facilitator or as a moderator in the student group discussions as well as the follow-up review of the particulars of the case and the assessment comments. It is critical that initiative be shown by the individual students (working together in small groups or alone) and that they (collectively and individually) are able to arrive at logical courses of action in light of the difficulties and circumstances posed by each case.

> **CASE STUDY TENET #14:** *Cases can be used to provide practice opportunities for decision making and problem solving (Shulman, J.J., 1992; Wassermann, 1994).*

Using small discussion groups as the focal point of a class setting enables students to explore a wide range of alternative behaviors and the corresponding consequences—both short and long term. It is this critical thinking and interaction process that is one of the more important objectives of the group discussion process associated with the case study method of instruction.

The Use of the Case Study Method by Individuals

However, it is not an absolute requirement that each case study be dealt with by the group discussion method. An alternative technique that has proven to be very effective is to assign different cases to different individuals and to request each student, working alone, to address each of the questions presented at the end of each case study. Subsequently, individual students are able to report back (verbally or in written form) to the larger group and/or to the instructor in terms of how each individual reacted to the case and what actions they would have initiated in dealing with the problem(s) as outlined.

However, these case studies can also be most helpful for the individual AD or would-be athletic administrator who wishes to work through the problem solving case study approach on an individual basis—without the benefit of a group of peers or an instructor. In this situation, the reader works, as an individual, through each of the cases by answering the questions provided at the end of each case study.

CONCLUDING STATEMENTS ON THE USE OF THE CASE STUDY METHOD

The use of case studies in the preparation of teachers have long been recognized in higher education as an appropriate method of *teaching students how to relate theory to the real world* (Shulman, L., 1992). Case studies have proven to be both effective and efficient in preparing competent teachers. The use of case studies in this way received national support when the Carnegie Task Force on Teaching as a Profession (1986) endorsed their use inclusive within the teacher preparation effort of American colleges and universities (Wright, 1997).

> **CASE STUDY TENET #15:** *Antidotal information as well as empirical research supports the use of the case method in the professional preparation of professionals within educational institutions.*

While the value of using case studies in the professional preparation of professionals within educational institutions (such as athletic directors and other athletic administrators) is still undergoing debate in certain circles, research into the advantages and benefits of such an approach is continuing to grow (Colbert, Trimble & Desberg, 1996). Antidotal information, experiences from educational institutions (and professors) employing case study techniques and methods as well as findings of initial empirical research pertaining to the materials and the methods associated with the case study method of education all seem to indicate that such educational strategies, techniques and methods have real benefits in the training and preparation of professionals in terms of problem solving, decision making and taking priority actions within the administrative arena of school-based athletics (Stier, 2000).

CONCLUSION

The use of case studies can be an effective and efficient method of preparing future school-based athletic administrators as well as helping those individuals who are already engaged in administration enhance their problem solving skills as managers and leaders. The use of case studies can play a significant role in enabling these individuals, male and female, to make the important connections between theory and real life, between principles, ideas or concepts and actual practice out there in the real world, on the firing line.

The true determination of just how effective and efficient the use of case studies can be in enabling future, as well as current athletic administrators (ADs, associate ADs, assistant ADs, etc.), to increase their knowledge base and to upgrade their level of competency, depends upon the commitment demonstrated by these same individuals as they work through the series of case studies. Those individuals who diligently work through the various problems and challenges presented by the 90 case study will be in a much better position to prevent, manage and resolve problematic situations, if and when they should occur.

EXERCISES FOR CHAPTER FIVE

A. Typically, what are the sources of problems facing athletic directors at schools?

_____

_____

_____

_____

_____

_____

B. Why would many problems currently facing athletic directors disappear if the ADs would hire competent and quality coaches?

_____

_____

_____

_____

_____

_____

C. Why can the use of case studies facilitate the development of problem solving skills for the reader/participant? Elaborate.

_____

_____

_____

_____

_____

_____

D. Why is the possession of a conceptual view of the world beneficial to the would-be problem solver within the athletic scene?

_____

_____

_____

_____

_____

_____

E. Describe the characteristics of a quality case study situation.

_____

_____

_____

_____

_____

_____

_____

F. When reviewing case studies, there are/aren't a variety of possible correct or appropriate answers or responses. Discuss and take a position and defend that position.

_____

_____

_____

_____

_____

_____

_____

G. What are the advantages of working individually as well as in a group setting when utilizing the case study approach to problem solving?

_____

_____

_____

_____

_____

_____

REFERENCES

Boyce, B.A. (1992). Making the case for the case-method approach in physical education peda-gogy classes. *Journal of Physical Education, Recreation and Dance, 63*(8), 17-20.

Carnegie Task Force on Teaching as a Profession. (1986). *A nation prepared: Teachers for the 21st century*. New York: Carnegie Forum on Education and the Economy, Carnegie Corpo-ration.

Colbert, J.A., Trimble, K., & Desbert, P. (Eds.). (1996). *The case for education*. New York. Teachers College Press, pp. 33-49.

Merseth, K.K. (1996, November). Cases, case methods, and the professional development of educators. *ERIC Digest*, 2 pp.

Palin, D. (2000). Now starting at coach. *Athletic management XI* (5), 51-42, 54, 56.

Pitts, B. (1998). (Ed.). *Case studies in sport marketing.* Morgantown, WV.: Fitness Information Technology.

Silverman, R., Welty, W.M., & Lyon, S. (1992). *Case studies for teacher problem solving*. New York: McGraw-Hill Inc.

Shulman, L. (1992). *Toward a pedagogy of cases*. In J. Shulman (Ed.), *Case methods in teacher education* (pp. 1-30). New York: Teachers College Press.

Shulman, J.J. (1992). *Case methods in teacher Education*. New York: Teachers College Press.

Sykes, G., & Bird, T. (1992). *Teacher education and the case idea*. In G. Grant (Ed.), *Review of research in education, 18,* pp. 457-521.

Stier, Jr., W.F. (1995). *Successful coaching—Strategies and tactics*. Boston. American Press, MA.

Stier, W.F., Jr. (1999). *Problem solving for coaches*. Boston: American Press.

Stier, W.F., Jr. (2000, November 30). *Fund-Raising and promotion secrets for the busy athletic administrator*. Presentation made at the 19th National Athletic Business Conference, Or-lando, Florida.

Stroot, S.A. (Ed.). (2000). *Case studies in physical education*. Scottsdale, Arizona: Holcomb Hathaway, Publishers.

Wassermann, S. (1994). Using cases to study teaching. *Phi Delta Kappan, 75*(8), 602-611. EJ481329.

Wright, S. (1997). Case-based instruction: Linking theory to practice. *The Physical Educator, 53*(4), 190-197.

CHAPTER SIX

Problems with Athletes

CHAPTER OBJECTIVES

After reading this chapter you will be able to:

- Be familiar with various problems relating to athletes
- Understand why and how athletes may be dismissed from teams
- Understand the challenges involved in attempting to prevent violence at athletic contests
- Research appropriate drug testing procedures for athlete
- Indicate steps an athletic director might take to assist coaches with problem athletes
- Be sensitive to the needs of athletes who seek to boycott the athletic scene
- Respond to student-athletes' request for adding an additional sport(s)
- Appreciate the importance of providing equal and appropriate meal money for athletic teams
- Outline a strategy for instituting a code of conduct and state the major components of such a code
- Establish appropriate transportation policies for injured athletes
- Justify the need for athletes to dress appropriately, on and off the playing field
- Explain to athletes and their parents the realities of collegiate recruitment of athletes
- Outline preventative measures that will prevent college athletes from dropping below the minimum number of credit hours to be eligible
- Develop policies pertaining to the conditioning of athletes by coaches
- Respond to athletes who issue unreasonable demands, i.e., firing of a coach

Coaching is teaching and motivation. [Courtesy of Washington State University]

CASE

1. The case of the athlete dismissed from the team
2. The case of violence in sports

3. The case of the code of conduct
4. The case of drug testing for athletes
5. The case of poor substituting during a contest
6. The case of the athletic team boycott
7. The case of athletes pushing for a new sport
8. The case of athletes demanding more meal money for away contests
9. The case of athletes damaging equipment and facilities
10. The case of the transportation problems for injured athletes
11. The case of athletes dressing like slobs
12. The case of the supersStar's recruitment for college
13. The case of the player's eligibility
14. The case of the questionable conditioning of athletes
15. The case of athletes demanding a coach be fired

CASE # 1

The Case of the Athlete Dismissed from the Team

Coach Allan Sampson was both a highly successful and highly demanding coach. He was not really a dictator but he had clear expectations of what he wanted of his athletes. And, he just would not tolerate deviation from what he thought athletes should be and should act like—on and off the proverbial playing field or court.

Thus, it was no surprise that young Joey Clarke, a senior standout on coach Sampson's soccer team, was in hot water one day when he violated several of the coach's sacred rules, for the third time. Coach Sampson had a saying that he was fond of using that went something like this: *Fool me once, shame on you. Fool me twice, shame on me. Fool me thrice, and you are gone.* Poor Joey. He knew he was letting the coach down but in his present state of mind he didn't care. He didn't care about the team or his teammates. He wasn't sure if he cared about anything or anyone—other than having a good time and not missing the fun of his senior year.

Well, Joey had been feeling his oats of late and he had what some people would call senioritis—that is, he was a senior, he wasn't going to be a professional athlete, he missed being with the girls, he missed what he saw as the fun-filled senior year and he was getting tired of all of the hard work and time required of him by his soccer participation. So, he started to slack off. He was late to practice. He missed a practice. He did not hustle in practice. And, he was giving a poor example. He was not the Joey of last year when he was a viable candidate for the team's most valuable player. But again, this was not last year. This year, there was a different team and a different circumstances. And, Joey had changed. He realized that soccer, during his senior year, was not at the top of his priority. In fact, it was not even close, and he acted that way.

So, it was no surprise that coach Sampson had a private talk with young Joey. When the student left the coach's office, Joey was no longer a member of the team.

Coach Sampson had removed other athletes from his teams over the years. However, he was never angry or mad at an athlete like Joey, whose priorities had changed. He was not really angry with Joey for the youngster's poor behavior, although he wished Joey had simply quit or, better yet, had not even come out for the team. The way things turned out, coach Sampson and his staff had now wasted many weeks of practice time working with Joey who now will not be with the team. He felt that the time Joey had taken from the team could have been spent working with a youngster(s) who will remain with the team.

Nevertheless, coach Sampson kept tabs on Joey through his fellow teachers as well as some of the students and athletes who the coach had in his classes and who remained on the team. Over the next six weeks Joey had gotten into some real serious trouble. He had some new friends who were a bad influence. His studies were going to pot. It was rumored that he was experimenting with alcohol and some drugs. All in all, Joey was in the fast lane and was fast becoming a mess.

Coach Sampson caught Joey in the school hallway one evening and asked him to stop by his office that afternoon during his study hall. When Joey arrived, the coach had a long talk with him. Over the next several weeks the coach and Joey visited often. Joey even came to the coach's home for an excellent dinner prepared by Mrs. Sampson. Mr. Sampson went to some of Joey's teachers and talked with them. He was even asked by Joey to come to his home and talk with Joey's parents and he did so. Soon, Joey began to get his life on the straight and narrow because of his former coach's efforts.

When asked by a fellow teacher why he had spent so much time on Joey the coach replied that: "Hey, I am a teacher and coach. Just because Joey was an 'idiot' in terms of not being able to adhere to the standards expected of an athlete (on my team) doesn't mean that as a human being he doesn't deserve my attention, my care and my love. That is what I do as a teacher/coach, I help and teach people to be contributing members of our society."   ·

The athletic director was confronted one afternoon after school by a parent of one of the athletes remaining on the coach's team complaining about how much time the coach was wasting on that dumb jackass who got kicked off the team. "Why, if the coach would spend half the time he spends with that stupid failure of a druggie with the kids remaining on the team, we would be having a winning season. Besides, the coach has never come to my house to talk to me about my son," added the distraught father.

The athletic director was dumbfounded. He thought about what he should say to the parent who was obviously upset. He decided to begin by . . .

QUESTIONS FOR DISCUSSION

1.   Why was the youngster kicked off the team?
2.   Is this situation in terms of the change in behavior from the junior to the senior year on behalf of Joey unusual in high schools today? Why or why not?
3.   What can *coaches as well as athletic directors* do to prevent youngsters from being removed from teams for cause.
4.   Should the athletic director have been involved in this situation at some early point of time? Explain.
5.   Was coach Sampson justified in removing Joey from the team? Why or why not? Did the coach give Joey sufficient notice? Was there adequate due process? Explain your position.
6.   Was the manner that the coach used in kicking Joey off the team appropriate? Why or why not? What tactic(s) would you encourage your coaches to follow in a situation in which the youngster was behaving so poorly as to actually be removed from the squad?
7.   Should the athletic director require that coaches notify the athletic director prior to removing an athlete from a squad? What rationale would you, as athletic director, provide to justify or not justify such a policy or practice?

8.   Should the coach had kept Joey on the team and tried to work with him? Should the coach have punished Joey in some other fashion and yet kept him on the squad? Provide a rationale for your thinking.

9.   What do you think most coaches do in terms of their relationships with former athletes whom they had removed, for cause, from their teams (or who had quit)?

10.   Why did coach Sampson go out of his way to help the youngster even after Joey was off the team? Did the coach have an obligation or a duty to help this young man? Justify your response in detail as an athletic administrator.

11.   What are the advantages to the coach and the sport as a result of the coach's willingness to help Joey even after the youngster is removed from the team? What are the disadvantages of such behavior?

12.   By helping Joey, is coach Sampson short-changing the remaining athletes on his team who might also need his help, his presence, and his individual attention? Elaborate.

13.   Is the distraught parent justified in the complaint against the coach? Why or why not?

14.   As athletic director, assume a role-playing posture and indicate what you would say to the complaining parent and what you might do.

15.   What general principles are applicable in this scenario in terms of (1) discipline and the establishment of rules and regulations, and (2) the obligations of a coach to current and former athletes?

16.   Comments . . .

RESPONSES FOR QUESTIONS FOR DISCUSSION

_____

_____

_____

_____

_____

_____

_____

_____

_____

CASE #2

The Case of Violence in Sports

During the third period of the home ice hockey game at Mohawk high school, a game involving two arch rivals (Mohawk high school and Tough high school) to determine the conference championship, a vicious fight erupted among the players. Players from Mohawk high school, behind 5 goals to 1, with less than 3 minutes to go, became frustrated and retaliated to the taunting of the players from Tough High School and their fans by pushing, shoving and then striking some of the opposing players. The instigators thought that since they were losing so badly that they had nothing to lose and therefore started the ruckus.

The altercation was so violent that not only did the athletes on the ice get into the brawl, but also players from both teams left their respective benches. After about 3 minutes (which seemed to be 30), and with the officials still not able to restore order, a fight erupted in the stands with the parents and fans on both sides becoming involved by throwing debris onto the ice, towards the opponents' bench. Some of the fans even threw punches at the opposing players on the bench. It was nearly 20 minutes before any sort of order was restored, and then only after the local police had been called to the ice rink.

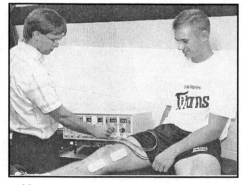

Athletic training rooms are an integral aspect of competitive sports. [Courtesy of University of Wisconsin-Oshkosh Sports Information Department]

In fact, the athletic director, who had gone down on the ice in an attempt to restore order, was severely injured when one of his own players hit him in the face with a stick. All in all, it was an ugly, ugly scene.

The next day the principal of Mohawk high school, Ms. June McKolsky, wanted to know how something like that could happen in her school. The athletic director was told in no uncertain terms to find out what happened, how to prevent it in the future, to punish those at fault, and to keep negative publicity away from the principal and the school.

The athletic director, steaming from the chewing out he received at the hands of the principal, really burned the ice hockey coach when he ran into his office and demanded: "What the @#$%&^$# are you doing with your ice hockey players? They acted like criminals out there. I almost got myself killed and you have the prime responsibility for controlling your charges. If you can't do that properly, I know there are plenty of other people just dying to assume your job and who will do it properly. I want you to solve this problem by reviewing the videotape and identifying those athletes who were the instigators, and especially the athlete who gave me these 17 stitches. Then, I want you to devise a suitable punishment for those at fault. Finally, you and I will meet this coming Friday to work out a plan to insure that a reoccurrence will NEVER, NEVER take place and embarrass me," concluded the athletic director.

QUESTIONS FOR DISCUSSION

1.   Who was at fault here? Elaborate.
2.   Was the athletic director wise in his reaction *to and* actions at the disturbance at the game? Explain.
3.   Why did the principal act as she did?
4. ˙ Is the principal treating the athletic director properly after the fight? Explain and justify your answer.
5.   Is the athletic director treating the ice hockey coach properly after the fight? Explain your answer.
6.   What proper course of action should the AD and the hockey coach (individually and together) now pursue? Be specific.
7.   As a consequence of the fight what should be done NOW? By Whom?
8.   How might the guilty parties be correctly identified?
9.   Who should decide the punishment for the athletes who were at fault? Elaborate.
10.   What might be suitable punishment for those athletes involved in the altercation? Will all those involved be punished identically or will the punishment vary depending upon any extenuating factors? What might be some extenuating factors?
11.   What can be done to the other individuals involved in inappropriate behavior (fans, parents, etc.)?
12.   What are some possible consequences (in and outside of school) resulting from such an unfortunate episode? Provide a detailed answer.
13.   What could the athletic director have done to prevent this whole, ugly experience on the ice from even happening? Outline a reasonable strategy and course of action.
14.   What could be done now to prevent this type of violence from occurring again?
15.   What are realistic objectives NOW in terms of the whole topic of *violence*?
16.   How (and when) can the crowds be educated in terms of proper behavior? Be specific in your response.
17.   What is wrong with the attitude of the athletes in this situation?
18.   Why do the athletes from Mohawk high school hold the attitude that they do?
19.   If a similar incident had occurred previously, what might this imply?
20.   Who should be involved in corrective action in this situation? When? How? Where? Be specific?
21.   Outline a suitable crowd control concept involving a so-called code of conduct.
22.   What general principles are applicable in terms of dealing with sport violence at the secondary level?
23.   Comments . . .

RESPONSES FOR QUESTIONS FOR DISCUSSION

_____

_____

_____

_____

_____

_____

_____

_____

_____

_____

_____

_____

_____

_____

_____

_____

_____

CASE #3

The Case of the Code of Conduct

Mr. Chuck Burnett, the school superintendent at Lemon Point Schools, was concerned with the growing problem with misbehaving student-athletes at all levels. He continued to read in the newspapers and see on television examples of all types of improper behavior (on and off the proverbial playing field) on behalf of athletes, at all levels from youth sports to the professional level. However, he was most concerned with how the athletes behaved in the classroom and on the proverbial playing fields within his own school district.

Since he didn't get to be school superintendent and keep the position for some twenty years by being stupid, or by closing barn doors after the cows walked out, he definitely wanted to nip this potential problem in the bud. He didn't want to have to deal with a situation after it became a public problem and a public embarrassment to him and to the school system and the school board.

Toward this end he called in the principals and the athletic directors of the three high schools and eight junior high schools for the express purpose of initiating a discussion on the topic of athletes' behavior. The meeting was started by Mr. Burnett indicating that he was concerned about the lack of respect and improper behavior that seems to be permeating all sports in this country. He further pointed out that he wanted his district to be proactive rather than reactive in terms of student-athlete behavior.

"Well, Chuck," said one of the junior high athletic directors, "our kids are pretty well behaved for the most part. I don't see any problem here. All of our coaches do a pretty good job in that respect."

Another athletic director pointed out that that was not always the situation in other schools, even in this district. "Although I believe that our schools and our athletes are no better or worse than in other districts, I can see where we can and should take some steps to insure that behavior associated with our athletic programs is beyond reproach," replied Louise Martin, the AD at McFadden High School.

"Are we talking about our *athletes*?" inquired one of the principals.

"Yes, and no," said Louise. "I am concerned in my program about our *athletes,* certainly. But, I am also concerned about our *coaches, our parents and our fans.*"

"What type of behavior are we talking about that would be considered inappropriate?" asked a junior high principal. "And, whose job is it to see that the athletes behave properly? Isn't that the job of the AD and the coaches?"

After much discussion, it was decided that something must be done now, before a really bad situation develops and the whole district becomes embroiled in a very public scandal. The superintendent suggested that a code of conduct for athletics be created.

One of the principals indicated that: "The difficult task is to determine how the code should be established, by whom, and what such a code should consist of and how to get people to abide by it."

"I agreed," added Joseph Banks, the athletic director/football coach at Midlakes high school. "Where should we start? Who should be involved? Any suggestions?" he added.

QUESTIONS FOR DISCUSSION

1. What is the current status regarding student-athlete behavior in competitive sport situations in *junior and senior high schools* in this country? At the *collegiate level*?

2. What is the status of student-athlete behavior in the high school you attended or where you now coach?

3. Is the superintendent wise to deal with this potential problem *before* a major incident occurs within the district or is all of this a whole lot of fuss about nothing? Provide a rational for your position.

4. Why is it important to deal not merely with student-athletes but also the behavior of other individuals in terms of attempting to insure proper behavior surrounding and involving athletic activities? Elaborate.

5. What should be the major components or elements of a code of conduct for (a) student-athletes, (b) athletic personnel, and (c) fans/general public?

6. What are some of the causes (as well as categories) of improper behavior within the so-called athletic arena? Be specific.

7. What type of behavior should such a code address for *student athletes*? Be specific and provide examples.

8. What type of behavior should such a code address for *athletic staff*? Be specific and provide examples.

9. What type of behavior should such a code address for *fans*? Be specific and provide examples.

10. How would you recommend that a conduct code be publicized and disseminated throughout the school, the district and the community? Provide examples.

11. What type of *admonition or punishment* (provide examples) should be implemented for improper behavior on behalf of:
    A. Student-athletes?
    B. Coaches?
    C. Athletic administrators?
    D. Parents?
    E. Fans and boosters?

12. How can proper behavior be encouraged and improper behavior discouraged in our school systems? Elaborate.

13. What should be the role of parents, coaches, fans, boosters and people in the community in terms of behavior associated with competitive sports?

14. Create an *abbreviated* athletic code of conduct for athletes that would be appropriate for a high school or school district, including punishments or consequences for violations of the code. The code should be no longer than a single sheet of paper.
15. What general principles are apropos in this situation?
16. Comments . . .

RESPONSES FOR QUESTIONS FOR DISCUSSION

_____

_____

_____

_____

_____

_____

_____

_____

_____

_____

_____

_____

_____

_____

_____

CASE #4

The Case of Drug Testing for Athletes

During a staff meeting the athletic director brought up the topic of drug misuse and abuse among the athletes. He indicated that drug problems were epidemic in schools throughout the nation and their school was no exception. He brought up the topic of drug education as well as drug detection (testing).

"It doesn't seem to me that merely having some type of drug education program is sufficient. We must have some type of detection program in place as well. And, of course, we must have an appropriate set of rules with corresponding series of consequences for violations of these rules," lectured the athletic director.

"What about the time and expenses involved in any type of drug testing program?" queried the women's basketball coach. My budget isn't sufficient now and if we add a drug testing program, which sport or sports will give up a percentage of their budget allocation to help pay for this new endeavor?

"Well, I am worried about the legal implications more than I am about the money factor," added the head football coach.

"Lets talk about the legal aspects of drug testing! Is anyone up-to-date with all the legal aspects of drug testing?" asked the AD.

"Before we get into that, shouldn't we talk about what type of drug testing we should be doing? There must be more than 100 possible drugs that we could test for. Which should we test for? And, what about the policy regarding the testing procedures? Who will be tested? When? Who will do the testing? You know, there must be a whole bunch of questions that we must be able to answer. I feel that we don't even know the questions, much less the answers, when we talk about drug education and drug testing. We won't be able to even scratch the surface in this meeting. Perhaps we should schedule a series of meetings to discuss this situation?" pointed out another coach.

"Well, what shall we do? Should we just do nothing and leave things the way they are? Or, should we take a reactive position and wait until something happens to one of our athletes or teams? Or, should we be proactive and try to nip this drug thing, this drug problem, in the bud?" responded the high school principal, who had been invited to the meeting by the athletic director.

QUESTIONS FOR DISCUSSION

1. Is *drug education* a necessary component of an athletic department's attack against drug misuse and abuse in today's society? Explain.

2. What about *drug testing*, is it a necessary component of a high school and/or college/ university athletic department's attack against drug misuse and abuse in today's society? Explain.

3. Summarize the pros and cons (and the *justifications*) regarding drug testing for athletes at the high school level. At the college level.

4. Whose responsibility is it to provide education about the dangers and problems associated with the improper use of drugs, etc., *to athletes*? Provide a rationale for your response.

5. Before a drug education program for athletes can be implemented, whom should the athletic department obtain permission from, if anyone? Be specific.

6. How might a typical drug-testing program operate? Specify the appropriate steps that would go to make up an acceptable drug-testing program?

7. Explain the so-called punishment or punitive aspect of drug testing. That is, what happens to the athlete who tests positive for drugs the first time? The second time? Subsequent times? Provide examples.

8. How would the athletic department provide for due process (and protection) for the individual athletes?

9. What are the legal implications (and potential problems) of a drug-testing program at the secondary level? At the collegiate level?

10. What about the costs of such a program? How are costs determined? Elaborate.

11. What drugs should be tested for at the high school level, the small college level and the NCAA division I level? Why?

12. How would a school insure confidentiality of the athletes being tested?

13. How would a school insure accuracy in the actual tests themselves?

14. Who would actually do the drug testing of the athletes? What firm or company might be sent the specimens? Be specific. How would the athletic director find out about such firms?

15. Do the athletes have to give their permission in order to be tested? Do their parents have to give permission to have their youngsters tested? Why or why not?

16. Does the athletic staff at this school even know if they truly have a drug problem or not? Or, are they just guessing or assuming that such a problem exists?

17. Do most high schools and colleges have drug problems? Do most *athletic programs* at the secondary and the collegiate levels have drug problems or the potential for problems? Elaborate.

18. What general principles are applicable in this scenario?

19. Comments . . .

RESPONSES FOR QUESTIONS FOR DISCUSSION

CASE #5

The Case of Poor Substituting during a Contest

Joseph Manolski, head varsity basketball coach at Milner's South High School in the state of Indiana, was experiencing both a stressful season as well as a highly productive and enjoyable season. The season was enjoyable in that the team was winning, sometimes by big margins. However, the season was simultaneously stressful because of one of the athletes, Larry Mallers, the best athlete and the best physical specimen on the team.

It seems that Larry not only was the most talented athlete for the Golden Bears but he knew he was the most talented athlete on the team as well. In fact, he had been giving coach Manolski some grief, more so in later weeks than earlier in the season. Recently, Larry (the Big Gun) Mallers had taken the attitude that he could out produce his teammates without really trying—and thus he stopped really trying (or trying as hard as he could or should) during practice.

This didn't set well with the coaching staff, especially with coach Manolski. Nor did it go over with a big bang with the other players even though there was no doubt that Larry was the best athlete on the squad, when he wanted to be. But Larry was taking the tack that he could produce in the games (when it really counted) without going through all of the stuff that the coaching staff was attempting to put him through during practice.

Before the next game coach Manolski met privately with the athletic director, Mary Sheltonn, and shared the entire situation abpit the prima donna (Larry Mallers). "Mary, I wanted to bring you up-to-date on this situation and ask your advice about not starting Larry at the next contest," stated coach Manolski. After being filled in on Larry's tactics, Mary replied: "Coach, don't give it a second thought. I appreciate the update and I support your move wholeheartedly. We cannot let such a situation continue and if you feel that he should sit and not start, then that is what happens and I am 100% behind you."

During the next home game, against archrival Mid-Town High School, Larry was kept out of the starting lineup. In fact, he did not play the entire first half. At half time, the team was behind by 4 points. During the half-time session none of the coaching staff said a word to Larry. They acted like nothing was wrong and devoted their time, comments and energies to the remaining players.

During the second half, the Golden Bears (with BG on the bench) surprisingly surged ahead in the latter part of the third quarter until the period ended with a 12-point lead. The last quarter started like the third quarter ended—with a devastating runaway fast break perfectly executed by the home team. With three minutes to play in the game and the team comfortably ahead by 22 points, coach Manolski looked down towards the end of the bench and motioned to Larry (who was sitting there, slouching and pouting).

"Larry, come on down here. I want you to go in for Jasper. Hurry up, we have less than three minutes till the end of the game," said coach Manolski.

Larry, still steaming from being left on the bench all of this time, just sat there, unmoving and glaring daggers at the head coach.

"Come on, Larry, you are holding up the whole team, just like in practice. Get a 'jump on it' and do your job, even though we don't need your big point production."

Larry, still sulking and angry about the fact that the team was winning without him, looked up from the floor directly at the eyes of the head coach and said: "Go @#$%&* yourself, you *&%$#@. You attempt to take away my manhood in front of all of my family and friends and then embarrass me by making me play with the team's scrubs at the end of this stupid game. Get a life and get out of here." With that Larry gave the coach the bird and walked off the court, all in full view of all of the spectators. He then headed to the showers—convinced in his own mind that he would never return.

QUESTIONS FOR DISCUSSION

1. What are the major problems in this scenario?
2. Why is Larry acting like he is before the big game? Is this normal?
3. Why did the situation with Larry develop to the extent that it has in this situation? Be specific.
4. How could coach Manolski have prevented Larry from acting like a prima donna? Provide specific recommendations.
5. What role might the athletic director play in preventing athletes from acting like Larry? Provide some concrete suggestions.
6. Why do Larry's teammates resent the way Larry is behaving—since they have a greater chance of winning games with Larry playing? Is this a normal reaction from one's peers?
7. Was the move by the coach to share information about the troublesome athlete with the athletic director a wise move? Why or why not?
8. What are the advantages of the coach informing the athletic director of a potential problem or of a possible course of action to be taken by the coach?
9. Did the athletic director respond appropriately? Be specific.
10. Did the athletic director tell the coach to act as the coach acted during the game? Elaborate.
11. What pressure does Larry's behavior place on the coaches of other sports? What concerns should be noted by the staff regarding their relationships (and expectations) with the rest of the athletes?
12. If the teammates did not mind the "games" Larry was playing with the staff and, in fact, supported (however reluctantly) Larry's actions, what pressure does this place upon the coaching staff and the athletic director? How should the coaching staff, especially the head coach, respond in this eventuality?
13. What principles are applicable in this situation in which the coach must deal with a prima donna who wants to play but not work hard in practice?

14. Did the head coach exercise proper judgment (and appropriate timing) when attempting to put Larry into the game? Why or why not? Is this what the coach had shared ahead of time with the athletic director?

15. Why do you think the head coached wanted to substitute Larry into the game during the last three minutes?

16. Why did Larry feel so indignant when asked to go into the game with only minutes remaining in the game?

17. What else could the head coach have done during the game to prevent this confrontation? Should the head coach have acted differently than he did during the first 37 minutes of the game? What about before the game?

18. What else could the head coach have done during the last three minutes of the game to prevent this confrontation? Should the coach have done something else? Why or why not?

19. Provide some ideas that the athletic director might encourage coaches to explore when considering which athletes to substitute into games at various times and under different circumstances.

20. What general principles, from the athletic director's perspective, are applicable in this situation in terms of handling individual athletes in light of their peculiar needs and wants?

21. Comments . . .

RESPONSES FOR QUESTIONS FOR DISCUSSION

CASE #6

The Case of the Athletic Team Boycott

On Friday afternoon, all but 2 of the 15 athletes who had made the team at Albertson College (NCAA division III) came to the athletic director, Mary Young, immediately after the basketball coach had announced who had made the team and who had not made it. These athletes were unanimous in their demand that their coach, Harry Haskins, be immediately fired. The reason given was that the coach was incompetent, did not know how to coach, was not nice, intimidated the players, did not listen to the players, *and cut two of the popular returning players (Dennis and David) from last season* (who happened to be last year's captains).

The thirteen players presented a unified stance from which they would not budge. The athletic director attempted to discuss the situation and explored all aspects of what had happened. The players were adamant. Either the coach would be fired immediately or there would be no team, it was that simple — no "ifs, ands or buts." The ringleader of the group stated: "Coach Haskins had no right to cut Dennis and David. They are our friends. They are our leaders. They know more than the coach does. Coach Haskins "oughta" drop off the face of this earth, the old @#$%&."

The athletic director indicated that she would investigate the matter and scheduled a later meeting with the dissenting student-athletes. The meeting was scheduled for two days hence.

The players subsequently went to the student council and attempted to get support for their position from that group as well as from the student body. The students also went to the principal in an effort to get administrative support as well as to exert additional pressure on the athletic director. The players even went to the news media and had several televised interviews resulting in a great deal of negative media coverage — print, radio and television. The controversy almost became the center of local news for a period of time. A great deal of attention was given to the situation, especially to the dissident students who were continually rallying as many constituency groups as possible to their cause. Parents, friends, other students, student-government representatives, news media, strangers, local business leaders, enemies of the coach (from early years as well as from recent events) — all became involved in this situation (on one side or the other).

The coach (as well as the athletic director) sought to mediate and defuse the situation. Coach Haskins attempted to meet individually with the boycotting players (excluding the two players who had not been selected for the team) in an attempt to resolve the situation and eliminate the anger, and the hatred. Alas, to no avail. Coach Haskins even offered complete amnesty or "forgiveness" to the 13 boycotting athletes if they would return to practice by the upcoming Friday—three days hence. Alas, to no avail.

The athletes wanted Mr. Haskins' scalp, his career, period. They were unbending. They were committed to professionally assassinate him — in public. They were going to "punish" him for his incompetence and audacity in cutting their two friends, Dennis and David, who were the so-called "leaders" of the players. Of the 13 boycotting athletes, 6 were seniors who were exerting tremendous pressure on the 7 sophomores to fall in line with the boycott. In reality, many of the 7 sophomores were just cowed into following the pack. The end result, however, was that all 13 basketball players were acting in apparent unison.

The athletic director had scheduled a final confidential meeting with the boycotting athletes. This followed three or four earlier group meetings with the 13 boycotting athletes and numerous individual counseling sessions with selected athletes. Prior to this final meeting the students (based on advice given by some community people) informed the media of the location and time of the confidential meeting. When the athletic director arrived for the supposedly private meeting with the athletes there were two television cameras all set up. There were also 5 or 6 reporters representing several newspapers and radio stations, in addition to the TV reporters.

When the athletic director made the announcement of her findings—which was that she could find no truth or basis in the charges that would indicate any need for disciplinary action on her part and that, indeed, the athletic director was in full support of the coach in his actions—the players all walked out and left the team.

QUESTIONS FOR DISCUSSION

1. What are the essential facts of the case?
2. Did the coach act appropriately, as far as you know, in dealing with the team and, in particular, with David and Dennis?
3. What could the coach have done, if anything, to prevent the situation?
4. Why could the coach not just let the two "cut" players return to the squad?
5. Why did the 13 students act as they did? Were they justified? Clarify.
6. Did the boycotting athletes behave professionally as they sought their objective? Explain.
7. Who were the so-called major "players" in this scenario? Evaluate their performances.
8. What negative consequences might come out of this situation? Affecting whom? Elaborate.
9. What positive consequences might come out of this situation? Affecting whom? Elaborate.
10. What social or group activity took place among the whole 15 member squad? Describe the ramifications of such activity.
11. What are the options of the coach NOW and what are the consequences of each of the options?
12. What options are now open to the athletic director (having shared her decision with the athletes) and what might be the consequences of each course of action?
13. What should the athletic director had done immediately after finding out about the boycott? Elaborate.

14. From the perspective of the head coach, what general principles might be appropriate in this case study?
15. Who has final authority in terms of picking members of a high school team? College team? Provide a rationale for your position.
16. Comments . . .

RESPONSES FOR QUESTIONS FOR DISCUSSION

_____

_____

_____

_____

_____

_____

_____

_____

_____

_____

_____

_____

_____

_____

_____

Case #7

The Case of Athletes Pushing for a New Sport

Jonathan Flakes has been the athletic director at Moonetone High School for some 15 years and thought that he had seen it all. He had gone through a lot during those years and had seen students cause not a few problems or controversies. However, the one he faces now has him stumped. It seems that last week he was presented with a petition from 35 male students asking (no, demanding) that lacrosse be added as a varsity sport.

Maybe if he had not been so abrupt (and dismissive) with the students when they had visited with him several months ago things would not have progressed to the stage where they are now, with a written petition. When the students had initially approached him he informed them that there was no money available for a new sport and if he had any extra money it would go to those sports that were not receiving sufficient money at the present time. He also told them that the next sport would be a women's sport due to Title IX requirements.

Now he has this ridiculous petition in his hand and, to top that, there was a rumor that there was another petition in the mix that could contain the signatures of as many as 500 students, parents and members of the general public. My, how he dreaded getting served with that document.

"Don't they know that there is not enough money in the budget now to adequately support the sports that we do offer at the present time," thought Mr. Flakes. "Why, even with all of the increased fundraising activities that we have been able to implement during the past two or three years, we are still only treading water, if even that."

The following Monday what the athletic director feared might happen actually happened, that is, a second petition with some 731 signatures (penned by both males and females) was formally handed to him, in front of representatives of the news media. It seems that one of the advisers of the student group pressuring for the new sport suggested to the students that if the media was made aware of what was going on in terms of the petitions that it would be just that much more difficult for the athletic director to refuse to honor the request for the addition of lacrosse (for males) as a new varsity sport.

As the athletic director walked down the hall toward his office, after receiving the petition, he wondered to himself whether any of the students or their parents had even given a second thought to the fact that the school was not even in compliance at the present time with Title IX, and with the addition of another male sport the athletic department would be even more out of kilter than it is now (in terms of proportionality of slots for males and females). In fact, if he had more money he would be inclined to spend it first on the existing sports, and if he had any money left over, he would then prefer to spend it for a new women's sport.

Sitting at his desk, he began to think in earnest about what he should do now that the cat was out of the bag, so to speak. He wondered what the superintendent and the school board might think about all of this. He sure did not want to be seen as someone who would give in to pressure from students and town people but he also did not want to alienate students, their parents or influential community people, not to mention the board. The first thing he decided to do was . . .

QUESTIONS FOR DISCUSSION

1. What are the problems facing the athletic director in this case?
2. Would this situation be different if the school was a college or university rather than a secondary school? Explain our position.
3. What might the athletic director have done earlier to prevent or head off the initial formal petition from being collected? How should he have reacted to the students' initial request for a new team?
4. What standards or criteria might a school (athletic department) use to determine whether a specific sport might be added (justified as a new sport)? Be specific. Also, provide a *process* whereby a sport(s) might be added to a school's stable of athletic offerings.
5. What factors, standards or occurrences might be present to warrant a sport to be discontinued by a school? Provide specific examples or instances. Also, provide a process whereby a sport(s) might be eliminated.
6. How can any high school be in compliance with Title IX? Specify the three common ways that a school can meet or satisfy the Title IX standards of the Office of Civil Rights (OCR)?
7. Why wouldn't a competent athletic director be able to secure the money through the formal budgetary process?
8. Would others view an athletic director, who is unable to raise sufficient money to implement new sports or sustain those that do exist, as incompetent? Why or why not?
9. What type of pressure might the news media bring to this whole *thing*?
10. Who is to blame in this whole situation? Why?
11. Why would so many parents and townspeople sign such a petition? Are they not aware of the current financial status of the athletic department? Speculate.
12. Are athletic directors susceptible to a great deal of pressure when faced with petitions signed by a large number of students, parents and community people?
13. What would happen to the athletic director if he did start a new male team in this situation? How might he be criticized?
14. How would the AD even attempt to fund a new team? Would not a competent athletic director be able to secure the needed money through outside fundraising and assistance from a booster club (or sport support group—SSG)?
15. If the athletic director did initiate a new team as a result of this blunt pressure, what message might that action give to students, parents and people in the community? Would there be other attempts to pressure the athletic director to action in other ways? Why or why not?

16. Should the athletic director attempt to shift the blame toward the school, the board or the superintendent by formally recommending the men's lacrosse team to the board and let the board decide whether to start the sport and how to fund it? Explain your position and the possible consequences of such an action by the athletic director.

17. Outline a plan of attack that the athletic director might pursue in handling this situation, keeping in mind that the school board and the superintendent are looking over his shoulder all the time.

18. Aren't athletic directors susceptible to all kinds and types of pressures? Should not athletic directors expect to deal with this type of controversy? Doesn't it come with the territory? Explain.

19. What general principles are suitable for this specific situation?

20. Comments . .

RESPONSES FOR QUESTIONS FOR DISCUSSION

_____

_____

_____

_____

_____

_____

_____

_____

_____

_____

_____

CASE #8

The Case of Athletes Demanding More Meal Money for Away Contests

The NCAA Division III women's basketball team had formally submitted a written complaint to the athletic director criticizing the fact that they had insufficient money for their meals on away trips. It seemed that they were tired of having to use their own funds to have sufficient money to purchase a decent meal, whether it be breakfast, lunch or dinner. In fact, the letter of complaint indicated that: "Over the past three years many of our team members have had to repeatedly use private funds to supplement the totally inadequate money that you, as athletic director, have made available to our team."

Some of the team members had even gone to some of the boosters, those who were sympathetic to the women's sports programs, and sought their help in securing an increase in the meal money allotted to the squad. However, one athlete, Neoma Welch, wanted to go even further. In fact, she told her teammates: "All of you just want to think about yourselves and your own meal money situation. To that I say 'phooey' because I want the meal money allotment for all of the women's teams to be increased to the point where we can all have a decent meal without having to spend any of our own hard earned money. Besides, I have a hunch that the guys have been getting more money than the gals just because they are bigger and stronger and supposedly need more caloric input."

The athletic director, Steve Strongsome, was dumbfounded. He couldn't understand what all the fuss was about. The meal allotment had been the same for all teams for the past four years and no one had complained before. Why now? He was confident that the meal money allotment was sufficient. "Those women, all they ever do is complain. If I gave them triple the amount of money they would still complain, no doubt," he concluded.

He also just didn't understand why the athletes had to complain about the meal money that they were given. This was Division III, after all, and the athletes were supposed to be involved in the sport for the fun of it, not for the scholarships (of which there were none) or for the large amount of meal money (of which there was not a lot). "Why, when I was an athlete at a school just like this one, I had to spend some of my own money if I wanted to have a full blown meal each and every time I ate on a road trip. It was expected. So what is the big deal now? It must be the times and these spoiled brats who act like athletes sure aren't athletes like we were at their ages," he thought to himself.

"But how to deal with these athletes?" he mused. "What should I do? How should I approach this situation now that I have this formal memo?"

QUESTIONS FOR DISCUSSION

1. Summarize the major elements in this problematic scenario?

2. Were the women on the team acting appropriately (including their approaching the boosters) in this situation in which they believed they were receiving inadequate meal money for away games? Explain your position.

3. What are your reactions to the thoughts of the athletic director and his reactions to the complaints of the athletes?

4. Do you know enough to make a decision as to whether the male athletes receive more money than the female athletes? Should males receive more because of their greater need of calories? Provide a rationale for your stance.

5. What should the athletic director do *now* having received the complaint letter? Be specific.

6. Is the athletic director realistic in comparing his own athletic experience as an athlete with modern day athletes? Provide a rational.

7. Would the reaction of the athletic director be different if he was positive, in his own mind, that the amount of money provided for away game meals was sufficient and that the complaint was merely a bogus gripe? Why or why not?

8. Should the athletic director meet with the athletes or is a simple letter appropriate? If a meeting is to be scheduled, what should the athletic director attempt to accomplish in this initial meeting?

9. Assume a role-playing posture and indicate what the athletic director might initially say in such a meeting.

10. From the athletic director's perspective, what is the role of the head coach of this team in this situation? Also, in the eyes of the AD, what should the head coach have done and/or not have done previously to this blow up, and what should the coach do now?

11. How might the athletic director deal with some of the boosters who had been approached by some of the athletes?

12. How might the athletic director have prevented this situation from developing to this stage? Be specific.

13. How would an athletic director go about determining the appropriate (proper, suitable) amount of meal money for breakfast, lunch and dinner for the athletes? What about the amount of money spent for lodging on overnight trips? That is, how would the athletic director go about establishing an appropriate amount to be spent for lodging?

14. How would the AD determine how many athletes should be lodged in a hotel/motel room? Should there be two athletes to a room? Three? Four? More? Should athletes ever sleep two to a bed on overnight trips? Should some athletes be expected to sleep on a cot in a room while others are in a bed? Justify your response.

15. Cite some general managerial principles that might apply in this sports situation.

16. Provide, on a separate sheet of paper, a complete departmental policy, including dollar figures, for meal money and lodging allocations for athletic teams at a high school or at a NCAA division III athletic program.

17. Comments . . .

RESPONSES FOR QUESTIONS FOR DISCUSSION

_____

_____

_____

_____

_____

_____

_____

_____

_____

_____

_____

_____

_____

_____

_____

_____

_____

CASE #9

The Case of Athletes Damaging Equipment and Facilities

Budget time was always a time of great consternation for Mary McDermitt, athletic director at Mayville College, a NAIA school located in the southeast. It seemed that there was never enough money for all of the sports. In fact, Mary often wondered how her coaches were able to be as successful as they were with the limited budget that she was able to secure through the normal budgetary process (budget request to the institution).

While she was contemplating how to begin to work on next year's budget construction she was struck by the report she received only that morning from the equipment room manager. The report, similar to ones she had been given the past three years since she was hired as athletic director from her previous post as volleyball coach at a junior college in upstate New York, indicated that the annual inventory of equipment and supplies revealed that there was over $16,000 in lost, stolen, damaged, or otherwise misplaced items from the previous year. In addition to the $16,000 in equipment and supplies, the equipment manager went on to indicate that there had been over $7,200 in damage during the previous 12 months (caused by athletes and/or fans) to various indoor and outdoor athletic facilities on the campus.

Finally, the proverbial light bulb lit up in Mary's mind and she connected the fact that the athletic department was severely short of funds on an annual basis and yet the department also had to replace some $16,000 in equipment and supplies and repair some $7,200 in damaged facilities. "I know what I should do," thought Mary.

"We can save money that the athletic department would have to otherwise use to replace the missing/stolen equipment and supplies (on an annual basis) by either eliminating or severely reducing the amount/value of missing/stolen items. In addition, we will make sure that the facilities are no longer damaged, or at least not damaged to the tune of some $7,000 each year. That way, the department would be able to save around $23,000 on an annual basis—but only if we are able to significantly reduce the amount of loss from missing items and damaged facilities," stated Mary to the coaches at a meeting she called shortly thereafter.

The coaches nodded their heads but several of them began to grumble. "What do you want us to do? How can we even begin to accomplish what you want to accomplish? How would we, in reality, cut down on the missing equipment and supplies and damage to facilities," asked the football coach.

QUESTIONS FOR DISCUSSION

1. Summarize the major elements in this case as they relate to the cited problems facing an athletic director.

2. Is the athletic director on the right track to solve this financial problem? Explain.

3. How else might the athletic director seek to solve the money crisis, that is, gain more money for the sports program other than by saving the money that would have to otherwise be spent on replacing the missing equipment/supplies and to repair damaged facilities? Be specific and explain your suggestions in full.

4. Outline a strategic plan of attack that the athletic department might pursue to eliminate or significantly reduce the amount of missing or stolen equipment and supplies.

5. Similarly, outline a strategic plan of attack that the athletic department might pursue to eliminate or significantly reduce the amount of damage to facilities. Be specific in terms of the plans and implementation tactics.

6. What policies might be put into place to help with the reduction of missing/stolen items and continual damage to facilities?

7. If the athletic director is able to significantly reduce the losses due to missing/stolen items and damage to the facilities, does this mean that she was incompetent during the previous three years when the athletic department lost about $23,000 each year? Explain.

8. How might the coaches be helpful in both tasks, i.e., reducing missing/stolen items and reducing damage to facilities?

9. How might Mary proceed to get the coaches on board in terms of really helping to reduce the amount of missing items and reduce the damage to the facilities? Provide a possible course of action in getting the coaches to buy into the concept of saving money this way.

10. How can an athletic department begin to get better control of equipment and supplies? What happens when such items end up missing? What about accountability? How can an athletic department keep track of who is responsible for missing items?

11. How can an athletic department make sure that the person responsible (athletes, coaches, others) for equipment and supplies that end of missing actually replace or pay for the missing items? Be specific.

12. If one has to pay for the stolen, lost or otherwise missing items, should the person pay full replacement cost or some other smaller amount? Justify your response.

13. What steps might the athletic director take to inform the athletes and the parents (as well as others) of the new emphasis on reducing missing items and damage to facilities?

14. Explain how Mary might publicize (and to whom) the success of the department in saving money this way? Why should she even bother to help spread the word on the success in this effort?

15. If the athletic director is successful in reducing the amount of losses stemming from lost or stolen equipment and supplies and from facility damage, how does this help the athletic director herself? How does it help her in the eyes of her superiors?

16. What general principles are appropriate in this situation for athletic administrators?

17. Comments . . .

RESPONSES FOR QUESTIONS FOR DISCUSSION

Case #10

The Case of the Transportation Problems for Injured Athletes

Johnnie Richards, star soccer player for McPherson High School in Midwestern, USA, was seriously injured during the first week of practice in the fall. It happened during a scrimmage with just minutes into the contest. Young Richards was attempting to score and in kicking the ball accidentally collided with another player and broke his leg. The head part-time coach, Marie Shipps, reflected: "Thank goodness it was not a compound fracture. That would have been truly ugly. And, we did finally get him to the hospital, even though it took a little while. But, now, we have that second problem, oh boy, what did I ever do to get myself into this mess."

Athletes today receive the very best in preventative medical care [Photo Courtesy of Bob Waldrop (Clemson University)]

It seemed that when Johnnie broke his leg the coach was visibly upset and not a little bit rattled. Coach Shipps, after about five minutes of wasting time and looking around and acting like she did not know what to do, Marie finally got the other athletes to carry Johnnie into her van and she personally drove the athlete to the hospital. As she drove off, she yelled to the players to continue the scrimmage and that she would be back shortly. When she dropped Johnnie off at the emergency room she immediately drove back to the soccer practice field only to find the whole team in a huddle in the middle of the field.

To Mary's horror she realized, when she ran onto the field, that another athlete had gotten hurt during the scrimmage while she was busy taking the first athlete to the hospital. Now, the day after the two accidents, Mary was waiting outside of the athletic director's (Dalton Knight) office. "What am I going to do to explain my actions or inactions," thought Mary. "I just plain forgot to call him."

The athletic director was fuming and wanted to calm down before bringing Marie into his office. "Why did she leave the field and allow the athletes to continue practice.

"And, why in the world did she just leave the injured athlete at the emergency room? What must she have been thinking? What an idiot. Didn't she read the athletic handbook that I gave her the day she was hired? I know that she is a part-time coach with no assistant, but my goodness, no one would do what she did and no one would fail to do what she failed to do," fumed the athletic director.

QUESTIONS FOR DISCUSSION

1. Summarize the situation outlined in this scenario.
2. What are the major problems presented in this situation?
3. As a result of what took place, what challenges and problems now face the athletic director?
4. What problems now face the soccer coach?
5. Who is responsible for what in this situation as outlined above? Explain in full.
6. Does the fact that there was no assistant coach assigned to the sport excuse the actions or inactions of the coach?
7. What specific policies, practices and procedures (relative to the list provided below) should have been in the athletic handbook that pertained to the situation in which an athlete is injured during practice?
   For example:
   a. Who to call/contact in event of an injury to a youngster in practice
   b. Availability of a phone on a practice field
   c. What other items should be available on the practice field in the event of an injury?
   d. How to get the injured athlete to the doctor/hospital
   e. What to do with the athletes who are not injured if the coach has to leave the field
   f. What the coach should do at the hospital when an injured athlete is taken there
   g. What follow-up steps should be taken by the coach and the athletic director
   h. Other . . .
8. Explain in detail the procedures and practices that outline the actions that coaches should take in the event of an injury in practice.
9. What should a coach do when an athlete is taken to a hospital in terms of the athlete? In terms of the parents of the athlete? In terms of the athletic director?
10. Why did the coach evidently not know what to do when the athlete was injured? Why did the coach not follow commonly accepted procedures in this case?
11. Was the athletic director correct in assuming that the coach should have known what to do since the AD had given the coach the athletic policy (*Policies, Procedures, Practices, Priorities and Philosophies—5Ps*) handbook? Why or why not?
12. What should the athletic director have done with the new part-time coach in terms of preparing the coach for a possible accident during a practice session? Be specific.
13. What general principles are appropriate to this situation for the athletic director and for the coach?
14. Comments . . .

RESPONSES FOR QUESTIONS FOR DISCUSSION

CASE #11

The Case of Athletes Dressing Like Slobs

The new athletic director, Rex Ranger, was embarrassed when he attended the first soccer game of the fall season. The away game was against a neighboring town and Rex had decided that he would accompany the team and the coaches on the school bus for the 25-mile trip to the opponent's school. When he entered the bus he was immediately surprised by the dress of the athletes. They were dressed like slobs; they were dressed like pigs; they were hardly the image of wholesome young athletes.

"Why would they not want to look and act like athletes," thought the athletic director. "And, why did the coaches not insist that their charges looked more presentable? Why, I am truly embarrassed by the way these kids look. They look pitiful. I will put a stop to that."

The next morning he called the head and assistant soccer coaches into his office just before the noon lunch period. "Hey, guys, what is with this sloppiness thing with the athletes? How in the world did you allow these kids to dress like they did? Weren't you embarrassed? I was. I just did not want to embarrass you or them during the game yesterday but believe me when I say that I really wanted to say something yesterday. I just bit my tongue."

"Hey, Rex," said Michael Williams, the head coach, "What do you expect us to do? With the ACLU around we just cannot force the athletes to dress up. Why, we would have out pants sued right off us in about 20 seconds."

"Wrong," said the athletic director. "I want our athletes to look and act like athletes should look and act—and I expect your help as coaches in getting this concept across to everyone, athletes, parents and our fans."

QUESTIONS FOR DISCUSSION

1. What are the major challenges facing an athletic director when faced with this type of problem? Be specific

2. Should athletic directors or coaches even be concerned with how athletes look and dress going to home and/or away games? What about how athletes look at school on the day of the game? At other times? Why or why not?

3. What can an athlete director actually do to get athletes to dress appropriately when going to an away and a home game?

4. Would the athletic director (school) be violating the rights of a youngster if the AD demanded that the athlete dress in a certain way? What about acting in a certain way?

5. Describe what the athletic director meant when he indicated that athletes should look like athletes and act like athletes? Provide specific examples.

6. What role(s) should the coaches play in having athletes dress appropriately? What can they do to insure that athletes dress appropriately (and act appropriately)?

7. What happens when individual athletes do not dress appropriately? What can the AD or coaches do in terms of disciplinary actions? Can athletes be denied playing time? Can they be dismissed for insubordination or other reasons? What other types of punishment or disciplinary actions can be administered?

8. What is the difference (if there is one) in expecting athletes to dress in a certain way and expecting them to act in a certain way at games/practices and in school?

9. What might the athletic director say or do with coaches to enlist their assistance in this goal?

10. Should the athletic director involve parents in this whole thing about establishing dress codes for athletes? Explain how the AD might approach parents and what he might share with them in terms of justifying the need for such a policy or practice.

11. Should the potential threat of a lawsuit from the ACLU or from parents discourage ADs or coaches from attempting to get athletes to dress in a specific fashion? Explain your position.

12. Should the athletic director confer with or get permission from other individuals (and if so, from whom) prior to attempting to implement a specific policy relating to dress codes and a behavioral code?

13. What general principles are involved in this case study for both coaches and for athletic administrators?

13. Comments . . .

RESPONSES FOR QUESTIONS FOR DISCUSSION

_____

_____

_____

_____

_____

_____

_____

CASE #12

The Case of the Super Star's Recruitment for College

David Treetop, a 6′ 11″ standout basketball player in high school, came to the athletic director, Maurice Murray, in early September, and indicated that he had received some phone calls and letters, addressed to him at his home, from several college coaches. David said he was confused and although he had asked his coach, Henry Hungry, for help, he was not sure that that had been a good idea.

"Why not?" asked the athletic director.

"Well," replied David, "coach Hungry indicated that he (the coach) would handle everything. He also told me that it was highly likely that he could see to it that I would receive a full scholarship guaranteed for four years at a 'big time' division I university. In fact, he also said that he might even be able to help more in that perhaps he might even be able to go to the same university that I go to—me as a star player and he as an assistant coach."

"What," inquired the athletic director. "Did I hear you correctly?"

David repeated what he had shared and added: "At a recent meeting with my parents, coach Hungry proceeded to outline a strategy regarding the handling of my recruitment including which rules and regulations to establish for recruiters, which schools to eliminate as well as when and how to handle the media and what press releases to leak. David added, "My parents didn't know what to expect since I am an only child and neither my father or mother had ever gone to college. They are inclined to just do whatever coach Hungry says."

It seems that both David and his parents were under strict orders from coach Hungry to never accept any phone calls or open any mail from the potential recruiters and colleges. Coach Hungry had indicated that he did not want David's concentration "broken" before or during the season with distractions. Instead, the coach said that he would handle everything and would tell David what to do, when to do it and how to do it, etc.

"Mr. Murray, I need your help. It is as simple as that. Are my parents doing the right thing in terms of trusting coach Hungry? Is Mr. Hungry correct in doing what he is doing and planning to do in the future? Can coach Hungry accompany me to college and coach me there? I am simply confused. HELP ME, PLEASE."

QUESTIONS FOR DISCUSSION

1. Was the basketball coach really knowledgeable about the scholarship rules of NCAA division I? Explain your answer.
2. What options were open to David before he confided in the coach in this matter? What options are open to him now that he has approached the athletic director?

3. What options were open to Coach Hungry when approached by David?
4. What are or should be the role(s) of the parents as described in this situation?
5. What could and/or should they do?
6. What is the role of the athletic director in this situation in terms of coach Hungry and in respect to David? Elaborate.
7. Assume the role of the athletic director and share what you would say to coach Hungry.
8. What advice would you as athletic director give to David? How would you answer his questions that he poised to Mr. Murray?
9. What is/are the role(s) of others in this situation? Who are the others? Specify their roles and responsibilities.
10. Should the actions that coach Hungry took in response to David's inquiry be considered proper or improper? Are these actions ethical or unethical (or questionable)? Explain in detail.
11. What are some of the factors that will have an effect upon whether or not David finds a suitable college to attend, whether he is offered a suitable (full ride) scholarship and whether or not David has his academic and athletic needs fully met? Explain in full.
12. Would the situation be different if the student was Mary Quickstop, star track athlete? If so, how? If not, why?
13. Would the situation be different if David was a 5' 11', 165 pound, average football player? Elaborate.
14. What pitfalls (what could go wrong) await David, the coach, the parents, and the athletic director?
15. What rules could or should be placed in effect to help David, the school, the parents, and the college recruiters? What ground rules might be appropriate school wide for a so-called STAR ATHLETE?
16. Who owes what obligations to whom in this recruitment process?
17. What ethical considerations should come into play in this situation?
18. What are the roles of the guidance personnel and the athletic director in this type of situation?
19. What guiding principles might be established to assist in the recruitment process of would-be college athletes—of all skill levels?
20. Comments . . .

RESPONSES FOR QUESTIONS FOR DISCUSSION

_____

_____

_____

CASE #13

The Case of the Player's Eligibility

Susan McCall, a sophomore at Southeastern College in Ohio, was really upset with herself, her volleyball team and life in general. How could she have been doing so poorly in school this first semester? It wasn't all her fault. Her teachers did not understand her. They didn't care about her. And, even her coaches did not go out of their way to support her when things really got tough. Gradually, throughout the fall, her grades have been fallen and just recently, at mid-term, her overall grades were well below a 2.0.

"I guess I really only have one choice. If I stay in the English class with the **F** that I now have there is really no possibility that I can bring that grade up to a passing mark. I guess I will have to just drop that class as well as the history class in which I am also just flat out flunking," moaned Susan.

The next afternoon, Friday, at 3:58 p.m., just before the team's vans left for a weekend volleyball tournament and just before the registrar's office closed for the weekend, Susan went over to the registrar's office and dropped the two 3-hour courses, bringing her total number of credits to 9. She then left with the rest of her teammates and participated in the two-day tournament, which her team eventually won, thereby maintaining their 4th place national ranking status according to the most recent NCAA poll. On the way home, Susan mentioned to her teammates in the van that she had dropped below the 12-hour minimum required by the NCAA in order to maintain one's eligibility. She said: "Hey people, I am sorry that I am not going to be traveling with you to any more contests, since I am no longer eligible."

One of her teammates replied: "Susan, don't you realize what you have just done to us, your teammates, and the team in general? Why, you have just caused us to forfeit every volleyball game that we just fought hard and long to win, as soon as the athletic director is notified on Monday morning that one of our athletes have dropped below the 12-hour minimum. How in the world could you do this to us?"

"Hey, I just wanted to play this weekend with you all," was the only retort Susan could utter. "It meant so much to be able to travel with you, to be with you, to be able to play in each of the games that we won. How could you have denied that experience to me? It wasn't my fault that my grades were failing and I had to drop the two @#%#^&% failing courses."

Her teammates sat in stunned silence the rest of the way back to the campus. Most of the young women were thinking of how this disaster was going to affect each of them, their athletic careers and the team's national ranking (and chances of post season play).

Early Monday morning the athletic director, Storm Norman, received an urgent phone from the assistant athletic director in charge of eligibility, Reba Robinson, who informed him of the disaster with the eligibility status of a volleyball player.

QUESTIONS FOR DISCUSSION

1.   What are the major elements in this scenario?
2.   What were the reasons that Susan did what she did?
3.   What could the athletic director have done, if anything, to prevent this type of situation from happening? Explain several different scenarios.
4.   Are there some things that athletic directors just cannot always prevent despite the best faith efforts to do so? Is this one of those instances? Elaborate and justify your position.
5.   Why did Susan drop the two classes at 3:58 p.m. on Friday? What did she fail to take into account?
6.   Will the NCAA give a break (benefit of the doubt) to the athletic department in light of the sneaky way in which Susan duped everyone? Explain.
7.   What will be the likely consequences of Susan dropping the two classes in respect to the athletic director, the athletic department, the volleyball team, the school, and to Susan?
8.   Explain the public relations nightmare that can result from this disaster.
9.   What should Storm Norman have done (if he did not do it) in an effort to prevent this situation from ever occurring? Be specific in your recommendations.
10. What options are now open to the athletic director upon learning of the problem with the volleyball team's eligibility?
11. What would you, as athletic director, do in terms of administering punishment to Susan? Should she be declared ineligible for volleyball for the rest of her time at the institution? Should she be declared ineligible for all collegiate sports for the rest of her time at the school? Why or why not?
12. Assume a role-playing position and indicate what you, as athletic director, would say to Susan, after the fact.
13. What would you, as the athletic director, say to the other team members?
14. Assume a role-playing stance and explain what you would say to the institution's President (your director superior) about this situation on Monday morning?
15. What are you trying to accomplish in your meeting with the president. Be specific.
16. How and when would you, as athletic director, inform the NCAA as well as your conference office of the infraction? Role play and indicate what you would say.
17. What type of damage control should the athletic director employ, starting Monday morning?
18. Write a news release for general distribution explaining the eligibility disaster/problem. When should it be released?
19. What general principles are applicable in this situation in terms of handling the eligibility status of athletes?
20. Comments . . .

RESPONSES FOR QUESTIONS FOR DISCUSSION

CASE #14

The Case of the Questionable Conditioning of Athletes

Stuart Smythe, head football coach at Westside High School, was beside himself. Here he was, in the last week of the preseason and a third athlete just went down with a serious injury, this time a leg problem. "What have I done to deserve this kind of trag-edy? Why me? Why, we have a good conditioning program. And, most of the athletes arrived at camp in pretty good shape. What is going on here?" decried the coach.

The athletic director, Johnnie Jones, was informed by the head trainer of the serious injury to the third would-be starter that same afternoon. A similar type of injury to all three athletes was of great concern to the athletic director. He asked the trainer: "Do you have any idea why this or any of the two earlier injuries occurred? Is there a pattern here? Whose fault is it that these terrible accidents/injuries have occurred? What could have been done to prevent these injuries?"

Conditioning is the one constant in competitive sports [Courtesy of West Virginia University]

The trainer, Joshua Breen, indicated that he was not sure as to the causes. He also did not know if the injuries were a result of something the coaching staff did not do properly or did do improperly. "But, I tell you what Johnnie, I will double check my records and start to review what has transpired in the way of other injuries and accidents as well as what type of condition-ing the athletes are experiencing under the eyes of the coaching staff," concluded the trainer.

"Ok Joshua, but when I start to see that many injuries (of the same general nature) I natu-rally start to wonder if there is something wrong with the conditioning program for the athletes and/or if the coaches are having the athletes do something stupid or inappropriate in practice that result in such injuries," concluded the AD. "Remember, I am going to hold you, in your role as athletic trainer, responsible (along with the coaches) for the conditioning programs for all the sports."

QUESTIONS FOR DISCUSSION

1. Summarize the main points in this case as they pertain to such problems faced by ath-letic administrators, coaches and trainers.

2. Whose fault might these injuries be? Should the trainer be held partially responsible (along with the coaches) for the conditioning and physical well-being of all athletes as this athletic director is doing? Provide a rationale for your stance.

3.   Is the appropriate response in this instance the statement that: "accidents happen all the time, it is just a case of an act of God." Why or why not?

4.   What can coaches do in an attempt to reduce such incidents and injuries? Be specific.

5.   Explain in detail what trainers can do in an attempt to reduce such incidents and injuries?

6.   What can athletic directors/administrators do in an attempt to reduce such incidents and injuries? Elaborate.

7.   Role play and state what you would do (and say), as athletic director, to the coaching staff before school starts to help emphasize the importance of preventing injuries to athletes? Be specific.

8.   Are repeated injuries to different athletes often a sign of inadequate conditioning by the coaching staff? Explain.

9.   Can repeated injuries to different athletes be a sign of weakness in coaching decisions? Why or why not?

10. What type of response or excuses might the athletic director expect from the coaching staff when questioned as to why so many injuries have occurred to different athletes? List such excuses.

11. How might an athletic director proceed during the preseason in terms of personally checking the physical and psychological conditioning of athletes on various teams?

12. What type of negative public relations might take place if such injuries prevent would-be starters from playing? How might such poor public relations be negated by the athletic administration?

13. If the athletic director deems that there is a problem with the type of conditioning carried out by the coaching staff, how might the AD proceed in terms of meeting with the coaches? Be specific.

14. Cite some general principles that are involved in this type of situation.

15. Comments . . .

RESPONSES FOR QUESTIONS FOR DISCUSSION

_____

_____

_____

_____

_____

_____

Case #15

The Case of Athletes Demanding a Coach Be Fired

The athletes had requested the meeting with the athletic director in a low key and polite fashion. It wasn't until Dalton Mead arrived at the meeting that he had scheduled in his office suite that afternoon that he realized that this meeting was going to be unlike any meeting he had had in a long, long time at this high school.

"Mr. Mead," said one of the youngsters, "we asked to meet with you because we just cannot take it any more. In fact, we are all so upset that we did not know what to do other than to approach you and to lay it all out for you to see and make the only decision possible."

Mr. Mead cautiously said: "Ok, let me in on what has happened. I need to know what has brought all of us here together."

"Well," said one of the kids, "you have to fire coach Scott, it is as simple as that. We won't play for him if he remains."

"Yea, chimed in another athlete, Bobby Smyth. "Coach Scott gives us no respect, he takes our 'manhood' away from us. Why, he treats us as if we don't know what we are doing and most of us know more than he does. The drills he has us run are outmoded and not fun. He even cut some of the players during tryouts, our best friends who made the team last year. How can that be, how can those guys make last year's teams and not this year's team?

The athletic director, sensing where this was going and where it might end, inquired: "Well, tell me something, what exactly has the coach done or not done that might warrant his firing in the middle of the season? Additionally, don't you realize that something like this happening to a young coach might ruin his career as a coach for the rest of his life?"

"We don't care. We don't care about his career; we are concerned about our careers, period. We just don't like the guy. He gives us no respect. He doesn't put our friends on the team and he is just not a nice person. He doesn't understand us, that is for sure. We will never win a game under his tutelage. It is either him or us," declared the co-captain.

Questions for Discussion

1. Summarize the situation facing the athletic director with these athletes.
2. Why would athletes act like this? Is this all that unusual? Explain.
3. Should the athletic director release the coach if the coach has lost the confidence of his athletes? Discuss.
4. Can the athletic director survive if the team members walk off the team and the end result is that there are no athletes (or insufficient numbers to field a team)?

5. Who, within the institution, might be looking at this situation with great concern? Why? What impact or influence might this have on the athletic director?

6. What would you recommend to the athletic director in terms of the next step(s) to take in this situation? Be specific and outline a series of steps that the AD might pursue. Explain WHY for each step or tactic.

7. With whom should the athletic director visit or meet with on an individual basis? Provide a list of such individuals and state why they should be communicated with in this situation?

8. Should the athletic director encourage the coach to quit? Why or why not?

9. Should the athletic director attempt to change the minds of the athletes? Why or why not?

10. Assume a role-playing position and state what you, as athletic director, would say (be specific) to the coach.

11. Are the athletes being reasonable and mature in their approach? What have they done correctly, if anything? What have they done that is inappropriate, if anything?

12. Is there a way out for the athletic director in this scenario, one that will allow the AD to look good?

13. Speculate as to why the athletes don't like the coach? Are these reactions justified? Appropriate? To be expected?

14. Is it important for athletes to like their coaches? Is it important for coaches to do things that will curry favor of athletes? Elaborate.

15. What might have been done much earlier in this school environment to prevent the current situation from occurring?

16. If the athletic director decides not to fire the coach, what might he say to the athletes in announcing his decision? Assume a role-playing position.

17. How might the athletic director deal with his boss or superior in the school? What is the danger at this level for the coach, for the athletic director, for the athletic department?

18. Would this situation be different if it occurred at a NCAA division III institution? Explain.

19. Cite some general principles and guidelines that are applicable in this situation relative to the administration of the athletic department.

20. Comments . . .

RESPONSES FOR QUESTIONS FOR DISCUSSION

_____

_____

_____

CHAPTER SEVEN

Problems with Athletic Coaches

CHAPTER OBJECTIVES

After reading this chapter you will be able to:

- Be familiar with various problems relating to athletic coaches
- List ways in which coaches might be motivated to take a more active role in school affairs
- Recommend a course of action to students who desire to become a coach and/or an athletic administrator
- Deal with coaches who live in the past and attempt to justify current actions based on the past
- Cite examples of how coaches might avoid the trap of being arrogant while being highly successful on the proverbial playing field
- Advise a coach who is having difficulty devoting sufficient time to one's professional life and personal life
- Recommend to coaches appropriate types of behavior in their role as athletic tutors, including how to become more organized
- Recommend to a coach steps to take to become more capable of dressing more appropriately as a professional and a coach

Major decisions at critical times comes with the territory.
[Courtesy of Washington State University]

- Explain how coaches should be evaluated as coaches in a high school setting
- Outline the improper methods used by coaches to motivate their athletes and to suggest appropriate strategies instead
- Differentiate between an overly aggressive coach and an overly conservative coach in terms of game/contest strategy and provide suggestions for a more appropriate course of action
- Suggest ways to deal with coaches who will not follow directions from higher administrators and whose actions border on insubordination
- Counsel coaches whose actions or inactions are indicative of insensitivity to others, adults and students

• Outline how an athletic department should operate its purchasing (and receipt) of equipment and supplies
• Understand the problems caused by teachers/coaches who resign from coaching once they have earned tenure (continuing contract)

CASE

16. Case of the uninvolved coach
17. Case of the future of the would-be coach
18. The case of the two coaches who worked closely together
19. The case of remembering the past
20. The first-time losing coach
21. The very unhappy coach
22. The case of handling the disorganized coach
23. The case of the coach's inappropriate appearance
24. The case of the expectations of coaches
25. The case of the negative motivation by the coach
26. The case of dealing with an overly conservative coach
27. The case of the coach who couldn't follow directions
28. The case of the inconsiderate and unthinking coach
29. The case of the altered purchase order
30. The case of the person who quits coaching but remains as a teacher

CASE #16

The Case of the Uninvolved Coach

Kevin Brown was the highly successful basketball and baseball coach at Central High located in a small community of 20,000 people. He has also taught history and physical education each of the 15 years that he has been at Central.

The new principal, Ms. Joanne McAllister, had been on the job for almost 4 months when she asked Kevin and the athletic director, Joe Smackler, to visit with her. During the meeting she broached the subject that had been a matter of discussion by the two previous principals, and which Kevin was rather adamant about. Specifically, Ms. McAllister wanted to know why Kevin, being such a successful and highly respected coach at the school, has never agreed to take part in any other official school activity. She also wanted to know why Mr. Smackler (who reported directly to the principal) had never been successful in getting the coach more involved in the total school activities. In point of fact, coach Brown had always gone out of his way to deliberately distance himself from the school, the faculty and the school programs—except of course when it came to the basketball and baseball programs.

On the other hand, coach Brown was always adamant that everyone else in the school (and the town) should certainly participate in and actively support his two teams and his athletes. In fact, he often complained that not enough faculty, staff and administrators were willing to help his two sports *and* his athletes. In addition, he was always asking for help and favors from others—both inside and outside of the school. However, he would never reciprocate the favor. He never attended a school art show. He never attended a school play. He never attended a school dance, much less serve as a chaperon. He never attended another sporting event, for that matter. He never volunteered to serve on any committee that did not directly affect his two teams. In reality, he never volunteered to do anything for the school or its programs, period. He only reluctantly attended faculty meetings and that was because the teaching contract required his attendance. However, he made sure that everyone knew he was displeased that he had to attend—and he certainly never did anything during these boring and useless meetings other than sit there and look bored to death.

In fact, he rarely attended the athletic meetings called by the athletic director. And, when he did attend, he was usually seen with his nose in a notebook working on his plays and his practice plans, never really paying attention to what was being discussed.

Right in front of the coach and the athletic director, the principal startled both by stating right up front: "Mr. Smackler, how in the world can you allow one of your premier coaches to distance himself from the school activities as well as from the athletic meetings. I don't think treating coach Brown as a prima donna is doing anyone any good—and I intend to do something about it, today."

In response to Ms. McAllister's inquiry about his attitude and his reluctance to be a team player coach Brown was a little irritated and became rather testy by replying: "Well, look. It is this way. I spend 18 hours a day, seven days a week, 52 weeks a year, working with my athletes—on and off the playing fields/courts. I don't have time to spend on non-essential things. The students, the faculty and administration, and the community, they all want our basketball and baseball programs to be successful. Well, the only way I know how to do that is to devote my entire being into making these programs what they are today. Why anyone can go to the art show or a school play. How many can coach like I do? How many can produce the winners like I do? How many can get our athletes to be as successful as they have become under my tutelage?"

Both the principal and the athletic director were a little taken back. The athletic director tried to support the position of the principal and attempted to motivate the coach to play more of an active role in the functions of the school. The AD tried to explain the reasons why it would be good for him and the school to have him more involved in non-athletic activities.

It seemed as if both the principal and athletic director were bound and determined that the coach was going to do more than he has in the past in terms of becoming involved in the school, its programs and its students. Seemingly, they were at an impasse.

QUESTIONS FOR DISCUSSION

1. Are the reasons given by the coach for his reluctance to become more involved in the school's activities *appropriate*? Are they *correct*? Why or why not?

2. Is it wrong or inappropriate for an athletic director to ever give highly successful (and temperamental) coaches preferential treatment? Elaborate.

3. Assume the role of the athletic director (role play) and explain the reasons why it would be good for the coach and the school to have coach Brown become more involved in non-athletic activities.

4. Why, do you think, did the athletic director not previously insist that the coach change his behavior in this area? Why did it take the principal to get involved before the AD got in on the act in a more forceful way?

5. Is it always important for the athletic director to support (publicly, privately) one's boss's position? In this case, what does it make the AD look like?

6. Why would the principal be concerned that one of the coaches, especially this one, is not actively involved in school activities? Should the AD be concerned with the situation, now that principal has expressed her opinion?

7. What role should the athletic director now play in this situation? Why?

8. Why have the previous principals failed to get coach Brown to change his attitude and his willingness to be part of the total school picture?

9. What might be the reaction of other faculty and staff in the school *toward coach Brown*? Why?

10. What might be the attitude of the other coaches and other teachers *toward the athletic director* who has allowed coach Brown to do pretty much what he wanted to do?

11. Is it really a big deal that this coach is not playing a more visible role in the school? Why or why not?

12. Who is hurt by the coach's current attitude and behavior? Why?

13. Is the coach being self-centered? Selfish? Why or why not?

14. What should be the expectations of head coaches in a high school setting in terms of their association with and involvement in the other activities of the school?

15. Why do you think coach Brown expects others in the school to be involved in his program but he is not willing to be involved in the program of others? Be specific. How would you counter coach Brown's argument?

16. If coach Brown is unwilling or unable to change his attitude or outlook, what should be done next by the athletic director? By the principal? Justify their actions.

17. Should the coach and the athletic director accepted some change in the status quo with the arrival of the new principal? If so, what should each have done as a result? Explain your position.

18. What general principles are applicable in this type of situation from the perspectives of both the principal *and* the athletic director?

19. Comments . . .

RESPONSES FOR QUESTIONS FOR DISCUSSION

_____

_____

_____

_____

_____

_____

_____

_____

_____

_____

Case #17

The Case of the Future of the Would-Be Coach

A freshman in college, Michelle Dickens, was attempting to get the hang on how to spend one's career. She was very interested in becoming an athletic coach, and eventually an athletic director. What she did know was that she thoroughly enjoyed her own athletic career in high school and at the college level. She wished more than anything that she could continue to have such a wonderful life that revolved around competitive sports, but as a coach (and, if she was lucky, as an AD), rather than as an athlete.

Michelle attempted to develop a plan of attack in which she would be able to review the pros and cons of coaching at the various levels. She wanted to find out how difficult it would be to break into coaching at the junior high, senior high and collegiate levels? What would be the odds of becoming a coach following graduation from college? What sport or sports should she coach? Should she become an assistant or a head coach at first? In what should she major in college if she desired to be a coach in public schools and/or at the collegiate level?

She also thought that it might be fun to become an athletic director at either the secondary or collegiate levels. So, she approached her athletic director at the college, Lori Meade, and sought her advice. The athletic director listened carefully to Michelle's comments and then, after careful consideration, started to respond by saying . . . .

QUESTIONS FOR DISCUSSION

1. Are Michelle's expectations realistic? Is she just in love with being an athlete or with sports in general? Or, is she actually interested in working within the athletic arena as a career optiion?
2. Should she major in physical education and become a teacher in order to become a coach? Should she major in physical education (teacher education) to increase her chances of securing a career (paid) coaching position? Why or why not?
3. Does it matter what teaching area she secures a teaching degree in terms of her desire to coach in middle or high school? Explain.
4. If she does major in physical education, would she be able to easily secure a teaching job without being able (required) to coach? Explain.
5. Should Michelle be prepared to coach more than one sport? If so, how many sports and which sports. Provide a rationale for your responses.
6. Is it important to be able to coach in more than one season? In more than two seasons? If so, why? If not, why? Be specific in your response and position.

7. How helpful will her successful college playing experience be in securing a coaching position?

8. Are there coaching positions plentiful in the public schools for would-be women coaches? Why?

9. What are some other reasons why an individual might desire to become an athletic coach?

10. Describe the various coaching options (both paid and volunteer) that Michelle might become involved in following her graduation from college?

11. What would be some of the facts and opinions that Lori Mead (the athletic director) might share with this would-be coach in an effort to help her create somewhat of an accurate insight into the future of one's career as a public school coach (as an assistant, as a head coach) and as an athletic director? What about at the college level?

12. Would the information be different if the student was a male rather than a female? Be specific if there are differences in terms of what males and females can expect when examining possibilities of becoming an athletic coach.

13. With whom might the athletic director suggest Michelle visit with to secure help in her career goals?

14. How could Michelle begin to expand her network of potential contacts in the coaching and teaching arenas? With whom should she attempt to develop network contacts?

15. What specific steps might the athletic director suggest that Michelle take to help insure better odds in getting a coaching position at the high school or junior high levels? In terms of:
    A. Courses taken
    B. Related experiences
    C. People to talk with
    D. Books to read
    E. Periodicals to glean
    F. Clinics or workshops to attend
    G. Other . . .

16. What would be some of the hurdles that any would-be coach might face—in getting a coaching job and then in keeping the position (being successful as a coach)?

17. Would being an elite high school and/or collegiate athlete be an advantage or a hindrance for one to be a successful coach? Explain your position.

18. What are the advantages and disadvantages (possible trials and tribulations) of coaching at each of the various levels?
    A. Junior high school
    B. Senior high school
    C. Junior college
    D. Small college (NCAA division III or NAIA)
    E. Medium size college or university (NCAA division III)
    F. Major university (NCAA division I)

19. What are the distinctive differences between being a head coach and an assistant coach in the eyes of the typical athletic director in a high school?

20. What are the important distinctions between coaching a so-called flagship or top tier sport and coaching a non-flagship sport at the secondary level? Be specific.

21. What are the various national or state organizations that the would-be secondary coach would be wise to be knowledgeable about and be a member of in the eyes of an AD?

22. What principles are applicable in this situation in which an individual desires to secure more information about a life long commitment to a professional career such as coaching and/or athletic administration.

23. Comments . . .

RESPONSES FOR QUESTIONS FOR DISCUSSION

_____

_____

_____

_____

_____

_____

_____

_____

_____

_____

_____

_____

_____

CASE #18

The Case of the Two Coaches
Who Worked Closely Together

Coach Terri Plumb was a striking young single woman who was serving as a head coach of the women's soccer team. She had been at the school for almost seven years and had moderate success. She was very, very popular with everyone—students and staff members alike.

Jack Newcomer was a first year coach hired to serve as the head soccer coach for the boys' soccer team at the same high school. He had just graduated from the state college the previous summer and had gotten married in July.

During the fall months, both Terri and Jack had numerous occasions to work together in teachers' and coaches' meetings. They were very often thrown together in terms of common practice times and late meetings at school. Before long they were seen meeting early before school, having coffee at the local donut shop in town and often meeting during free hours in the faculty lounge where they were observed laughing and thoroughly enjoying each other's company. They were even seen leaving the school together in the afternoon ostensibly going on scouting trips.

Eventually, it became common knowledge that when one saw Terri you also saw Jack (and vice versa). There was some talk downtown as well as among the staff (and even the students, according to some adults in the community) at the school about their relationship.

One afternoon, the athletic director was called by a member of the board and asked what was going on with two of his staff members, one of who is married?

QUESTIONS FOR DISCUSSION

1. What is the central issue in this scenario?
2. What is wrong in this situation, if anything?
3. What is the perceived difficulty? Elaborate.
4. Should male and female coaches be careful in terms of how much they are seen together? Should they be concerned with what other people (staff, students, parents, community members) think about them and their actions? Why or why not?
5. If there is nothing wrong in reality, could there still be a perception of improper conduct and is this perception something that the school, the athletic director or the central administration should be concerned about? Explain your rationale.
6. Why do you think the board member is calling the athletic director?
7. Is the board member acting properly or improperly? Explain.

8. How could things be defused at this point in time?

9. What could have been done to prevent the present situation from developing? By whom?

10. What should the athletic director do (say) in response to the board member? Should the athletic director talk with the principal? The superintendent? The board? Justify your position.

11. Should the athletic director talk to Terri and Jack? Why or why not? What might be the essence of this conversation?

12. Is the athletic director responsible for this situation with the two coaches? Could the athletic director find himself under fire for this type of behavior? Explain.

13. What would be the result, in addition to the above situation, if one or more of the following came into play?

   a. Both coaches were seen dancing at a Elks Clubs dance in a nearby town

   b. Both coaches were seen dancing at a social gathering at a coaching clinic held in conjunction with the state coaches' convention

   c. Coach Terri Plumb complained to the athletic director that Jack Newcomer was forcing his attention upon her

   d. Coach Newcomer complained to the athletic director that Terri Plumb was forcing her attention upon him

   e. The athletic director noticed, on several occasions, that both Terri and Jack had walked down the school hallway holding hands

   f. The athletic director suspected that Terri and Jack were having an affair

   g. The athletic director knew Terri and Jack were not having an affair but were just good friends

   h. Jack Newcomer was not presently married

14. What principles are applicable in the situation where coaches of the opposite sex must work in close proximity with one another in the conduct of their professional duties?

15. Comments . . .

RESPONSES FOR QUESTIONS FOR DISCUSSION

_____

_____

_____

_____

_____

_____

CASE #19

The Case of Remembering the Past

Bobby Hindsight, the head football coach at Newtown High School, was enjoying a rather stressful experience as a relatively new head football coach. Previously, he had a very successful career as an assistant football coach at Oldtime High School for some 12 years. Only recently, some two years ago in fact, he had been appointed as head coach of Newtown.

The first two seasons at Newtown had been an awakening for him. First of all, Newtown High is a somewhat smaller school and the athletic operation has certainly enjoyed less success in sport competition than the school where coach Hindsight previously came. Second, Bobby Hindsight is now the head coach instead of an assistant. Third, there really is no tradition of success at Newtown High. Of course, that is why he was brought to Newtown High, to build a winning program.

Since arriving at Newtown High, coach Hindsight had the habit of always using the phrase ("well, at Oldtown we did it this way . . ."). In fact, the only justification that he seemed to use when attempting to accomplish anything, whether to establish or change a policy, to implement a plan, or to do ANYTHING, was to indicate, "that was the way it was done at Oldtown."

It became obvious after some 6 months that this behavior was going to be a continual pattern. In fact, if anything, coach Hindsight's propensity to use the ill-conceived phrase increased. In addition, not infrequently the ideas presented by coach Hindsight with this so-called supporting justification just did not fit with the new school because the two schools were significantly different. The personnel were different, athletes were different, the facilities were different, the financial resources were different, the expectations were different, the history was different, the boosters and fans were different, etc. Finally, coach Hindsight had been caught more than once using the now overly familiar justification ("it was done that way at my previous school") in situations in which that just was not the truth.

After a while, the athletic administration and staff as well as other school personnel began to get tired of the consistent crying and whining of the football coach. They became less sympathetic that the present coaching situation wasn't exactly like the athletic situation at coach Hindsight's previous school. They were also less and less in agreement with the coach that the current football program was evidently going to the dogs (at least in the eyes of the football coach) unless things were changed and done like things were done at Oldtime High School. And, they seemingly became even less concerned that the football coach had his feelings hurt when he realized that he was not receiving the support from the administration and athletic people (especially the athletic director) that he "knew" he certainly deserved.

As a result, coach Hindsight became very concerned about the fact that he was having less and less impact upon the athletic decision makers (read athletic director) in the school. He began to realize that fewer and fewer individuals were evidently listening to him and even fewer were actually accepting what he was saying to them. In fact, he felt betrayed by the athletic director whom he now viewed as a potential threat, enemy and adversary.

QUESTIONS FOR DISCUSSION

1. What are your initial reactions to this situation?
2. What are coach Hindsight's goals? Are his goals worthwhile? Elaborate.
3. How would you describe his tactics?
4. How should coach Hindsight view his current athletic director? Elaborate.
5. What did the athletic director do or fail to do when coach Hindsight was interviewed that might have contributed to this situation?
6. What suggestions would you, as the athletic director, have provided coach Hindsight *when he first arrived* at his new school? Be specific and provide a justification for your position.
7. What could be the motivation of coach Hindsight? Why does he act as he does?
8. Are his actions disruptive to the main issue(s) at stake or supportive of said issues? Explain in detail.
9. What about coach Hindsight's ethics? Is his behavior ethical? Explain.
10. How does coach Hindsight think of himself? What does he think of others?
11. How do you feel the coach now thinks others view him? Elaborate.
12. Is he going to be effective? If so, explain. If not, explain.
13. Once it became evident that coach Hindsight was going to continue to act as he has, what should the athletic do, when should he do it, and how?
14. Should there be other people involved in straightening this coach out?
15. How do you feel other coaches at this school feel about coach Hindsight? Be specific.
16. How might coach Hindsight alter his behavior now to be more effective, if this is possible? How can the athletic director help him now?
17. What negative consequences could come out of all of this? What good could possibly come out of all of this? What are some factors that will (or could) determine whether or not the outcome might be positive or negative?
18. What general administrative principles are applicable in this scenario? Discuss.
19. Comments . . .

RESPONSES FOR QUESTIONS FOR DISCUSSION

CASE #20

The First-Time Losing Coach

For many years, Mr. Jack Wallace had been a highly successful athletic coach in a flagship sport at a school that had a history (and expectation) of successful teams. In fact, Mr. Wallace has never had a losing season, that is until the present season. His football team just concluded the season with the worse won/loss situation in his career—the team garnered a single victory with 9 defeats. It has just been a disaster from all perspectives for poor coach Wallace.

In the past, Mr. Wallace had been able to do pretty much what he pleased, partly because he was successful, rather his teams were successful. The football team had won many conference championships and 8 years ago made it to the quarterfinals of the state tournament.

However, coach Wallace had some severe faults—which were generally overlooked because his teams always won and because he had the support (because of his winning teams) of powerful people in the school and the community. One of his faults was that he had an abrasive personality. He was also rather bossy; he had to have things his way. Nor was he very patient with or tolerate of others (staff or athletes) all the while giving the impression that he thought that he was worthy of great adulation and respect. His status within the school system was evident whenever budget time came around each year. He would inevitably attempt to pressure the school administrators to give him whatever

A close call and excitement for all
[Courtesy of Cornell Athletics]

monies he wanted for his team, even if it meant that other coaches in his school had to sacrifice and do without. He often went over the head of the previous athletic director, directly to the superintendent or to the individual board members.

And, it worked. Everyone knew it worked. Everyone knew that Jack Wallace was a jerk, an egotistical jackass, but no one was in a position to do anything about it since the winning football team was all-important. It seemed that coach Wallace usually got his way, one way or another.

Now, according to some people, that might begin to change. The losing football team was a landmine on which Jack Wallace just planted both feet, asserted some of the little people who had been stepped on in the past by this bully of a coach. The new AD (who had arrived from a different school just before school and the football season started) saw a weakness in coach Wallace's supposedly bulletproof armor.

With his team losing, coach Wallace began to experience something he had never felt before. That is, hostility and resentment and even a lack of respect from a growing number of people. Even some of his ardent supporters and fans were less visible in their support, while a few of them were actually critical of his coaching performance as well as his irascibility. One of his coaching colleagues made a statement: "You know, it is like vultures just waiting until the old jackal makes one mistake too many—and with the enemies coach Wallace has made in his 15 years on the job it is no wonder that he is vulnerable now that his team has been unsuccessful." Another colleague added that coach Wallace evidently forgot the adage that one should be nice to people on the way up the career ladder for one is very likely to meet the same individuals on the slide down.

Even the local newspapers and radio stations were beginning to question his competency and questioned whether or not the coach had lost his touch.

Coach Wallace, however, couldn't understand what was going on. He also was confused that people would have the audacity to come out into the open and actually criticize him. In the past these little people just stayed out of his way or he would have simply crushed them. He just did not understand how people could treat him differently, now that he was not winning. After all, he had one losing season. Next year he was confident that he would be back on top, if that idiot athletic director doesn't get in his way. "Then I will show those idiots, those ingrates, a thing or two. How dare they criticize me. Why I have done more for this school, for this town, than anyone in the past 30 years," thought coach Wallace.

QUESTIONS FOR DISCUSSION

1. What does coach Wallace's usual behavior teach you about relationships between coaches and other individuals (including the athletic director) within a school setting and within a community?
2. How could the previous athletic director allow such a situation to develop? What might the previous athletic director have done earlier to stop or prevent this type of situation from developing?
3. What should Mr. Wallace have done (besides win) to prevent the current situation?
4. Why wouldn't coach Wallace want to change his behavior in the above scenario?
5. What role might the new athletic director now play in this entire situation? Be specific in your recommendations for his actions now.
6. Should the new athletic director now go for the jugular vein and try to get rid of the coach? Explain.
7. With whom should the athletic director speak to in terms of coach Wallace's prior habit of jumping the chain of command? What should the athletic director say?
8. What should or could coach Wallace do now to help rectify the situation in terms of interpersonal relationships? Provide a rational for such strategy.
9. What should he not do now in light of the present situation? Why?
10. Why would having a winning team SOMETIMES enable a coach to get away with actions or inactions that normally would not be tolerated—even by mature and sane individuals? Elaborate.

11. How would other coaches react to coach Wallace usually getting his way in respect to the annual budget process? Elaborate.
12. What can the new athletic director do in terms of working with other coaches?
13. Cite some principles that are applicable here?
14. Comments . . .

RESPONSES FOR QUESTIONS FOR DISCUSSION

_____

_____

_____

_____

_____

_____

_____

_____

_____

_____

_____

_____

_____

_____

_____

CASE #21

The Very Unhappy Coach

Coach David Crabapple came home from teaching and coaching one afternoon and was very, very unhappy. It seems like almost everything went wrong during the past week. His classes (he taught mathematics) were really becoming taxing since there were so many students in his classes—so many students who did not really want to learn but were merely taking up space.

And today, of all days, the star player on his JV soccer squad came to him and indicated that he was unhappy and was not going to play anymore because of the strict rules that the athletic director had established for all athletes (at all levels) in that sport. Finally, just before coach Crabapple left for home, he was approached by Mr. Eversuccessful, the head varsity coach, who indicated that he wanted coach Crabapple to scout an opponent tomorrow evening (Wednesday) and also another opponent this coming Saturday. This Saturday happened to be the 5th wedding anniversary of the Crabapples.

So it was not unexpected that coach Crabapple was not in the best of moods as he drove the 45 minutes home from school. Now in his 5th year as teacher/coach in this school, he had chosen not to live in the town in which he taught and coached since he wanted his free time (whatever free time he really had) to be his own. Also, he didn't want to live under a microscope by living in the same town or community where he taught and coached. He did not want to always have to be called back to school for every little emergency. Unfortunately, this did not always work because the head coach as well as the athletic director kept calling him back anyway—which made the 45 minute drive (each way) all the more difficult.

And to top it all off, his wife, Mary Miserable Crabapple, kept complaining about all the time David spent away from home. She resented his time spent coaching when he could be spending time with her. She kept indicating, whenever she became very frustrated and irritated, that if she knew what life with a coach was going to be like prior to their marriage that perhaps the marriage would never have taken place. Anyway, Mary Miserable kept pressuring David to do something so that she would be able to see him more than just a few hours each evening.

Coach Crabapple knew something must be done. He was becoming painfully aware that his teaching and his coaching were suffering, not to mention his family life. He was beginning to resent the fact that his coaching was interfering with his life at home (or was it the other way around?). On the other hand, he loved the coaching part of his life (especially game day). He didn't know what he would do if he did not have that respite from his teaching responsibilities. He knew that coaching was an essential element in his life. He also was resentful of his wife and her nagging and whining about the time his coaching took. In general, he was just a very unhappy person.

He thought about the stupid rules that the athletic director had established. Even his players, especially the star JV player, resented these regulations. "If only the athletic director would stay out of my way and not interfere with my JV program with his asinine rules, I would be a happy man. And, if the varsity coach would not hint that the JV team should play a specific style and use the varsity strategies, my JV program could be a lot more successful," thought coach Crabapple. In fact, he also resented the athletic director for everything that is wrong with the sports program in general and his team situation in particular.

He was even resentful toward the varsity head coach (Mr. Eversuccessful) of soccer. The head coach was always assigning menial tasks to him and always making him do the micky mouse type of grunt work. "What am I—a slave to Mr. Eversuccessful? He gets all the credit when the varsity team wins with the players I have trained as JV athletes," bemoaned the coach. Of course Coach Crabapple could only express this attitude to himself since he was unwilling to bring himself to communicate such feelings openly. And, it was eating his guts out.

"And, Mr. Knowitall, the high school principal, that pompous jerk. Where does he get off insisting that my lesson plans must be up-to-date *and* on file in his office? No one ever looks at those lesson plans—just a lot of busy-busy work. I wish Mr. Knowitall would just leave me alone so that I can get my teaching out of the way in time for what I really love to do—coach and win," reflected coach Crabapple, who entertains this thought to himself whenever he gets angry at the principal, which is frequent.

Basically, coach Crabapple was just an unhappy man and he really did not know why. But, he was not enjoying life as he had anticipated when he decided he wanted to coach and teach in high school. And, he wife was not the happiest woman in the town either—not by a long shot.

Over the next few months the athletic director became aware of coach Crabapple's problems. He told himself that he was determined to do something about the situation.

DISCUSSION ITEMS

1. What exactly are the problems here? Specify each difficulty or challenge.
2. For each of the problems, who is at fault (or who has responsibility)? Elaborate.
3. What did the JV coach evidently do wrong (or not do at all) which might have contributed to this situation developing at the school?
4. What did the JV coach evidently do wrong (or not do at all) which might have contributed to this situation developing at his home?
5. Is coach Crabapple correct in his feelings and reactions toward the athletic director? Explain in full your response and provide suggested courses of action that the coach should take to improve the situation in terms of the AD.
6. Is Mrs. Crabapple being unreasonable in her concerns and expectations? Elaborate.
7. What steps should coach Crabapple have taken to prevent this situation from developing to this point?
8. What might Mrs. Crabapple have done differently prior to this point in time?

9. What should Mrs. Crabapple attempt to do now?

10. Has the athletic director acted properly up to this point? Why or why not?

11. What is the role of the athletic director in terms of helping coaches become more comfortable in their athletic responsibilities? Be specific in providing strategies and tactics that athletic directors might implement.

12. Has the principal acted properly? Why or why not? Be specific in your explanation.

13. Has the varsity head coach acted properly? Why or why not? Provide a rationale.

14. What could coach Crabapple had done much earlier to help prevent this situation from developing?

15. What steps are open to coach Crabapple, at this point in time? Outline the options and strategies in detail as to how he should or might now proceed.

16. What should the athletic director have done in the past, especially when coach Crabapple was hired? What steps should the AD take at the present time?

17. What principles should govern the handling of this type of situation? What rules of thumb should govern any action that might be taken by each of the central characters in this scenario?

18. Comments . . .

RESPONSES FOR QUESTIONS FOR DISCUSSION

_____

_____

_____

_____

_____

_____

_____

_____

_____

Case #22

The Case of Handling the Disorganized Coach

The new boys' basketball coach, Murray Taylor, had just started preseason practice at the beginning of the previous week. However, already there were mumblings among the players and their parents after only about eight practice sessions.

It seems that the head coach simply comes to practice without any definitive plan as to what the athletes and the coaches are going to do that day. Coach Taylor certainly had never arrived at any of the previous eight practices with any notes or other evident plan(s) as to what should take place that day. Instead, it seems as if he is literally flying by the seat of his pants. He just gives the impression of deciding to do whatever pops into his head at any particular time. He will tell his assistant, Andy Newbody, to do one thing and then two minutes later will change his mind and have Andy (and some athletes) do something entirely different, for no apparent rhyme or reason.

Andy, an experienced assistant coach, had worked with and for the previous head coach for six years. The previous head coach, in contrast to his replacement, was extremely well organized and who always knew exactly what the coaches and the athletes would be doing during almost every moment of every practice. Andy was experiencing withdrawal pains in his new working relationship with his new head coach. He also was feeling left out of the planning and organizing of the practices since there wasn't any apparent advance planning and organizing going on. Coach Newbody did not know what to do. He felt that he couldn't really complain to anyone. And, he was hesitant to have a private talk with the head coach until he knew coach Taylor better. As a result, Andy kept his feelings to himself and he felt the worse for it.

However, the grumbling and complaining did not cease to exist among the athletes, and their parents. Soon the athletic director, Mr. William Taft, was on the receiving end of several pointed criticisms of coach Taylor's coaching, especially his lack of organization and structure.

In a private meeting between coach Taylor and William Taft the subject of the apparent disorganization of the basketball practices was discreetly brought up. Coach Taylor indicated that he did not feel the least bit uncomfortable in the way he was conducting his practices. "It will just take the players and Andy some time to get use to my style. I may look disorganized but that is just the way I coach. You know my record. I have not been as successful as I have been during the past decade by being incompetent. No, I know what I am doing. It just may look to the uninformed that I don't. I just like to be a free spirit and make decisions as I go along. After all, what really counts are the wins and loses. Just give me some slack and I will produce a winner here," added coach Taylor.

QUESTIONS FOR DISCUSSION

1. Is coach Taylor's position an appropriate one? Elaborate.
2. Is it important that coach Taylor be better organized? Why or why not?
3. It is important that he *appear* to be better organized? Why or why not?
4. What difference does it make if coach Taylor is organized or not?
5. Isn't the most important factor associated with this team whether or not it will be victorious on the court? Elaborate. Why try to fix what isn't broken?
6. Why are the athletes uncomfortable in the way the head coach is currently operating? Does it matter?
7. Why does the assistant coach feel so uncomfortable in his role as an assistant? To what extent does it matter?
8. Why are the parents so upset with coach Taylor's organizational skills or the lack thereof?
9. Does it matter what the parents feel about the coach's organizational skills? Explain.
10. How would you suggest the athletic director respond to coach Taylor's comments? Be specific and role-play your answer.
11. Is it appropriate for the athletic director to become involved in this situation? Why or why not?
12. How might the athletic director get (appropriately) involved in this situation with a head coach and the coach's coaching style *during the early weeks of practice*? Be specific?
13. What would be the advantages and the disadvantages of coach Taylor altering his organizational tactics during the practices, at this point in time?
14. What could coach Taylor do to create a *perception* of being organized? Provide specific examples of how the head coach might change his practices and strategies in practice to provide the image and create an impression of an organized and competent mentor.
15. What are some elements that make a practice session well organized? Be specific.
16. How might coach Taylor alter his working relationships with his assistant in this case?
17. What general principles are applicable in this scenario, specifically as they relate to a coach's organization, the perception of being organized, the working relationship between the head and the assistant coach; and, the possibility of the AD being held responsible for one's coaches?
18. Comments . . .

RESPONSES FOR QUESTIONS FOR DISCUSSION

_____

_____

CASE #23

The Case of the Coach's Inappropriate Appearance

Coach Dennis Bulge was a fairly successful coach during his 19 years at Casa Bella High. However, in recent years he has not been paying as close attention to his personal appearance as he did in his early years of teaching and coaching. In fact, during the past 5 years or so he has let himself go in terms of how he presents himself.

It wasn't just that his choice of clothes was not up to par. And, indeed, his choice of clothes could use a modern update. The fact that he wore the same clothes over and over again did not help at all. But, his severe weight problem also became a topic of great notice, especially to his students and to his fellow teachers and coaches. When he began his career at Casa Bella High he weighed 175 pounds and stood at 6' 2". Today, he tops the scale at 265 pounds—and the weight was not exactly evenly distributed. The *Junk Food Addict*, as coach Bulge was frequently referred to, even had a habit of eating junk food and downing numerous soft drinks (non-diet) during practice sessions, a fact that has not gone unnoticed by others.

The result has been that the students in the school, including his athletes, have been poking fun at him (behind his back) for the past 2-3 years. They made up very unkind names and critical jokes about coach Bulge regarding the coach's lack of fashion sense, his inability to change clothes during any given week and his immense physical size. Youngsters can be very cruel and in this situation they began to practice this attribute to the utmost. The end result has been that his effectiveness in the classroom where he taught social studies and mathematics has been compromised. And, in the opinion of some of the coaches and the athletic director, even Dennis Bulge's coaching effectiveness might have been compromised due to the overwhelming emphasis being placed by his athletes on how their coach looks and what he would wear.

Some of the athletes have complained to their parents and to others in the community that they felt embarrassed for themselves and for their coach because of the poor or unprofessional image that their coach presents wherever he goes. "He is not a very good representative of our team, our players and the school," complained one of the tri-captains to the athletic director, Michael Jacobs.

Even his colleagues, in his own school as well as at other schools, have quietly commented in a negative vein about how coach Bulge is letting himself go. Coach Bulge has also become a frequent topic of discussion in the faculty lounge where even his friends took part in the negative discussion and ridicule of the coach.

Finally, the athletic director decided that he would have a confidential conversation with coach Bulge about his appearance and eating habits. Mike Jacobs wanted to be very careful lest he unnecessarily hurt the coach's feelings and/or be accused of discrimination in his criticism of the coach's excess weight, eating and drinking at practices, and apparent lack of a professional image. But, nevertheless, for the benefit of the coach, the athletes, the sport program, the AD decided to approach the subject with coach Bulge.

QUESTIONS FOR DISCUSSION

1. Summarize the salient elements of this scenario?
2. Does the athletic director have a right or an obligation to approach coach Bulge about his apparent excess weight, about the coach's apparent inappropriate dress, about the coach's eating and drinking at practices? What is the responsibility of the athletic director in this situation? Explain your rationale.
3. Why should anyone be concerned with the coach's appearance or image? Is it important? Elaborate.
4. Is the fact that an individual is grossly overweight a matter that falls outside the purview of that person's competency as a teacher? As a coach? Explain.
5. What are some possible reasons that the coach has let himself go?
6. Do you anticipate that the coach is aware of the fact that he has let himself go? Is he aware of the behind the back criticism and ridicule taking place among the students, among the athletes, and among his peers? Elaborate.
7. Why would the student-athletes be so critical of their own coach (behind his back)? Why do you think kids are especially cruel, if you do?
8. Why would the coach's peers in his own school be willing to criticize him, behind his back, when they are in the faculty lounge? Why are peers so cruel?
9. What should the AD have done or said to the student-athlete who complained to him about coach Bulge? Be specific, assume a role-playing posture and indicate what you would say if you were the AD?
10. What exactly should the AD say to coach Bulge in the confidential meeting called by Mr. Jacobs for the purpose of discussing the coach's appearance (and behavior)? Be specific by assuming the role of the AD and indicating what you would say (role play) to the coach.
11. What would be the AD's response if coach Bulge indicated that his weight was his own problem and no one else's? What if the coach's response was that his weight was a medical matter and should not even be discussed as an aspect of his job performance?
12. How else might coach Bulge respond to the comments of the AD? Provide different scenarios spanning the entire spectrum of possible responses. What might be some of the AD's responses if the coach becomes defensive or angry?
13. Assuming that coach Bulge did elect to change, what suggestions do you have to aid him in changing his appearance, image and behavior? Be specific in your suggestions as to various strategies and tactics?
14. From whom might the coach seek assistance in this effort? Why?

15. What principles or guidelines might be applicable in this situation regarding a coach's behavior, appearance and image?

16. Comments . . .

RESPONSES FOR QUESTIONS FOR DISCUSSION

_____

_____

_____

_____

_____

_____

_____

_____

_____

_____

_____

_____

_____

_____

_____

Case #24

The Case of the Expectations of Coaches

The athletic director at the very large Southtown High School, Mr. Experience, recently hired Stacy Newbody (head tennis), Mike Newsome (assistant football), Virginia Phoob (head gymnastics), David Lee (head basketball) and George Toothsome (assistant wrestling), as coaches and teachers. During one of the early orientation meetings that Mr. Experience had with all new coaches, the athletic director was reviewing some of the expectations of all coaches in terms of their individual job responsibilities.

After the rather lengthy sharing of information by the athletic director with the five new coaches, Virginia Phoob asked what were the expectations in terms of winning and losing contests and being rehired by the school. In response, the athletic director said something to the effect of how important it is for all coaches to have teams that everyone can be proud of, both on and off the court or field. He emphasized the importance of having good student-athletes who the people in the community can look up to and be proud of, etc. He indicated how important it is for the community to be proud of the teams, the athletes and their achievements.

Soccer, a sport that everyone can play and enjoy.
[Courtesy of University of Delaware Sports Information Office]

He concluded by saying: "I am sure that with all of your areas of expertise and your willingness to work hard and to produce, that each of you will have no problem at all during your stint here."

Near the end of the school year the athletic director met individually with Stacy Newbody, Mike Newsome, Virginia Phoob, David Lee and George Toothsome to review the past year and their status for the future.

To Stacy Newbody (tennis is not and has never been and never will be of much interest at the school) and Virginia Phoob (the chief administrator's daughter had a super experience on her squad, the first time for this sport in the school), he indicated that he was pleased and asked whether or not they had any questions. Meeting concluded.

To Mike Newsome (whose football team went 8-1 and tied for the conference championship) he indicated the same as he had to Stacy and Virginia.

To David Lee and George Toothsome, however, the athletic director indicated, individually, that their teaching and coaching contracts would not be renewed. It seems that the basketball team suffered through a 2-19 season, which was the worse ever in the history of the program. Likewise, the wrestling program did not register a single win for the school and the head coach had therefore "resigned." Thus, the athletic director indicated to George that he did not measure up to expectations.

Later, the five coaches (Stacy, Virginia, Mike, David and George), who had developed somewhat of a close friendship during the year—all being new and whatever, got together and compared notes and . . .

QUESTIONS FOR DISCUSSION

1. What is wrong with this situation?
2. Why do you think the athletic director said what he did to:
   A. Stacy Newbody (head tennis)
   B. Mike Newsome (assistant football)
   C. Virginia Phoob (head gymnastics)
   D. David Lee (head basketball)
   E. George Toothsome (assistant wrestling)
3. Did the athletic director share sufficient pertinent information with the coaches in terms of expectations? Explain your response.
4. What were the specific expectations shared with the new coaches?
5. What do you suspect (and the coaches now suspect) the expectations to be NOW?
6. What could or should (if anything) the coaches have done differently at the start of the school year and/or later during the school year?
7. What could the two dismissed coaches do now? What recourse is open to them now?
8. Were the coaches dismissed (not rehired; non-renewed, etc.) on valid grounds? Why or why not?
9. What would be valid/invalid grounds for dismissal or non-renewal?
10. Did the athletic director act in good faith and in a professional fashion? Why or why not?
11. What would be different, if anything, if this had happened at the college level instead of the high school level?
12. What would be appropriate expectations for secondary coaches and teachers, in terms of their being renewed, continued in their positions?
13. What would be appropriate expectations for collegiate coaches at the NCAA divisions I, II and III in terms of their being renewed, continued in their positions?
14. What general principles are applicable in terms of criteria for evaluation of coaches (who also teach) at the secondary level?
15. Comments . . .

RESPONSES FOR QUESTIONS FOR DISCUSSION

CASE #25

The Case of the Negative Motivation by the Coach

The new head coach, Margaret Millstone, was excited about her new teaching and coaching position at her new high school. She had served as an assistant coach long enough, five years in an adjacent state. Now, she was in a position to be her own person, to be the head mentor, to be the one making the decisions and building a program just as successful, if not more so, than the program her former boss had built over his 30-year career.

The major problem that Margaret was experiencing in her first season had to do with how she treated her athletes. The previous coach at Margaret's new post was very laid back and hardly ever yelled at her athletes. The previous coach asked rather than tell, coaxed rather than demanded, cajoled rather than required, and spoke softly rather than yelled. However, the won/loss record of the previous coach was barely over .500 for a 10-year period.

That way of coaching, however, was not Margaret's style. And Margaret was bound and determined not to settle for such a mediocre record of half wins and half losses. She was the product of the so-called old school of coaching. She was a screamer. She was demanding, to the point of being extreme. She was a perfectionist. And she was going to make her athletes highly successful.

She was also a strict disciplinarian and expected her charges to be up in the air asking "how high, coach?" whenever she yelled, "jump!!!!!!" She expected, no demanded that her athletes do their best, always. She expected, insisted, that her athletes perform expertly in everything they did. And, she was not very intolerant of mistakes by her players.

In her efforts to motivate, correct and mold her athletes to do what she wanted them to do and to perform at the level that she knew they were capable of performing, she not infrequently utilized vulgarity. In fact, she was fond of attempting to shame any athlete who failed to live up to the expectation that the coach had of the athlete by spouting a series of four letter words.

The problem was that after 10 games the team's record was not very good. In fact, the team had only won three games. The result has been most traumatic on Margaret. And, consequently, the impact on the players had been nothing short of catastrophic.

Margaret was not only verbally abusive, with cutting remarks about individual athletes whenever a youngster made a mistake or failed to live up to the coach's expectations, but vulgar and foul language was creeping into almost every attempt at communication with the kids. To make matters worse, the coach also began to publicly humiliate players who failed to measure up. Of course, losing games or making mistakes were never the fault of the coach, but always someone else's—the previous coach, an athlete, an official, the athletic director or even the principal, etc.

Several of the girls complained to their parents. Some of the parents as well as some athletes met independently with Robert DeSota, the athletic director who had been in that post for a decade, to officially register complaints. The girls indicated that they felt humiliated by the new coach. They complained about verbal and physical abuse (being made to run laps until they almost dropped, for no apparent reason other than not playing well or because of a simple mistake). They also felt intimidated by the coach's cursing and foul language. "She is like lighting," said one of the athletes, "we never know when or where she will strike next but she is deadly, she is devastating. She never, but never, says anything nice to us. And, everything is always our fault, period. All she does is yell, criticize, threaten and punish. She makes us feel like we are walking on egg shells."

The athletic director called the coach into his office for a private meeting during which he broached her conduct (being careful not to let Margaret know that some athletes have complained about her). After asking about her conduct and its appropriateness, the coach said: "Well, you never hear anything negative from the athletes so I don't know why you are concerned. I am just a hard driving and aggressive motivator. The girls will do just fine. I know what I am doing. The girls respect me, I know that for a fact."

QUESTIONS FOR DISCUSSION

1. What is exactly wrong in this situation?
2. Why is the head coach acting like she is? Be specific.
3. Is there ever any excuse for foul or vulgar language from a coach in this type of school setting? Even for special effect? Why or why not?
4. Is there anything wrong about being a dictator as a coach? Anything wrong with being demanding as a coach? Why or why not?
5. Why might the girls be so upset with such an aggressive coach as Margaret? Elaborate.
6. Is the fact that the previous coach was so different from Margaret the source of the problem? Explain.
7. Are the athletes being realistic when they complain about being humiliated or intimidated by the coach? Don't all coaches yell at athletes and aren't all athletes put under pressure by their coaches? Explain the difference between appropriate pressure and inappropriate pressure by the coach?
8. What type of motivation is coach Millstone utilizing? Is this type appropriate at the secondary level? Why or why not? At the collegiate level? Why or why not?
9. What type of motivation is best suited for high school athletes? For college athletes? Provide specific examples of how high school coaches can successfully motivate individual athletes as well as entire teams. Do the same for the college level.
10. Did the athletic director act appropriately in bringing the coach in for a conversation? Why or why not?
11. What steps should the athletic director take to confirm that the accusations made by the parents and the athletes are accurate and correct? Elaborate.

12. What would you suggest that the athletic director say to the coach to broach the subject of her behavior and her motivational tactics? Be specific. Assume a role-playing position of the athletic director and communicate with the head coach.

13. Should the athletic director have told the coach that the athletes (and parents) had complained to him about her before their meeting started or soon thereafter? Why or Why not?

14. After the coach had started to defend herself and after she had indicated that the girls were not complaining, assume the role of the athletic director (role play) and indicate what you, as athletic director, would say to the coach.

15. In your opinion, what should Margaret do now to counteract the negative atmosphere she has established with the team and with the individual athletes? Be specific.

16. How can the athletic director help Margaret at this point in time? Outline an appropriate strategy.

17. How might this entire unfortunate situation have been avoided? What mighty the athletic director had done at an earlier point in time? Be specific.

18. What responsibility (blame) rests on the shoulders of the athletic director for this situation developing as it has? Why?

19. What principles are applicable in this scenario in terms of coaching behavior and in terms of the actions and duties of an athletic director?

20. Comments . . .

RESPONSES FOR QUESTIONS FOR DISCUSSION

Case #26

The Case of Dealing with an Overly Conservative Coach

The newly appointed head football coach, Al Buffet, of the Red Hawks of Eastside High School, had just finished his fifth game of the season and the team stood at a disappointing 2 and 3 record. Even the two wins were not very satisfactory, either to the coach or to others. These two victories were considered by many, and rightly so, more as gifts from heaven than earned victories.

Whenever a team, especially a team of a flagship or top tier sport, does not win as many games as others think the team should, the first person to feel the blunt of the criticism is the head coach. And, the second person to feel the blunt of the negative comments and criticism is the athletic director.

In this case, a lot of this criticism had to do with how Al Buffet coaches. It seems that Al believes in the so-called Woody Hayes brand of football, that is three yards and a cloud of dust. In short, Al Buffet had the philosophy that if his team was going to end up on the short end of the score, his players were not going to beat themselves. And, his players were never going to be embarrassed.

Thus, to say that his game strategy was conservative would be a severe understatement. His team rarely passed. He never went 3rd and long. He always kept the score down believing that his squad would never be embarrassed even if they lost as long as the score was close. And, he was also firmly convinced that his players would never really be out of many games because as long as he could keep the score close, his players would always be within striking distance of an opponent.

Some called him conservative. Some referred to him as ultraconservative. His loudest critics called him gutless. And still others pointed out that: "We would really not be complaining if we were 5-0 at this point in the season. Do we really care about the process or are we really concerned only with the result. And in this case, the result is an embarrassing 2-3 record with even the two wins being questionable."

The athletic director, Billy Bob, met with coach Buffet on Monday morning. The athletic director shared that there was a combined community and booster club meeting next Sunday night to address the situation of the pending football disaster. He pointed out the school was located in a small community where football is king and where the pride of the town rests to some degree on how successful the athletic program is, especially the football team.

During this meeting the two men started to examine all of the facts pertinent to the current football controversy. They agreed that they had two objectives. First, to see what, if anything, might be done to help salvage the season in terms of wins and losses. And, second, what could be done to appease or otherwise address the concerns of some the people in the community, especially the more important and influential booster club members.

QUESTIONS FOR DISCUSSION

1. What are the real problems in this scenario?
2. Why is the team not winning? Justify your position.
3. Why would anyone in the community be unhappy *with how* a team or individual athlete wins? Is this reasonable? Does this attitude exist in a significant number of communities and among a significant number of fans? After all, isn't a win a win? Explain your position, as an athletic director, in detail.
4. Who, if anyone, is at fault here? Elaborate.
5. Is the head coach using an appropriate coaching philosophy? Why or why not? If not, what would be an appropriate philosophy? Why?
6. What would your philosophy be as athletic director regarding how the coach is coaching this football team and the matter of winning versus losing?
7. Is the head coach using appropriate coaching tactics or strategy in terms of being conservative? Explain in detail.
8. Is it really true that people in this community are unhappy with the coach's conservative strategy *only* because the team is 2-3 and if the team had a 5-0 record there would be no significant or major complaints at all? Does this make sense? Elaborate.
9. Regardless of one's coaching philosophy, what suggestions would you, as athletic director, provide for this coach in terms of dealing with members of the community, especially the booster club (and its influential members)?
10. Are the people in this small community being fair in how they view the football team and the head coach? Is their criticism appropriate and justified? Why or why not?
11. Is the athletic director acting appropriately in meeting with the head coach and sharing the information that he did? Why or why not? What would you share with the coach in this meeting?
12. What is the role of the athletic director in this type of situation?
13. Should coaches have to pay attention to what people in the community, even booster club members, think about the team and the coaching staff? Elaborate.
14. Is winning really important in today's high schools? Is winning really important in schools located in small, medium or large cities? Elaborate.
15. What makes some schools and communities different from others in terms of how they feel about the won/loss record of the athletic teams in their high schools? Can athletic directors, with the power and influence that they possess, play a major role in affecting how fans, supporters, boosters and others in the community view coaches, winning and the whole sports scene? How? Be specific.
16. What general principles are applicable with this type of situation?
17. Comments . . .

RESPONSES FOR QUESTIONS FOR DISCUSSION

Case #27

The Case of the Coach Who Couldn't Follow Directions

Dennis Blatz was always an individual with a mind of his own. Ever since he was a youngster he had to do things his way. It was ironic that as a coach he would never allow his own team members to do things that he had done as a youngster and as an athlete. To the contrary. His athletes had to do things his way or else there was always the highway—he just didn't stand for athletes *or* subordinates to disagree with him (in private or in public). His assistant coach of 3 years, Chelsie Ashley, could attest to that. Quite early in their professional relationship he set her straight in terms of who was the head coach and who was the assistant coach.

Thus, it was amazing to Frank Cohn, the athletic director, that coach Blatz was rather stubborn and headstrong when he, Dennis Blatz, was in the role of a subordinate to others. Specifically, Mr. Cohn found it ironic indeed that coach Blatz would insist that his players and assistant coaches adhere to the so-called party line but, that as head coach, found it extremely uncomfortable (some would say impossible) for him to assume a similar role. In fact, coach Blatz has, in recent years, increasingly become almost insubordinate upon occasion when it came to following the directives of the athletic director.

It seemed that coach Blatz believed that following the policies, procedures and practices of higher authority only applied when he, Dennis Blatz, was the higher authority. It wasn't that Dennis was outright disobedient—not directly to the face of the AD anyway.

No, instead Dennis was rather sneaky in that he believed in the philosophy that forgiveness was easier to obtain than permission. Hence, he frequently forgot to do things he was supposed to do. At other times he just neglected to follow through. And, in still other instances, the coach just never heard or never became aware of directives or of expectations. In short, the coach was his own person even within the hierarchy of the athletic department. Perhaps two of the reasons he could get away with this type of behavior was that he had extremely successful teams and the athletic director was nearing retirement and didn't want to make any waves at this point in the twilight of his career.

However, things changed a few years later when a new athletic director, Toni Waickman arrived on the scene. She had had 5 years experience as an athletic administrator in an adjacent state and wasn't about to put up with such foolishness by coach Blatz. But before she did anything with the coach she met with the principal and brought him up-to-date on the historical behavior (misbehavior) of coach Blatz.

QUESTIONS FOR DISCUSSION

1. What is the essential substance of this scenario?
2. Why is the coach so determined to have things his way as head coach (insofar as his athletes and his assistant coaches)?
3. Explain (from an athletic director's viewpoint) the coach's behavior and attitude in terms of the concept of "forgiveness was easier to obtain than permission" and cite examples.
4. Is the coach acting within proper parameters in his dealings with his team, his players and his assistants from the perspective of an athletic director? Why or why not?
5. If the coach felt so strongly about his athletes and his assistants following his orders, why did he not adhere to the same thinking for himself when it came to his relationship with his superior, the athletic Director? Elaborate. What factors might have contributed to the coach's behavior?
6. Would this situation have been any different if the coach was a woman? Why or why not?
7. Why didn't Frank Cohn, the experienced athletic director, do something about the coach during all of these years? Be specific.
8. What might Frank Cohn have done with this obstinate coach in earlier years? Elaborate and provide the possible (positive and/or negative) consequences of each course of action.
9. With the arrival of the new athletic director, what might the head coach had anticipated? Why?
10. What should the head coach have done when the new athletic director arrived on the scene? Why? Stipulate several different scenarios and possible consequences.
11. Could Toni Waickman, as athletic director, accept the continuation of the behavior of this coach? Why or why not?
12. Does the fact that Toni is a woman plays a role in this situation? Explain.
13. What were the reasons that Toni Waickman went to visit the principal? What do you think she said to the principal? Why? What did she want from the principal? What were her options in terms of coach Blatz?
14. What do you anticipate that Ms. Waickman, as athletic director, might now say to the coach? Assume the role of the AD and share your comments with the coach in a role-playing situation.
15. What are the options of the coach now that the new AD has arrived and sought changes in his behavior? Cite various options open to the coach and the possible consequences (positive or negative) emanating from each course of action.
16. What general principles are pertinent to this case?
17. Comments . . .

RESPONSES FOR QUESTIONS FOR DISCUSSION

_____

_____

_____

_____

_____

_____

_____

_____

_____

_____

_____

_____

_____

_____

_____

_____

_____

_____

_____

CASE #28

The Case of the Inconsiderate and Unthinking Coach

The high school gymnastics coach, Jennifer Mueller, was in a fit. She had the first big gymnastics meet tomorrow, Saturday. She was suppose to get the tape for the mats out of her team's storage room so the custodian could tape the mats together for the big meet. However, to her horror, she just realized that she had failed to include any special tape among the recommended/needed items she had given to the AD so that he could have ordered the supplies last spring. She double-checked her storage area in the fervent hope that she might have some extra rolls, but alas, no. She then rushed to the main athletic equipment room only to find that there were no extra roles of tape there either. She was really in a fix. She had a big problem. But it wasn't her fault, not really, she thought.

"It was the fault of that stupid athletic director. Why, if he would have just ordered the equipment himself and had not burdened the coachers with all of this terrible paper work we would not be in this pickle now," thought he coach. Oh, how she wished that the athletic director didn't require each coach to request each and every item of supplies that might be needed for that particular sport. All she wanted to do was coach, period. Why were coaches given this extra responsibility? That was the job of the AD, wasn't it? She turned around, thinking of whom she might be able to lay the blame for this fiasco. What to do? The meet was tomorrow?

While she was storming around the hallway, the wrestling coach, David Stammer, overheard her complaining to her athletes about how stupid the athletic director was, how terrible the school was and how tough life was overall. "Coach Mueller, I can let you have some tape. My kids and I have just finished taping all of our three mats together for our wrestling tournament Sunday. I will have them take/tear the tape up and we can move the tape to your mats in the gymnastics room. In the meantime, I will go to one of my coaching buddies at East High School and borrow some tape from him tonight and then my guys and I will retape our mats tomorrow in time for our Sunday meet."

"O.K. Give me the tape," snorted coach Mueller.

When the weekend came, both the gymnastics competition and wrestling meet went well. However, coach Jennifer Mueller was still upset that she was put in this position and was going to really give it to the AD when she had cooled down. "It is just ridiculous that I be put upon like this by this stupid policy. What a waste of my valuable time having to worry about this and having to get the tape this way. Why, how demeaning. It is no wonder that my girls lost the competition, it is all the AD's fault," fumed the gymnastics coach.

Weeks went by and coach Mueller never once said thanks to the wrestling coach or to the wrestlers who had come to the rescue of the gymnastics coach and team.

To the contrary, Jennifer was too busy complaining to her athletes, their parents and anyone else who would listen about the stupid policy (imposed from above by the athletic director) that makes the coaches responsible for ordering and storing such items as tapes for their mats. "Why, I, the coach, actually had to supervise the wrestlers and the janitors while they taped the mats together. Hey, I was hired to coach gymnastics, not a janitor or a supervisor of janitors. Why can't the AD just let me coach and take care of all of this Mickey Mouse stuff himself," moaned Jennifer, to anyone and everyone (in and outside of school) who would listen.

About a month after that fateful weekend the wrestling coach was talking with the AD and brought up the subject of that weekend's mix-up. "Coach, I wanted to compliment you on your thoughtfulness and willingness to help Jennifer get out of that mess she made for herself," added the AD. In response, the wrestling coach replied: "Well, you know, you are the only person to even say anything positive to me about my efforts to help her and her team. Jennifer has never even said 'boo' to me much less 'thanks'—I think she was and is still upset that she has to have duties or responsibilities other than just coaching her athletes. We should all be so lucky, right?"

The athletic director replied by indicating that . . .

QUESTIONS FOR DISCUSSION

1. What are the key elements in this case?
2. How would you describe the gymnastics coach's behavior? Elaborate in detail.
3. How would you describe the wrestling coach's behavior? Why?
4. Does the gymnastics coach have a point about being asked to be responsible for such unreasonable duties and responsibilities? Why or why not? What are normal duties and expectations of a coach at the high school level other than actual coaching on the field, court or in the pool
5. Do many high schools require coaches to have other responsibilities besides merely coaching youngsters, such as submitting orders for equipment and supplies to the AD? What about being responsible for storing such items in their team's equipment room(s)? Describe what these other duties might include, if any, and provide a justification.
6. Why did the wrestling coach even bother to help the gymnastics coach? Be specific. Might it have been out of the goodness of his heart? Might it have been for a selfish reason? If so, what selfish reason? Might it have been for a combination of reasons? Elaborate.
7. Will the wrestling coach be so quick to help Jennifer the next time? Speculate and provide a reason for any future action on his part.
8. Will any other coach be anxious to help Jennifer out the next time she needs assistance? Why or why not?
9. In high schools, small or not, is the rumor mill pretty effective in sharing what happens within the school, whether it deals with faculty, coaches or with students? If this is true, what implications does this have for coaches in the performance of their duties and in their relationships with others, in and outside of school? Elaborate.

10. Is Jennifer thinking of her public relations with others? Is she concerned with how she is being mistreated? Is she concerned with what other people think about her? Is she wise in her thinking and actions? What is first and foremost in her mind? Elaborate.

11. Why is the gymnastics coach blaming the AD? Is the way she is going about expressing her viewpoints politically wise, expedient and/or professional?

12. Why did Jennifer not say "thank you" *immediately* to the wrestling coach and his athletes who had helped with the taping? Why didn't Jennifer *ever* say "thanks" to the coach and the players?

13. What unethical actions did Jennifer engage in regarding this whole case, if any? Elaborate.

14. What would have happened if the wrestling coach did not help Jennifer?

15. What would the athletic director share now with the wrestling coach following the revelation from the coach that the gymnastics coach never thanked anyone?

16. What are the general principles that are appropriate in this specific case?

17. What should the athletic director have done with the gymnastics coach much earlier? What should the AD now do with the gymnastics coach at this point or time? Why?

18. Comments . . .

RESPONSES FOR QUESTIONS FOR DISCUSSION

_____

_____

_____

_____

_____

_____

_____

_____

_____

_____

_____

CASE #29

The Case of the Altered Purchase Order

Mr. Larry Grightwell had served as athletic director at the small NCAA division III university for almost thirty years. Following the end of the current school year, May 31st to be exact, he will officially retire and his replacement will be a relatively young gentleman, Doug Bunisher, who will assume his new duties on June 1st.

On January 15th of Mr. Grightwell's last year as AD, all of the coaches had to submit their customary budget request for the subsequent year's equipment and supplies. Mr. Steve Floshmour, the long time head football coach, submitted an equipment and supply budget request of some $45,500—which was approved (after a careful scrutiny and evaluation) by the outgoing athletic director.

Athletic conditioning and training often requires year-round commitment for the elite athlete. [Courtesy of Oklahoma State University Athletics]

When the new athletic director arrived on campus it did not take him long to review and assess existing policies, practices and procedures. One of the few changes he wanted to implement almost immediately had to do with how ordered equipment and supply items were to be shipped to the school. Under the previous administration all items ordered on behalf of individual sports, from the various sporting goods stores and other vendors, went directly to the head coaches of the various sports. Changing this procedure, Mr. Floshmour directed that, effective June 10th, i.e., almost immediately, all equipment and supplies would be received in one central location. The athletic director also gave the responsibility for checking the items shipped from the vendors against the purchase orders to one of the assistant athletic directors.

On August 1st, the football items that were ordered much earlier (back around March 1st) arrived on campus. The very next day the assistant AD in charge of the equipment room and the previously ordered equipment/supplies came to the athletic director and said: "Doug, we have a problem. We have been *shorted* on the equipment and supplies and have received some items never ordered. In fact, we are missing 10 helmets, 6 pairs of jerseys and 6 pairs of pants as well as 8 pairs of shoes. Instead, we received items that we never ordered. For example, we have 7 wind breakers, 7 coaching shirts, 7 coaching pants, 8 pairs of coaching shoes, 16 pairs of socks, plus 14 baseball/coaching hats."

When the athletic director approached the head football coach inquiring about the discrepancy, the coach replied that: "Oh, those items that were on the original purchase order were changed. I needed some coaching items for my staff and the old athletic director never allowed us to include them on the school's official purchase order (PO). So, I have always called my good buddy George Fastmann, who is the salesman at Brooks Sporting Goods, and told him to substitute the items I needed (but the school wouldn't purchase) for some of the items that I really did not need."

Coach Steve Floshmour was completely unrepentant that he had been caught substituting unordered items for officially approved items to be bought via the official purchase order (PO). In fact, he was rather indignant that he was even being approached in this manner by the new AD.

"Since you have arrived here you have preached how important it is that all of us coaches be professional in appearance. Well, now we have our new coaching uniforms and can be dressed head to toe in professional attire. That is what you wanted, isn't it? The old AD, that old stuffed shirt, just never would approve the school paying for the coaching uniforms for the football staff," concluded the annoyed football coach." Besides," he added, "you just told us at the last staff meeting that you would approve the purchase of appropriate coaching uniforms for all of the coaching staff."

The athletic director responded by . . .

QUESTIONS FOR DISCUSSION

1. What are the problems in this situation? Be specific.
2. Did the previous athletic director make the proper decisions regarding purchasing priorities, especially his refusal to purchase the coaches' apparel items? Explain.
3. Did the new athletic director make the proper decision regarding the *change* in the procedure dealing with the receipt of purchased items? Was the process of making and implementing the change appropriate? Explain your answers in full.
4. What were the possible reasons behind the change in terms of where the ordered items were to be received from the vendors? Explain the rationale. Were the reasons valid and appropriate?
5. Shouldn't the coaching staff have appropriate attire to coach in? Does this warrant the football coach's actions? If you were the athletic director, would you have the department budget now pay for these items or would you require the coaches to pay for their own items that had been ordered in this manner? Provide a rationale to support your position.
6. Do you agree, and if so, why, with the new athletic director's belief that the school should pay for the coaching attire for each coach at the school?
7. Under what conditions and using what process, if any, could or should the head football coach be able to alter items ordered on an original purchase order? Be specific in your comments.

8. What should the athletic director say in response to the football coach's comments above? Describe in detail in your own words, by assuming a role-playing position, and share your comments to the football coach.

9. What should the head football coach have done (or said) when he first became aware of the new athletic director's change in policy regarding the receiving of ordered/purchased items? Role-play a response by the head coach.

10. Is what the football coach did in terms of altering the purchase order the equivalent of a death-dealing blow to his career? Discuss.

11. What do you think might become of the professional relationship between the head football coach and the athletic director? Between the athletic director and the other football coaches?

Figure 7.1. Cheating—a death dealing blow to one's career.

12. How could or should the athletic director and/or the coach act towards each other so that a healthy and positive relationship might be the result?

13. Should the athletic director involve his immediate boss or other members of higher administration? Why or why not?

14. After the meeting with the head football coach, what steps should the athletic director take in response to the:
    A. Head football coach
    B. The other football coaches
    C. Higher administrators (especially the athletic director's boss)
    D. Sporting goods vendors
    E. Others

15. What punishment, if any, should the athletic director administer to the head football coach? To the assistant football coaches?

16. What principles are applicable in this situation regarding the purchase of the equipment and supplies?

17. Comments . . .

RESPONSES FOR QUESTIONS FOR DISCUSSION

_____

_____

_____

_____

Case #30

The Case of the Person Who Quits Coaching But Remains as a Teacher

What a mess, a true mess. What had gone wrong? After all, coach Jessie Robins sure looked like a great hire three years ago. When she arrived for the job interview she presented herself as the ideal college graduate, all ready and willing to begin a long and successful teaching career in history—and also certified to coach volleyball and softball. In fact, it was that combination (teaching and coaching) that finally landed her the job over some more experienced and qualified teachers who were not inclined to coach. One of the other candidates, Mary Youngston, had actually been a better candidate as a teacher but indicated less than an energetic attitude about coaching. In fact, she had indicated that she would coach if she had to but would not really want to. And she would not give any guarantee as to how long she might coach (especially after she earned tenure in three years).

Well, as it has happened, Jessie did just what the search committee (including the AD) was afraid that Mary would have done had she been hired. Jessie had just handed in her resignation from coaching, but not from teaching, the week after she got the letter from the school superintendent notifying her that she had been granted a continuing contract, i.e., tenure (tenure = lifetime contract in teaching).

"What had really gone wrong in that job interview? Did Jessie really lead us all down the primrose path, did she really pull the wool over all of our eyes?" the athletic director, Timmy Morrison, asked himself. "Where there any signs in that interview or in her application or in her past that might have alerted us to this disastrous resignation?" wondered Timmy. "Or, did she just deliberately mislead us all and lie to us. Did she know all along that she would give up coaching once she had the lifetime teaching contract (tenure)? And, how can I prevent this from ever happening again?" concluded the athletic director to himself.

The next day the superintendent called Timmy and asked him to bring him up-to-date on the disaster of yesterday in terms of the coaching resignation. He began the phone conversation by saying: "You know, Timmy, you made your own bed this time and you have to sleep in it. You now have no head coach for two important teams and I don't foresee any teaching vacancies that we are going to be advertising this year. This means that you are going to have to fill these posts with either teachers who are already on staff – and good luck on that effort – or you are going to end up with a rent-a-coach as a head coach in both volleyball and softball. What a mess you have gotten us into Timmy. Couldn't you and the search committee done a little better job when hiring the coach/teacher in the first place? Why, I just dread the phone calls from parents on this one that I know I am going to be getting. Darn you Timmy . . ."

QUESTIONS FOR DISCUSSION

1. Outline the relevant components in this particular situation.
2. In your opinion, why did Jessie indicate a firm commitment to both coaching and teaching? Was this honest, ethical?
3. Is it inappropriate or sneaky or dishonest or unethical for a coach to indicate that one wants to coach for a long time when, in reality, the individual intends to coach only until tenure or a continuing contract is earned, and then coaching goes by the wayside?
4. Why is the athletic director so upset with the resignation? Be specific.
5. Why is the superintendent breathing down so hard on the AD's neck?
6. What is wrong with having so-called rent-a-coaches involved in coaching, either as a head coach or as an assistant? Provide a complete response.
7. What might a search committee do before, during and after an interview with a prospective teacher/coach candidate to determine the candidate's real commitment and intentions insofar as coaching is concerned? Outline such a strategy associated with securing a person on one's staff who is willing to coach for a long period of time in addition to teaching.
8. What might a search committee and/or an athletic director *say* or *ask* the candidate that might help discern those who really want to coach for a relatively long period of time? What might be said or asked of the candidate to differentiate the "short timer" coach and the "long term" coach?
9. Is there anything that could be done or pursued to help the athletic department retain people (the AD wishes to retain) who coach, i.e., to prevent individuals from resigning from coaching while remaining as a full time teacher? Explain in detail.
10. Is it fair to the candidate(s) to press for a commitment or inclination to coaching for a long period of time (as long as the school wants the coach)? Explain your rationale.
11. What does the athletic director now say to the superintendent in response to the latter's phone conversation? Assume a role playing posture and respond in kind.
12. What negative consequences might now face the athletic director in terms of: (1) the athletes, (2) parents, (3) principal, (4) superintendent, (5) school board, and (6) others?
13. What specific concepts or principles might be applicable in this situation in which an athletic director seeks to fill an important coaching spot with an individual who would also teach in addition to coach?
14. Comments . . .

RESPONSES FOR QUESTIONS FOR DISCUSSION

Problems with Other Individuals

CHAPTER OBJECTIVES

After reading this chapter you will be able to:

Crowd control is essential for a successful athletic event at all levels
[Courtesy of University of Southern California Sports Information]

- Be familiar with various problems relating to other individuals
- Avoid making major decisions too quickly, especially when new to the job
- Deal with other administrators who might not be professional in their actions and dealings with people
- Respond to an influential *center of influence* who attempts to inappropriately influence athletic decisions, especially personnel decisions
- Cite the dangers of managing via the crisis mode
- Evaluate fairly the performance of coaches and not succumb to outside pressures to interfere with the personnel process
- Appreciate the role and importance of maintenance personnel in the overall operation of an athletic program
- Realize the potential changes and dangers that might crop up when a new boss arrives on the scene
- Explain why it is advisable for an athletic administrator to remember people's names, especially those close to the athletic program
- Enumerate ways *centers of influence* can appropriately help the athletic director in terms of fundraising and the general operation of the program
- Be familiar with potential problems in dealing with the news media
- Outline some things that an athletic director can do to help make oneself indispensable to the school and sports program
- Offer suggestions for the athletic director who has an unreasonable boss or superior

- Characterize a properly designed and constructed athletic newsletter and indicate some major problems that should be avoided
- Define the term *delegation* and outline different ways to delegate to a subordinate

CASE STUDY

31. The case of the and making important decisions too quickly
32. The case of the impolite non-athletic administrator
33. The case of the would-be head coach
34. The case of crisis management
35. The case of the athletic director faced with the tough decision
36. The case of the broken-down coach
37. The case of the problem between the coach and the custodian
38. The case of impressing the new boss
39. The case of the forgetful athletic director
40. The case of the lack of influential fundraising contacts
41. The case of the problem with the media
42. The case of the indispensable athletic director
43. The case of the athletic director with the difficult superior/boss
44. The case of the sloppily made newsletter
45. The case of the improper delegation

CASE #31

The Case of the Athletic Director
Making Important Decisions Too Quickly

Will Siegnfield, the new athletic director at the largest high school in the state, Boatman South High School, had been at his new school for less than three weeks. In that time he was put into the inevitable position of having to make not a few major decisions, decisions that had the potential for significant consequences, if the wrong decisions were made.

Jerry Fireman and Terry Mansfield, his two part-time, assistant athletic administrators, were only too happy to help their new boss. Both Jerry and Terry were not hesitant or reluctant to share their opinions on what should be done. In fact, they were eager to advise their new boss as to what to do. And Will, being new and unfamiliar with the school, its history, the so-called political scene as well as the people associated with the program, was only too happy to rely upon his assistants for advice and counsel.

It came time for Will to submit the athletic department's new global team rules to the principal (for submission to the school board). Will relied on Jerry and Terry to draw up the regulations along with how transgressions would be handled. Looking at the two page sheets of rules and punishments Will said: "Do you two really think these rules are appropriate here, for all of the teams? And, regarding the punishments for each of the rules broken, are you sure that these consequences are appropriate here?"

"Oh yes," echoed Terry and Jerry in unison. And the document was mailed, without further discussion or review, to the principal via inner office mail.

Two days later another situation developed in which Will had to make a decision. Again Jerry and Terry were *Johnnies on the Spot* in terms of being willing and able to give the new athletic director advice and input. Again, Will accepted the recommendation(s) of his two part-time assistants. This time the situation that developed had to do with the booster club's inquiry as to whether Will knew of any special needs that the football coaches had in terms of equipment and supplies. It seems that the booster club might be able to help out by purchasing same. With advice from his seemingly experienced and capable assistants, Will was provided a list with some twenty items on it totaling over $10,000 for the football squad, which he relayed to the club's president.

"Are you guys sure that this is the acceptable procedure to follow in respect to the booster club and the purchase of equipment?" asked Will. And the reply by Terry and Jerry, in unison, was: "Of course, these items are needed and this seems to be a great way to get the items."

About five days later the principal, Jim Welch, called the new athletic director to his office for a private meeting. "Will," said the principal, "I know that you are new to this school and new to how we do things here, but I am astounded that two of the biggest decisions that you made since your arrival were such poor decisions. I don't think I have ever seen a new athletic director come into a school and alienate more people than you did in just three weeks."

"What do you mean, Jim?" replied Will, nervously fidgeting in his chair.

"Well, for starters, the rules and the attached punishments are rather harsh, don't you think? Those rules sound more like Jerry's and Terry's wacko philosophies than yours. I just didn't get the impression during your job interview that you, with all of your experience, were going to be so dictatorial and extreme with the athletes. If that is not enough, lets talk about you and the booster club. What do you mean by going behind my back requesting monies for just football from that group. The booster club doesn't get to decide how much money goes to what sports. Why naturally, the club wants to give the bulk of the money to their favorite sport, football. But, what about the other sports? I don't like end runs around here, period. That is not being loyal, period."

QUESTIONS FOR DISCUSSION

1. Summarize the fundamental issues in this scenario?
2. Are there dangers in an administrator being required to make decisions before the person is ready to make wise and appropriate decisions? Explain in detail and provide examples.
3. Why were Terry and Jerry so willing to be helpful? Elaborate?
4. Did these two part-time assistants have a secret agenda? Did they deliberately attempt to make their boss look bad? Explain.
5. Why was Will so willing to accept Terry's and Jerry's advice and suggestions?
6. Who really made the decisions put forth by Will to the principal, in reality?
7. What should athletic directors do in terms of seeking and/or accepting suggestions and input from subordinates? Provide concrete suggestions.
8. What should Will Siegnfield have done in terms of the decision dealing with team rules? Why? Be specific.
9. Why did the booster club people ask Will if there were any needed items that the club could purchase for the team? Speculate.
10. What should Mr. Siegnfield have done in terms of the booster club decision? Why? Be specific.
11. Why is the principal so angry? Explain in detail. Is the principal justified in being upset with the athletic director? Why or why not?
12. Should the athletic director be upset with his assistants? Why or why not?
13. What should Will have done, when Terry and Jerry offered advice and suggestions, which might have prevented these problems from developing and still not hurt the two assistants' feelings? Elaborate.
14. How could this whole unfortunate situation been avoided, if indeed it could have been? Be specific.

15. What general principles are applicable in this situation where the athletic director is new to the job and is faced with the situation in which important decisions must be made, made before the AD has had time to become acclimated to the position and the politics of the job?

16. Comments . . .

RESPONSES FOR QUESTIONS FOR DISCUSSION

Case #32

The Case of the Impolite Non-athletic Administrator

The director of the food service operation at the college called the athletic director on a Thursday and informed him there was a big problem. It seems that the assistant athletic director had had the fall sport coaches send a letter to all of the incoming athletes (prior to the pre-season tryouts and conditioning sessions) indicating that the athlete could charge their meals at the cafeteria while receiving a summary bill at their homes sometime thereafter.

Mr. Heartless, the administrator in charge of food service at the college, indicated that this would not be the case. In fact, after the athletes were in camp for a day, he told the athletic director that the athletes were already being turned away from the cafeteria lines because some of them had not brought any money with them from home (expecting to eat on campus now and being billed later).

Jeani Goodperson, the athletic director, immediately obtained a three-way telephone hookup between herself, the assistant athletic director and Mr. Heartless. The assistant athletic director, Jerry Spoon, confirmed that he indeed had informed the coaches to include that information in the letters sent to all of the fall teams because that is what he had been told by a staff member in Mr. Heartless' own office. Mr. Heartless, almost losing his cool, said that that was certainly not correct.

The assistant athletic director obtained, from his records, a summary of the conversation he had had with a Mr. Accurate, a staff person in Mr. Heartless' office, and read aloud the summary statement—which confirmed that Mr. Accurate did indeed tell the assistant athletic director that it would be all right to charge the meals for later payment. At that point, Mr. Heartless did lose his cool. He (in a semi-polite manner, but nevertheless pointed fashion) indicated that the assistant athletic director was most certainly either a liar or very, very confused because Mr. Heartless knew Mr. Accurate would never reveal such idiotic information, having worked in the food service office for a number of years.

Further, Mr. Heartless informed the athletic director that whether or not his staff member made a mistake was of no significance. What did matter is that he (Mr. Heartless) was not going to provide credit to the athletes, period. "It is just bad luck for the student-athletes. It is something you, as athletic director, will have to solve. Don't count on me to do your job and solve your problems for you," screamed Mr. Heartless.

The athletic director told the food service director that it might not be a real good political or public relations situation if parents started calling the President or other central administrators asking why their youngsters were being denied food (credit) when they had received written information to the contrary. In reply, Mr. Heartless said: "My job is to run the food service and to make a profit. The welfare of your pampered athletes does not concern me in the least. It is just not my concern, not my business. I am in the food service business. Jeani, this is your problem. That is why you people in athletics get the big bucks."

QUESTIONS FOR DISCUSSION

1. What are the facts of the case? Briefly summarize the situation.
2. Who is responsible for the initial problem or mix up? Be Specific.
3. What could the athletic administrators and/or coaches have done to prevent this situation from developing into the fiasco it has become?
4. What could Mr. Heartless have done to prevent this problem?
5. Why do you think the assistant athletic director had kept a written summary of his conversation with Mr. Accurate? Implications? Did it work? with whom?
6. Why did Mr. Heartless act as he did? Speculate.
7. What should be done to prevent this type of situation from reoccurring in the future?
8. What negative consequences might result from this situation, if any?
9. What positive consequences might result from this situation, if any?
10. What should the athletic director do now? What about the assistant athletic director? What are the consequences of these options? Justify your stance.
11. Who is to *blame* in this situation? Provide a rationale for your position?
12. Does it make any difference who is to blame, at this point in time?
13. What would happen if the President became aware of this situation from upset parents?
14. Should either the athletic director or the food service director contact their superiors? Why or why not?
15. What general principles might be appropriate in this case study?
16. Comments . . .

RESPONSES FOR QUESTIONS FOR DISCUSSION

_____

_____

_____

_____

_____

_____

CASE #33

The Case of the Would-Be Head Coach

Mary Inbetween, the assistant women's soccer coach at Farfield high school, was approached by one of the school board members, Mr. BIG, one afternoon after practice. He asked her if she had ever thought about becoming a head coach of soccer.

Mary Inbetween had graduated from State University only five (5) years earlier and had been a star athlete in both soccer and softball (fast pitch). Upon earning her B.A. degree she took the job that she presently held—assistant soccer coach and assistant softball coach as well as teacher of physical education in the junior and senior high school.

She explained to Mr. BIG that, yes, she had always desired to be a head coach in both soccer and softball. She also inquired: "Why do you ask?"

Mr. BIG then explained that he was only curious and had wondered if she had any aspirations regarding the head coaching position at Farfield high school. "You never know when opportunity might come knocking, do you?" he added.

Nothing else was said for two weeks. Then one evening, as Mary was arriving home, she received a call on her cell phone from the principal, Mr. Johnny Butler, asking if she would mind coming in early the next morning, before school, to discuss some matters. When the coach inquired as to the purpose of the meeting she was told it had to do with the head soccer position.

The next morning she met with the principle and Mr. BIG, both of whom asked all kinds of leading questions about the current women's head coach (Mr. Oldtimer). Many of the questions were phrased in such a way as to lead to a negative response. For example: "Now, Miss Inbetween, what would you say are the reasons for the poor showing of the players, is it because the coach is out of touch, or is it because he doesn't care anymore?" asked Mr. BIG.

She was further asked if the athletes liked the head coach, if the head coach had ever sworn in front of the players, if the head coach had ever acted unprofessionally (in front of the players or when alone with his staff), whether the opposing coaches respected the head coach, whether the parents liked the head coach, and whether Ms. Inbetween thought the head coach was still competent as head coach?

The principal indicated that they knew that they were putting her between a rock and a hard place but that she had to remember that the ultimate good and the ultimate goal revolved around providing the very best learning experience for the athletes. And hence, she should feel comfortable in sharing her personal and professional thoughts (in a confidential fashion) with them.

Figure 8.1: Between rock and a hard place

Finally Mr. BIG asked the final question: "Will you take the head coaching position in soccer next fall if the head coach is relieved of his post or resigned his post?"

QUESTIONS FOR DISCUSSION

1. What are the essential elements of this scenario?
2. What might Ms. Inbetween try to do early on in this series of events? Why?
3. What should coach Inbetween do now after she has heard everything from these two gentlemen? Be specific and provide a rationale for your decisions.
4. Should she talk with (and if so, when):
   A. Coach Oldtimer?
   B. The athletes on the team?
   C. The principal (alone)
   D. Mr. Big (alone)
   E. Members of the school board?
   F. Others? Who?
5. Would it make any difference if the head coach was indeed an unprofessional and incompetent coach OR a professional and competent coach? Why or why not?
6. What did Mr. BIG and the principal do right (if anything)?
7. What did both individuals do wrong (if anything)?
8. What was the motivation behind all of this maneuvering?
9. What general rules of thumb are applicable here in terms of professionalism, loyalty, chain of command, honesty, professional advancement, etc.?
10. Is coach Inbetween at risk here in this situation? Elaborate.
    A. What could happen to her that might be positive?
    B. What could happen to her that might be negative?
11. What should Ms. Inbetween say if coach Oldtimer came to her and indicated that he had heard that she (Mary Inbetween) had been saying negative things about him in order to get the head coaching job?
12. Would there be any differences if the head coach had been a woman instead of a man (coaching a women's team)? Explain.
13. What might happen if the players somehow became aware of the attempt to dump the head coach and took the stance of supporting the potential change in coaches?
14. What would be the situation if the players threatened to quit the team after they had been told that Mary Inbetween was in line for the job and old coach Oldtimer was out? In this eventuality, what might happen? And what can be done? By whom?
15. What are some general principles that are appropriate in this type of situation? Be specific.
16. Comments . . .

RESPONSES FOR QUESTIONS FOR DISCUSSION

_____

_____

_____

_____

_____

_____

_____

_____

_____

_____

_____

_____

_____

_____

_____

_____

_____

CASE #34

The Case of Crisis Management

The athletic director, Mortimer Kazwalski, was like most athletic administrators. That is, he was almost constantly being faced with challenges, problems and difficulties in the performance of his responsibilities. Some problems are more serious than others. Some problems are mere challenges or difficulties. And, some problems are indeed big, big problems. However, he was different in one respect, his administrative mode of operation was invariably one of reaction, rather than proaction. His anticipation skills were certainly wanting in the severe.

Injuries can occur in spite of one's best efforts [Courtesy of Washington State University]

The new head wrestling coach, Ted Watson, was halfway through his season and was having trouble adjusting to the administrative style of Mortimer. Ted's previous athletic administrator at a different school was just the opposite of the one he was stuck with presently. Poor Mort, thought Ted Watson. "He can't seem to find the forest for the trees. Almost every day I see the poor man running around the building as if he were a chicken with its head cut off, always attending to some kind of emergency, problem, difficulty or challenge. He spends so much time putting out fires, no wonder he can't do his real job well."

His assistant coach, Billy Davis, added: "Well, if we conducted our practices like he attempts to run the athletic department we would be in deep trouble, wouldn't we?"

"Yea, the problem is that he cannot anticipate the sun coming up tomorrow. He just seems to wait until something bad happens and then he gets all upset and confused. And, then to top it all off, all he seems to worry about in the face of any big problem is to find someone to blame, to crucify," added the head mentor.

"I agree," his assistant said. "And I am getting sick and tired of his trying to find fault with people whenever there is a problem. His blaming people for problems just exacerbates the problems. It is almost as if he doesn't trust us or doesn't have any confidence in what we are doing. Doesn't he know that we, as coaches, are the experts in our respective sports?"

From the athletic director's perspective, things were going as usual. He knew that he was competent because problems were dealt with in an expedient fashion and problems came with the territory. As much as he wanted the problems to go away, he knew that he and his staff would still be faced with problems, day in and day out.

Mort's attitude was that he was going to visibly attack each and every problem vigorously and aggressively (and visibly) until the problem was solved, resolved or went away. And, he was going to hold everyone accountable ("accountability is a buzz word in our society isn't it?") for errors or oversights. That was the *only way to prevent problems* from occurring again. He also wanted to improve his image so he made sure that he was seen visibly active in solving problems for his department and his coaches. In this, he saw himself as a father seeking to protect his children from the problems of the real world.

QUESTIONS FOR DISCUSSION

1. What are the typical and primary jobs, duties and responsibilities of a so-called athletic administrator? Elaborate.

2. What kind of image is Mort projecting to his coaches? Is it appropriate? Is it positive? Elaborate.

3. What are the real problems and challenges that Mort now faces as an athletic director? Explain in detail.

4. What do you think might be the present relationship between Mort and his coaches? Why?

5. How does an individual get others to have confidence in oneself?

6. What are some of the negative consequences of constantly being in a reacting mode in terms of doing one's job? What are some positive consequences, if any?

7. How can Mort anticipate problems, well in advance?

8. What suggestions would you share with him in terms of being more proactive rather than reactive in terms of dealing with problems? Elaborate.

9. Who has more problems to solve in their jobs, athletic directors or coaches? Or, is it just that both athletic directors and coaches have their share of problems but the problems are just different in their nature? Explain your position.

10. How can problems and difficulties facing athletic directors best be dealt with, in general terms?

11. One of the ways to successfully exist and survive as an athletic administrator is to be able to deal with problems. What suggestions might you provide to Mort in terms of his preventing problems from occurring in the first place?

12. List five of the typical problems or difficulties that face the average athletic director at the junior high level? At the high school level? At the collegiate level?

13. Why does the AD attempt to blame people for problems or mistakes? Why is this behavior itself a problem?

14. What should the athletic director do instead of initially attempting to blame people for a problem? Why?

15. Accountability is important in administration and in coaching. Differentiate between *accountability* and *just faulting* or *blaming people*.

16. Why is Ted Watson having an especially difficult time adjusting to the administrative style of Mort? What suggestions might you provide the head wrestling coach in dealing with his current athletic director?

17. What does the athletic director think about himself? Why? Does Mort believe that he is an effective administrator? Is he? Explain your stance.

18. What might the head wrestling coach do in order to make the transition from working with one type of athletic director (at his former school) and working with his current athletic director (who has a different administrative style)?

19. What general principles are appropriate in this situation for both coaches and for athletic administrators?

20. Comments . . .

RESPONSES FOR QUESTIONS FOR DISCUSSION

_____

_____

_____

_____

_____

_____

_____

_____

_____

_____

_____

_____

_____

_____

Case #35

The Case of the Athletic Director
Faced with the Tough Decision

Coach Tyler Redman was a well-respected teacher. In fact he was well-respected throughout the small town community. He had coached basketball for almost 20 years during which time he had his share of successful teams. However, in the last few years his teams have really struggled. In fact, they had not had a winning season in the last five years and last year was just abominable.

There was some talk in the town of how the coach may have allowed the game to pass him by. Some felt that he had lost touch with the kids. Others just felt that some teams go through cycles and this was his turn to have some down years and that the team under his leadership and tutorage would eventually (sooner or later) be back on top.

His defenders, although vocal, were not many. They pointed out that he had accomplished much in his 20-plus years as a teacher and coach at McPhelps High School. "His student-athletes are all so polite. You never see one of his kids in trouble, either in school or with the police. He really teaches them to become good citizens. He doesn't just talk about helping kids but he actually helps them on the court and off the court. Look at how well his former athletes have done on and off the court," commented one supporter.

A current school board member retorted that there was a lot of evidence that indicated that coach Redman was a quality teacher/coach. "Why just look at some of the things that will show you he is top notch," said the board member.

However, his detractors were quick to point out that every coach was suppose to do those things—and win as well. "Coach Redman just doesn't have it any more. The game has passed him by and the team's record shows it," cried Mr. Ralph Weimer, the president of the booster club and a very wealthy and influential businessman in the community."

To Sammy Balinsky, the relatively new (and untenured as a teacher) athletic director, Mr. Weimer pointed out that: "You know, there are a lot of important people in the community that agree with me that the coach should go, he should go back to the classroom where no one keeps score. In fact, if something isn't done soon, you may find yourself in the line of fire. It might turn out that it is either you or him that have to go because I don't intend to have my son subjected to that kind of coaching when he moves up to the varsity level next year. Think about it. What is the best course of action, a decision to replace an obvious incompetent coach or securing a new leader of the athletic program, one who is not afraid to make the tough decision, a decision that everyone knows must be made to save the program and to insure that the athletes receive the type of quality coaching and teaching that they deserve."

Sammy was in a dilemma for sure and he thought that he knew the consequences of an inappropriate move. But what should he do? What was the ethical situation? He was married, had two children, a new house with a large mortgage, two cars (not paid for), one cat and two dogs.

QUESTIONS FOR DISCUSSION

1. Can a coach today, of a flagship sport, survive as a coach in high school with several successive years of sub-par team performance (below .500)? Does the size of the school make a difference? Explain in detail.

2. ` What could be some of the reasons why coach Redman's teams have not won more games? Elaborate.

3. What might an athletic director do to help a high school coach become more successful in the win/loss column? Be specific and explore all possibilities.

4. Is it the coach's fault that his teams have not been more successful in winning games? Why or why not?

5. What are some examples of things that the athletic director and/or head coach could do or publicize that might enable others to view the coach in a more positive light? Be specific and provide at least seven strategies or tactics.

6. At the high school level, is and should the athletic director held accountable for a team's failure to win in a flagship sport? What about the NCAA division III level? What about at the big-time, NCAA division I level? Elaborate.

7. Should the athletic director, in this situation, go ahead and sacrifice the coach and re-place him with a new coach because of the pressure being exerted by Mr. Wimmer? Explain.

8. Would the athletic director be seriously contemplating the coach's replacement if there had not been such severe pressure to dump the coach and a threat to the athletic director himself? Why or why not?

9. What is wrong, if anything, with firing a high school coach in a flagship sport who is not winning? Justify your position.

10. What does the athletic director really have at risk in this situation?

11. Explore the ethical dimensions of this situation for the athletic director.

12. Is there any realistic way that the athletic director can attempt to save the job of the coach? Elaborate.

13. What are some criteria that athletic directors evaluate their coaches on? Be specific.

14. Should the athletic director sacrifice his own job/career in this situation since the coach would lose his job anyway if a new athletic director came into the picture? Assume a position and justify it.

15. What are some general principles that are befitting this particular scenario?

16. Comments . . .

RESPONSES FOR QUESTIONS FOR DISCUSSION

_____

_____

_____

_____

_____

_____

_____

_____

_____

_____

_____

_____

_____

_____

_____

_____

_____

_____

_____

CASE #36

The Case of the Broken-down Coach

Coach Tired Brokendown, 47 years old, had been coaching and teaching for almost twenty-five years. He had been coaching in Maintown High School for twenty-one of those years and had enjoyed exceptional success as a coach and as a teacher in the so-called early years. In fact, he had won one state championship shortly after arriving in town. He had coached football as an assistant, was head coach of basketball and baseball but really concentrated on basketball.

However, in the past decade, things had changed for Coach Brokendown. Maybe it was the messy divorce. Maybe it was just that things had passed the old coach by. Times have changed and coaching has changed. Coach Brokendown has not kept up-to-date in either basketball or his teaching responsibilities. He has certainly not carried his share of the load in terms of extra duties such as monitoring dances, volunteering to help on committees, etc. In fact, he frequently gives the impression of just hanging in there for the next twenty years until retirement.

The long time athletic director, Mr. Frankensmith, has been getting some pressure from the principal and some board members concerning Coach Brokendown. There has been concern expressed that the basketball team is not only not progressing but also actually declining even further, if that is possible. Fewer and fewer students are trying out for the team. More kids are quitting, being kicked off the team, and sustaining serious injuries in practices. And, there is hardly any fan enthusiasm for the sport as there had been in the coach's early years.

The problem reached a climax when the booster club presidency passed to Mr. Banker who was an influential money person in the community. He also happened to have a son who was going into high school and who was supposed to be a great basketball player (so says his father). Almost immediately following his election to the presidency, Mr. Banker got busy gathering support for a change in the coaching staff, namely, the head basketball position. However, since Mr. Brokendown has a continuing contract (like tenure), Mr. Brokendown will always have a teaching post at the high school. This is more than can be said for the athletic director who is not a teacher at this school, but is a full time athletic director with no job protection other than a two-year contract. In fact, he will be coming up for his contract review during the next four months.

Mr. Banker and the principal (Mr. Gutless) walked into the office of Mr. Frankensmith, the athletic director, on a Monday morning whereupon they broached the subject of what might be done to upgrade the basketball program. It seems that they both wanted the basketball coach released (fired) from the coaching post, period. And, they want the AD to do it without any reference to the booster club or to the principal having had any part in the decision to get rid of the coach.

QUESTIONS FOR DISCUSSION

1. What are the important elements or factors in this scenario?

2. What has happened to Coach Brokendown? What evidence is there that the coach is less than competent? Why has he become what he has become?

3. What does Mr. Banker want? Why?

4. Is Mr. Banker justified in his actions and motives? Aren't coaches supposed to be competent? Aren't they supposed to have winning teams? Elaborate.

5. What might the athletic director say to Mr. Banker and the principal that Monday morning? Role-play your comments. Offer justification for your recommendations.

6. What can the athletic director do now to solve this situation or problem? Be specific.

7. What should or might the athletic director have done previously? What has the athletic director done wrong in the past in this coaching situation?

8. How can the athletic director save face for all of the parties?

9. What should be the role of the principal in this scenario?

10. What pitfalls await the athletic director in terms of:
    A. The coach
    B. The principal
    C. Mr. Banker
    D. Other coaches
    E. His own career
    F. Others . . .

11. What can the AD do to remotivate Coach Brokendown? Is it too late? Why or why not?

12. Explore how the basketball coach might be fairly and justly evaluated in terms of his competency by the AD.

13. Can and/or should a coach who is *fairly assessed* and found to be wanting be removed from coaching duties? How? Under what circumstances. What is meant by fairly assessed?

14. How can the athletic director be fair to the coach, the athletes, the school and himself in this situation?

15. What general principles might be applicable here in terms of proper management of the basketball situation from the athletic director's perspective? From the school's perspective?

16. Other . . .

RESPONSES FOR QUESTIONS FOR DISCUSSION

_____

_____

_____

_____

_____

_____

_____

_____

_____

_____

_____

_____

_____

_____

_____

_____

Case #37

The Case of the Problem Between the Coach and the Custodian

It was Monday morning and Mike Spelgrand, one of the janitors assigned to the athletic facilities in Winterfield High School, was angry, very angry. And, he was not beyond sharing his feelings of frustration and bitterness with some of the other janitorial staff during their customary mid-morning break.

It seems as if the head football coach, Wally Walartz, was especially critical of the maintenance staff and loudly complained to the athletic director over the weekend about the terrible job that the staff had been doing with the practice and game fields throughout the fall. In fact, coach Walartz not only vented his frustration to the athletic director, but he was very free with his critical remarks with others, including his coaching staff, the players, members of the booster club and with even some of his close social friends.

Needless to say, such comments, especially in a small community, quickly found their way back to Mike Spelgrand via the community grapevine—which was really humming over the past weekend. In fact, Mike was so angry Saturday evening, upon hearing the criticism that the football coach was seemingly spreading throughout the community, that he decided to confront the coach immediately.

And he did. He happened to run into coach Walartz at the bar at the local Moose club. When he saw Wally Walartz, the football coach was drinking his customary beer and whisky among his customary cronies.

Upon approaching the football coach amidst the coach's supporters and admirers the janitor wasted no time nailing the coach to the proverbial wall. Not only did the janitor berate the football coach for criticizing him and his fellow maintenance staff, but was really upset that the coach had been free with his criticism to everyone under the sun and then some.

"Why didn't you just come to me if you had a problem with me, my staff or with our work? Why did you have to go behind my back and stab me? You are always stressing teamwork and honesty with your team and athletes and then you act like this. Why can't you act in a professional manner instead of talking a good game, you fat @#$%^@ fraud. You just make me sick, you are just an old stuck-up, egoistical slob!!!!!"

Coach Walartz had been feeling pretty good since he had more than several drinks under his ever-expanding belt. He was not about to have someone like a lowly janitor attempt to embarrass him in front of his supporters and admirers. In no time at all coach Walartz got into an angry shouting match and traded verbal charges as well as a push or two with the janitor, claiming that Mike and his staff were lazy goof-offs and that if they were really competent they most certainly would not have ended up as common janitors.

Finally, after about five minutes of ever escalating barbs and threats, charges and counter-chargers being thrown at each other, they were both forcefully pulled away from each other by the crowd that had congregated, lest they end up trading full blown punches in the bar—right in front of everyone. Needless to say, everyone in the place had heard the angry exchange and it did not take long for the rumor mill to have spread the news of the confrontation throughout town.

By Monday morning, it seemed that everyone who was anyone in town had heard about the blowup between the janitor and the head football coach.

So, the other janitors were not surprised in the least when Mike, early Monday morning at work, began his tirade about the bumbling, incompetent football coach. In fact, they were as incensed as he was, if not even more so since they had heard about the incident at the Moose club through the grapevine (and the story got more blown out of proportion with each telling).

During the morning break they began to share with each other how unappreciated they really were and how high and mighty **all** those stupid, stuck-up coaches always acted. They proceeded to discuss how sorry all the coaches would be if they, the custodial and maintenance personnel (engineers), did not go out of their way, almost on a daily basis, to help those lazy, egotistical coaches. "Besides, they always get the press, the praise and the glory (and the big salaries) and what do we ever get? We get the short end of the proverbial stick, that is what we get. Wonder what would happen if we really *worked to rule*, if we really followed our union contract to the letter. Bet those idiot coaches couldn't survive one week without one of us holding their hands and wiping their noses," replied one of the maintenance engineers.

Later that Monday morning the athletic director got a phone call from the superintendent who wondered what all the fuss was about down there in athletics. "Why can't you control what your people are doing down there," asked the superintendent. "My goodness, my phone has been ringing off the wall with board members and boosters wanting to know what happened and why. I think we need to meet. Lets say at 4:30 this afternoon," he concluded.

QUESTIONS FOR DISCUSSION

1. What are the sources of the problems in this situation? Be specific.
2. Describe the attitude of the football coach towards the maintenance personnel. Implications? Summarize the attitude of the maintenance engineers toward the football coach and the other coaches? Implications?
3. What did the football coach do wrong? Cite chapter and verse.
4. Why do you think the football coach complained to the athletic director without first approaching Mike Spelgrand?
5. What should the athletic director have done when the coach complained about the maintenance staff? Why?
6. Why did the football coach share his negative feelings about the maintenance staff with others, especially those within the community?

7. How might this entire situation have been prevented? What role should the athletic director have played in this scenario to prevent this situation from developing in the first place?

8. Does Mike Spelgrand, the head janitor, have a point(s) in his verbal criticism of the football coach in the bar? Be specific.

9. What did Mike Spelgrand do wrong in this whole situation? Is there any justification for Mike's actions in the bar? Why or why not?

10. How important is the relationship between coaches and janitors or maintenance personnel in any sports program?

11. Could the janitorial and maintenance staff members make life especially tough for the coaches? Elaborate.

12. How would the superintendent view the athletic director in light of all that has happened? Why might the athletic director be vulnerable? Elaborate?

13. What can the athletic director do now, after the episode in the Moose club, to defuse the situation between the coaches and the maintenance engineers or janitors? Outline a specific course of action with possible consequences.

14. What might be the immediate and long-term fallout in terms of the people in the community, with school personnel and with the athletes as a result of what has happened?

15. What does *working to rule* mean in terms of unions? Provide examples.

16. What general principles are applicable in this type of situation?

17. Comments . . .

RESPONSES FOR QUESTIONS FOR DISCUSSION

_____

_____

_____

_____

_____

_____

_____

_____

_____

CASE #38

The Case of Impressing the New Boss

With the announcement of the new superintendent, Dr. Samuel Houserman, Samantha Muzic was not a little bit concerned. It was not that Samantha didn't have confidence in her performance as athletic director for the large school district, Messano, Ohio. No, it was just a natural concern whenever one receives word that there was going to be a new boss in charge of one's own area. And, in this school district, the athletic director reported directly to the superintendent on a bi-weekly basis.

Figure 8.2: Impressing one's superior

"I wonder if the reporting arrangement will remain the same, with me reporting every other week to the superintendent on the state of the athletic program or will this Dr. Houserman change things around?" wondered Samantha. The athletic director was concerned about how much the new superintendent might view athletics (and the athletic director) on the secondary level and how interested he really is in the athletic program.

"How am I going to go about meeting my new boss? How should I go about finding out information about him? I sure don't want to meet him and start to work for him without knowing what type of person he is. I wonder what "the book" is on him?" she mused.

"I sure don't want the new superintendent to develop incorrect impressions of me and my abilities, but how do I insure this? What if others convey to him biased and incorrect information with the result being that the superintendent thinks I am a dummy? I had better be assertive in self-promoting myself in the eyes of my new boss," she concluded.

QUESTIONS OR DISCUSSION

1. What are the important aspects of this case?
2. Is it unusual for an athletic director to report directly to the superintendent? What is the usual reporting structure at the high school level? As an athletic director in a high school, to whom would you like to report to?
3. Should Samantha be concerned with the appointment of a new boss? Explain in detail.
4. How important is it that the athletic director takes a proactive approach in making sure that the new boss is fully aware of her value, her past accomplishments and her competency? Justify your response.

5. If Samantha doesn't do anything to inform her new boss of how competent she is, what might be the consequences? Elaborate.

6. What information and/or documentation might (or should) Samantha want to share with Dr. Houserman?

7. What, specifically, should the athletic director deliberately do (and when) in an effort to acquaint the new superintendent with her range of duties, her competency level, and her value to the athletic program as well as to the school?

8. Are there cautions you would give to Samantha in this situation? Be specific.

9. Would the new superintendent not be aware that those persons who would be reporting to him would be attempting to place themselves in a positive light? What do you think the superintendent might think or do in response to someone attempting to toot his or her own horn?

10. Assume the role of the athletic director (role play) and share what you would say (and perhaps give) to your new boss in one of your earliest meeting. What specifically would you want to share with this person?

11. Is it important to find out information about the superintendent? What can the athletic director do (what strategies and tactics) to get the low down on the new superintendent? Suggest strategies that would not only be effective but professionally acceptable.

12. What general administrative principles or managerial guidelines are applicable here?

13. Comments . . .

RESPONSES FOR QUESTIONS FOR DISCUSSION

_____

_____

_____

_____

_____

_____

_____

_____

CASE #39

The Case of the Forgetful Athletic Director

Jimmie Albert, athletic director, has a problem, a big problem. And, he was aware of it. It seems that he was forever forgetting people's names. He would forget names of student-athletes, parents, booster club members, teachers, and even of coaches. In fact, everyone he ever met was in danger of being forgotten in terms of name recognition.

And, it was getting worse. Jimmie, no matter how hard he said he was trying, just could not remember people's names. When introduced to someone, he was always thinking of what he was about to say instead of listening to the person's name and attempting to associate the name with that individual.

In recent years, the athletes began to take notice of this flaw and it was not uncommon for athletes to make fun of the athletic director and his memory lapses, behind his back. In point of fact, it was beginning to become a big embarrassment to the AD and the department.

Upon reflection, Jimmie thought: "Well, I had better admit that I have a big problem and deal with it. If I don't, I am going to be the laughing stock of the school and my position might even be in jeopardy. But how should I deal with this problem. It seems that no matter what I try to do, I still cannot remember people's names."

The athletic director approached one of his trusted assistants and asked: "Steve, can you help me. Would you be willing to prompt me in terms of the names of the various boosters at the next booster club meeting? I know that you know almost everyone's name in the club and with you at my side I will have ready access to everyone's names."

QUESTIONS FOR DISCUSSION

1. Summarize the essential elements of this case.
2. Is the athletic director correct in his assessment of the situation? Explain.
3. Is it enough that the athletic director recognizes that he has a problem? Why or why not?
4. Is it wise for the athletic director to confide in Steve and solicit Steve's help at the next booster club meeting? Elaborate.
5. Why do you think the athletic director is so forgetful of names?
6. What might people think when another person fails to remember that person's name?
7. Should the athletic director seek professional help? From whom?
8. Is this deficiency a matter that can or cannot be changed? Is it a matter of a physical problem or disease? Explain.

9. Outline an overall *strategic plan* that might help the athletic director improve his memory insofar as people's names are concerned, especially at formal gatherings and events.

10. Provide some specific *tactics* that might be helpful to the athletic director in terms of remembering names of people he meets.

11. Will the athletic director's superior(s) evaluate him and his performance in a negative manner because of this forgetfulness? Under what circumstances? Elaborate.

12. What general principles are applicable in dealing with this case scenario?

13. Comments . . .

RESPONSES FOR QUESTIONS FOR DISCUSSION

_____

_____

_____

_____

_____

_____

_____

_____

_____

_____

_____

_____

_____

_____

CASE #40

The Case of Influential Fundraising Contacts

Jack McLinklock had been the athletic director for almost five years and he was pretty happy with what he has accomplished. Being hired by the previous president to get the department into some sort of order, Jack went about the formidable challenge with skill and enthusiasm. He spent almost all of the next five years working diligently within the department. In fact, almost all of his activities were internal in contrast to external activities. And, this was fine under the previous administration.

Now, however, there was a new president on the scene and this individual (Ralph Maasen) was anything but an internal administrator. He very quickly gained a well-deserved reputation as an outside administrator/manager and, in short order, let the athletic director know that he too was to be more active in outside activities, outside of the AD's office and outside of the school—with one goal in mind, i.e., generating significant funds and resources for the intercollegiate athletic program.

Celebrities can help promotional and fundraising efforts for athletic programs.[Courtesy of University of Tennessee — Chattanooga Athletics]

"But to actually raise the $100,000 in the next twelve months like Ralph says he wants me to do is ridiculous," declared the athletic director. "I have tried now for some months to raise some money but to get that much money in such a short time, why, you cannot get that money by means of car washes."

It seemed that Jack had tried to contact some wealthy people in the community with the goal being to ask them to donate money for the athletic program. But, to his dismay, hardly anyone would even take his calls and even less would allow him into their offices. They did not know the athletic director. He did not travel in their social or financial circles. He was a stranger to these wealthy, important and influential people even though he had lived in the community for almost half a decade.

Realizing that he could not gain access to these heavy hitters he looked around to see who could help him. One of his assistants pointed out that he needed a bridge or step stone with which to gain access to these important would-be donors to the athletic department. "Well, who are these people?" cried Jack. He was told of a number of people that he, as athletic director, might be able to secure access and who might, in turn, be able to open doors to these wealthy, potential donors.

"But, you know, you need to start cultivating these intermediaries right now. You should have done so four years ago, in fact," stated the assistant, who had lived in the community all of his life and was well respected by most who lived in the town.

"OK, right, but what do I do now? What are the steps I can take right now to save my job?" pleaded the athletic director.

QUESTIONS FOR DISCUSSION

1. Explain the challenges now facing the athletic director.
2. Why didn't the athletic director become more of a fundraiser and promoter earlier? Was this a wise decision at the time?
3. Is it common today that presidents are demanding that athletic directors (at the NCAA I, II, III levels) to be effective fundraisers? Why or why not? Is this reasonable or even fair in light of all of the other tasks that ADs are involved in at the NCAA I, II and III levels?
4. Even if the athletic director was not told to fundraise earlier during his tenure, what might he had done or accomplished at that time to become better known and respected within the community? Provide examples that clearly outline some reasonable strategies and tactics.
5. What are the expected roles of *centers of influence?* Provide examples.
6. Why weren't the influential and wealthy people receptive to the overtures of the athletic director? Why did they not even allow him access to them? Explain in full your position.
7. What would have had to happen in the past to change the situation today in terms of gaining access to these so-called heavy hitters?
8. If the athletic director does not run in the same financial or social circles of the people he wants to gain access to, what is the answer? How can the AD gain access to such high, important and influential people? Provide a rationale.
9. What can the athletic director do now that he is in this predicament? Be specific and provide several courses of action that might benefit the AD and the athletic program?
10. To whom should or could the athletic director rely upon or seek help from in terms of assisting in the fundraising process and in terms of gaining access to important people?
11. What general principles or guidelines are applicable in dealing with this case scenario—in terms of steps that an athletic director might pursue to establish oneself as one who is well known and respected within the community by those in positions of power and influence.
12. Comments . . .

RESPONSES FOR QUESTIONS FOR DISCUSSION

CASE #41

The Case of the Problem with the Media

Michael McCormick, the local news media sports reporter, attempted again to call the athletic director (Philip Adams) at the lone local city high school. This was his third try and he was getting more than a little anxious. In fact, Michael was getting angry. Was the athletic director deliberately avoiding him or was the athletic director just never available to people, especially the news media? If he wasn't so committed to the athletes and the sports program in the town he would just let it go and let the AD hang himself, his coaches and the whole darn athletic program. But no, he was going to force a confrontation of the issue with the athletic director if it took all week and a hundred more phone calls.

Philip, the athletic director, kept finding the written notes from his secretary every time he came back from an urgent and essential meeting for two days now. Each note indicated that it was vitally important that the AD give the sports writer a call back as soon as possible. "What is with this guy?" thought the athletic director? It wasn't that Philip was goofing around. It wasn't that he had nothing else to do but call Michael back, he was busy as a bee and was dealing with really important problems on the campus that dealt with student-athletes, his coaches and his boss. He would get back to the sports reporter later in the week. Right now he had much more important things to address and he had better do just that or he would find himself and his sports programs in deep trouble.

So it happened that finally the reporter drove out to the AD's office on the offhand change of running into the elusive athletic director. And, wouldn't you know just after lunch, he caught Philip walking into the building where his office was.

"Phil, why haven't you returned my calls?" cried out the sports writer. "I have been trying to reach you all week. You know, I have better things to do than to chase you all over town. Finally, I had to drive all the way over here to catch you."

"Hey, Mike, I have been busy. I have a job to do, you know, and I was going to give you a call—it is just that I have a lot on my plate right now and I have to establish priorities and deal with important things first."

With that remark Mike went ballistic and declared: "Hey, you jerk, what I am attempting to do is to save your old butt and to save the school some embarrassment. If you don't have time to accept some friendly advice and help, then you deserve what you and your program get." And, with that, the reported started to head toward his car.

"Now wait a minute, Mike," said the athletic director. "Listen, lets talk now, we can go into my office and I will fix us a cup of coffee and we can have a real down to earth, two-way conversation on any subject you want—and I promise I will pay attention and listen. All I care about is the school, the sports program and the kids, just like I know you do."

With that both the writer and the athletic director went into the latter's office where the news reporter shared the following: (1) most of the coaches were calling in the final scores to his desk after the home/away contests—but the basketball coach was only calling in when his team won, (2) the football coach, in the fall, never had the stats organized when his assistant called in the scores for the away games ("he just rambled on and on all over the place and it took forever to get the stats from him"), (3) the wrestling coach would forbid his athletes from talking with the news media if the coach was displeased with almost anything, (4) there was almost a complete lack of cooperation between the AD's office and the sports writer (it was almost as if the writer had to pull teeth to get any real information, instead of pure pabulum), and (5) no one would talk to the sports writer when the star swimmer was arrested for allegedly shoplifting at a local fast food convenience store.

"Well," asked Michael, "what do you think?"

QUESTIONS FOR DISCUSSION

1. Summarize some of the more important problems that face the athletic director in this scenario.
2. How important is it that the AD pay special attention to keeping the sports media happy? Explain.
3. What might the athletic director have done in terms of being more accessible or being perceived as being more accessible to the public and the media?
4. Is Michael correct in his assessment of the AD's intentions? Does it make any difference if the perception is correct as long as the sports writer holds the perception? Elaborate.
5. Is it ever permissible to only call in scores when one wins? Elaborate.
6. Who has responsibility for calling in the scores to one's home media for away games? For home games? Why? Who decides? Elaborate.
7. When a basketball coach or staff member calls in the stats for the game, what does the sports writer mean by sharing the stats in a very disorganized fashion? What can a coach or staff member do to expedite the sharing of pertinent stats with the media?
8. In the sport of basketball or baseball provide an example of a box score form that could be used in calling in the scores/stats of a game.
9. Whose responsibility is it to get the correct stats to the media? Justify your position!
10. What type of policies might an athletic director impose upon the coaches in terms of dealing with the press, in terms of making athletes and staff members available to the media following contests as well as during the week? Be specific.
11. Summarize how an athletic administrator might go about developing and maintaining a sound, professional relationship with the sports writer and news media.
12. Cite one or more general principles or guidelines that are applicable to this case in terms of dealing with the news media.
13. Comments . . .

RESPONSES FOR QUESTIONS FOR DISCUSSION

_____

_____

_____

_____

_____

_____

_____

_____

_____

_____

_____

_____

_____

_____

_____

_____

CASE #42

The Case of the Indispensable Athletic Director

Casey Tillemann had been an athletic administrator for some years now. He had started out as an athletic coach, and not too poorly a coach at that. However, it did not take him long to decide that his real future, his real love, had been being involved in organizing and planning and facilitating the management of sports and sport activities. So, after coaching for some 5 years he found himself being mentored by an athletic director and a principal who allowed and encouraged him to, at first, volunteer to take on specific administrative duties and responsibilities. Later, when there was an opening for a paid position as an assistant athletic director, Casey jumped at the chance and gave up coaching for good.

That was 15 years ago. During the intervening years he moved from assistant AD to an associate AD at a junior college and now, in his present position, serves as an athletic director at the fairly prestigious and successful NCAA division III institution. Casey had a positive reputation among his peers, the athletes and the higher administration.

When the new president of the university arrived on campus, Dr. Joseph Smithsonn, it was rumored that there would be a lot of changes in the higher administrative ranks because at Dr. Smithsoon's previous two institutions that is what he did as president, i.e., he cleaned house of senior administrators and brought in new people, people who would be beholding to him as president.

When Dr. Smithsonn inquired about the general state of the athletic program, and particularly about the athletic director, he was surprised to find that the consensus was that the program was excellent and that the athletic director was not only a competent administrator but was, in point of fact, doing the work of two, if not three people (or at least it seemed like that was the case, to most of the people he spoke to).

One of the middle management administrators, Neoma Spellman, cautioned the new president that he shouldn't try to fix what wasn't broken. "You know," she said, "Casey is one of those people who has become not merely a mainstay in the arena of athletics on this campus but, in point of fact, has become the proverbial indispensable person for the athletic program. Why, if you let him go you would literally have to hire at least two people to do his job."

The president asked: "Do you mean that he is the only person who can do that job? I don't believe it. I can hire any athletic director and he or she would do just fine."

"No, you don't understand," replied Neoma. "Sure there are people out there who could do the job of an AD, but not as well as Casey can do it and not as quickly and not with as little fuss or problems as when Casey is in charge. He has made extremely strong alliances within the institution, the community and even regionally and nationally. I dare say that if he resigned his post and then turned around and immediately applied for the same job, we would certainly hire him—which is more than I would dare say for many of our current staff members. His departure would be noticed in more ways than one. In a nutshell, I think the institution and the athletic program, as well as yourself, would be in for some challenging times if he were not the athletic director."

QUESTIONS FOR DISCUSSION

1. Explain the challenges now facing the president.
2. Is it all that unusual for a new chief executive officer to want to clean house and bring in or elevate one's own senior level administrators?
3. Expound on the idea or concept of becoming an indispensable person (administrator) within an athletic department (within an institution or organization).
4. Provide some specific examples of what an athletic director could do within a high school or a college to make oneself indispensable to the chief executive office and/or the program. Elaborate.
5. Why is it important for an athletic administrator to develop a positive reputation among co-workers and colleagues, in and outside of the athletic department?
6. Explain some very specific strategies and tactics that an athletic director might pursue in creating, developing and fostering such a positive reputation and image among co-workers within an institution or school system?
7. If you were the athletic director and had a conversation with the president, assume a role-playing posture and indicate what and how you would explain your value to the program/school and what you actually do.
8. Comments . . .

RESPONSES FOR QUESTIONS FOR DISCUSSION

_____

_____

_____

_____

_____

_____

_____

Case #43

The Case of the Athletic Director
With the Difficult Superior/Boss

The athletic director, Reba Smallsky, was really in a seemingly unsolvable pickle. It seems that when she was hired a member of the search committee was openly hostile toward her and, in point of fact, demonstrated a disdain for her, if not an outright display of hostility. It seems that this search committee member, Terry (Short Tempered) Territown wanted a friend of his to be appointed as the new athletic director and made a very hard case in favor of this friend.

Thus, it was no surprise to some that when Reba was eventually appointed as athletic director (she was clearly heads and tails above the rest of the field who were being evaluated/interviewed by the search committee) that Terry was outraged and secretly confided to his friends that Reba would rule the day that she had the audacity to even apply for the position of AD, much less accept the offer from the institution.

It did not take long for Terry to lay down a concerted effort of sabotage against the new athletic director. And, to make it worse, Terry, in a very short time span, was promoted (the promotion had people in the know shaking their collective heads) to an administrative position that oversaw the overall operations of the athletic department, making Terry the direct supervisor of Reba.

With this sudden thrust of power, control and influence, Terry did everything he could to make life miserable for the athletic director. Nothing Reba did was good enough. Periodic evaluations for the AD included negative comments and assessments. The most menial jobs and ridiculous tasks were assigned to Reba and traps were laid periodically in the hope that the AD would step on one of the many landmines that were being laid for her in the proverbial mine field by Terry. In short, it seemed that Terry was carrying out his threat to make life miserable for the AD and to get rid of her so that his buddy would replace her.

The question remaining for Reba, who was not oblivious to the whole ridiculous situation, was how to deal with this environment, this vindictive monster, this unprofessional person who was in a position of power. "What have I done in my life to deserve this crap from this despicable excuse of a human being?" asked Reba. "Now what do I do? What are my options? To whom do I turn for help, if anyone? I have to map out a plan or strategy or else my goose is cooked by this idiot. How in the world did he ever get to a position of power and authority?" thought Reba.

QUESTIONS FOR DISCUSSION

1. It is all that unusual that a boss or superior might "have it in" for a subordinate in today's political educational environment on the (A) high school level and/or (B) collegiate level? Explain.

2. What might Reba have done before accepting the offer of employment to prevent or diminish the seriousness of the situation she now finds herself in?

3. Could Reba have foreseen that Terry would end up as her director superior? Elaborate.

4. Why is Terry so upset with Reba?

5. Should Reba confront Terry? What should she say to Terry? Assume a role playing posture and reveal what the AD might say in meeting with Terry?

6. What can Reba do now that she has taken the job to protect herself? Be specific and outline a plan involving:
    A.   Those who might be approached for help
    B.   The steps that might be taken by the AD to survive in this position
    C.   The avenues that are open to Reba in terms of looking elsewhere for a position

7. If Reba thought about moving on to another position, what challenges face her?

8. To whom might Reba approach in the school or organization for assistance? Should the AD go to the presidentat a college or the principalsSuperintendent if at a high school? If so, under what conditions? How and what should be said/shared?

9. If Terry is successful in getting Reba removed from the post as athletic director, what are Reba's options?

10. What are some general principles that are appropriate in this scenario that are applicable for Reba's survival?

11. Comments . . .

RESPONSES FOR QUESTIONS FOR DISCUSSION

_____

_____

_____

_____

_____

_____

CASE #44

The Case of the Sloppily Made Newsletter

The athletic director, Bobby Boo Reebason, knew that one of the major problems facing the athletic department was the lack of awareness among the general public, the alumni and even many fans about the total athletic program and many, if not all, of the athletic teams. "If only there was a way to make these people aware of all of the good things that are going on within this department, why, we would have much fewer problems in terms of public relations and image," confided Bobby to his assistant, Mary Jane Janson.

"Why don't we initiate a newsletter that we can send free to everyone in the community?" responded Mary Jane.

"Great, I think I will start one. I always wanted to be a writer, and I think I know exactly what should be done," declared the athletic director. "I will appoint you as editor and I will write a column each issue that will go in on the very front page."

A month later the athletic director was wishing that he had never heard of the newsletter idea. It seemed that almost anything that could go wrong went wrong—and then some. The first issue of the newsletter had been prepared and proofed by Mary Jane and distributed free to everyone at the various homecoming games that weekend. In addition, copies were mailed to all members of the booster club and to all of the school officials. Finally, the really important people in town had all gotten complimentary copies as well. The following Monday he had gotten a phone call from his boss, the superintendent, who asked that he come immediately to his office and to bring copies of the athletic newsletter.

"What a mess, Bobby, you have laid at my feet. What a disaster. Look at this garbage that you have the audacity to call an athletic newsletter. Why, it is terrible. The registration is all off. The spelling is terrible, why a fifth grader could do better. And, there are even mistakes in facts, wrong dates, misspelled names and incorrect titles. Even the photos that you have stuck in there are lousy. Did you know that Mrs. Johnson, the school board treasurer, called me at home last night to complain about that terrible picture of her in the background of the action shot taken at last week's basketball game. I had three phone calls last night from parents who were wondering why their children's names were not included when the names of some of the other athletes were. All in all, you have made just a "lovely start"with this newsletter for this school, for the athletic department, and for yourself. Well, what do you have to say for yourself?" squealed the superintendent.

QUESTIONS FOR DISCUSSION

1. Summarize the essential problematic elements of this situation facing the athletic director?

2. Who should be the editor of the newsletter? Why? What role should the athletic director normally play in terms of the creation, preparation, proofing and distribution of the newsletter?

3. Is there a need to seek permission prior to initiating a departmental or program newsletter? From whom? Why?

4. Should the newsletter be sent free of charge to various constituencies? Should the newsletter be a benefit included as part of a membership package in the booster club or the sport support group (SSG)? Justify your position.

5. What other mechanism could be used to distribute copies of the newsletter to the appropriate individuals, groups and businesses.

6. Should everyone in the community receive a free copy or have one made available to them for easy viewing? How could this be accomplished?

7. What should comprise the essence (contents, etc.) of this type of newsletter? Be specific.

8. What is(are) the basic purpose(s) of an athletic department's newsletter? Provide a list of possible contents and topics.

9. What are the cardinal rules governing the creation and distribution of a newsletter for an athletic department? List these rules and explain each.

10. Who should be printing this newsletter (on or off campus)? Share some thoughts as to how the athletic director or others might approach a printer in respect to securing the services of the printer at a reasonable cost or at a greatly reduced (or free) cost?

11. Should the newsletter have paid advertisements to help offset the cost of the newsletter? Why or why not? Justify your stance.

12. Share your insights into the type of paper, the color of inks, the size of paper, the use of photos, use of half tones, etc., in the creation of the newsletter.

13. What are the various purposes of the newsletter in addition to distributing information to others (on the high school level; on the collegiate level)?

14. Cite the general principles that are applicable in this scenario? Be specific.

15. Comments . . .

RESPONSES FOR QUESTIONS FOR DISCUSSION

_____

_____

CASE #45

The Case of the Improper Delegation

Allison Albot, the athletic director at McBell Junior College, was initially worried about how she was going to actually accomplish what had to be accomplished during the upcoming year. "How are we going to do everything the President said he wanted done?" thought Allison. "My goodness, he has absolutely no clue how an athletic department is run, how the programs are organized, structured and implemented. Why, with only a single assistant athletic administrator (new to the position) to help me, how am I going to even oversee everything much less do everything?"

Thomas Dent, her new assistant, had been a head soccer coach at a previous school. When he became aware of Allison's concerns, he said: "Why don't we just get some help, some volunteer help. There are always people around who seem anxious to get involved in the athletic program. We could just use them as 'official volunteer helpers' or as volunteer athletic staff to do those things that we don't have time or the inclination to do."

After some further discussion, both agreed to solicit volunteers and to train them to get involved in some of the more mundane, but nevertheless essential, tasks associated with the success of any athletic department. It did not take too long to attract some seemingly dedicated and, on the surface, talented and motivated individuals who wanted to be officially associated with the athletic department and one or more teams. There were individuals who were trained and assigned to staff different areas by helping out in terms of selling game tickets, site preparation, post game roundup, concessions, accompanying teams to away games as supervisors, drivers for away contests, greeters for visiting teams and officials, supervision of the inventory set-up, etc.

Things went fairly well with the arrangements with these volunteers. The volunteers seemed happy and content with the arrangement. After all, they were now athletic staff and enjoyed the prestige of being associated with a college sports program. And, Allison or Thomas trained them in how to handle their various duties and responsibilities.

However, there were several problems that all occurred on the same weekend, the same weekend that the AD was out of town attending a conference meeting. Allison heard about it Monday morning when the President's secretary called at 8:05 a.m. and requested that Allison come to the President's office at nine that same morning. It seems that during Friday's away basketball game the bus broke down and the team members (along with the chaperone) were stranded overnight. There was no one with the team who had a school credit card to pay for the unanticipated motel and meal charges that the team incurred. Then, at Saturday's home wrestling match there was a problem with the mats not being placed down the previous day. As a result, the match was postponed for over 2 hours while the wrestlers from the home and away teams lugged the mats out and prepared the site for competition. Evidently, the volunteer athletic staff person assigned as site overseer failed to convince the custodian that he had the power and authority to direct the maintenance staff to prepare the good mats for the following day's competition. The third (and final straw . . .) disaster took place later that night when the volleyball team was to start its 8-team tournament in the same gym that held the wrestling match earlier that day. When the wrestling match was over everyone evidently went home and the volunteer staff member either did not know that the mats had to be put away or had no influence over the athletes in terms of motivating them to put away the mats. Even the home coach was of no help as the coach said he had to get home for dinner, as he was 2 hours late already.

QUESTIONS FOR DISCUSSION

1. Summarize the essential elements of this problematic situation?
2. Who is going to be blamed by the president? Why? Is this logical? Is this fair?
3. How might the president blame the athletic director for the overnight fiasco with the missing credit card? Elaborate.
4. Who is really at fault for these areas and problems?
5. Can the athletic director successfully pass along the blame to the various volunteer staff members? Why or why not?
6. What could have been done to prevent the big problems associated with Friday night? Be specific.
7. What could have been done to avoid the problem with the wrestling mats? What should have been done by whom and why?
8. The volleyball situation developed because the mats remained on the floor and in the way of the volleyball competition. Whose fault was this? Who is going to be (partially or fully) blamed? Justify your position.
9. What was the problem with delegation in terms of the wrestling situation?
10. What was the real culprit that caused the difficulties for the volleyball team? Elaborate.
11. Whenever an athletic director is not physically present for a home game or for an away competition, what should the AD do in terms of delegation for those events and activities, both at home and away sites? Provide examples.
12. What general administrative principles or managerial guidelines in terms of (A) delegation, (B) training, and (C) preparation for unforeseen events/challenges are applicable here?
13. Comments . . .

RESPONSES FOR QUESTIONS FOR DISCUSSION

CHAPTER NINE

Problems with Controversial Issues

CHAPTER OBJECTIVES

After reading this chapter you will be able to:

- Be familiar with various problems relating to controversial issues
- Differentiate between actions that are sexual harassment and those that are not
- Explain the proper method of dealing with profits and contributions to an athletic team
- Protect an assistant coach who has an unreasonable and demanding boss (head coach)
- Outline to a future spouse of a coach the challenges and sacrifices that spouses often face being the spouse of an athletic coach

Nothing excites the crowd like a successful play on the field.
[Courtesy of Central Michigan University Public Relations]

- Deal with the rent-a-coach problem facing school districts
- Be familiar with the steps to take in response to a charge or accusation made against a coach
- Explain how to respond to a complaint when the person making the charge wants to keep the person's identity a secret
- Be aware of the pitfalls that might exist in a school's faculty lounge
- Describe the acronym ABWA insofar as it pertains to an athletic director's desire to become more visible
- Assess the pros and cons of keeping the budget process and the budget itself a secret on the school's campus (high school and college)
- Prevent athletic facilities and equipment from being damaged
- Explain the essential elements of Title IX and the three prong test for compliance

- Summarize the essence of a quality run concession stand
- Be familiar with the recommendations as to the number of major annual fundraising projects a school should initiate

CASE

46. The case of Mime Beautiful
47. The case of the anxious coach
48. The case of the potential rival and a new boss
49. The case of the impending marriage
50. The case of the rent-a-coach problem
51. The case of the partying coach
52. The case of the unfair treatment charge
53. The case of reluctant complainer
54. The case of the negative atmosphere
55. The case of an ad administering by walking around (ABWA)
56. The case of the secret budget process
57. The case of the missing equipment and supplies
58. The case of the sneaky Title IX compliance
59. The case of the inefficient concession stand
60. The case of too many fundraising projects

CASE #46

The Case of the Mime Beautiful

Miss Mimi Beautiful, who had been in the teaching and coaching profession for four years, was a new addition to Maple Valley High School. She was hired as the assistant coach of basketball and a teacher of physical education in the high school. Her head coach was Big Blue Eyes, a 32 year-old bachelor. In the 11 years as head coach at Maple Valley he had earned a reputation as an outstanding and dedicated coach as well as quite a ladies man. He had dated several teachers in the school system where he worked but nothing serious had ever developed.

During the fall, Coach Blue Eyes asked Mimi Beautiful if they could get together to discuss and plan for the upcoming season. "We need to spend some time together to work out the details for the season since we are going to have a super team. Why, we could even vie for the conference championship," said the head coach.

The night of the first meeting, Mimi Beautiful met with Coach Blue Eyes at his apartment. She arrived around 6 p.m. Throughout the evening he kept inching closer and closer to her and sat very, very close to her. Frequently, he touched her hands and arms as he spoke. He was very demonstrative with his hands whenever he spoke, i.e., he talked as much with his arms and hands as he did with his voice. She began to feel uncomfortable, but said and did nothing. After all, she was new to the school, hardly knew anyone, did not know the lay of the land, and did not have tenure or continuing contract (and would not for another three years).

Mimi got through the evening – and they were able to discuss some basketball – but it was a trying evening for the assistant coach. Later that night, at home, Mimi thought over the evening's activities and wondered if it was just her imagination or what? Was Coach Blue Eyes just being a good old boy or was there more to the situation?

During the next few weeks both Coach Blue Eyes and Mimi Beautiful had occasion to meet together at school, at the local restaurant in town and at his apartment, to discuss basketball and other school related topics. Even at school, Coach Blue Eyes continued to be that touchy-feely type of communicator—as Mimi found he was with everyone.

Throughout the basketball season they were inseparable, going to and from games, going on scouting trips, to basketball clinics, etc. For Christmas, Coach Blue Eyes bought a beautiful swim suit for Mimi and gave it to her as a present with a remark: "I sure would like to see you model this for me but I bet you are too bashful, ha, ha." Mimi just smiled and said "thanks, but no thanks."

During January, Coach Blue Eyes invited himself over to Mimi's apartment and brought a bottle of wine and some Chinese take-out food. Not much was accomplished in terms of basketball as they spent the evening eating, drinking the wine and watching television as well as listening to music.

This relationship continued for some weeks and then in early February, during a meeting at his apartment that was scheduled for the purpose of viewing some video tapes of past games, Coach Mimi Beautiful found herself being asked out by Coach Blue Eyes for an actual date. She was asked if she wanted to accompany the head coach for dinner at an expensive restaurant and then a popular play in a nearby city. She found herself in a dilemma. She did not know what to do. She had never thought that things would progress to this stage. She picked up her purse and keys and ran out of the door and headed home, as fast as she could. She thought to herself: "What had I done to bring this situation to this stage?"

QUESTIONS FOR DISCUSSION

1. What are the central issues in this situation? Is there anything to be concerned about here? Elaborate and fully justify your position.
2. Was there impropriety here? If so, specify. If so, on whose part? Elaborate.
3. Were there examples of poor judgment being used in this situation? Be specific? If so, by whom?
4. What should men and women look out for in terms of working together as professionals, especially in those situations in which the men and women must have close contact in the conduct of their professional responsibilities?
5. What constitutes sexual harassment? Define sexual harassment under the law.
6. Is this a situation of sexual harassment? Explain and provide details.
7. Some educational institutions or school systems have a policy against fraternization or social relationships among faculty and staff, especially those individuals who have a relationship in which one person reports to another as part of the job description. What are the advantages and disadvantages of such a policy? Discuss.
8. Why did coach Blue Eyes act like he did throughout the whole time frame?
9. Were there some danger signs in this relationship? If so, specify.
10. What should be the relationship between a head coach and assistant coach? How can coaches of the opposite sex be sure that their working relationships are proper and appropriate?
11. What might be some perceptions (false or true) held by others of coaches of the opposite sex who work closely together?
12. How can coaches, those who must work closely together with the opposite sex, work to insure that others hold only proper perceptions of them and their relationships with their colleagues who are of the opposite sex? That is, how do such coaches prevent negative or nasty rumors from being initiated and perpetuated?
13. What could any female and any male (working closely together in a professional situation) do to insure that the working relationship(s) remain just that, professional?
14. What might Mimi had done to prevent from being in such a situation as she finally found herself in?

15. What should Coach Mimi do now?
16. Was coach Blue Eyes acting properly and appropriately in everything that he did? If not, identify actions that were improper. Explain.
17. What should coach Blue Eyes do now?
18. What general guidelines or principles are applicable here for both men and women?
19. Comments . . .

RESPONSES FOR QUESTIONS FOR DISCUSSION

_____

_____

_____

_____

_____

_____

_____

_____

_____

_____

_____

_____

_____

_____

CASE #47

The Case of the Promotion
of the Would-be Big Time Program

Coach Youngman was a new basketball coach at Westwood High School. Although he had served as an assistant coach for almost 10 years at two other schools out of state, he was new to this high school and to the state.

Coach Youngman wanted to be sure that his basketball program looked every bit like the big-time basketball programs he always saw on television. Hence, he almost immediately went to work, upon arriving at his new school, to develop a promotional and fund raising operation which would rival the best of them—as he got fond of saying to his two assistant coaches.

Part of his plan was to involve the basketball team with a new booster club that would be devoted strictly to the boys' basketball team. In terms of the booster club (THE ROUNDBALLERS)—he was able to control the activities of the members of that club (some of the most influential members of the community) with an iron fist. This is spite of the surprise and wishes of his fellow coaches and his athletic administration.

Another of his innovations at this school was his effort to have special game programs for his team. He even set about to sell advertising for the printed piece to local and area merchants. Many times, he himself sold the ads and at other times his assistants, and cronies from the community, as well as his players, actually sold the ads and collected the money (which was deposited in the coach's personal checking account) to be used only for the basketball team.

After only about 18 months, Coach Youngman found himself in a position of controlling a bank account (on behalf of THE ROUNDBALLERS) worth some $15,000.00 and started to really provide some special things for his team, such as special pre-game and post-game meals, special uniforms, special scouting trips, etc. He was often quoted as saying that he was the savior for the basketball program.

In response to comments from the athletic director who revealed that the other coaches at his school were upset with all of the special treatment being reaped by the boys' basketball program, coach Youngman simply replied that that was not his problem. His job was to win basketball games—not be buddy-buddy with other coaches (especially those who did not have winning teams). "**And, I am winning games, right!!!!**," stated Youngman.

"Besides," coach Youngman said, "any of those coaches could have done what I have done. But no, all they do is complain and gripe about why they cannot compete with THE ROUNDBALLERS in terms of fundraising, gathering support, etc. And most of them are losers to boot."

Not much was officially said for the first three years when Coach Youngman's teams finished as sectional champs, one year actually winning the state championship. With winning came even stronger and more visible support from influential members of the community, as well as a few influential school board members. And with winning, coach Youngman was more frequently criticized (behind his back) by his ever-growing antagonists—within the community and, not infrequently, even within the school.

However, the fourth, fifth and six years were different. The basketball team's fortunes came upon hard times. The last year was a complete disaster with the team finishing last in the conference and several of the games being complete routs, much to the embarrassment and consternation of coach Youngman. As a result, there were ever-increased criticisms from fellow coaches, athletic administrators, parents, townspeople, and even some booster club members, to mention only a few groups. Those coaches who were stepped upon earlier by coach Youngman now saw their opportunity to have the table turned—and they jumped at the opportunity. They made life truly miserable for coach Youngman every opportunity they got.

QUESTIONS FOR DISCUSSION

1. Summarize the problems here? Who are the significant players in this scenario?
2. Enumerate some of the areas in which Coach Youngman might not have utilized his best judgment. Be specific and provide details.
3. Is coach Youngman being unreasonable in his desire to be so actively involved in promotions and fundraising for his basketball team at this level? Is he attempting to be what he should not be (and never should be) or is he using initiative as a high school coach?
4. Is coach Youngman acting appropriately in his effort to secure special treatment and support for his team from the booster club members and other influential people in the community?
5. Why are the other coaches at Westwood High upset? Do they have a right to be? Why or why not?
6. Has the athletic administration assumed a proper role throughout this entire scenario? What options are open to the athletic director in light of coach Youngman's activities and attitude *in the first three years* of the fundraising efforts?
7. What should have the athletic director done when coach Youngman was initially hired?
8. What should be the relationship between the athletic director and the boosters club as well as the coach and the booster club?
9. What options are open to the athletic director dur*ing the last three years of coach Youngman's activities and attitudes* when the team was not winning?
10. Why do you think coach Youngman was able to exhibit such great control over the members of THE ROUNDBALLERS? Was this a good thing or was it negative?
11. What are the three major purposes of the booster club at the secondary level?

12. Is it ever a good idea to handle (deposit) the money as coach Youngman has done? Elabprate.

13. What could Coach Youngman have done to endear himself more to the various constituencies, especially his coaching peers at his high school?

14. Describe Coach Youngman's level of interpersonal skills.

15. Now that the basketball team is experiencing tough times it seems that the fortunes of coach Youngman are changing, for the worse. How could coach Youngman have foreseen this? What could he have done in anticipation of such events?

16. What could or should coach Youngman do *now* to reduce some of the problems that are so obvious? How can the AD hel now?

17. Cite general principles in terms of public relations, promotions and fundraising in light of this scenario? Provide justification for doing things one way or another (coach Youngman's way or other ways). .

18. Comments . . .

RESPONSES FOR QUESTIONS FOR DISCUSSION

_____

_____

_____

_____

_____

_____

_____

_____

_____

_____

_____

CASE #48

The Case of the Potential Rival and a New Boss

Coach Barry Bulba was a very powerful figure in the community as well as in the school system. He was almost a legend to not a few people. To others, he was a spoiled brat, a bullying skunk, but one who was able to make powerful friends in the right places and who won basketball games—and championships.

Head girl's basketball coach Jessica Bree Brandey was new to the school system and to the school. Coach Brandey had had two year's prior coaching and teaching experience at another school and was moderately successful. Hence, she was hired in her present position as head varsity coach at Briarwood high school.

Figure 9.1:A bullying skunk

Almost immediately upon arriving at the new school, Jessica Bree found herself in a private conversation with coach Bulba, physically a big, imposing man. He went out of his way to show her the way "it is around here" in this athletically oriented basketball hotbed. He conveyed, in very frank terms, that boys' basketball was king around this town and he welcomed having someone who coached women's basketball to the school, someone who appreciated the pecking order and who would not make waves. "Youngster, if you listen to me, I will show you the ropes. Just don't rock the boat or else you will be the one who will be looking for the life preserver," he said.

It did not take long to convince coach Brandey that coach Bulba was indeed a very powerful person to be dealt with, both in school and in the community. It seemed to coach Brandey that it was up to her whether the relationship would be adversarial or not—and whether or not she would be willing to confront and/or antagonize coach Bulba.

Within the first four weeks of the school year, coach Brandey discovered that coach Bulba received preferential treatment in terms of workload (he taught less than anyone else in the high school); he received a disproportionate budget (in his favor); he has less preparation for classes that coach Brandey was assigned; he received better quality uniforms for his team and more frequently than other teams; he had first call on the video tape system; he had more assistants than coach Brandey did (he had two while she had none); he even seemed to have an inordinate amount of influence over the actions and decisions of the athletic director; he seemed to exert actual control over many members of the booster club and its officers; and, always had a winning team.

However, there was also a new principal who joined the school at the same time coach Brandey did. This principal, during the first few weeks of school, kept emphasizing, during the faculty initial orientation gathering, during the regular faculty meetings, and even in informal one-on-one sessions, that every single segment of the school program was equally important and there were to be no sacred cows.

The principal, Ms. Goodintentions, had never been a principal before. Rather, she had moved to her new position from a nearby town where she had served as an assistant principal for some five years. The book on Ms. Goodintentions was that she was fair and was a very, very strong willed person, once she had made up her mind.

QUESTIONS FOR DISCUSSION

1. Why did coach Bulba act the way he did when he shared his thoughts with coach Brandey? What was the agenda, i.e., what was he really trying to accomplish?
2. Is there anything sexist in coach Bulba's attitude and treatment of coach Brandey? Elaborate.
3. Explain the strengths and weaknesses of coach Bulba?
4. How much real power does coach Bulba possess and how did he get the power he does have?
5. Who are the other so-called role players (what about the athletic director?) in this drama? What should be their responsibilities, their roles and their possible actions as this drama unfolds? Provide details.
6. Why does the AD allow this situation to continue? Is this appropriate given the situation in that school and in light of the booster group and other supporters?
7. What should the athletic director have done when coach Brandey arrived as a new teacher and coach? Why?
8. What options are open to coach Brandey in face of her potential rival's attitude and actions?
9. What should be the immediate and long range goals of coach Brandey (in all areas)?
10. What do you suggest that coach Brandey should have done in response to coach Bulba's initial efforts at communication? Why?
11. What are the implications of various courses of action open to coach Brandey? Be specific.
12. What does coach Brandey have at risk in her current predicament?
13. What options are open to the new principal? Be specific and provide potential consequences for various courses of action.
14. Are the roles of a principal and an assistant principal significantly different?
15. Can coach Brandey count on the new principal or the athletic director to support her position, her requests? Can she take the new principal at her word? Elaborate on possible consequences.
16. What insight or suggestions might you share with coach Brandey in terms of dealing with the principal and the athletic director?

17. What are the dangers that the new principal faces?
18. What should the AD do now that the new principal has voiced her philosophy in terms of priorities within the school? Why?
19. What should ADs always do when a new superior (boss) comes on the scene? Elaborate and be specific.
20. What general principles come into play in this situation?
21. Comments . . .

RESPONSES FOR QUESTIONS FOR DISCUSSION

_____

_____

_____

_____

_____

_____

_____

_____

_____

_____

_____

_____

_____

Case #49

The Case of the Impending Marriage

Coach Harry Hustle was a very successful coach as well as a confirmed bachelor. He had a won/loss record over some 17 years of nearly 70%, including four trips to the state playoffs with one state championship. The high school, Southwest Suburban High, was located some 25 miles from the nearest major metropolitan center. He lives in a large six-bedroom house in the small farming community that he had owned for some 12 years. For the past ten years he has rented five of the bedrooms to bachelor teachers in his school system as well as teachers employed in a neighboring school system.

Modern Mary was a most successful businesswoman in her own right. In fact, she was known as one of the best business people (male or female) in the area, she was indeed a rising star in the business community. She had spent the past fifteen years developing quite a successful business as an owner of three very profitable boutique shops in the general metropolitan area. Just last year the Chamber of Commerce for the metropolitan center selected her as businesswoman of the year. She lived in an extremely exclusive apartment complex in downtown Metro. However, the closest she ever got to competitive athletics was when she turned on the television at night and heard the sports commentator provide the local scores.

During the summer months, some nine months away, Harry Hustle and Modern Mary were planning to be married. They had been dating for about six months after having been introduced by a mutual friend. Both indicated that they wanted a family and to live the life of the typical suburban couple, barbeque and all.

In attempting to explain to his future bride what life married to a successful, high school mentor, might be like, Harry tried to tell Modern Mary what his daily routine consisted of.

Modern Mary, also concerned about her lifestyle and Harry's expectations, explained to him what her daily commitments (and interests) were.

They both agreed that it was important to prepare each other and themselves for possible changes in their lifestyles once they tied the marriage knot. However, they also understood that it was much easier talking about mutual understandings and being flexible than it was to actually do it.

Coach Harry Hustle made an appointment with Big Jim Stewart, the athletic director, in an effort to get some advice from an older, more experienced and (hopefully) wiser athletic icon in terms of what Modern Mary should be told about being married to a coach. Coach Harry Hustle asked the AD, who had been a highly successful coach in his own right for decades as well as a happily married family man for 30 years, what he might share with Modern Mary and what he should do *as a married man and a coach.*

QUESTIONS FOR DISCUSSION

1. What might the AD recommend that coach Hustle share with his future bride that would make her fully aware of the commitments that coach Hustle has in his job as a coach? What might the AD share with the coach to bring the coach back to reality?

2. What might be some erroneous expectations of the future bride of coach Hustle without additional input from Harry (and additional insight from the AD)? Elaborate.

3. What role should the athletic director play and what can the athletic director do in terms of helping current and would-be spouses of coaches cope with being married to a coach?

4. Why is it important for an athletic director to have coaches, who are married, to have an understanding spouse? Be specific.

5. What might be some erroneous expectations of the coach without pertinent input from Mary? Elaborate.

6. What should Mary share with coach Hustle that would make him aware of her commitments as a successful entrepreneur and businesswoman?

7. What would be some of the dangers and pitfalls for a marriage involving *any* coach *from the perspective of the spouse of the coach*? Be specific and explain your rationale.

8. What would be some of the dangers and pitfalls for a marriage involving *any* coach *from the perspective of the coach*? Be specific and explain your rationale.

9. What type of understandings might both Mary and Harry establish with each other to provide for a smoother transition into marriage? What might be some potential trouble (rough) spots for both Harry and Mary?

10. What sacrifices might be necessary for both of them? Elaborate.

11. What would be a good arrangement and mutual understanding for both Harry Hustle and Modern Mary that might facilitate a happy marriage? Be very specific in your recommendations. That is, what can both the coach and the non-coach spouse do to help one another and to reinforce and support the other in this marriage?

12. Should Modern Mary visit with the AD to get a first hand insight into the life of a successful coach? Explain.

13. Should coach Hustle attempt to involve his wife in his career and interests? If so, how?

14. Should Mary to involve her husband in her career and interests? If so, how?

15. What general principles are applicable in this type of situation? Elaborate.

16. Comments . . .

RESPONSES FOR QUESTIONS FOR DISCUSSION

CASE #50

The Case of the Rent-a-Coach Problem

Westview High School was experiencing a challenging time insofar as its athletic program was concerned. The number of teachers who also wanted to coach had decreased significantly in recent years. It seemed to Jack Tillsome, principal, that as soon as a full time teacher/coach had earned tenure as a teacher that individual began to contemplate the possibilities of not coaching any longer. Perhaps the young teachers were initially willing to coach (as well as do anything else asked of them) when they were originally hired; however, it did not take long for many of them to tire of the challenges and problems presented as a result of coaching one or more sports.

Of course, there were exceptions. Many of the so-called flagship sports were coached by full time teachers who had coached for many years and who wished to continue to coach for many more.

But, for many, if not most, of the non-flagship sports the athletic director and the principal were having great difficulty in keeping full time teachers as coaches. As a result, the school found itself facing the ever-increasing prospect of hiring more part-time coaches. And, this fact was very disagreeable to the athletic director, Maury Fixbinger. "These so-called rent-a-coaches really don't have what it takes, in my opinion, to be quality coaches over the long haul," he complained to the principal.

"Nonsense, Maury," replied the principal. "There are advantages and disadvantages of having full time teachers who coach just as there are advantages and disadvantage of having part-time coaches as part of your staff. In my opinion, it usually depends upon the individual."

"That is easy for you to say, Jack. My problem is that we may be hiring teachers who are willing to coach and we may actually hire them because they are willing and minimally qualified to do both. But then these individuals opt out of their coaching obligations while retaining their full time teaching duties once they get that lifetime contract (tenure or continuing contract). That leaves me with the option of only hiring a part-time person to coach. We may end up with 90-95% of our 83 coaches as part-timers. We have to do something about this situation. Either we have to try to keep full time teachers as coaches or we have to get better-qualified part-timers to assume coaching positions. And that is the rub. It is hard to get qualified part-timers," bemoaned the athletic director.

The principal, kidded good naturally: "Listen, I know you have problems and challenges in your job. We all do. But Maury, if there were not such problems and challenges in your line of work we wouldn't need someone as good as you are with your skills and experiences to be our athletic director. You can resolve this situation so that our youngsters will have qualified coaches, whether they are full time employees or part-time employees of our school system."

QUESTIONS FOR DISCUSSION

1. What are the problems presented by this case? Summarize the essential elements.
2. Why would full time teachers (especially younger teachers) who coach be willing to give up their coaching responsibilities? Elaborate.
3. Do not part-time coaches have the same problems and challenges as full time teachers who coach? Provide a rationale for your position.
4. What are some of the major challenges and problems of full time teachers who coach? Of part-time coaches?
5. Why does the athletic director feel as he does towards part-time coaches? Why does he refer to them as rent-a-coaches?
6. Are the part-time coaches in your state required to satisfy specific requirements in order to become a coach? If so, what are these requirements?
7. Are you in agreement with the position of the principal in respect to the challenge of getting quality coaches? Why or why not?
8. What are the advantages of having full time teachers also coach one or more sports? Elaborate.
9. What are the disadvantages (from the perspectives of the athletic director and/or principal) of full time teachers who also coach?
10. What are the advantages of having individuals who only coach part-time involved as coaches in our schools? Elaborate.
11. What are the disadvantages of having individuals who only coach part-time involved as mentors in our schools? Elaborate.
12. Why is it difficult to hire highly qualified part-time coaches on the secondary level? On the collegiate level?
13. What are some possible solutions for the athletic director to pursue in terms of securing better-qualified and more experienced part-time coaches? Elaborate.
14. What might the athletic director do during the search and interview process for coaches, both part-time and fulltime?
15. What might the principal and/or athletic director do to convince full time teachers who coach to keep their coaching responsibilities? Be specific.
16. In your area or state, is there a greater problem securing women as coaches than men (as full time teachers/coaches and/or as part time coaches)? Why?
17. Should the athletic director be thankful for such problems and challenges in that that is why the school had hired someone of such quality and experience as Maury?
18. Specify general principles that are applicable to this particular scenario.
19. Comments . . .

RESPONSES FOR QUESTIONS FOR DISCUSSION

Case #51

The Case of the Partying Coach

Ms. Ginny Partygirl (unmarried) was a new coach at South Ridgemont high school. She was moving from a nearby school system where she had coached softball for ten years. She had a reputation as an excellent coach who had a very, very close relationship with her team members. She was also known as a frequenter of drinking establishments according to the "book" around town.

During the preseason tryout period, coach Ginny had been working the girls really hard. There were three girls in particular who were having a very difficult time, especially with the coach. They were continually in the doghouse because they had not performed up to expectations either in terms of attitude or in terms of performance. The result was that there were several confrontations between the three youngsters and the coach during the early tryout period. In fact, the coach and the three athletes had had several blow-ups, one episode taking place in front of the whole team.

On Friday night, during the weekend before the final day of the tryouts, the coach was invited to a party that some of the athletes were having at one of the girl's home. Unbeknownst to the coach, the parents of the youngster were to be away for the weekend, on a business trip, so the party was on. All of the girls who were trying out for the team were in attendance for the big party. Even coach Partygirl showed up for a time at the party. However, she did not stay all that long and left after an hour or so.

The following Monday, the final tryouts were held. On Tuesday afternoon, the coach put up the list of names of the students who had made the team on the bulletin board inside the locker room. The three athletes who had been giving the coach a hard time during tryouts were truly shocked and dismayed to learn that they did not make the team.

On Friday, these same three athletes (the three trouble makers) went to see the athletic director. During the meeting, the three girls expressed shock, dismay and disgust in sharing that there was drinking going on at the party held the previous Saturday, the party that the "coach probably helped plan and even attended." In addition, there was an accusation of improper activities of a sexual nature taking place during the party, a party at which attendance was actually *mandated* (implied) if a person really expected to make the team. Specifically, there were reports that skits were performed that had sexual implications or connotations.

All three players demanded that some action be taken against Coach Ginny Partygirl because:

1. The coach (Ginny) attended the party of the softball team where drinking was condoned (and the coach was probably drinking as well).

2. The coach probably organized the party (as part of an initiation rite).
3. The coach was involved with the sex skit while at the party.
4. The coach is a lesbian and has tried to pressure or recruit players to this lifestyle.
5. The coach was punishing the three girls by cutting them from the team because:

    A. The three girls left the softball team party early and were not considered as part of the in group—those who made the team
    B. The three girls did not drink alcohol at the party
    C. The three girls did not participate in the sexual skits and other reportedly offensive activity
    D. The three girls had several confrontations with the coach and publicly disagreed with some of the coach's decisions during the preseason practice period
    E. The coach has been dishonest in her relationship with the players, favoring some and treating others like @#$#%$#.

Several days later, the athletic director received several phone calls from the parents of the three athletes as well as a phone call from the editor of the town paper—inquiring as to the facts of the case and what actions, if any, the school was going to take regarding these allegations.

QUESTIONS FOR DISCUSSION

1. What are the central issues here? Be specific in your listing.
2. What are the actual *known facts* in this case?
3. Are all of the accusations of the athletes known to be accurate? Be specific.
4. What can the athletic director do to ascertain the facts? How might the athletic director go about finding out the actual facts in this case? With whom should the athletic director deal with in getting to the bottom of this case? Suggest a course of action.
5. What improper actions have taken place here, if any? Elaborate.
6. Should the head coach have gone to the party (if indeed she actually went to it)?
7. Should a coach ever go to a student party? Explain your answer.
8. Why are the three athletes coming forth with their complaints now? Might the accusations be true, false or half truths? Discuss.
9. What should the athletic director do now? Be specific in your recommended courses of action in terms of:
    A. The athletes
    B. Coach Ginny Partygirl
    C. The parents of the athletes
    D. The school principal and other central administrators
    E. The editor of the town paper
    F. The general public

G. The members of the booster club
H. The accusation that the coach is a lesbian
I. The accusation that the coach is pressuring members of the team to a specific lifestyle

10. How could this situation have been prevented? Who could have been involved in the prevention process? Elaborate.

11. Who is at fault in this scenario? Define responsibilities.

12. How could this situation be defused now?

13. How can the athletic director see that both justice and protection of one's rights be insured in terms of:
A. Coach Ginny Partygirl
B. The three athletes
C. The other members of the team
D. The team members in attendance at the alleged party

14. How can coaches prevent misperceptions being drawn by others?

15. What general principles are applicable in this situation?

16. Comments . . .

RESPONSES FOR QUESTIONS FOR DISCUSSION

_____

_____

_____

_____

_____

_____

_____

_____

_____

_____

CASE #52

The Case of the Unfair Treatment Charge

Ms. Theresa Urgent, a standout basketball athlete at McInhereny High School, made an appointment to see the athletic director in his office on a very urgent matter. At the meeting, Theresa shared several severe charges, in confidence, against one of the male coaches, Mr. Charlie Niceguy, the head basketball coach and teacher of history.

Specifically, the charges included:

1. Mr. Niceguy had kicked Theresa off of the basketball team because she had refused his improper advances.
2. Mr. Niceguy had often made comments about the way Theresa wore her clothes and complimented her about how pretty her clothes were.
3. Mr. Niceguy would sometimes touch Theresa's arm when he was talking to her—both in history class and in practice sessions.
4. Mr. Niceguy, during practices and early season games, patted her on her shoulder when she was going on the floor from the bench.
5. Mr. Niceguy offered her a ride home from practice several times during the season (until she got kicked off for breaking rules about drinking).
6. Mr. Niceguy often had her sit next to him on the bus on the way to and from athletic contests.
7. Mr. Niceguy often had meetings with Theresa in his office (with the door closed and no windows in the office), before, during and after school.
8. Mr. Niceguy had presented a gift for Theresa at the end of last season and gave it to her at the team's banquet.
9. Being kicked off the team will hurt her chances for a college scholarship.
10. She was humiliated by Mr. Niceguy by being told, "you are not the type of girl we want to be a member of this team" during the final disciplinary meeting held in his office.

QUESTIONS FOR DISCUSSION

1. What are the essential elements of this situation?
2. Why is Theresa coming to the athletic director now? Explore the possible options.
3. Why did Theresa get removed from the team? Do we really know why? What are the Implications?
4. In the eyes of the athletic director, what did Mr. Niceguy evidently do wrong (either through omission or commission), if anything? How do we know?

5. Could the coach be unjustly charged because the youngster was angry at being dismissed from the team? Discuss and explain you rationale.

6. Did Coach Niceguy use good judgement in his dealings with this student-athlete (as described above)? Why or why not? Be specific.

7. How could this whole situation have been prevented?

8. If the gift given to Theresa by the coach at the team banquet was the same as each athlete received, would that fact have any bearing on the situation?

9. If the reason Mr. Niceguy offered Theresa a ride was because the youngster's mother had failed to pick up her daughter and Theresa had no other way to get home, would this have any impact upon the situation? Explain.

10. What should the athletic director **say**, during the meeting with Theresa? Assume a role playing stance and state what you intend to share.

11. What might the athletic director have done **much earlier** to prevent or diffuse the situation?

12. What can the athletic director do to defuse the situation now? Elaborate.

13. With whom should the athletic director work with at this point? Why? What about the confidentiality factor?

14. What does the athletic director do (if anything) in terms of communicating with . . .?
    A. The head coach
    B. Other team members
    C. Parents of the athlete
    D. Parents of other athletes
    E. Other coaches
    F. Other teachers
    G. Principal
    H. News media
    I. Others

15. Can the rights of both the athlete and the coach be protected in this situation? How?

16. How does the athletic director insure that the truth is made known? Is this the primary goal? If not, what is?

17. If the parents of the athlete become involved (and how can they not be involved????), what are the implications?

18. When coach Niceguy finds out about the charges, what are his options? List the options and possible consequences of each.

19. From the perspective of the head coach, what principles are applicable in this type of situation?

20. From the perspective of the athletic director, what principles are applicable in this type of situation?

21. Comments . . .

RESPONSES FOR QUESTIONS FOR DISCUSSION

_____

_____

_____

_____

_____

_____

_____

_____

_____

_____

_____

_____

_____

_____

_____

_____

_____

_____

CASE #53

The Case of the Reluctant Complainer

Traci Concerned, a two-sport athlete, called the athletic director several times but the athletic director was out of town at a conference so Traci kept missing him. When asked by the secretary if someone else could help, she indicated, "very definitely not." *Initially, Traci would not leave a message, a number or even a last name.*

Finally, frustrated, she blurted out over the phone to the secretary that:

"Well, if he doesn't have time to see me maybe he will like to see it spread all out in the paper about the improper behavior of Coach Very Established."

The next day the athletic director returned from the athletic conference and was in the office when Traci Concerned called and was able to speak with her. Over the phone Traci made an appointment to come in and meet with the athletic director the very next day.

The next day, at the appointed time, Traci came to the meeting but indicated to the athletic director that she did not want to make any waves. She explained that she was just upset about what she viewed as improper behavior by Coach Very Established. Now, however, having thought of it further, she just did not want to become involved but did want to let the athletic director know what was going on. "Thus, everything I am telling you must be treated in the strictest confidence. I don't want Coach Very Established or anyone to know that we had this conversation," said Traci. She added: "Never use my name in any way or fashion, as I would just deny that I said anything to you."

It seems that coach Very Established, had been her coach for three years (she was a senior) and that lately the coach had been overly friendly. That is, the coach kept touching her on the arms and neck, saying things that might have a double meaning to some, dropping hints that could have inappropriate overtones, etc. In the last few months it had gotten worse, with more blatant references to going out together and going to the coach's apartment where they could review some old basketball video tapes.

Traci indicated that the straw that broke the camel's back was the other day when Coach Very Established came up behind her and actually fondled her from behind.

However, with graduation approaching and with her need for a good recommendation and further help from the coach (a well known and highly successful mentor in the state and even nationally) Traci indicated that she wanted things dropped. In fact, she emphasized once again:

"Please, never use my name in any of this. I just hope that someone in the future will be the Joan of Arc and will take the coach to task because of how he humiliates women. The worse part of it all is that the coach doesn't see such behavior as wrong. H always makes sure whatever happens is in complete privacy, always without witnesses."

QUESTIONS FOR DISCUSSION

1. What are the essential elements of this situation?

2. How should the athletic director proceed in light of the fact that Traci will not pursue matters publicly or officially?

3. What about promising confidentiality to Traci in this situation? Explain the pros and cons.

4. Does the fact that Traci has chosen not to press charges create difficulties for the athletic administration in terms of possible options to pursue? Explain.

5. In this situation in which the coach is being accused behind the coach's back, how can the coach's rights be protected? Will or should the coach even be apprised of the accusations in this particular case?

6. What should the athletic director do now in terms of:

    A. Traci Concerned—what would or should the athletic director do in terms of advising Traci as to her further options?

    B. Coach Very Established—when and how should the athletic director approach this coach?

    C. Other athletes—should other athletes be involved in any way? Explain.

    D. Central administrators—should any other administrators be made aware of the surreptitious charges against the coach? Explain.

    E. Other individuals? Specify whom and what actions the athletic director might pursue.

7. What would be the course(s) of action open to the athletic director if Traci wanted to actively and publicly pursue the matter against Coach Very Established?

8. How can the athletic director prevent further problems? What potential fallout might occur in the immediate and long range future?

9. How could the athletic director prevent this type of behavior from happening in the first place? In the future?

10. What general principles are applicable in this type of situation in terms of proper administrative and coaching (professional) conduct and the handling of unofficial and official complaints?

11. Comments . . .

RESPONSES FOR QUESTIONS FOR DISCUSSION

_____

_____

_____

CASE #54

The Case of the Negative Atmosphere

Jackie Mansky was getting more than a little embarrassed of the atmosphere that she found in the faculty lounge. Maybe it was always there and she was just more sensitive to it in recent weeks. But today was really bad. Today, coach Ted Speckalski did it again—did it with the new coach of softball (Jean). Today, coach Speckalski really put Jean Muzic down, like a ton of bricks, in front of everyone in the lounge.

It was shortly after Jean Muzic arrived in the crowded faculty lounge that coach Speckalski started on his daily routine of cracking rather insensitive, offensive jokes and telling stories, which usually revolved around the supposedly inadequacies of women and which almost always included references to the female anatomy. Today he was again very blunt, so very cruel, in his remarks about Jean and the young girls on her high school team. He had the faculty members (both men and women) in stitches. Finally, Jean left the room almost in tears—angry and frightened at the same time.

Later that afternoon, Jean confided in Jackie that she really felt behind the proverbial eight ball in that she was offended by the remarks by this bully and was equally afraid and disgusted that no one else in the room (or on the faculty—teacher or administrator) would speak out against this constant string of insults. Jean indicated that she felt threatened in that she feared retaliation from coach Speckalski who was also her department chair (History) and who evidently had the confidence of both the athletic director and the principal.

In short, Jean indicated that she was not going to go to the faculty lounge in the future even though this would perhaps cause her to reduce her networking with her professional colleagues. She just couldn't continue to be the blunt of the jokes and/or comments. "The level of the conversation is always in the gutter and no one seems to give a hoot," cried Jean.

Jackie revealed that coach Speckalski had just always been that way and that no one had ever stood up and said that anything was wrong. After all, he was just one of the good old boys and if anyone wanted to be accepted as one of the group then one had better accept it. Jackie counseled Jean to just bear up and take it like we have always taken it. "It is the only way to survive in this school, to get your pay raises and other perks which these jerks have control of," said Jackie. She continued: ". . . those of us who have taught here for any length of time have survived haven't we? All you have to do is to mind your own business and play the game and before long coach Speckalski will find someone else to be the blunt of his attention. You are just giving him fuel for his action by reacting as you are."

Jean replied that she did not know what to do and that Jackie wasn't much help. Jean indicated that she was looking for concrete suggestions on how to resolve the dilemma—not suggestions on how to continue to endure the threatening experience that was beginning to affect her work at school as well as her life at home. Jean finally decided that she would . . .

QUESTIONS FOR DISCUSSION

1.   What are the essential elements of this situation?
2.   What is wrong here? Be specific.
3.   Who is at fault here? Be specific and explain your position.
4.   Summarize what constitutes sexual harassment in schools and athletic programs.
5.   If the actions of coach Speckalski are offensive, who else is to blame (if anyone) beside himself?
6.   Why are there differences of opinion in this situation between Jackie and Jean?
7.   Why was Jackie Mansky of such little help? What would you, if you were Jackie Mansky, do in response to Jean's plea for help? Be specific and provide a rationale for your position.
8.   Why is Jackie acting as she is? Elaborate.
9.   Could this situation have been prevented? How? Be specific.
10. Who shares responsibility for what takes place in the faculty lounge? Why?
11. What responsibilities do the other teachers/coaches and athletic administrators have in this situation? What about the educational process for staff?
12. What might Jean do in this scenario? In terms of herself? In terms of Jackie Mansky? In terms of coach Speckalski? In terms of others? What are Jean's options?
13. In each of the options asked for in # 12 above:
     A.   What might be the negative consequences of actions taken by Jean?
     B.   What might be some possible positive results of actions taken by Jean?
14. What role can the following people play in this situation (in terms of prevention and in terms of corrective actions)?
     A.   The athletic director
     B.   The Principal
     C.   The other teachers and coaches in the faculty lounge
     D.   Jackie Mansky
15. Why has coach Speckalski acted as he has?
16. Is the description of coach Speckalski as stated by Jackie Mansky accurate? Elaborate.
17. What has to be done to make coach Speckalski aware of the consequences of his actions?
18. Why hasn't coach Speckalski stopped his offensive behavior?
19. What general principles are appropriate in this type of situation in terms of proper administrative and professional conduct by all who are involved?
20. What steps are open to Jean if she wanted to bring specific charges against the head coach? How should or could she proceed?
21. Comments . . .

RESPONSES FOR QUESTIONS FOR DISCUSSION

Case #55

The Case of an AD Administering by Walking Around (ABWA)

Mathew McDonalds, the newly appointed athletic director at the Division II university was determined that he was not going to fall into the trap of his predecessor. For almost seven years he endured a boss who, as athletic director, exemplified all that was wrong with an athletic administrator. For this period of time he did everything he could as the assistant athletic director to both help the athletes enjoy their athletic experiences and to help the woefully inadequate athletic director survive in his job as athletic manager of the fairly good size athletic program (26 teams in all).

He was sure that he would not be in the position that he was today (that is, appointed as the new AD) if the powers to be (both on and off campus) did not recognize his good faith efforts to do all that was in his power to salvage the athletic department from what had gradually become an untenable situation. If only the previous athletic director had listened to him and had wanted to change from the bad habits that he fell into—perhaps the firing would not have been necessary.

Anyway, today he was contemplating what he should do in his initial month on the job as the new athletic director. "I must be very careful to make my own distinctive mark on the athletic program as the new AD," he mused. "I must be careful not to follow in the exact footprints of my predecessor. In fact, I might consider doing the exact opposite of what he did just so that people will take notice that I am different than my prior boss, the person who was fired after having been on staff for some 30 years"

One of the complaints that athletes and coaches had voiced about the previous AD was that he was never very visible, either at practice or at games, especially away games. Complaints were also registered that the previous AD often hid in his office whenever controversial situations came up in the hope that problems would simply go away. And, the previous AD never seemed to know (or even care) what was going on in his own department since he was desk bound so often (and for long periods of time).

"I had better demonstrate a distinctive style of administering this department and managing the resources available to me as athletic director," concluded Mathew. "Perhaps I had better consider following that old acronym (ABWA) that my university professor use to always talk about. At least that way people will be able to see a very real and visible difference between my predecessor and myself. I will begin next week to *administer by walking around* on a consistent basis. I will be sure and be seen by all of my constituents, I want to be visible", he vowed.

QUESTIONS FOR DISCUSSION

1. What are the major problematic elements in this situation?
2. How important is it for any new athletic director to be one's own person when accepting the position of an athletic director (manager/administrator)? Why?
3. Is it a good idea to attempt to deliberately attempt to differentiate oneself from one's predecessor if the prior administrator was judged to be incompetent or less than competent? Justify your stance.
4. How appropriate was it that Mathew attempted to help out his prior boss during his tenure as the assistant athletic director? Explain in full. Ramifications?
5. What might Mathew have done (*be specific*) in an effort to help his former boss overcome the weaknesses that evidently led to his boss's eventual dismissal?
6. Do you think that Mathew was able to learn a lot about being a successful athletic director by being observant of the successes *and* failures of his previous boss? Explain your position *and provide examples*.
7. Why would any athletic director operate by hiding in his office on a frequent basis?
8. Speculate as to why the previous athletic director became less than competent the longer he stayed in his job as athletic director?
9. Why did Mathew get promoted to the top job of athletic director when he had served for so long as the previous athletic director's (who was judged less than competent at the end) right hand man within the department?
10. Explain what you interpret the acronym *ABWA* means in terms of describing the behavior of an athletic director on a college or university level? Would it involve anything significantly different if the situation involved a high school athletic program? Explain.
11. What are the benefits or advantages of following the *ABWA* philosophy in terms of student-athletes, parents, and coaches? Summarize these benefits and advantages.
12. Provide **specific examples** of what you might suggest that Mathew do in order to follow the tenets of the *ABWA* philosophy? Include the time elements and schedule plans that Mathew might want to follow in light of the *ABWA* philosophy.
13. What are some general administrative principles or guidelines that are applicable in this situation?
14. Comments . . .

RESPONSES FOR QUESTIONS FOR DISCUSSION

_____

_____

_____

CASE #56

The Case of the Secret Budget Process

Jacob Ellisen had developed a reputation of a most secretive athletic administrator in the school's history since his arrival several years ago. In fact, his nickname among the staff was Mr. Secret.

It seems that the whole budget process was a great big secret. Practically no one knew what was going on with the budget besides Jacob and his immediate supervisor, James Frank. The coaches sure didn't know what was going on with the total budget. They felt lucky that they even knew what their own budget was for the current year. They certainly were never told what the other sports' budgets were and they were not allowed to see what the total budget figures were either.

When it was time for the budget to be put together, the AD generally asked each coach what was needed for that particular sport but that was the last each coach heard of in terms of the budget until the athletic director sent a note back to each coach with the amount of that coach's next year's budget. And, invariably, the budget increase, if there was any increase, was something like 2% to 3%, period. There was never any possibility of appeal or special consideration.

And, if the coaches were in the dark with the budget process and the final budget figures for all of the teams, other people (teachers, parents, boosters, athletes, etc.) had no idea at all what was happening with the budget. It was all very secretive. "It is nobody's business what the sports' budget is. It is no one's business how the budget is put together. And it is sure no one's business how the money is spent. That is why they hired me, to be the decision maker in this matter. As long as I satisfy my boss (James Frank), I am doing my job and doing it quite well, I might add. Mr. Frank signs off on my budget request and the higher administrators and the board always seems to approve my budget requests. What more could we all ask for?" responded the athletic director when questioned by one of the parents as to why the budget and the budget process was not more in the open.

One of the new coaches, Michelle Younster, was surprised when she arrived on campus with all of the secrecy surrounding the budget. At her previous school the athletic director had demonstrated the opposite philosophy towards the whole budgetary process. At that school, every coach, every athlete, every student in the school, everyone who wanted to see the actual budget figures for each sport as well as for the overall athletic program—could simply request permission to view the documents and they would be able to do so. Even the budget process by which the individual budget of each sport was determined was diametrically opposed to Mr. Secret's practice.

As time passed, Mr. Secret's budget philosophy came under greater scrutiny and received more and more criticism from those who were not allowed to have access to the process and the completed document (and that involved a large number of people). Several coaches were openly upset that they could not have access to the budget figures for all sports, so they might compare what they had been budgeted in light of what other teams had been allocated. Several of the coaches of women sports were especially eager to be able to compare the individual team budgets. Additionally, a student government leader who happened to be an outstanding athlete on the field hockey team also joined the fracas by officially requesting, in writing, that the students have access to the athletic budget, under the so-called Sunshine Laws of the state.

Things were getting hectic for Mr. Secret. The pressure was building up. Then one day the superintendent called Mr. Secret into his office and asked: "What is this that I hear about the budget controversy over in your department? You know how I hate to have problems or controversy. Now what is going on here? I want this potential blow-up resolved before it becomes a big scandal"

QUESTIONS FOR DISCUSSION

1. What are the basic areas of contention in this situation?
2. Why does Mr. Secret conduct the budget as outlined above? Elaborate.
3. What are the advantages and disadvantages of the way Mr. Secret works with the budget? Is this a common method or an acceptable method of working with an athletic budget with some successful athletic directors?
4. What are the possible reactions of the coaches when they become aware of the budgetary facts to which they had previously been forbidden to view? Provide several scenarios.
5. If the athletic director allowed all coaches to view other coach's budgets could this not create jealousy and serious resentment among the coaches? Explore this possibility.
6. What do other people (parents, athletes, students, boosters) think when they realize how secretive the budgetary process really is? Do they normally even care? Do people care because of the secretive nature of the process? Do people care about the actual budget allocation to various sports? Elaborate.
7. Should Mr. Secret have initiated the budget process as he has in this situation? Would it make a difference if the school were a college rather than a high school? Why or why not?
8. Why would the coaches of the women's sports be interested in comparing their budgets with the budgets of men's sports?
9. Traditionally, what male and female sports could be considered very similar in terms of budgetary allocations and needs?
10. Is it appropriate for Michelle Younster to feel uncomfortable enough with Mr. Secret's budget operation to attempt to have it changed? Explain.
11. How would a coach attempt to change the budgetary process?
12. At Michelle Younster's former school, why was the budgetary process almost the opposite of Mr. Secret's?

13. How can two so entirely different methods of handling the budgetary process be successful at different schools?

14. What are the advantages and disadvantages of having a so-called open budgetary process? Elaborate.

15. What are the advantages and disadvantages of having a so-called closed budgetary process? Elaborate.

16. Does the individual situation (the specific school and history associated with the school) have a great deal to do with how the budget process is approached? Explain.

17. Which is better (from *your* perspective as an athletic director) to have, a closed or open budgetary process? Compare both systems and the possible consequences.

18. What are some suggestions that you might make to the athletic director in terms of better steps that might prove to be more beneficial in the whole budgetary process? Include in your suggestions steps that might be used in the creation of the individual sport budgets, the approval process of each sport budget, and how special needs might be met.

19. Why is the superintendent involved now? What might the athletic director say in response to the superintendent's inquiry?

20. What general principles are applicable for the athletic director in this situation?

21. Comments . . .

RESPONSES FOR QUESTIONS FOR DISCUSSION

_____

_____

_____

_____

_____

_____

_____

_____

CASE #57

The Case of the Missing Equipment and Supplies

The athletic director at Beaverton High School, Joanne Wandsen, was upset. No, she was angry, really angry. Here she was, in a budget crunch for the second year in a row and now she finds out that Jessie Murphy, the head ice hockey coach, is missing a significant amount of equipment and supplies. And this after the big talk she made at last fall's coaches' meeting about how everyone was going to have to watch the pennies and be very careful about what resources are available to the athletic program.

If the report she has in her hands is accurate, the hockey team was missing almost $5,000 worth of items since the start of the current season. How can that much be lost, misplaced or stolen in one season? Now that the season has ended last week she decided that she had to talk with coach Jessie Murphy.

During the meeting between Joanne and Jessie, the AD asked if the report of the missing items was accurate as she handed the sheet of paper to him. Looking it over he mused and said: "Well, you know, before last year each of us coaches kept tabs

Elite athletes deserve the best in equipment and supplies. [Courtesy of Kansas State Athletics]

on our own inventory. You were the one who took that responsibility out of our hands. Now, your new equipment manager has the responsibility for the inventory. Ask him."

"Coach Murphy, I am not talking about the inventory per se. I am talking about your responsibility, as head coach, to maintain and safeguard your team's equipment and supplies. You know very well why the change in policy was made regarding who has responsibility for taking inventory for each sport. I want to know why your team is missing equipment!"

"I don't know. How would I know? I am suppose to coach, not be a bean counter. What do you want from me?"

"Coach, let me tell you something. You are responsible for the missing items. Every head coach is responsible for the items that are used for their sport. Now, what I want you to do is this. Review how you, your assistants and your athletes handle and treat the equipment. I would like to know how the missing jerseys, helmets, sticks and other items might have walked since the beginning of the season. I would also like to know how you plan on recouping the missing items or getting the money to replace them. You know, I suspect that the items might be in your players' little hot hands."

"What do you want me to do, keep tabs on each little item of equipment and supplies that the kids get?" asked the coach. "You know, we have to trust our athletes when we give them stuff. Besides, I sure don't have time to be an equipment manager myself in addition to all of my coaching and teaching responsibilities. There are not enough hours in the day for that," he concluded as he just sat there like a bump on the log.

QUESTIONS FOR DISCUSSION

1. Does the AD have a right to be upset at coach Murphy? Why or why not?
2. What are the typical responsibilities of a high school head coach (in the eyes of the athletic director) in terms of safeguarding equipment and supplies distributed to athletes, and the return of same? At the college or university level?
3. What can be done with athletes prior to the season starting, during the season, and after the season has concluded, that will aid in retrieving loaned equipment and supplies? Be specific in recommending policies, procedures and practices.
4. Why do you suppose the change was made regarding who was to take the annual inventory? Elaborate. What are the advantages of having an equipment manager in charge of the equipment and supplies in terms of the inventory and checking in of purchased items?
5. Whose fault is it that the items are missing? Is it the individual athletes (if indeed the athletes have the missing items)? Is it the coach? Is it the equipment manager? Is the AD correct in her statement or assumption in this regard?
6. Should athletes be held responsible for the equipment and supplies issued to them? Why or why not? If they should, what does this mean in reality?
7. Should the coach have the primary responsibility for seeing to it that the *athletes return* items of equipment that they checked out back to the school?
8. What steps might coach Murphy take now to try and track down the missing items? Be specific.
9. How might the missing items be missing? Elaborate.
10. Can athletes be trusted with athletic equipment? Can anyone be trusted when it comes to athletic equipment and supplies? Why or why not?
11. What steps might this coach, or any coach, have taken in terms of keeping track of jerseys, pants and helmets and insure that all items issued to athletes are returned in suitable condition? Be specific.
12. Should the athletes be required to pay for their lost items? Elaborate. Why or why not?
13. Should the head coaches be held responsible for the equipment and supplies used in their sports? Why or why not? What does this responsibility mean in real life?
14. Should the head coaches be made to pay for missing items not returned by individual athletes? Why or Why not? If so, under what conditions?
15. Should the athletic director be held responsible for the missing items? Why or why not?
16. If the items have to be replaced, how is the athletic director going to get the money for such expenditures? Speculate. To whom does the athletic director have to report to in

terms of justifying the next year's ice hockey expenditures? What could the AD say to justify spending so much money on items that were lost, missing or stolen?

17. Why is an accurate inventory so essential to the successful operation of an athletic department? Elaborate.

18. What general principles are appropriate to this situation?

19. Comments . . .

RESPONSES FOR QUESTIONS FOR DISCUSSION

_____

_____

_____

_____

_____

_____

_____

_____

_____

_____

_____

_____

_____

_____

CASE #58

The Case of the Sneaky title IX Compliance

The president of the university, Carmen Shepherd, had just concluded the meeting with her athletic director, Joshua Janacanna, and felt pretty good about what she had set into motion. She had always been in favor of equal opportunities for all people and especially when it came to women's opportunities in this society. However, she also was keenly aware that the AD was correct in that football was somewhat of a sacred cow on this campus and brought in a lot of money from alumni and other fans. In fact, she owed her job to the two biggest football boosters at the university who went to bat for her as an individual who understood the importance of football for this university as well as the need for appropriate opportunities for women and men in sports. The fact that she, as president, was expected to accomplish both, i.e., insure that football had all of the resources that the coaches (and boosters) deemed necessary **and** insure that the institution met the requirements of Title IX was not lost on the president. That is why she smiled as the AD left her office.

The president had suggested to the AD that perhaps a sport might be added to the athletic offerings in an effort to counterbalance the unevenness of male versus female athletes that currently existed. The fact that football had some 120 athletes and wrestling had another 20 athletes (so-called *participatory slots*) really hurt the proportionality test. She had emphasized to the AD that if the university could find (and add) a woman's sport(s) that had 140 female athletes, this would help balance the male/female ratio that was one of the three key points in meeting the requirements of Title IX, according to the Office of Civil Rights (OCR). She hoped that the AD would interpret her suggestions correctly and come back with the recommendation that she wanted. After all, she wanted the school to be in legal compliance with Title IX and also wanted to insure that football was not touched in a negative way.

When Joshua got back to his office, he called his administrative staff and several coaches together and shared the essence of his meeting with the president. Together, they all worked hard in several brainstorming sessions on the subject of how to solve the Title IX challenge, especially the imbalance in the number of male and female athletes on various teams. The result of this and several other subsequent meetings was the recommendation that rowing be added as a woman's sport, with some 140 slots for athletes. "The addition of rowing will – in one broad stroke – solve our Title IX problem once and for all," stated the athletic director. He added: "I knew immediately what the president was hinting at when she suggested we find a team or teams that had the potential for a very, very large team roster. Well, we found one, with rowing."

One of the women (Jeannie Bumgarden, volleyball coach) in the group asked: "Yea, but aren't we just stretching the rules in reality? Are we really obeying the intent of Title IX with this 140-roster team? Why, what team has 140 athletes? Aren't we just throwing out (adding) the 140 *participatory slots* so that we can say we have equal slots (participation) for men and women? This move may meet the legal interpretation of the law but, in my mind, such a move doesn't do anything for the intent of the legislation. To be blunt, this is just a sham."

"No, this is a legitimate effort to add a sport and a large number of female athletes to the overall scheme of things. The fact that our roster involves 140 females is just an added bonus. Besides, who says we can't add a team with a large roster. Rowing has to be attractive for us because it involves both fall and spring competitive seasons coupled with winter months of continuous conditioning. In fact, if we are smart, we could carry open-weight rowers and light-weight rowers (less that 130 pounds). We could also further break down the 140 athletes into varsity and non-varsity teams. In this way we can meet the needs of a very large group of female athletes and would-be or wannabe athletes (at a reasonable cost in terms of people power and money) while we also solve the potential problem of appropriate participatory slots (Title IX)," chimed in the football coach.

"Yea, remember a few years back when the University of Wisconsin (Madison) initiated rowing and immediately solved their Title IX problems," reminded the women's basketball coach, Carol Simmons. (Steinbach, 2002).

"Ok," stated the athletic director, "lets get with it and work out the details so that I can get back to the president with the recommendation that she really wanted in the first place. We should be able to satisfy everyone with this plan of attack."

REFERENCES

Steinbach, P. (2002). Open Oar Policy, *Athletic Business*, 26(11), pp. 32, 34.

QUESTIONS FOR DISCUSSION

1. Summarize the salient elements of this case.
2. Is it common for presidents of colleges and universities to feel such pressure from outside groups or forces as Dr. Shepherd felt in this situation? Elaborate.
3. Why does the president feel so strongly that football must be successful on this campus?
4. Is Dr. Shepherd being honest in her approach to solving the Title IX potential problem? Explain your position.
5. What are the three prongs or methods by which institutions can show that they are in compliance with Title IX?
6. In your opinion, did the athletic director approach his challenge appropriately when he returned to his office? Why or why not?
7. Is the addition of a single women's sport that involves such a large number of athletes (140) legitimate in terms of meeting the proportionality test of Title IX? Explain your rationale.

8. Why can't schools just add more roster slots (participatory slots) to a women's sport (for example, increase women's basketball to 55 instead of the normal 12-16 athletes) in an effort to increase slots for women?

9. What makes this situation in which 140 slots are added for rowing more acceptable than merely increasing the basketball roster for women from 15 or 16 to 55? Be specific.

10. Is the president, as well as the athletic director, acting in good faith (following the intent as well as the letter of the law of Title IX) by proceeding as described above? Justify your position.

11. Are the volleyball coach's statements accurate or is she off base? Elaborate.

12. What general administrative principles or managerial guidelines are applicable here?

13. Comments . .

RESPONSES FOR QUESTIONS FOR DISCUSSION

CASE #59

The Case of the Inefficient Concession Stand

The athletic director, Jerome Sullivan, thought that he had the solution of the problem of what to do with the concession stand. In the past, the concession stand at the college's athletic contests had been anything but a success. In fact, in the decade before Jerome took his new job (just 25 days ago), the concession stand had been operated by student groups who submitted bids to run the concession operations at various events; by the managers of the food service operation; by the athletic department itself; and, during one year by an outside firm (really one guy who ran the hot dog stand in town and submitted a bid to run the concessions for the athletic department and to share in the net proceeds).

However, none of these past efforts had positive results. In fact, they had all been judged as failures by almost anyone who you would ask. Jerome had to figure out what to do with the whole concession operation, quickly, and it had better work. He knew he was under the microscope from above and that his actions in this endeavor would be carefully scrutinized, as would his chances of remaining as athletic director.

After consulting with his staff, he took the suggestion of one of his assistants who had been on staff for a decade and who was also a coach of a flagship sport. The suggestion had this coach assuming total responsibility for the concession operations during the year and would be given one-third release time from his other athletic administrative duties. Jerome told the coach: "Donald, I trust you to make a sizeable profit for the year or you need to tell me immediately so that I can change things and go in a different direction. Just make us some money and don't cause us any problems, " the AD concluded.

Through the year the athletic director periodically received a short written note or a phone call from Don who reassured Jerome that the concession operation was a big success. However, when the end of the school year came and the AD glanced at the final financial report for the fall, winter and spring seasons—he was horrified. He realized that he had made a critical error and now had an even bigger problem.

It became abundantly clear that what had happen was merely a shell game. Specifically, the overall net profit under Donald was in the neighborhood of $15,000, a fact that Don was extremely proud. However, Don's attitude was quickly one of horror when he was told by the athletic director that this profit was all smoke and mirrors because Don had forgotten to add in the one-third release time that he had received for assuming responsibility for the entire concession operation. Since Don's annual salary was some $60,000, a one-third release time meant that the department allocated (expended) some $20,000 to give the coach time to oversee the concession operations and this $20,000 just wiped out the supposed profit of $15,000 and, in point of fact, placed the concessions operations in a deficit position to the tune of around $5,000.

QUESTIONS FOR DISCUSSION

1. Provide a summary statement outlining the problems in this scenario as well as the resultant challenges facing the athletic director.

2. What other decisions might the athletic director had made when considering what to do with the concession operations?

3. What are the typical arrangements that outside vendors make with an athletic department in attempting to secure the rights to operate concessions?

4. What are the advantages and disadvantages of allowing student groups or athletic teams to oversee the concession operations for specific teams? Be specific.

5. What are the athletic department's general objectives with any concession operation?

6. What mistake(s) or omissions did the athletic director make early on? Be specific.

7. Why did the AD accept the recommendation from one of his assistants? What general principal does this act violate in terms of administrative behavior? Explain.

8. As the year went on, were the periodic reports that the AD received adequate? Should the AD have accepted this reports as he did? If not, what should Jerome have done and/ or required? And why?

9. What did Jerome and Don forget when thinking in terms of net profit?

10. When Don was given one-third release time from his other administrative duties, what does this mean in actuality?

11. This one-third release time creates a hardship on the athletic department in that the department must then do what?

12. What should the athletic director do now when confronted with the reality of the situation?

13. What are some general principles and concepts that are applicable in this type of situation from the perspective of the athletic department and the athletic administration?

14. Comments . . .

RESPONSES FOR QUESTIONS FOR DISCUSSION

_____

_____

_____

_____

_____

Case #60

The Case of Too Many Fundraising Projects

Dr. Newton Quarterman, the new president of the institution, was very explicit in his discussion with the athletic director, Mary Young Turtle, when he said: "Although I know you were hired by my predecessor and he might not have had the same philosophy as I do, but that is neither here nor there. The point is, I am the president and I expect you to raise money for the athletic department. If there is any department or unit on campus that can generate money it seems to me that it is intercollegiate athletics. And, as the leader of athletics, I am going to hold you accountable to do just that, to raise some sizeable bucks. I don't really care how you go about doing it, just do it and don't embarrass yourself, the athletic department, the institution, or me."

Game promotions and enthusiastic fan support can lend much to the athletic experience
[Courtesy of Washington State University]

After getting back to his office, Mary Young called her staff together to discuss the challenges presented by the president's edict. After much discussion and sharing of ideas, it was decided (mainly because the AD wanted to be sure that sufficient monies would be raised and that he wanted no stone to be left unturned) that the department would initiate some 17 different fundraising projects or efforts during the next twelve months. Five of these would be in the fall semester. Another five would be kicked off in the spring while seven would be engaged in during the winter months. Some of the fundraisers would hopefully generate some big bucks while others were more modest in their reach.

As the year went on problems began to emerge. The paid staff of the athletic department (administrators and coaches alike) was being stretched to their limits in terms of time and energy. They were also being burned out due to the extra work that all of the fundraising projects required. If that was not enough, some of the projects were running into trouble, embarrassing trouble, some said because people were trying to do too much in too short a period of time with too few resources. Even some of the youngsters, students and student-athletes, were having trouble being involved in so many different activities, including a number of different fundraising projects.

And, to top it off, the AD and the president both received complaints (in person as well as via phone) from people in the community indicating that they were more than a little annoyed by the fact that every time they seemed to turn around they were being badgered by someone from the college/athletic department/athletic teams seeking money. Some of the local business owners were especially perturbed with the number of calls or contacts that they received from representatives of the athletic arena.

Finally, in March, the organizers of the spring fundraisers indicated that they were having just an impossible time attempting to solicit volunteers from the community to help with the new fundraising projects, as most of the people being approached had already been involved in other projects for the department earlier in the year. As a result, they were all worn out and unable or unwilling to volunteer their time, services and expertise to the athletic department again.

QUESTIONS FOR DISCUSSION

1. Summarize this scenario and the challenges presented.
2. Is it fair for the president to change the rules in terms of what is expected of the athletic director?
3. Is it reasonable to expect the athletic department to raise significant monies when it has not done so in the past? Elaborate.
4. What is the major fundraising principal that is being violated in this scenario?
5. What should the athletic director have done when faced with the directive of the president? Be specific.
6. What is the minimum percentage of needed funding that each fundraising project should generate for the department within a given calendar year? That is, each fundraising project must generate what percentage (_____%) of the total amount needed to be raised annually through outside fundraising efforts? Explain your rationale.
7. How many major fundraising projects should the athletic department undertake in a calendar year, that is, what is the maximum number?
8. What steps might have the athletic director taken to prevent the problems with:
   A. Paid staff being over worked
   B. The students and student-athletes not having time to do what was expected
   C. Volunteers being burned out
   D. Community people complaining to the AD and president about being hit by solicitors
9. What is the solution to his situation?
10. What might the athletic director now say to the president in response to the community people and business owners complaining about being bothered by solicitors?
11. What general principals are applicable in this type of situation from the vantage point of the athletic administration?
12. Comments . . .

RESPONSES FOR QUESTIONS FOR DISCUSSION

Problems with Policies, Practices, Procedures, Priorities and Philosophies

CHAPTER OBJECTIVES

After reading this chapter you will be able to:

- Be familiar with various problems relating to athletic policies, practices, procedures, priorities and philosophies
- Outline a suitable *pass to play* policy for a school athletic program
- Establish a *vacation policy* (acceptable excuses) for spring sport participation
- Be familiar with pros and cons relative to establishing travel squad limitations
- Provide a list of potential sources for job vacancies for individuals who would apply for administrative positions
- Assess appropriate coaching actions and practices both on and off the proverbial athletic field
- Write a complete *pay to pay* policy at a high school and explain the pros and cons of such a policy
- Summarize the essential elements of an evaluation system for coaches at the secondary as well as collegiate levels

Fundraising projects can be an annual event at many athletic program [Courtesy of James Frank]

- Describe the benefits and difficulties of allowing full time teachers to bump part-time coaches
- Comprehend the ethical dilemma facing athletic directors when coaches accept free shoes under a variety of different circumstances
- List the components of a policy for crowd control at athletic events
- Summarize the table of contents for a high school departmental handbook

- Recommend who should accompany high school team members on the team bus to an away contests other than the players, coaches and administrators
- Outline an athletic department's plan advantages and disadvantages for having one or more athletic banquets for the athletic teams as well as a policy for individual athletic awards (criteria for letter awards, etc.) for individual teams
- Differentiate between the various types of corporate sponsorships and enumerate the benefits of each

CASE

61. The case of having to pass to play
62. The case o the problematic vacation policies
63. The case of the questionable travel squad
64. The case of applying for an administrative position
65. The case involving the coach's little kids
66. The case of having to pay to play
67. The case of accountability in evaluating coaches
68. The case of the awards ceremony
69. The case of the part-time coach being bumped by a full time teacher
70. The case of the athletic shoe purchases
71. The case of inadequate crowd control
72. The case of the problematic departmental handbook
73. The case of the request for the cheerleading squad to accompany the basketball team on the team bus
74. The case of planning for the athletic banquet
75. The case of crating corporate sponsorships

CASE #61

The Case of Having to Pass to Play

Abraham Lincoln High School was having a problem, a problem that was both an internal concern as well as a public relations nightmare. It seems that for the past three years the average GPA of the student athletes was well below (embarrassingly low) the average of the general student body. In addition, a sizeable proportion of the athletes, at all grades, did not have a **C** average during the semesters in which they competed.

As if the existence of such low grades by athletes was not enough, the local newspaper, that was read statewide, just ran a series of articles on abuses that frequently occur within the athletic arena and brought up the question of whether or not the student athletes at Abraham Lincoln High School were successful in the classroom as they have been on the proverbial playing fields. The series in the newspaper brought to the surface a renewed concern about academic progress and academic success by student athletes.

In a staff meeting of all athletic staff, called by the school principal and the athletic director, the general topic of student-athletes' academic progress was the central topic. "As you all can see from the data I have passed out, Abraham Lincoln High School's past record of athletes' academic achievement leaves much to be desired. In fact, it is both embarrassing and atrocious. Needless to say, something must be done. Something will be done. This initial meeting is being held to initiate a dialogue among us as to what might be done, what can be done and what will be done in terms of helping our student athletes, both as students as well as athletes," began Mr. Henry Grades, principal.

The athletic director, George Gaines, then added: "Henry, I think that I can speak for all of our athletic staff when I say that we all agree that something must be done in terms of our athletes' academic achievements. We must do a better job of seeing to it that the kids do well in the classroom for the benefit of the youngsters themselves as well as for publicity reasons. My goodness, if we don't do something, and soon, we will end up as the laughing stock of the entire state."

"What can be done to motivate our athletes?" inquired Nancy Meagan, the varsity volleyball coach. "What are our options? Isn't it the responsibility of the individual student and that student's parents (and the classroom teachers) to see to it that the student does well in the classroom?"

"I think that is correct, for the most part, Nancy," responded the athletic director. But, lets examine all of our options. "I do feel that we as athletic personnel are going to be held accountable for what a student does in the classroom."

"Well, we could implement a closer watch on the athletes' academic progress. That way we might know earlier if a student is not performing well," pointed out Jay Jenkins, the basketball coach.

"We could also have a study hall for the kids," echoed another coach.

"What about special academic advisers?" chimed in another.

"Well, if not academic advisers, what about mentors, student mentors?" suggested the softball coach.

"Tutors, what about tutors. I always had tutors when I was in college," added Philip Moores, the head football coach.

"What about working with the kids themselves? How do we motivate them to do better," asked someone.

"You don't," pointed out the gymnastic coach, Susan Baskins. "There are some kids that just don't want to spend time in the classroom. They don't care about academics; all they care about is sports. You can't force them to earn **A**'s can you?"

"Well, maybe that is one way we attempt to motivate them," suggested the principal. "Lets make the youngsters do well in class if they are going to be able to take advantage of the privilege of athletic participation."

"You mean institute a pass to play policy?" asked someone.

"Maybe, lets look at the possibility," replied the athletic director.

QUESTIONS FOR DISCUSSION

1. Summarize the specific challenges facing the athletic staff and the school in this case.

2. What are the typical causes of substandard academic achievement by student-athletes? Justify your responses.

3. Who is (are) responsible for seeing to it that student-athletes do well academically? Explain.

4. What are some of the reasons that some school personnel are concerned with the poor academic performance of the student-athletes? Are these legitimate reasons? Explain.

5. What are the advantages and disadvantages of tactics that you can think of that can be used to insure a *closer watch* on the athletes' academic progress?

6. What are the advantages and disadvantages of implementing a *study hall* for the athletes?

7. What are the advantages and disadvantages of providing *special academic advisers* for the athletes?

8. What are the advantages and disadvantages of having *special faculty or community mentors* work with the athletes?

9. What are the advantages and disadvantages of providing *tutors* for those student-athletes who are in need of such assistance?

10. What other tactics or strategies might be implemented to help student-athletes do better in terms of grades? List and explain.

11. Outline the essential elements of a pass to play policy.

12. How did pass to play policies get started in this country, as a national movement? Where did it get its start and why. Who were the people involved at the grass roots level in terms of getting this concept accepted?

13. What are the advantages and disadvantages of a pass to play policy? Elaborate?

14. Do pass to play policies actually work? That is, do such policies actually motivate (force) student-athletes to do acceptable work in the classroom? Or, do such practices just exclude the marginal student-athlete from the athletic arena or competition due to low grades? Elaborate and explain your responses.

15. What should be the ultimate goal of a sound pass to play policy?

16. What are some objections that might be raised by the general public to such a policy? By the parents? By the athletes? What would be the rebuttal to each of these objections?

17. Why are pass to play policies becoming more prevalent in the United States? Implications.

18. Prior to implementing a pass to play policy what steps should be taken by the administration, the faculty, and the coaches?

19. What other options (besides a pass to play policy) are available to the school and the staff in terms of increasing the academic advance (success) of the student-athletes? Elaborate as to the advantages and disadvantages of each option you suggest.

20. What general principles are applicable in terms of attempts to enable student-athletes to experience academic success?

21. Comments . . .

RESPONSES FOR QUESTIONS FOR DISCUSSION

_____

_____

_____

_____

_____

_____

_____

_____

CASE #62

The Case of the Problematic Vacation Policies

The baseball coach, Coach McCormick was getting sick and tired of having his charges take off for vacation every year during the spring break at JFK High School in Northern Michigan. It seems that every spring during preseason or during the actual season some of his athletes would simply take advantage of the school's spring break (sometimes lasting 9 whole days) and take a spring vacation with their parents. "Don't these idiots know that by leaving practice and missing actual games that they are helping to destroy the season for the rest of the players, for the whole team, for the school?" complained coach McCormick to his new athletic director, Ann Martin.

Ms. Martin, new to the school but already an experienced athletic administrator with some 5 years of managerial experience at a high school in the deep south, responded by saying: "Well coach, what type of policy do you have when kids leave for vacation during the annual break? Do you allow them to come back without any consequences? Or, do they have to sit out so many games? Do the starters who leave lose their starting spots? What are the significant consequences, if any?"

Coach McCormick thought a few moments and then responded: "You know, I never thought about it from the perspective of punitive action against the kids. I just let them go and had hoped that my pep talk would discourage most of my players from ever leaving on the break. After all, playing baseball is the most important thing a youngster can do in the spring and no real athlete would want to leave one's teammates in a bind by skipping out on practice or, heaven forbid, actual games. I think I might institute some type of punishment or consequences for those who miss practices and games during this spring season. Thanks Ms. Martin for the help."

When baseball season rolled around and tryouts took place, coach McCormick was very careful to make it plain to everyone, parents, athletes and the booster club members, that this spring would be different in that he expected everyone to remain with the team throughout the entire season, spring vacation notwithstanding. In fact, his new rules included the following consequences for missing practices or games during the official spring vacation period: (1) for every practice missed, one would have to sit out one game and (2) for every game missed one would have to miss three games—once the athletes returned to school.

There was some grumbling from athletes and parents alike when they were initially informed of these new expectations/rules/punishments but no great outcries. This was not the case however when the spring vacation came around and two sets of parents decided to take their two sons on an extended vacation, one to Europe for 8 days and the other to Canada for an extended camping experience in the wilderness of the Canadian Northwest Territory. The parents howled to no end to their friends, the coach, to anyone who would listen. The commotion reached the AD and the school principal. The ruckus even reached the ears of various members of the school board (one school board member was a neighbor of one of the parents who had planned the vacation) and the superintendent.

Finally, the athletic director received a call from the superintendent who shared the following: "Ann, what in heaven's name is going on with you and the baseball coach? You don't know how many phone calls I have received in the past few days regarding the fact that your policy of **forbidding** athletes to go with their parents on vacation during our school's spring break is causing havoc with everyone's credibility, mine included. I want you in my office this afternoon right after school, let us say at 3:45 p.m. See you here."

QUESTIONS FOR DISCUSSION

1. Summarize the problems and challenges facing both the coach and the athletic director. Be specific.

2. Did the coach act properly by bringing his concerns to the athletic director? Explain your position.

3. Did the athletic director respond appropriately to the coach's concerns and did the AD provide adequate assistance and advice? Was the athletic director specific in her comments or was their much room for interpretation in what she was conveying to the coach?

4. What are the essential elements on both sides of the argument for and against letting athletes go on vacation during official break periods in the school year, if this means that these athletes will miss practices and games?

5. Should the athletic director be concerned about the health and status of the physical conditioning of athletes who have missed multiple days (a week or so) of practice and then return expecting to take up where they have left off, or is it not a big concern?

6. What about those athletes who do not miss practices or games during vacations? Is it fair to allow those who do miss a week or more to return and immediately take their starting spots back (if they happened to be starters)?

7. Can athletic directors implement a policy across the board that provides for punishment for those athletes who miss practices/games because of family vacation plans, when the youngsters return to school? Why or why not. Provide a rationale.

8. What are the advantages and disadvantages of implementing a school wide policy versus having different teams institute their own policy regarding missed practices and games *during vacation periods*.

9. What should the athletic director have done when the coach approached her about this challenge? What recommendations would you have made as the AD regarding the appropriate steps to take in response to the coach complaining?

10. If the superintendent said that no athlete could be kicked off the team for going on vacation what should the athletic director do? What should the AD and coach do if the superintendent or board instituted a policy that no athlete should be prevented from

trying out for a team even if that athlete knew in advance that he would be going on vacation?

11. What would be, in your opinion, an acceptable policy in this situation, from the perspective of the athletic director? Be specific and actually create a policy statement regarding vacation policies for athletes at the high school level.

12. Would this situation be different if it was at a NCAA division III college? What about if it was at a NCAA division I school (and some of the athletes had scholarships and some did not)?

13. Why did the parents not complain earlier? Why did they complain after the season began and the vacation period approached? Why did the parents complain to just about everyone?

14. Who is at fault for this situation developing to this point? Why?

15. What general managerial principles or guidelines are appropriate in this type of situation? Be specific.

16. Comments . . .

RESPONSES FOR QUESTIONS FOR DISCUSSION

CASE #63

The Case of the Questionable Travel Squad

Coach Joanna Kelvin, head softball coach at Southbell High School, was again feeling angry and upset not only with herself but with the whole athletic department. Here she was, one of the most successful coaches in the school system and with a team that should be competing not only for the conference championship, but perhaps even a high finish in the state tournament, and yet she had a big problem.

With the season set to start in less than a week, Joanna had a dilemma. Specifically, she had at least 24 outstanding young ladies seeking to make her team. In fact, she had an exceptional roster of outstanding pitchers, seven in all. Of the 24 athletes, only four were seniors and eight were juniors. The rest were sophomores. All told, coach Kelvin had an exceedingly talented group of very young, impressionable athletes. However, the problem was that the stupid athletic director, John MacMasters, had a travel squad limitation of 16. That meant that she would have to leave a total of eight players home for each away game. "That is ridiculous. These players are all young; they need to have the experience of traveling to all of my away games. I just have to have 24 players travel with me. It is for the good of the program. If MacMasters understood softball like he thinks he knows football there would be no problem in having my travel limitations raised to 24, in light of the unusual circumstances our team finds itself in this spring," mused coach Joanna Kelvin.

After some serious thought on the matter, coach Kelvin knew what she must do. She would just not tell the athletic director how many young women she will be taking to the away games. She had an extra six uniforms so she could actually suit up six of the extra eight athletes and the other two could join her on the bench—at least they would feel a part of the team. To solve the difficulty of how to get the extra athletes to the away games she would just drive her own van so that the extra eight athletes could have a ride there. Or, she would get one of the softball boosters to drive a vehicle. Additionally, she would pay for the meals for the extra athletes out of her own pocket. "The athletic director will never even know about all of this and what he doesn't know won't hurt him. After all, it is easier to receive forgiveness than it is to receive permission. And, it will certainly help our softball program," concluded the coach.

Everything worked just dandy for the first five games of the season. Not only was the team undefeated, but all 24 young athletes were having the time of their lives. The comradely among the players and the coach was excellent and all of the youngsters were developing into excellent athletes.

Then the roof fell in. Mr. MacMasters called coach Kelvin into his office on a Monday morning and said: "Coach, I have received complaints from the parents of one of your athletes who accused you of improper behavior. Specifically, that you have been forcing some of your athletes to travel by unauthorized vehicles. Additionally, they claim that you do not allow all of your athletes to dress for a game but rather make some of them sit in their street clothes with you on the bench, further humiliating them. What do you have to say for yourself, coach?" inquired the athletic director.

Coach Kelvin was flabbergasted. How could her best intentions come to this? What could have possibly gone wrong to create such an erroneous impression among these parents? All she wanted to do was to help her athletes and her team. And now, here she was, her deception has been found out by her boss, and she is being accused by parents of unprofessional conduct. "It is all the fault of this stupid athletic director and his stupid limitations with the travel squad," concluded the coach.

DISCUSSION ITEMS

1. What are the problematic elements in this scenario?
2. Are the intentions of coach Kelvin proper? Elaborate.
3. If coach Kelvin's actions are not proper, how serious are her actions? Explain.
4. Why do you suppose the athletic director established such limitations on the team's travel squad?
5. Assuming that the athletes on the team were aware of the restrictions on the maximum number of athletes traveling with a team, how would coach Kelvin address the fact that she is violating this policy and practice? How is the head coach going to resolve the situation in which she knowingly provides a bad example by not following the publicized rules and regulations governing travel squads?
6. Would this situation have been different if the team had been the baseball team (involving male athletes)? Why or why not?
7. Has the athletic director been acting appropriately in this situation? Explain.
8. Why have the parents complained to the athletic director? How do you suppose they found out about this situation?
9. What else could possibly go wrong with the practice of coach Kelvin taking eight more athletes to away games than permissible? Be specific.
10. What would other coaches in the school think about this practice, if and when they find out what coach Kelvin has done?
11. What should coach Kelvin have done if she wanted to take more than the allowable number of athletes to an away game? Be specific.
12. What should coach Kelvin do now that she has been found out?
13. What should the athletic director do now that the coach has been found out? What about punishment or disciplinary action? Create a role-playing situation in which you are the athletic director speaking to the coach?
14. How should the head coach deal with the parents who are complaining about the allegedly inappropriate actions?
15. How should the head coach deal with the players now that she has been found out and will no longer be allowed to take the extra eight players to away games?

16. What general principles of coaching and administration are applicable in this situation? Be specific.
17. Comments . . .

RESPONSES FOR QUESTIONS FOR DISCUSSION

_____

_____

_____

_____

_____

_____

_____

_____

_____

_____

_____

_____

_____

_____

_____

Case #64

Applying for an Administrative Position

Ralph Newsome was a new college graduate and wanted to secure a teaching and coaching position in the worst way. However, his biggest challenge, as he viewed it, was his inability to always know about job vacancies. In fact, several times he became aware of a job opening only when the announcement appeared in the paper in which the school gave the name of the newly hired athletic administrator. "How can I apply for jobs if I can't even find out about them? I feel like I have a 'ball and chain' attached to me whenever I try to improve myself, " complained Newsome.

One of his friends, Harry Thompson, who had coached on the college level for some years, told him that many times the advertisements for jobs (especially at the collegiate level) were phony. In fact, some schools have already decided on who was to be the new administrator or coach but went ahead with the advertisement and search process anyway just to make it look good. Ralph Newsome asked: "Is that legal? Is that ethical? How can they do that?"

Figure 10.1: "Ball & Chain" Obstacle

Not to be discouraged, Ralph approached several other friends, some of whom were athletic directors or assistant athletic directors, who were employed on the high school and college levels. They were only too happy to help Ralph with a number of very good ideas that might aid him in becoming aware of athletic administrative openings in the area, as well as around the state and even in different parts of the country. These strategies and tactics would enable Ralph to take a proactive stance in terms of securing information about potential or actual job vacancies and included the following:

1. _____
2. _____
3. _____
4. _____
5. _____
6. _____

QUESTIONS FOR DISCUSSION

1. Of the six statements that you completed above, which would be the best (most productive) in finding out about athletic administrative vacancies in smaller colleges? Why? Which would be the least effective? Why?
2. What are some sources that might provide information on athletic administrative vacancies at the NCAA division I collegiate level?
3. Were there any other techniques or strategies that you thought of but discarded due to ethical reasons? If so, what were these techniques or strategies and why were they not appropriate? Be specific.
4. Is it true that some searches for coaching and athletic administrative positions are not on the up and up? How can this be in today's society????? Is this fair? Is this honest? Is this ethical?
5. Why do some school authorities evidently advertise and search for a future member of the athletic administrative staff when these same individuals already know whom they will hire for the vacancy?
6. What general suggestions could you give to any person who is seeking a new position?
7. What suggestions would you share with coach Newsome in terms of how to dress for an administrative job interview? Be specific.
8. What suggestions would you share with coach Newsome in terms of actually interviewing for an athletic administrative job?
9. What steps should an athletic director or central administrator (on the high school or on the collegiate level) do to insure a wide range of suitable and qualified prospects (create an appropriate prospect pool) to review, consider and possibly interview for an administrative or coaching position? Provide a comprehensive outline of the steps involved in the selection of an athletic staff (administrative) member for a college as well as for a high school situation.
10. Cite some general principles that are pertinent in terms of seeking an appropriate job as an athletic administrator? As a coach?
11. Comments . . .

RESPONSES FOR QUESTIONS FOR DISCUSSION

_____

_____

_____

_____

CASE #65

The Case Involving the Coach's Little Kids

Coach Goodnatured Specalski, the head basketball coach at Smithtown High School, wanted to involve his two young children in the sport. He decided to invite his son Dalton, age 10, to serve as his assistant student-manager. And, he asked his little daughter Joani, age six, to dress up in a cheerleading outfit and to stand with the regular cheerleaders during the games.

Coach Specalski's wife, Dolores, thought that the idea was o.k. as long as the youngsters behaved themselves and didn't get in the way.

After the season had begun and the team was into the 6th game of the season the coach brought along his two children (his daughter was all dressed up in a miniature cheerleading outfit and his son had on a sweater with the school's mascot and colors) along with him to the gymnasium for an away trip. Coach Specalski told the cheerleaders: "Watch my daughter for me, Joani, while we are going to the game and until we get back to the high school." He then deposited his son with the senior student manager, told him to watch his son for the evening, and indicated it was o.k. if his son was given errands to perform during the night.

During the evening ride to the away game (45 minutes away) the coach did not have time to deal with his children. In fact, they were under the total supervision of the high school students. Of course, during the game, coach Specalski certainly couldn't be bothered with watching or even paying attention to the kids, as he was busy coaching and attending to other tasks. On the way home he did remember to look around and see whether or not both children made it back on the bus. Seeing both on the bus, he said: "Lets head for home, people."

Having arrived at home he got into his car and started to drive away— without his children. Suddenly both his son and daughter came rushing up to the car banging their little hands against the side windows. Letting both children into the car he asked if they had a good time and whether they would like to come again to spend time with daddy.

On the drive home the daughter asked if they could stop to eat since they did not have anything to eat since lunch because they were rushed out of the house after school and they had no money in their pockets to buy food at **Micky Ds** when the team stopped following the game.

Upon arriving home the mother asked the little one how things went. Looking up at their father the children replied, in unison: "Oh, alright, I guess."

The next week brought some criticism of the coach's actions to the attention of the athletic director. Some of the parents of the high school students with whom the children were left thought this was totally unacceptable behavior for the coach. One parent told the AD: "It is not my daughter's job to watch the coach's child during the game or before or after the game. Besides, the coach's children should not be involved in any way with the team at either home or away games."

Another taxpayer, who had no direct relationship with the people involved, nevertheless heard about this situation at the local barbershop and decided to get involved. She called one of the board members and proceeded to fill this individual in on what had really happened. She demanded that the real person who is at fault be called on the carpet, i.e., that incompetent athletic director. "After all, it happened on his watch and it is his responsibility to see that this type of thing does not happened. Why, one of those kids might have been injured, or even worse—killed."

DISCUSSION ITEMS

1. What is acceptable and unacceptable about the concept of involving one's children in such game situations (in the roles of cheerleader and assistant manager or ball boy/ball girl)?

2. What was the intention of the coach? Was it a positive goal? Was the attempt successful? Explain.

3. What went wrong, if anything? Be specific and justify your position.

4. What went right, if anything? Be specific and justify your position.

5. Should coaches involve their children as ball boys/girls or helpers or as mini-cheerleaders? If so, under what situations. Explain in full.

6. What should the coach have done in this scenario? What should the coach not done? Be specific and provide a rationale for your answers.

7. What should the athletic director have done to prevent this situation from turning out like it did?

8. What policy or policies might be in place that might cover this situation before the school year even started? Clearly present such a policy or policies and explain your rationale.

9. What legal ramifications come into play here? Provide examples and possible consequences.

10. What do you think the principal might think of this situation in terms of the decision-making ability of both the coach and the athletic director?

11. What could have been done to improve things in this situation now that this incident had come to light? By whom and when?

12. What could be the worse case scenario in this situation?

13. How do you think the children felt about their experience with father?

14. Is it ever appropriate to involve one's children in one's coaching activities *in some way*? If so, cite some examples. If not, explain why.

15. What general principles come into play in this situation regarding what the coach tried to do?

16. Comments . . .

RESPONSES FOR QUESTIONS FOR DISCUSSION

_____

_____

_____

_____

_____

_____

_____

_____

_____

_____

_____

_____

_____

_____

_____

_____

_____

_____

The Case of Having to Pay to Play

Mrs. Melinda Handwringer, the mother of three daughters and one son, all of whom are currently student-athletes at Montrose East High School, approached Sharron Richards, assistant athletic director and cross country coach, just as Sharron was standing in the checkout line at the local grocery store. "Ms. Richards, how glad I am to have this opportunity to catch up with you. You are such a hard person to reach. I have been attempting to reach you all week," cried out the mother.

Ms. Richards, not exactly enthralled with the prospects of having a lengthy or in-depth discussion with this mother at this particular time and place, politely replied: "Why, Mrs. Handwringer, how nice it is to run into you. How are the children?"

"That is why I wanted to talk with you. Have you heard what the idiots are up to now? Have you heard? What do you think about their idiotic plan?"

Sharron had an inkling what the mother was driving at but didn't want to let on. Instead, she merely said: "What is it that has gotten you so upset?"

"Why you know dearie, those stupid central administrators have proposed that all students who want to play athletics will have to pay for the privilege of representing this town and this school. How ridiculous can one get? Don't they know what a hardship that places on the students and their parents? Now don't get me wrong, I am not complaining just because my husband, Bert, and I will have four children next fall—all of whom will be out for at least one athletic team and perhaps more. No, No, I am speaking for all of the parents in this town who are shocked, outraged and just stupefied at this ridiculous proposal."

Mrs. Handwringer went on. "Why, if that incompetent athletic director, Marty Bullguster, would know how to handle a budget as well as be half-way competent in terms of raising funds, the school would not be in this situation in which there is not enough money to support our fine children as they represent all of us and the school. Don't you agree that our children and their parents shouldn't be burdened with this extra financial cost? Why it is unbelievable, isn't it!!! I know that you totally agree with me, why you have always been so supportive of the athletes and the total athletic program."

Sharron Richards was obviously having a hard time getting a word in edgewise. As she was about to respond, the mother again interrupted her by adding: "Sharron, what is going to happen to those youngsters whose parents are unable to pay the required amount? I bet that if an athlete is one of the so-called stars or blue chippers that the school will somehow find a way to get around this stupid, idiotic rule and will let those highly skilled kids play without paying—don't you think? And, my goodness, what about those athletes from large families? My own for example, will all four of my youngsters have to pay the same amount? My goodness, my goodness. And, by the way, I hear that the athletic director even made the suggestion that every sport will cost the same—thereby the cost would be the same for each child. My goodness. My goodness. Do you mean to tell me that it costs as much to run cross-country as it does to play football? Even I know that that is a bunch of hogwash, don't you agree, Sharron?"

Sharron started to say: "Well, I . . ." when she was cut off and Mrs. Handwringer interrupted again by inserting the comments "One other thing, dearie, even the JV and frosh teams will have participation fees the equal of the varsity competition—even with the younger teams having fewer coaches and fewer contests. How can they justify that tactic? How?"

"Well, I believe . . . " Sharron attempted to say before she was interrupted by the cashier at the checkout station who indicated that her bill for the groceries was $67.66. Paying in cash, Sharron was escorted to the door by the bag boy as Mrs. Handwringer shouted out: "It was great having this conversation with you. You have reinforced my belief that you really care about the athletes and understand how dumb the athletic director really is. Thank you for agreeing with my position. It makes me feel very good to have your continued support."

DISCUSSION ITEMS

1. Explain the essentials of this scenario?
2. Under what circumstances (within a school district) will the pay to play scenario develop? How can such an eventuality be prevented? Once installed, how can you get rid of the policy, once it has been established?
3. Does Mrs. Handwringer have any valid points in her arguments against the pay to play concept? Elaborate.
4. Does Mrs. Handwringer really speak for all or a majority of other parents? Elaborate.
5. Should Sharon have openly defended the athletic director in response to Mrs. Handwringer's overt criticism? Explain fully the ramifications of keeping quiet, as well as speaking up in defense of the athletic director.
6. What are the various options typically available to athletic administrators as they evaluate how to or whether or not to pursue the pay to play concept? Be specific and provide various alternatives.
7. What are the typical advantages and disadvantages of instituting a pay to play policy as viewed by the athletic administrators?
8. What are the advantages and disadvantages to charging the same amount for all athletes regarding of the sport in which they compete? Elaborate.
9. What are the advantages and disadvantages to charging the same amount for both varsity athletes as well as non-varsity athletes (JV and Frosh)? Elaborate.
10. Explain various ways to take into account the situation in which an athlete (and parents) is (are) unable to pay the amount charged? Address the pros and cons.
11. What are the advantages and disadvantages to charging the same amount for each youngster in the same family regardless of the number of children in any single family? Elaborate.

12. What are the advantages and disadvantages to charging the same amount for any single youngster regardless of the number of teams the student plays on? Elaborate.
13. What dangers are present for Sharon Richards in the above situation? Be specific.
14. What should coach Richards have done when initially approached by the mother in the grocery store? Why?
15. What do you think are the impressions that Mrs. Handwringer has of Sharon at the present time? Could or might the mother share with others that Ms. Richards is in full agreement with everything that the mother has been saying, including that the athletic is less than a genius in running the total athletic program? Why or why not?
16. What might happen if word of this conversation gets back to the athletic administration? Could Ms. Richards find herself in a sticky situation, one in which she might have a lot of explaining to do to Mr. Marty Bullguster?
17. What are some tactics or strategies that the athletic administration might want to consider pursuing if the pay to play concept might indeed become a necessity? Explain the rationale for each tactic or strategy.
18. Is it even *legal* in your state to have a pay for play program?
19. What should coach Richards do now as she walks out of the grocery store? With whom? Why?
20. What general principles might be applicable in this situation in which the mother attempts to communicate as shown in this scenario? Elaborate.
21. Comments . . .

RESPONSES FOR QUESTIONS FOR DISCUSSION

_____

_____

_____

_____

_____

_____

_____

_____

CASE #67

The Case of Accountability in Evaluating Coaches

On October 10th, Mr. Helpful, the new principal of Pullman High School in Plainview, Minnesota, approached the athletic director on the topic of evaluating the coaching staff. The athletic director, Mr. Harry Jello, indicated that in the past he was just happy to be able to find warm bodies who would be willing to serve as coaches. And, in terms of evaluation, he (as athletic director) had always given positive recommendations for just about all the coaches at the end of the school year.

The athletic director further asked why there was a need for a change? "With the rent-a-coach problem, how can we attempt to actually establish any type of evaluation system? All that would happen would be to lose some coaches—either because the coaches would not stand for *it* or because the coaches would be *fired*. And we all know how difficult it is to get coaches in the first place," moaned Harry Jello.

Mr. Helpful, the principal, indicated that in the school of 2000 students (grades 9-12) there were 19 varsity teams, 12 junior varsity teams, 10 frosh teams and two cheerleading squads. Each of these teams had a so-called head coach (someone in charge) and several teams had assistants (ice hockey had a four-person staff while the football staff numbered nine).

The athletic director was given a charge, i.e., to work out a plan (for review and possible approval by the principal and the board of education) for the evaluation and assessment of all coaches of athletic teams, including those individuals in charge of the cheerleaders. The deadline for the written report was determined to be a week before school was out in the spring (June 16th).

The principal wanted to know from Mr. Jello how he, the athletic director, was going to proceed in terms of the process of setting up or structuring such a plan, etc., before actually proceeding to the next step of implementing the plan of attack. "I want to know, in advance, how you are going to begin to tackle this sensitive project before you jump in with two feet, is that clear?" said the principal.

Harry responded by saying, "Sure, you want not only to have a written plan outlining a proposed system of evaluation or assessment for all coaches, but I have to check with you before even working on the plan. I need to let you know how I intend to begin to work on the plan itself."

"Right on," replied Mr. Helpful. "Good luck. I look forward to seeing your progress in the near future."

QUESTIONS FOR DISCUSSION

1. What *misperceptions* might the athletic director possess presently?
2. What steps do you suggest Mr. Jello follow immediately following the meeting with the principal? Be specific.
3. What does the athletic director need to do now regarding an actual evaluation system? Be specific.
4. Why is it important for the principal to know, in advance, about the proposed process that the AD intends to pursue in this matter?
5. Is there a possible hidden agenda in this scenario? Is it that the principal wants to fire some coaches? Be specific in examining all possible options and goals. Prioritize the possible objectives and goals in terms of those that are preferred over those that have lessor priority.
6. What specific steps might be recommended in respect to the process of working on such a proposed system? Provide details and be specific.
7. Who should be involved in the proposed process? When? In what fashion? Why?
8. What are two major goals of establishing the process itself? In other words, why is the process of working on an evaluation system so important, if not as important, as the actual evaluation system itself?
9. What are some of the pitfalls that await the AD, the principal, the school and the coaches in terms of working out a process for a proposed evaluation system—if care is not taken?
10. If there is a teachers' union at the school, how might this affect the goals of (1) establishing a *process of working out a system of evaluation* and (2) *actually developing a system of evaluation for coaches*? Provide a justification for your answers.
11. What would be the advantages of a real evaluation system for coaches?
12. What would be the disadvantages of such a system? From the standpoint of the coaches, the school and the athletes—if any?
13. Would you expect that there might be resistance on the behalf of the coaches on staff to the concept of an evaluation system being implemented now? Why or why not?
14. What might be some of the major objections raised by the coaches? Are they justified in raising the objections? Are any of the objections really valid? Which ones? Explain.
15. What is the single, most threatening aspect of a comprehensive coaches' evaluation system insofar as coaches are concerned?
16. What might be done to help alleviate the coaches' fears about any proposed evaluation or assessment system?
17. What is wrong with the system as it currently exists in this school?
18. What pitfalls do you foresee in the attempt to implement any evaluation system?
19. Outline what you feel might be a defensible evaluation system for coaches at the secondary level. Include any *special instruments* or *forms* that might be utilized.

20. *Who* should be evaluating the coaches? Parents? The athletic director? Current athletes? Past athletes? Booster club members? News media? The principal? Others? Provide a rationale for your recommendations.

21. *When* should evaluation of coaches take place?

22. *What* are the justifiable purposes of any evaluation of coaches?

23. Prioritize the different criteria that coaches should be evaluated in light of.

24. Once a coaches' evaluation system is in place, is it set in stone or should it be flexible? Explain.

25. What general principles might be applicable in terms of any evaluation system for coaches? That is, what are the essentials of an appropriate and just evaluation system of coaches (head, assistant, full and part-time coaches)?

26. Comments . . .

RESPONSES FOR QUESTIONS FOR DISCUSSION

_____

_____

_____

_____

_____

_____

_____

_____

_____

_____

_____

_____

CASE #68

The Case of the Awards Ceremony

The annual spring athletic banquet at North Springville High School is only a few months away. The athletic director, James Franks, has decreed that each coach shall provide, in writing, the criteria upon which each of the athletes on each of their teams shall be able to earn awards for their successful athletic participation. This directive was given to the head coaches at the start of the school year, some 5 months ago.

At that time, James Frank indicated that: "Each sport (coach) will be able to provide various individual awards, including letter awards, for that sport. Each head coach will have the responsibility for establishing the criteria for each award. Further, different sports can use different criteria for their own awards. All I want to mandate is that the criteria should be appropriate, fair and just—and that I, as athletic director, *approve each individual sport's award system prior to the awards being approved.*"

At the athletic staff meeting called to discuss the AD's request, the football coach indicated that he appreciated the fact that different sports could have different criteria that determined whether or not individual athletes would be able to earn varsity letters, etc. He added: "I certainly support the idea that sports are different and that awards should or could be different in terms of the actual type of awards to be given to the kids as well as what the athletes have to do to earn the awards, including the very, very important letter awards."

"You mean that the football players can earn varsity or sub-varsity letters by satisfying different performance standards than those on the baseball team?" asked Billy Tillstone, the baseball mentor? "Is that fair?" he added. "What happens if the tennis player only is required to play in one-half of the matches while my baseball players are required to hit .300 and to have played three-fourths of the innings? Is that fair?" he asked.

"No, that is not what the AD has in mind" chimed in the gymnastics' coach. "Each sport is so different, we are just being asked to take into account our distinct differences in the awarding of letter awards as well as the distribution of other special awards, such as 'most valuable' player, 'most improved' athlete, etc. We just have to be sure that each of us, as coaches, make up *appropriate awards* and *establish the suitable standards* that govern whether or not the athletes deserve specific awards."

"Well, I just don't like the fact that some athletes will be able to earn some awards in an easier fashion than others. Kids talk you know," complained the basketball coach. He then added: "My kids will really have to work to earn their awards. I can just imagine what the golf athletes will have to do."

"Why does the AD have to approve each of our set of standards? Doesn't he trust us? Are we not the experts in each of our sports? What does he know about gymnastics anyway, nothing," offered Charlie Honeycutt, the gymnastics coach.

QUESTIONS FOR DISCUSSION

1. What are the advantages and disadvantages of involving the coaches in helping to establish awards and criteria for awards? Why doesn't the AD merely institute or implement the criteria and the awards that he feels are appropriate or best?

2. What is to prevent a coach from establishing standards or criteria that are too weak or inappropriate for the athletes on that team? Elaborate.

3. Will athletes compare criteria among sports and be aware that some athletes will earn awards more easily (or the perception will be that they can)? Is this important? What difference does it make if this becomes the case?

4. What are some appropriate awards, other than the traditional letter awards, that might be earned by individual athletes on various teams? Be specific in terms of awards and in terms of sports.

5. Might there be some criteria that would be appropriate for all sports (that is, in order for an athlete to earn a letter in any sport an athlete must satisfy one or more criteria or standards regardless of what sport the youngster participates in)? Explain in detail and provide examples.

6. What might be some of the *general criteria* for an athlete to earn the traditional letter awards for different sports? Specify the sports.

7. What might be some specific criteria for the freshman (1st) letter award to be earned by an athlete [specify the sport]?

8. What might be some specific criteria for the sophomore (or 2nd) letter award to be earned by an athlete [in the same sport]?

9. What might be some specific criteria for the junior (or 3rd) letter award to be earned by an athlete [in the same sport]?

10. What might be some specific criteria for the (senior or 4th) letter award to be earned by an athlete [in the same sport]?

11. What would you, as the athletic director, recommend for seniors who don't actually meet the stated *physical requirements* for a letter award? Specify the type of policy you would recommend or implement.

12. What are the reasons for having an awards program for athletes? Elaborate.

13. What are some pitfalls that might arise in terms of an athletic department attempting to *institute an overall awards policy* such as outlined in this scenario? How can these potential problems or pitfalls be avoided? Be specific.

14. Does the athletic director have the right or the obligation to demand that all awards and all criteria be approved by the AD's office prior to being put into place? Elaborate.

15. What general principles might be appropriate in establishing a comprehensive awards program for a high school?

16. Comments . . .

RESPONSES FOR QUESTIONS FOR DISCUSSION

_____

_____

_____

_____

_____

_____

_____

_____

_____

_____

_____

_____

_____

_____

_____

_____

_____

_____

CASE #69

The Case of the Part-time Coach being Bumped By a Full-time Teacher

The basketball team had just finished with the best record in the history of Thomas Jefferson High School, situated in a quaint little river town along the banks of the Mississippi. Cody Bennett, the head coach, had finally been rewarded for his five years of hard work and dedication when his chargers advanced to the quarterfinals of the state tournament with an overall record of 21 and 3, before losing in double overtime to the eventual state champions. This achievement was all the more remarkable considering that Cody was only a part-time coach. His full time job was as a salesman for a large manufacturing firm located in a nearby metropolitan area.

The future of the team looked bright indeed since four of the starters will be returning next season. However, not all was well in River City since the teachers' union contract had a little known clause that indicated that any part-time coach could be replaced (bumped) by any full time teacher within that school system who wanted that coaching position and who met minimum requirements. While this clause had not been utilized in many years it was still in effect when Mr. Henry Keatings, the shop teacher, walked into the office of the athletic director (Billy Bob Spider) and announced that he wanted to be appointed the head basketball coach next season.

"You know, *I am qualified for the post* because of my playing days back 20 years ago. Plus, I took a 'Theory of Coaching Basketball' class while a freshman in college. And, of course, I have had actual coaching experience since I coached my son's little league baseball team several summers ago," reported Henry Keatings.

"Are you sure that you want to do this?" asked Billy Bob. "I mean, you haven't coached basketball. You have never coached high school athletes. And almost the whole team is returning next year. Why, we have a good chance to win a state championship next year. And, coach Bennett has spent five years of his life building this team to this point."

"Why do you think I am so excited about being the head coach next year. With all of the talent coming back, how hard could it be to coach these guys? Besides, I have several starters on the team in my industrial arts class and we get along just fine. You know, the school administration is always crying about the lack of full time teachers who also want to coach—well, here I am, ready, willing and able to coach the team," added the would-be coach. "Besides, the union contract stipulates that I have to be appointed since I am a full time teacher and have met the so-called minimum requirements," added Keatings, almost as an afterthought.

QUESTIONS FOR DISCUSSION

1.   Why might this rule be in effect within this school system? Elaborate.
2.   Is this rule of real value? Why or why not? To whom?
3.   What is the real problem with such an agreement?
4.   What might be the downside of adhering to this union agreement?
5.   What might happen if the athletic director ignored the union agreement and refused to make Mr. Keatings the new basketball coach?
6.   With whom might the athletic director confer with in this sticky situation? Why?
7.   If you were the athletic director, explain how you would handle this hot potato.
8.   What effect do you think the implementation of this union rule will have on the athletic staff (especially other part-time coaches) if Billy Bob actually bumps coach Bennett in favor of the full time teacher? Explain your rationale.
9.   Why does Mr. Keatings want to be the coach? Are his reasons valid?
10. Are the needs of the athletes being met by making a change in coaches at this point? Why or why not?
11. Is Keatings really qualified to become the coach of this team? Of any varsity basketball team? Explain your rationale.
12. What is your opinion of the so-called minimum qualifications aspect of the union agreement?
13. What might be the reactions of the players when they hear of the coaching change? Speculate. What might be the reactions of the people in the community to this coaching change? What about the booster club members?
14. Should the athletic director attempt to talk Mr. Keatings out of this course of action? Why or why not? What might be the consequences of such an attempt on behalf of the athletic director? Provide several different scenarios.
15. Assume the role of the athletic director (role play) and attempt to talk Mr. Keatings out of wanting to coach the team.
16. Assume the role of the athletic director (role play) and explain what you would say to coach Bennett in giving him the bad news, assuming that this is the final decision.
17. What would you, as athletic director, want to share with the returning players about the coaching change?
18. How do you suspect coach Bennett will feel when informed by the athletic director that he has been bumped by Keatings just because this teacher is a full time teacher and Mr. Bennett is not? Elaborate.
19. Is this fair? Is this Just? Why or why not?
20. What recourse is open to coach Bennett at this point in time?
21. What general principles are appropriate in dealing with this situation?
22. Comments . . .

RESPONSES FOR QUESTIONS FOR DISCUSSION

CASE #70

The Case of the Athletic Shoe Purchase

Jane Smoot, head girl's basketball coach at Easyside High School, desired to assist her athletes purchase their shoes (Nike) for basketball before the season. She worked out an arrangement for the athletes to buy the shoes—as a group—from a local vender, unbeknownst to her athletic director, Marcia Zimmerman. Coach Smoot always required her athletes to wear the same matching style shoes.

Coach Smoot worked out an agreement that all 20 of her athletes could pay $105.00 for a pair of basketball shoes (these shoes normally sell for $135.00 at retail) at the start of the season. Each of the youngsters could also buy a second pair of shoes for another $105.00 sometime in early January, if they so desired.

The owner of the sporting goods store, Mr. Nice Guy, was a favorite fan of Coach Smoot and of the girls' basketball team. Mr. Nice Guy told Jane, a week after the two of them agreed, once again, upon the details of the purchases, that he would also give free of charge to Coach Smoot and her assistant (June Alley) two pairs of shoes (retail price $165.00 each) because:

1. The team was buying so many shoes, and
2. He really wanted to help the team and the two coaches by providing matching Nike shoes

Coach Smoot agreed and thanked Mr. Nice Guy over the phone and then, the next day, informed her assistant, June Alley, who was very excited with the prospect of getting two free pair of Nike basketball shoes *again* this season.

Before the practice sessions began, Mr. Nice Guy came to the gymnasium and fitted each of the athletes, then gave them their shoes and took the cash for each of the shoes from the coaches (who had collected the cash money ahead of time from each of the athletes). Before Mr. Nice Guy left the school, he went to the coaches' office and dropped off a pair of Nike shoes for each (he already knew their sizes since this type of arrangement had been done before). On his way out of the office, he turned and wished the coaches good luck and said: "If you two ever wanted to go (part-time) into the sporting goods business as saleswomen, just give me a call. I can always use good workers like you."

QUESTIONS FOR DISCUSSION

1. Did Coach Smoot act properly? What specific issues faced the head coach in this situation?
2. Did the assistant coach act properly? What specific issues faced the assistant coach in this situation?

3. What position does this situation place the athletic director?

4. Should the coach (or assistant) even be involved in assisting the athletes purchase the shoes?

5. Enumerate different ways in which coaches might prearrange for their athletes to take advantage of lower than retail prices of athletic equipment or supplies from specific vendors. Be specific in the details *and* cite advantages and disadvantages of each.

6. Should the head coach keep the free shoes? Why or why not? Should she give them away? Why? To Whom? What about the assistant coach? What should she do? Why?

7. Is there an ethical question or questions involved in this type of situation? Explain in detail.

8. What would happen if one of the parents called the athletic director or principal and complained about the fact that the coaches were getting free shoes while the athletes had to pay for theirs? How would you, as athletic director, respond to such charges?

9. What would happen if one or more parents complained that they could not afford to pay $105.00 for the Nike shoes? Is it fair to embarrass an athlete who cannot afford the designated shoes?

10. Should the agreement, understanding or practice with the vendor be shared with athletic director and/or the principal? Why or why not?

11. Is the athletic director at fault for not knowing about this special arrangement? Discuss in detail.

12. How could the athletic director have prevented this situation from happening in the first place?

13. What specific policies or procedures might be placed into being which could have an affect upon this type of situation?

14. What about the central administration? Should the members of the school board and/or superintendent now be involved?

15. Should the agreement or understanding with the vendor be made public? Would the coaches (and the athletic director) feel comfortable in having the parents and others in the community know that the coaches were involved in these types of activities and had made these types of decisions? Explain the rationale. Were the reasons valid?

16. Cite some principles or guidelines applicable here.

17. Comments . . .

RESPONSES FOR QUESTIONS FOR DISCUSSION

_____

_____

_____

CASE #71

The Case of Inadequate Crowd Control

The hockey coaches always prided themselves on having an exciting team on the ice. They also felt a deep sense of self-satisfaction from the atmosphere that always seems to surround the games. It was the crowds that made the games so electric. It was the crowds that made the games so exciting. The players could feel it. The coaches could feel it. And, the fans could feel it.

Big-time athletics often necessitate sophisticated and updated facilities. [Courtesy of University of Wisconsin Sports Information]

The head ice hockey coach, Willy Hemptser, was especially effective in getting the fans in the stands to become a real part of the competitive spirit. He could work the crowd into a frenzy during an important contest. He was known to address the crowd during the pregame warm-ups if the spectators were too quiet or subdued. Once, between the first and second periods of a very important game, he even stayed on the ice, took the microphone, and attempted to rile up the crowd into a frenzy, which he did.

During the last game of the season, one in which the conference championship was at stake, Willy was especially hyper. Maybe it was because the athletic director stayed at home that night to watch the season ending show of his favorite television series. He also was remarkably effective that evening in getting the crowd into the game. In fact, the crowd became so enthusiastic, so excitable, that the sound was almost deafening.

The game was a hard fought contest and the score was tied during the late minutes of the game when it happened. A call went against coach Willy's team. As a result, a winning goal for his team was nullified. The two opposing teams on the ice got into a pushing match and Willy went absolutely ballistic. He did nothing to stop the rest of his team from leaving the bench and going onto the ice to join the fray. Coach Willy even turned to the crowd, exciting them to attempt to intimidate the officials and the opposing team.

The end result was almost catastrophic. Some of the more rowdy fans and boosters began to really get out of control. Objects were thrown onto the ice. Some of the spectators even threw objects into the penalty box hitting one of the opposing players in the face, cutting his nose severely.

One thing led to another (as things usually happens) and the violence escalated rapidly. The ice became a battlefield with the officials being helpless to stop to the fighting among the teams.

The hometown fans, seeing some of their players getting beaten, actually went onto the ice and started to mob the opposing players, who quickly became greatly outnumbered.

It took almost 15 minutes for the disturbance to quiet down. As a result, the officials canceled the contest, and this fact only excited the crowd to greater frenzy. After the game, the opponents' bus was trashed with windows broken and baseball bats taken to dent the sides of the vehicle. All in all, it was a very ugly scene.

QUESTIONS FOR DISCUSSION

1. Who shares responsibility for this fiasco? Be specific and provide a rationale for your position.
2. Could this unfortunate situation have been anticipated? Why or why not?
3. What role should the athletic director have played in this scenario? What should the athletic director have done earlier in the season, before the game, during the game? Be specific.
4. Should the athletic director have been at that contest? Why or why not? Should the AD be at every home game? Is this even possible?
5. If the athletic director was not at this contest, what steps should he have taken? Be specific.
6. What did the head ice hockey coach do wrong? When? Be specific. .
7. How might the crowd (fans, spectators, booster) be involved with the team without having these same individuals going overboard in their reactions? Provide some suggestions.
8. How might an effective crowd control policy be established in this school now that such a disgraceful event has taken place?
9. What are the essentials of an effective crowd control policy?
10. Create a sample crowd control policy and explain how it might be implemented for a typical secondary school.
11. Might the head hockey coach and/or athletic director be held responsible in terms of legal liability? Why or why not?
12. What might the ice hockey coach and/or the athletic director have done to prevent this situation from developing or becoming as serious as it was? Be specific.
13. What should the head coach do now after the game? Be specific.
14. Elaborate on what the AD might do now, after the fact, to mitigate the negative consequences that developed during the game? What should the AD do now in regard to the behavior of the head coach?
15. What might other school officials (principal, superintendent, the board members) do now that this disgusting episode is over with? Elaborate.
16. What general principles are suitable for consideration in this type of situation?
17. Comments . . .

RESPONSES FOR QUESTIONS FOR DISCUSSION

_____

_____

_____

_____

_____

_____

_____

_____

_____

_____

_____

_____

_____

_____

_____

_____

CASE #72

The Case of the Problematic Departmental Handbook

The athletic department was not unlike any other athletic entity at any large high school in any medium size city in the United States. However, William Robert Linder, the athletic director at Crystal City high school continued to feel as if he was always operating in a crisis mode. He felt like the little kid with fingers stuck in the various holes in the proverbial dike attempting to stem the rush tide of water (problems).

It wasn't that his school had any more problems than other schools, he was sure. But then why did he feel so helpless or put upon every time there was a problem or controversy? Why did every little bump in the road (and there were a lot of them) seem like an insurmountable problem that had to be addressed as if no one had ever anticipated that such a situation might occur? Why did it have to happen to him?

One day the new football coach had come and asked why he could not take an additional 22 athletes to an away varsity game since he had extra uniforms. He also requested that all of his traveling athletes (all 85 of them) receive an additional $2.75 for meal money after the upcoming Saturday game.

The AD did not know what to say. How to respond to the new coach? "If only I had some guideline to help me formulate a response," mused William Linder.

"You know," interjected his part-time secretary, "if you had some established policies, some guidelines or procedures and practices that you could use to guide you in your decision making, you would have a much easier time. Why, at my husband's place of work there is a departmental handbook with all kinds of policies, procedures and practices outlined, in writing, that everyone has access to. People know what the policies are and the handbook guides the decision making of the administrators in charge of the office or division."

"You know what, you hit the nail on the head replied the athletic director. Why didn't I think of that? Why, I can develop such a handbook and it would help me with decisions that need to be made because it would include important policies and procedures of the whole athletic department. It would state, in print, how many athletes should be on each team's travel squad. It would specify the amount of money for meals for each team, etc. Why, it would save me so much time and effort. I could always just say: 'it is a policy, it is in the policy handbook.' It would enable me to have an excuse for decisions that I make as I could just say that it is policy and that we have to follow policy."

"And, as my husband tells me," added the secretary, "when you don't want to do what is in the handbook, you can always make an exception. My husband tells me that his boss, the divisional manager, always uses the excuse or rationale that that is why managers or administrators exist, i.e., to make exceptions to policies, practices and procedures."

QUESTIONS FOR DISCUSSION

1. Summarize the major elements of this situation.
2. How would you suggest the athletic director go about creating such a handbook? Should he write it himself? Why or why not? If not, what alternative is open to him?
3. What could the athletic director do or where could he go to see how other schools have developed and implemented such a tool as a handbook?
4. Should the athletic director pay any attention to the business world and the handbook idea? Is there any similarity between the business world and the world of education that would provide a link or linkage between the two that would enable the athletic director to borrow an idea or a tool (such as a handbook)?
5. Discuss: "*Handbooks should contain policies that show that the planners/writers anticipated potential problems and controversial situations and developed, in advance, policies, procedures and practices (as well as a philosophy[ies] and priorities—the 5Ps) that will facilitate future decision making and problem solving.*"
6. What is(are) the real purpose(s) of the departmental handbook for a high school?
7. How can such a handbook be used to prevent problems? Provide a rational and examples.
8. In the situation outlined above, how might the handbook be used to help the athletic director create a response to the football coach regarding the travel squad and the amount of meal money?
9. Who might *want* to provide input into the handbook? Who should have input?
10. Who would have to approve the contents of such a handbook for a public high school? Be specific and explain the process of approval. What about in a college or university? Explain fully.
11. What is your position on the statement that: *managers or administrators exist to make exceptions to policies, practices and procedures*? Can administrators unilaterally make exceptions to the printed handbook? Why or why not? When might it be appropriate? Give an example of when it might not be appropriate.
12. Develop and write below a **detailed** *table of contents* for a typical high school athletic department's handbook.
13. How would the athletic director go about disseminating the handbook to others? How should the handbook be bound? Why? To whom should the handbook be given?
14. What steps should be taken in terms of anticipating changes in the contents of the handbook? Explain in full what the athletic director might do (physically) to make potential changes in the handbook easier and to make sure that people who are in possession of various copies of the handbooks are made aware of such changes and can keep the changes handy and in an appropriate place.
15. What principles or guidelines might be appropriate in this case?
16. Comments . . .

RESPONSES FOR QUESTIONS FOR DISCUSSION

_____

_____

_____

_____

_____

_____

_____

_____

_____

_____

_____

_____

_____

_____

_____

_____

_____

CASE #73

The Case of the Request for the Cheerleading Squad To Accompany the Basketball Team on the Team Bus

At first glance the request seemed innocuous at best. At least it seemed that way to the adviser of the cheerleading squad for the men's basketball team, Susan Babblott. Susan had been approached about this very subject by the cheerleading captains (Pattie and Jeanie) who had been elected by being the most popular women on the squad. They asked coach Babblott why they, as a cheerleading squad, could not accompany the guys' basketball team to away games—on the same bus.

"After all, we are recognized as an athletic team by the school board, we are treated like athletes in terms of rules and regulations and eligibility, etc., we are expected to adhere to the same high standards as all athletes are—why can't we also go on the same bus for those athletes we are to cheer for?" echoed Pattie and Jeanie.

Coach Babblott responded by asking why they and their cohorts wanted to accompany the athletes on the team bus. "Because we are as much members of the team as any of the players. Besides, this will build team unity. And, besides, one of the parents told us that the school and the AD cannot discriminate against females by preventing us from going to a single away game. And, we want to go the same way the athletes do to the games," the response came.

The next day coach Babblott was in the office of the athletic director, Larry Tripplit, and presented her case by repeating everything that had happened in her meeting with the captains. "Well, Susan," asked Mr. Tripplit, "what are your thoughts on the topic? Should the cheerleaders be allowed to ride the team bus with the boys? What do you think the basketball coach would say?"

"I already saw him in the hall and he about took my head off, that ogre. Why, he had the audacity to say that the cheerleaders were as much a part of his basketball team as the old oak tree out near the parking lot. I don't think he appreciates the situation that I am in as cheerleader adviser. I don't think he understands how much the girls want to be on the team bus that the guys ride on," she concluded.

"Well, I tell you what my thoughts are right now. The cheerleaders ride now in a school vehicle right behind the team bus (which I grant you is not full). I don't understand why they want to be with the guys for other than to engage in horseplay and to socialize. And, I don't think the coach or I want that type of behavior on the bus, do you?" opinioned the athletic director.

"Listen Larry," intoned coach Babblott, "I don't want to seem pushy here but there are parents who are involved in this situation." To which the athletic director responded by . . .

QUESTIONS FOR DISCUSSION

1. Outline the critical elements in this case that confront the athletic director.
2. Should the coach have attempted to nip this situation in the bud if she really did not think this was a good idea? Elaborate.
3. If you were the athletic director, would *you* think this is a good idea? Why or why not?
4. Why is the cheerleading coach acting as she is doing in this scenario? Cite the possible pressures she might be feeling.
5. Is the reaction of the basketball coach to be expected? Why or why not?
6. Was the cheerleading coach smart to catch the basketball coach in the hallway? Discuss.
7. Does the fact that a parent evidently is supporting the effort by the cheerleaders to ride on the bus enter into this equation when viewed by the AD? To what extent?
8. Should the athletic director override the wishes of the basketball coach? Ever? Provide a rationale for your position.
9. What should the athletic director do now in this scenario? Provide a timeline and an outline of activities or actions that the athletic director might be involved in to resolve this situation?
10. If there had been a predetermination of such a policy governing this situation and if such a policy or procedure had been included in the departmental handbook, would this situation be as much of a problem as it seemingly is now? Explain.
11. How might the athletic director go about attempting to reduce the negative consequences of any unpopular decision made by him?
12. What does the AD do when one finds oneself in a situation in which any decision (apparently) will offend one constituency or another constituency?
13. Describe some principles, concepts or guidelines that might govern the athletic director's decision-making and actions in this scenario.
14. Comments . . .

RESPONSES FOR QUESTIONS FOR DISCUSSION

_____

_____

_____

_____

_____

CASE #74

The Case of Planning for the Athletic Banquet

"Believe it or not, we have never had a formal athletic banquet here at our high school," explained the principal, Jessup Johnson, to the new athletic director. "In the past, for a variety of different reasons, we seemed to only have a hodge-podge of different mini-gatherings for some of the teams while other teams have just never bothered with any season ending experience. And, you know what, the school and especially the athletic department has survived just fine. That is why I am not really in favor of your suggestion that we start sponsoring an athletic banquet that would somehow involve each and every team. I know that your previous school had such a banquet and it must have been very successful for you to be pushing so soon and so hard for a banquet to be initiated here."

"Yes, I know that there might be some resentment from some individuals and groups any time something is changed within the athletic department. But, I think having one big banquet at the end of school will satisfy most of the people and it will be a huge success. At my previous school, such an arrangement worked well. It had always worked well, for over 40 years. Even though, I grant you, a majority of the coaches are against this one banquet for all concept, I am sure they will survive this little bump in the road," concluded the athletic director.

"Well, ok. But let me tell you this. If this whole thing blows up in your face, don't tell me that I did not warn you. It is hard to change what people have gotten use to, believe me. I should know. I have been principal here for 14 years."

"Look, I will guarantee you that the banquet will be a great success. The athletes, the parents, the staff and fans will really enjoy it," offered the athletic director.

"Fine, but I don't want you to allow what happened at East High a couple of years ago when some jerk donated a $45 MVP trophy and had the perpetual (annual) trophy named for himself. What a laughing stock their athletic director became. Imagine, some idiot getting a trophy named for himself in perpetuity for a measly $45. What a laughable situation," claimed the principal.

QUESTIONS FOR DISCUSSION

1. Why would an athletic director want to initiate a new athletic banquet type situation in a school such as this?

2. Why would there be some resentment among some individuals, teams, fans and parents to having a single banquet for all teams scheduled at the end of the school year? How might the athletic director respond to this resentment and opposition (i.e., objections)?

3. Is it wise to attempt to initiate something that a majority of the coaches are against?

Why or why not? Under what circumstances might it be worth it?

4. What is the danger of the athletic director attempting to initiate what worked at one's previous school at a new school?

5. How would you, as athletic director, attempt to get the coaches in favor of this move? What about the athletes? The parents? The booster club?

6. What are the traditional objectives and goals of an athletic banquet? That is, what are the major purposes of a banquet or banquets?

7. There are traditionally three types of organizational structures that any athletic director might consider when planning/scheduling such season ending activities as banquets. Name and explain these three types of banquets in terms of timing and scheduling—and provide the plus and minuses for each.

8. Explain your philosophy about awards to various people and the criteria for such awards. As athletic director, would you allow individual coaches to give whatever awards they wish to whomever they wish? Explain your philosophy and any limiting factors you might establish.

9. How would you respond as athletic director to the complaint from parents that having one banquet would take too much time and that the big sports with large numbers would monopolize all of the time at the banquet?

10. Is there a point in time in which the athletic director might back off and admit that a change in the so-called banquet scenario might not be appropriate? Under what condition would you, as athletic director, retreat and back off from your publicized move for one annual banquet in late spring.

11. What are some negative elements that might accompany the initiation of a single athletic banquet held at the end of the school year?

12. Who would you prevent coaches from "giving away the store" in terms of donors wishing to donate trophies/awards (in perpetuity) for a measly donation?

13. Where would you hold the banquet and why?

14. Who would be invited guests and why?

15. What are some common elements that are usually part of every athletic banquet? Elaborate.

16. Would you plan for a special speaker? Who? Why?

17. What principles are applicable in this situation with the banquet and in such a situation where there are perceived problems or resistance to a major change in practice or policy?

18. Comments . . .

RESPONSES FOR QUESTIONS FOR DISCUSSION

_____

_____

_____

_____

_____

_____

_____

_____

_____

_____

_____

_____

_____

_____

_____

_____

CASE #75

The Case of Creating Corporate Sponsorship

The athletic department just needed an infusion of funds. It was clear that there were insufficient monies in the budget to accomplish all that needed to be done. And, it was clear that there had not been much foresight in terms of fundraising in the past that might have alleviated this disastrous situation.

Joseph McMillian, the athletic director, was faced with a dilemma. The President, Mary Louise Smith, was not very knowledgeable and was really suspicious of the athletic program in general and any special or unusual methods of financing the program and activities. She was especially worried about getting involved in any situation in which one or two individuals might gain unacceptable power or influence over the athletic arena through their donations or financial contributions to the sports program. As a result, the edict came down that any effort to increase funding had to be accomplished through means other than simply securing a sugar daddy to cough up the money.

Successful corporate sponsorship agreements often means significant financial resources for the athletic program. [Courtesy of Scrolling Score-Rite Tables by PowerAd Company, Inc., Salina, Kansas]

"Ok, so I cannot get some wealthy guy or gal to simply give me the money, what can I do?" thought Joseph. "Where is the money, who has the money, who has the money who would not assume the sugar daddy role," Joseph mused. Finally, he hit upon the idea, i.e., soliciting companies and businesses to donate money through the vehicle commonly referred to as *corporate sponsors*.

He approached several businesses and eventually got through to the general manager of the local soft drink wholesale and distribution company. He offered the general manager an arrangement whereby in exchange for a large sum of money for each of the next few years, the company would be able to lay claim to being a *corporate sponsor*. After the arrangement had been signed by the AD and the general manager, money changed hands. Ads in the local paper, celebrating the corporate sponsorship, between the soft drink company and the school, appeared within three days.

Two weeks later, the AD made a similar arrangement with a car dealer. However, after it became known that the local automobile dealership was promoting the fact that it was THE corporate sponsor of the athletic department the AD got a phone call from a very disturbed general manager at the soft drink company. "Hey, I thought we had a deal, a written contract, that specified that Coke was your corporate sponsor?" complained the representative. Shortly thereafter, the automobile representative called and complained about being upstaged by the C soft drink radio promo that said that the soft drink distributor was THE corporate sponsor of the college's athletic program. "What a mess," thought the AD.

The athletic director tried to explain (in two different meetings with a representative of both firms) that the corporate sponsorship agreement did not specify exclusive rights to being a corporate sponsorship, just to be a corporate sponsor. "Well, hopefully, I have finally solved this potentially embarrassing situation," thought the AD, after he placated both businessmen.

However, the peace did not last long when both business representatives came to see Joseph, in person, to complain about the latest fiasco, that is, when a different automobile dealer ran an ad in the local newspaper stating it was a corporate sponsor and a second soft drink company did the same thing. "What in the world is going on here?" echoed both people representing the first two sponsors. "Not only are there more sponsors but there are more sponsors in the same industry or business that we are in. It was bad enough that there are more sponsors than each of us thought, but to have as additional sponsors companies in our own field of endeavor is just too much. We are embarrassed with the public, and worse, we look bad to our superiors at headquarters. Either you solve this or we both will be visiting your President in the very near future."

QUESTIONS FOR DISCUSSION

1. Outline the essential elements of this scenario that cause the problems for the AD.
2. What did Joseph do wrong initially in his attempt to develop a corporate sponsorship arrangement with businesses? Be specific.
3. Does the initial soft drink manager have a justifiable grievance? Explain.
4. If the initial soft drink was the only sponsor to be engaged, what type of corporate sponsorship is this called?
5. Does the first car dealer manager have the same grievance? Why or why not?
6. What does the AD say to these initial sponsors to make them happy?
7. Now that the latest two companies have come on board, are the managers at the initial sponsoring companies justified in being unhappy? Explain.
8. The fact that a corporate sponsorship with the second car dealer was consummated meant what kind of corporate sponsorship was in effect?
9. Summarize the advantages of the three types of corporate sponsorships.
10. What should the AD have done along the way to make sure that all four sponsors would be happy?
11. What are some of the essential elements in any corporate sponsorship agreement?
12. Cite some general guidelines or principles that pertain to the establishment of corporate sponsorships in this type of scenario.
13. Comments . . .

RESPONSES FOR QUESTIONS FOR DISCUSSION

_____

_____

_____

_____

_____

_____

_____

_____

_____

_____

_____

_____

_____

_____

_____

_____

Problems with Special Situations

CHAPTER OBJECTIVES

After reading this chapter you will be able to:

- Assist coaches in their efforts to work with athletes on goal setting
- Enumerate the duties and responsibilities of a publicity director for a school and an athletic league at the college level
- Provide to high school and college students career information about coaching and athletic administration
- Help individuals overcome the *glass ceiling* in their search for a suitable career position
- Outline the things that a quality mentor might be able to do for an individual in terms of professional assistance

Student enthusiasm is contagious.
[Courtesy of John Carroll Sports Information]

- Identify the possible landmines waiting the coach who retires from coaching and assumes the position of athletic director
- Reveal the problems with athletic directors keeping to themselves and to their offices
- Conceptualize the professional office of an athletic director and recommend specific steps to take to maintain a professionally looking office and appropriate personal image
- Explain the policies to establish when planning to rent out an athletic facility to an organization not affiliated with the school system
- Indicate why *padding the budget* should never be done by the coaches or by the athletic administration
- Understand the legal liability risk of the athletic department in the conduct of athletic contests
- Stipulate how the athletic department should plan for a major upgrade or creation to an athletic facility
- Reveal the negative consequences of unkempt athletic facilities insofar as the athletic director and the department are concerned

- Outline a suitable inventory process and storage system for a high school including steps to take in ordering items, receiving items and storing items purchased
- Recognize the elements that make up a quality game promotion

CASE STUDY

76. The case of the lack of goal setting
77. The case of the new publicity director
78. The case of the confused would-be athletic coach
79. The case of the glass ceiling
80. The case of the well-meaning mentor
81. The case of the coach being told how to do his job
82. The case of the athletic director hiding in his office
83. The case of the messy athletic director
84. The case of the problems associated with renting a facility
85. The case of fiscal irresponsibility
86. The case of the unsafe practice site
87. The case of the upgrade to the facility
88. The case of the unkempt facilities
89. The case of the poorly organized inventory setup
90. The case of the poorly organized game promotion

CASE #76

The Case of the Lack of Goal Setting

Coach Henry Wallace was disturbed. His junior high basketball players seem confused. In fact, they seemed to just be going through the motions throughout the entire season. They played the games but none of the players seemed very focused. Nor did many of the athletes seem to be capable of working towards specific objectives. Rather, they just seemed to come to practices and go through the motions. And, after the practices, they would stop and leave and that would be that. At the next practice, individual athletes would take part but without enthusiasm, without focus and without visible commitment. The same with games and pre-game warm-ups. The athletes looked like they did not care about what they were doing even warming up for the game.

Finally, with half of the season completed, the athletic director, Carolyn Ault, decided that she had seen enough and called the coach in for a meeting to discuss the situation, a situation that had become noticeable to many people, in and out of school. During the meeting the AD expressed concern for the situation, asked some questions, and offered some suggestions.

During the meeting the coach was a little defensive at first, declaring: "What do you mean my kids don't care. They are in middle school, their hormones are running rampant and they have a thousand things going on in their lives. Why shouldn't they be distracted? Why, what do you expect of me?"

The athletic director tried to calm the coach down. After about 30 minutes, the coach was mollified slightly and left the meeting not in anger but with a deep feeling of concern and not a little self-doubt in his own ability as a coach and mentor. "Maybe I have lost it," thought the coach. "Maybe it is time for me to hang it up and do something else with my time. It is not that I don't have other things to spend my time on."

Following the meeting with the athletic director, coach Wallace decided to call in several of his more experienced players for a short talk. During the 40-minute session with four of his 7th and 8th grade athletes, the coach attempted to bring up different topics relating to how the youngsters viewed their sport, their own participation and their achievements in the sport. It did not take long to discern that the kids were not really focusing on their sport and their own participation.

One of the major things coach Wallace learned from the discussion was that the young athletes failed to be focused in terms of what they really were supposed to do and to be working on. In short, the players did not exhibit any specific or general goals, either for themselves as individuals or as a team unit. This was evident the more the coach asked the players about why they were participating and what they saw themselves doing and achieving in the near and distant future.

Following this exploratory meeting the head coach met with his assistant, Jimmy Ulter. They talked about how to get their youngsters to focus on specific and general goals. "We need to do something to help these kids understand that they need to have something to shoot at, something to aim at," said the head coach.

"You mean, they need to set goals," added assistant Jimmy Ulter.

"Yes, goals. They are essential. But how do we proceed? What should we do? How do we get the players to be more goal oriented and more focused?" added coach Wallace.

QUESTIONS FOR DISCUSSION

1. What are the major problems outlined above for the coach? What are the major challenges facing the athletic director in this situation?
2. Do athletic directors have an obligation to help coaches be better coaches? To what extent? Provide examples.
3. Assume the role of the athletic director and indicate how you might have expressed *concern* for the situation at the first meeting and at the follow-up meetings.
4. Again assuming the role of the athletic director, what *questions* would you have asked in the initial meeting that you called?
5. Should athletic directors have successful coaching experiences themselves? Why or why not?
6. How can an athletic director who has not coached (at all or successfully) overcome that seemingly significant deficiency?
7. And, in the meeting, what would be some *suggestions* you might provide to the coach to help him in this situation?
8. Did coach Wallace do the right thing in scheduling a meeting with some of his players to see what might be the problem? What would you have done differently, if anything? Explain your reasoning.
9. What are some of the visible signs that may be indicative of individual athletes failing to have established goals?
10. How would you suggest the two coaches should approach the team to introduce the players to the whole topic of appropriate goal setting? Be specific.
11. In general, what are the roles of coaches in terms of individual athletes attempting to become involved in goal setting? Provide examples.
12. What is the role of the athletic director in helping coaches understand their athletes better? Specify what the athletic director can do to continue to help her coach(es) in this situation.
13. Can coaches be so close to the situation that they can't see the trees for the forest? Explain this statement.
14. How might individual athletes at this age level go about the task of developing or establishing appropriate goals? Should the athletic director be involved with athletes directly in this situation? Why or why not? Be specific.

15. What is the time element when goal setting is involved? How much time should be devoted to goal setting? When? Why?

16. What administrative principles or guidelines are applicable here insofar as the athletic director is concerned?

17. Comments . . .

RESPONSES FOR QUESTIONS FOR DISCUSSION

_____

_____

_____

_____

_____

_____

_____

_____

_____

_____

_____

_____

_____

_____

CASE #77

The Case of the New Publicity Director

Coach Joan Grant, the assistant head coach of one of the more successful field hockey teams within NCAA division III, was given the additional responsibility (by the league secretary) to serve as the publicity director for the entire league, involving some 14 different teams in nine different cities, located along the east coast. The position was a non-paying, part-time position. Joan was able to continue in her teaching and coaching jobs at Westwood College.

Coach Grant was informed that one of her tasks was to have the league become more visible to the general public so that (A) more people would come to see the games as paying spectators and (B) it would be easier to raise money from different segments of the various communities and the general public(s). The full time league commissioner told her: "Joan, we need your help to make this league the talk of the country, the pride of the sports federation, the excitement of the community. This will be easier than in most leagues since we have had exceptional success in terms of our league members achieving excellent won/loss records, with several teams having earned top ten spots nationally in the polls."

QUESTIONS FOR DISCUSSION

1. What are some challenges or potential problems that might face Joan in her new position as publicity director for the league?
2. What are some pluses that Joan might want to take advantage of?
3. What should Coach Grant do upon learning of her new appointment?
4. What should she be careful of avoiding in her new position?
5. What concerns might the athletic director at Westwood College have in this situation? Be specific.
6. What should the athletic director share with the coach when apprised of this new responsibility? What specific guidelines might the athletic director set down for the coach to follow to insure that her college duties would not suffer?
7. How should Joan proceed INITIALLY to fulfill her new responsibilities?
8. How shall Joan balance her coaching duties, teaching responsibilities and her new publicity obligations? Outline some definite suggestions.
9. What exactly is involved in her new responsibilities? Be specific.
10. Define the terms publicity, promotions and public relations in terms of Joan's new responsibilities. What are differences between each term? Provide examples of each.
11. As publicity director, what skills should she possess? Explain in detail.

12. Outline a tentative PLAN OF ATTACK to cover a two-year period in terms of promotions, publicity and public relations for the league.

13. How can she separate her coaching and other responsibilities at Westwood College and her league duties and responsibilities?

14. What are some general principles of promotions, publicity and public relations that are applicable in this situation?

15. Comments . . .

RESPONSES FOR QUESTIONS FOR DISCUSSION

_____

_____

_____

_____

_____

_____

_____

_____

_____

_____

_____

_____

_____

Case #78

The Case of the Confused Would-be Athletic Coach

Mary Goodwish, a junior in college, had thought all her life about being involved in some fashion with collegiate athletics, as a full time job. She was an outstanding athlete in high school and an average college athlete. In terms of grades, she was – like most people – average with a 2.7 cumulative GPA average through 4 semesters of college.

Now, however, Mary Goodwish began to think quite seriously about her career options once she had graduated from college. She was also at that point in her life where she had to pick a so-called major in college so that she would be able to graduate from college in the traditional 4-5 year time period. She began to search for some answers to what kind of life she would like to have as an adult wage earner. She was beginning to search out for herself answers to questions that would help her in her career planning. She told her mom that she was going top ask her high school athletic director for some information . . .

DISCUSSION ITEMS

1. What kind of education does Mary need to have to be involved in coaching or some other aspect of sport, such as becoming an athletic administrator, or even an athletic director?
2. What academic field of study might Mary major in so that her career aspirations (becoming employed in sports) might be facilitated? Does majoring in physical education significantly help or impede one's possible employment in the sports world (in a school setting) either as a coach or as an athletic administrator? Explain your rationale.
3. What kind of skills and competencies does Mary need *to enter* the job market as well as *to remain there and begin to move* up the ladder of success (coaching career ladder or the athletic administration ladder)?
4. What does the phrase *ladder of success* mean and what does it consist of in the world of sport? Provide examples.
5. What steps should she take *now* to get a head start on her career?
6. What kind of sport jobs (reasonable opportunities) are out there in the world of sport for someone like Mary? Be specific.
7. What factors should she consider in becoming a coach? An athletic administrator?
8. What makes for a successful coach? Why do some coaches fail? Be specific and provide examples.
9. What makes for a successful athletic administrator? Why do some administrators fail? Be specific and provide examples.

10. *From the perspective of an athletic director*—what is it like to become a coach in a junior high or high school on a full time basis? What about on a part-time basis? What are the differences in being a full or a part-time coach? What challenges and advantages are there in each situation?

11. Does one have to be a coach or should one have had coaching (successful) experience to be a quality athletic administrator (director) at the high school level? At the junior college level? At the small college level? At the big-time (NCAA division I) level? Explain your answers.

12. How does one become a high school coach in this state? In other states? What are the legal requirements to become a coach? How does one find out this information? Be specific.

13. How does one become a coach in the junior college ranks? What is the difference in becoming a coach at the high school level and the junior college level?

14. How does one become a coach in the small college ranks? What is the difference in becoming a coach at the high school level and the small college level?

15. If Mary wants to become an athletic administrator at the big time university level, how does she prepare herself and what does she have to do to get there—and stay there? Be specific in your suggestions and recommendations.

16. Is there discrimination against minorities and/or women in terms of securing head coaching positions and/or athletic director type posts? Explain.

17. What principles are applicable in terms of being marketable in the sports world within an educational setting?

18. Comments . . .

RESPONSES FOR QUESTIONS FOR DISCUSSION

_____

_____

_____

_____

_____

_____

_____

CASE #79

The Case of the Glass Ceiling

Ginny Visin had always dreamed of becoming a high school coach of softball. Ever since she was a youngster playing ball in the sandlots of Chicago she wanted to be involved in sports. She was a gifted athlete, even at an early age. And, she only increased her athletic prowess, as she grew older.

Outstanding coaches can have tremendous influence on their athletes for a lifetime.
[Courtesy of Washington State University]

She was lucky that she lived in the age of expanding sport's opportunity for women. For if she had lived in her mother's time, she would have been relegated to participating in so-called *play days* for the girls that were more recreational in nature than real competitive opportunities. However, this is now the 21st century and she had taken advantage of every opportunity thrown her way in terms of athletic involvement. She played little league sports. She was a standout on the junior high level in three sports, basketball, softball and volleyball. And, in high school she earned All-State honors in basketball and softball. She was so good, in fact, that she earned a coveted full athletic scholarship to a big-time university where she continued her record pace as an exceptional athlete. She graduated as one of the most successful female athletes to ever wear the uniforms for the Falcons. Throughout all of her athletic life as a competitor she had been successful.

Unfortunately, although she was a great collegiate athlete she did not possess the ultimate skills to play professional sports. As a result, Ginny elected to do the next best thing and pursue a coaching and teaching career. That way she would at least be able to stay in the thick of things athletic-wise. Besides, she could also play basketball and softball in various city leagues that were beginning to blossom around the country. Nevertheless, it was a far step from the professional leagues for women that now existed—but for Ginny it would have to do.

After some five years as a teacher of physical education and as an assistant coach of girl's volleyball, basketball and softball, Ginny was able to reduce her athletic involvement and concentrate just on basketball and softball (for girls)—her two best sports as a participant and as a coach. And, she continued to teach as well. However, she was still an assistant coach. Her head coaches, David and Steve, were both relatively young and highly successful as teachers and coaches. Thus, they were not going to retire and thus create an opening for her to step into. Thus, it became obvious that if Ginny was ever going to be a head coach she would have to move to a different high school or seek a coaching position at the college or university level.

Her head coaches indicated that they were always willing to help her in terms of her career moves by recommending her for a head job. So, Ginny started applying for head positions at other high schools and at a variety of small and medium sized colleges. She was determined to become a head coach in one or both of her favorite sports. She was sure that her experience as an athlete and as an assistant coach in highly successful high school programs would make it possible for her to get a suitable post.

However, to no avail. Over the next two years she was infrequently interviewed for some high school positions. To her it seemed that every job that she really wanted at the big-time high school level went to a male coach who had had head coaching experience. It seemed that principals and athletic directors were reluctant to hire a woman as head coach who had only been an assistant coach previously. The story was similar at the college level, only worst. Ginny was getting tired of being told that it was too bad that she had had no head coaching experience. She was caught in the classic Catch-22 situation. And Ginny was starting to continually bang against the proverbial glass ceiling and could seemingly get no higher in her chosen profession.

QUESTIONS FOR DISCUSSION

1. Is Ginny's predicament a common situation today in high school and/or college coaching? Explain.
2. Should the head coach of a female sport be a woman? Why or why not?
3. What factors should be considered when evaluating candidates for a head coaching position of a female sport? Of any sport?
4. How would you, as athletic director, go about insuring that the applicant pool for a head coaching position (for females) contain women?
5. What responsibility, if any, do you have as an athletic director, to see that women become head coaches and assistant coaches of female sports?
6. Would you, as athletic director, hire a woman with lesser (but still minimum) qualifications/experience over a man with better qualifications/experience for a job of coaching a female team? Provide a rationale for your response.
7. What questions might the athletic director ask of candidates in a job interview for this type of position? What type of questions cannot be asked? Provide examples.
8. Why doesn't Ginny just stay at the school where she is currently teaching and coaching? Elaborate.
9. Is Ginny seeking to move too fast too quickly? Is she expecting special treatment because of her prior success in sports?
10. Is her timing appropriate? That is, is this the right time for her to seek a head coaching position?
11. Are Ginny's goals appropriate? Why or why not?
12. What can David and Steve do to help Ginny in her quest? Be specific.
13. Why did the open positions outlined in this case study go to male coaches? Speculate.

14. What else can Ginny do to make herself more marketable? To help her crack the glass ceiling?

15. How might Ginny respond to those athletic directors who interview her and question the fact that she has never been a head coach before and was now applying for a head coach? Assume the role of Ginny and indicate specifically (role play) what and how you would communicate your message(s).

16. How does any woman make the giant step from being an assistant coach to the head coaching post at the high school level? Be specific.

17. How does any woman make the super giant step from being an assistant coach on the high school level to a college head coaching position? Explain your rationale.

18. What skills, competencies and experiences would you, as athletic director, look for in potential head coach candidates?

19. What can you, as an athletic director, do to insure that women are given a fair shot at vacancies and that women are actually hired as coaches?

20. Is Ginny being treated differently than male coaches in similar positions (that is, seeking head posts while having only served at the assistant level)? If so, why?

21. Is it fair for Ginny to be treated as she has been? Is this really an example of the glass ceiling in the marketplace? Elaborate.

22. Is this merely a case that there are many more qualified applicants for the number of head coaching posts and Ginny just doesn't have as good a resume (experience) as other candidates?

23. Now that Ginny has experienced failure in her attempts to get a head coaching position, what should she do? Be specific.

24. Should Ginny hire a lawyer and attempt to force a district or a college to hire her? Is this a case of discrimination from the facts presented?

25. What general principles are appropriate or applicable in this situation for the athletic director's perspective?

26. Comments . . .

RESPONSES FOR QUESTIONS FOR DISCUSSION

_____

_____

_____

_____

_____

CASE #80

The Case of the Well-Meaning Mentor

Missy Linder was an energetic young lady of 27 who had just completed her 5th year as varsity volleyball coach, assistant basketball coach and assistant softball coach at Eastmann High School in Alabama. She also taught health and physical education. Needless to say, Missy was pretty busy.

Nevertheless, she somehow always found time for each and every one of the students who wanted to visit with her—and she was a very popular teacher and coach. Perhaps it was because of her age or her enthusiasm. Whatever the reason, Missy was well thought of by almost every-one.

Harley Fletch, the athletic director and girl's head basketball coach, really appreciated the professionalism that Ms. Linder displayed. He was similarly impressed with her growing body of knowledge. He acknowledged that many people could try very hard but effort was only half the battle. One also had to have competency and an ever-deepening level of skill. And, in Missy he thought that the school, the students and the parents were very, very lucky to have someone of her caliber on staff.

Sometimes when he relaxed and thought of his younger days he saw a lot of himself in Missy. That is, he recognized her burning desire to achieve, her willingness to take on difficult tasks, her unselfishness in volunteering to help others and to help the school itself, and her ability to actually get the job done through skill and wise decision-making. He knew that she deserved to advance far in her chosen professions of teaching and coaching. He also recognized that although she was a top notch professional for someone of her age and experience, she still could benefit from help from competent professionals, individuals who would look out for her welfare and feel comfortable in providing advice when appropriate—without being upset if the advice is not followed.

During the next 18 months, Harley Fletch took advantage of being in the right place at the right time to help coach Linder in various areas. He politely and discreetly gave her good advice in professional areas in an effort to prevent her from making professional boo-boos (as he had done in his early career). He also provided her with opportunities to gain additional experiences as an assistant coach in basketball. He even began to give her some administrative tasks to perform because in his heart he felt that she might, someday, want to further her career in the area of athletic administration. And, he wanted to help her be all that she could possibly be as a person, as a coach and as a teacher.

In reality, Mr. Fletch became the assistant coach's unofficial mentor (both in coaching and in the area of administration) although neither he nor Missy would have ever used that term. Rather, he became a confidant in whom Missy began to place great trust. Their professional association and relationship blossomed over the next two years to the point where Ms. Linder felt comfortable in sharing confidences as well as in seeking advice both of a professional and personal nature. They became good friends as well as professional colleagues.

QUESTIONS FOR DISCUSSION

1. Why is it advantageous for Missy Linder to have Mr. Fletcher as a mentor? What are some positive concrete benefits for Missy?
2. Why did Mr. Fletcher feel so positive about Miss Linder as a coach, a person, as a potential administrator? Elaborate.
3. What exactly is a mentor? What does a mentor do? Be specific.
4. How can a coach today hope to attract a mentor who will professionally help that individual as a coach and/or as a future administrator? Explain your answers.
5. Is Ms. Linder acting in a professional manner in terms of Mr. Fletcher? What about Mr. Fletcher; is he acting in a suitable and appropriate fashion for someone in his position? Why or why not?
6. Is Mr. Fletcher being unfair to other staff members by serving as the unofficial capacity of mentor to Ms. Linder? Why or why not?
7. What might other people think of the relationship between Ms. Linder and Mr. Fletcher? Why? What potential dangers might exist in this relationship between a male and a female?
8. What must both Missy and Harley be sure to do in order to keep their relationship on a professional and appropriate level? Be specific.
9. Did Missy seek out Mr. Fletcher to serve as a mentor? How did he become someone who looked upon Missy with favor and professional pride?
10. What would happen to this relationship if Mr. Fletch provided advice and Missy failed to accept the advice? Why?
11. What general principles are applicable in this specific case?
12. Comments . . .

RESPONSES FOR QUESTIONS FOR DISCUSSION

CASE #81

The Case of the Coach Being Told How to Do His Job

Richard Cummings had not regretted the day he decided to give up coaching basketball and take the position of athletic director at Boomtown High. Although he certainly missed the excitement of the game, the comradely association with his players and the thrill of winning athletic contests, he certainly didn't miss the pressure that the basketball coach at that school was subjected to. And, he didn't miss all of the long hours spent on the non-coaching aspects of being a successful basketball coach.

But the athletic director had paid his dues. He had been a winner for 25 years at Boomtown. And, as a result, he has been rewarded with the post of AD. Actually, he has been pretty competent as the athletic administrator, but not as good as he was a coach. But he was learning. If only the school and the coaches would have patience until he got it right, he and the athletic program would survive and eventually prosper.

Most of the coaches on the staff felt rather fondly of old Richard because as a former coach he understood the challenges and the trials and tribulations that they experience in the everyday conduct of their jobs. However, at the present time, the basketball coach, Teddy Tolbert, was not one of Richard's favorite fans. It seems Richard couldn't quite get the coaching blood out of his system. As a consequence, he kept critiquing Teddy's coaching efforts throughout the season. In the early part of the season Teddy thought that the former coach was just trying to be helpful. But as the season progressed, Mr. Cummings expanded his comments to include rather critical and even caustic remarks about some of the coach's decisions and strategy. Additionally, Mr. Cummings actually started to suggest to Teddy what the coach should do (in terms of tactics and strategies) in upcoming games.

The straw that broke the camel's back was when the athletic director caught coach Tolbert during half-time of a very tight game and started to tell the coach who he should start for the second half and what defense the team should use to attack the visitors.

The next day coach Tolbert made an appointment to visit with the athletic director. His intention was to try and get the athletic director to act like an athletic director and not as an old frustrated former basketball coach reliving his golden years through the actions of the new coach. However, he was not sure what or how he was going to accomplish this. He wondered about how the athletic director would react and whether or not he should even take a chance by approaching the athletic director with his concern.

QUESTIONS FOR DISCUSSION

1. What is the big deal about the athletic director retaining an interest in the basketball team? Is this what this situation is all about? Why or why not?
2. Why is the athletic director acting as he is? Elaborate.
3. Is the relationship between the athletic director and the basketball coach anything more than a minor annoyance? Why or why not?
4. Why do you think the athletic director gave up the basketball coaching position?
5. Should Richard Cummings have given up coaching basketball *and* assumed the position of athletic director? Why or why not?
6. Is this type of behavior by Mr. Cummings common among athletic directors who were previously head coaches? Speculate.
7. Could this situation have been avoided? If so, how? By whom? When? Be specific.
8. Should not the athletic director have foreseen this eventuality? If so, what could the AD have done to prevent this interference?
9. What might the current basketball coach have done to prevent this situation from developing to the stage where it is now?
10. What should be the professional relationship between the head coach of a sport and the athletic director who had coached that particular sport? Elaborate.
11. If this situation continues what might be the consequences for the athletic director *and* the basketball coach?
12. What should the basketball coach say to the AD in their meeting? Be specific. Examine the various possibilities through role-playing.
13. What might be the appropriate response(s) of the athletic director? Speculate.
14. Does the current basketball coach take a risk by approaching the athletic director with his concern? Explain your position.
15. What general principles are suitable for this specific situation?
16. Comments . . .

RESPONSES FOR QUESTIONS FOR DISCUSSION

_____

_____

_____

_____

_____

CASE #82

The Case of the Athletic Director Hiding in His Office

It had not been a very good year for Michael Buntley, the athletic director at Parkridge High School in Middletown, Indiana. In fact, it had been a terrible year. First of all, the majority of the experienced coaches were upset with him because they felt that he was weak when dealing with the boosters and the administration.

If that was not enough, the athletes were on his case because they felt that he was a no-show when it came to athletics. In fact, the joke among the athletes was that the AD was a missing person since he only infrequently was seen at sporting events, and then only at flagship sports, and then only ever so briefly.

The parents were also on the "beat up on the AD bandwagon" because they viewed him as a poor money manager. He was always crying about the lack of funds, yet never did anything about getting more funds—other than ask for more money through the regular budgetary process.

The boosters were not exactly enthralled with Mr. Buntley either. He had failed to make them feel important, worthwhile or significant in terms of the support of the sports program. Most of the officers and so-called bigwigs in town recognized that if it were not for the Booster Club, the athletic program at Parkridge High School would be in a lot worse financial shape that it was in now. However, they were never given the respect and accolades that they felt they deserved by the AD.

And, the principal, Ms. Elmilda Swanson, wasn't exactly a fan of Mr. Buntley ever since that time in the fall when she learned that the AD had been especially critical of her at a booster club meeting. In fact, she had heard through the grapevine that the athletic director had referred to her as all mouth and no action in terms of providing financial support for the sports program.

Poor Mr. Buntley felt that he needed a flak jacket when he walked around the halls of the school. He felt that way even when he walked downtown in the small comunity. It seemed that he was the lighting rod of criticism, and he couldn't understand why.

Well, he would fix that. People wouldn't have him around (at least not as visible as before) to kick and beat up as much. He would simply get of their way for a while. He would remain unseen, therefore providing less of a target for carping from the ever-growing number of unreasonable and ignorant critics. He would rely on Mrs. Judith Sampson, his secretary, as a go-between with those people who might want to see him or get him to do things.

So, for the next 6-8 weeks, good old Buntley stayed in his office unless it was absolutely necessary to venture out. He was not going to talk to athletes, to coaches, to boosters or to people in the comunity. He would even stay out of the way of the principal, if that was possible. He felt that he was pretty smart with this new strategy as he was sure that when things died down he would be able to resurface and things might be back to semi-normalcy.

QUESTIONS FOR DISCUSSION

1. Are athletic directors normally under pressure from one or more groups of individuals? Explain.
2. List some of the controversial areas that athletic directors at the high school level should be on the alert for in terms of potential problematic situations?
3. What can athletic directors do to gain the respect of the coaches on their staff?
4. How can an athletic director present an image of being strong in relationships with booster clubs, boosters, and the school administration? Elaborate.
5. In respect to athletes, what can an athletic director do to maintain a positive yet professional relationship? What steps should an AD take to be respected by athletes?
6. Why is *perception* often times as important (if not more important) than *reality*? Discuss.
7. How can Mr. Buntley create and maintain better relationships with parents, especially in terms of budgets and money management?
8. What might be some possible courses of action that the athletic director might take to mend fences with the booster club and important members? Be specific.
9. How did Mr. Buntley get on the principal's bad side? How could this situation have been avoided? What might he do to rectify this situation, if anything?
10. Is the particular strategy hatched by the harassed athletic director an appropriate one for this athletic director? Why or why not?
11. What might happen to the athletic director as a result of this strategy?
12. Can an athletic director survive for long when a significant number of constituencies feel that the AD is less than competent? Elaborate.
13. Cite some general principles or guidelines that are applicable in this particular case?
14. Coments . . .

RESPONSES FOR QUESTIONS FOR DISCUSSION

_____

_____

_____

_____

_____

_____

CASE #83

The Case of the Messy Athletic Director

Athletic director Maurice Thompson had been a highly successful football coach for over 20 years. He had a reputation during this time of juggling a 1001 things at once—while serving as a teacher, coach, husband and father, etc. Now, entering his 2nd year as the athletic director at the same high school where he had enjoyed many decades of success as a coach, he was not a little upset with his boss, Jake Klukas, the principal who had been at the school for 5 years. Mr. Thompson had just returned from a meeting with the principal and the meeting had not gone well at all. In fact, Maurice was steaming with barely controllable anger.

"The audacity of that man telling me how to dress, how to act, how to keep my office," fumed Maurice. "Where does he get off telling me that I have to present a better image of myself now that I am the athletic director and not merely a coach. Why, I am insulted that he told me my office looked like a jungle," thought Maurice.

Figure 11.1. An office like a jungle

The meeting between the athletic director and the principal had taken about 25 minutes but it seemed to both gentlemen that it had lasted much longer. The principal had realized early on in the meeting when he had tried to help the athletic director understand the importance of presenting a proper and professional image (both on and off the job) that things were not going well. In fact, it was obvious that the athletic director had no clue about the need to be professionally dressed and to have a professional office.

It wasn't that the former coach/newly appointed athletic director was a slob. He wasn't. It was just that Maurice was a little sloppy and certainly did not go out of his way to present himself as a true white collar professional person overseeing a very large and important educational unit (with a fairly significant budget to boot) within the large school district.

Maurice continued to dress like he did when he coached. He liked his old coaching duds and wasn't about to change now at his age. He still attempted to juggle many things at once, but now as athletic director he found that the things he faced as AD were more complicated, time consuming and distracting that the challenges he faced as football coach. Also, his autocratic style as football coach did not go over well with the coaches under his command now. They resented his do it my way or else style and were not reluctant to share their displeasure with the principal and the superintendent.

The AD's office was something else. It was not only not neat, it was a MESS; everything seemed to be in total disarray. However, the AD knew where every sheet of paper was in that office, it just looked like a gopher lived there with papers strewed everywhere, including on the floor. He greeted guests and staff in his old coaching sweatshirt and coaching shoes, he placed his feet on his desk, he chewed gum, his hair was rarely combed, and he incessantly talked about his successful days as a winning football coach. As a highly successful football coach, this image had always been accepted, even encouraged by fans, friends and some members of the news media. However, this type of behavior was not accepted by the principal who expected a more professional business approach by the leader of a large athletic program.

QUESTIONS FOR DISCUSSION

1. Summarize the major problems now facing Maurice Thompson as an athletic director.
2. Why might the tactics used by an individual who coaches not work when that same person advances to the position of athletic director? Elaborate.
3. Why doesn't Maurice simply change now that he is an athletic director?
4. What might the principal and/or the superintendent have done earlier to avert this situation from developing to the point where it has now?
5. When a coach considers moving up to the post of athletic director, what are some of the considerations that the individual might want to consider in terms of changes or differences to be faced in the new role?
6. Why should an athletic director be concerned with having a neat office? Is it important to attempt to impress visitors to one's office? If so, why?
7. What are some suggestions you might give to Maurice in terms of undergoing a complete makeover in terms of (A) personal appearance; (B) personal behavior, (C) office management, and (D) appearance of the office, etc.?
8. Describe the expected physical appearance (and behavior) of a professional athletic director at the high school level. Is there a difference between how a high school athletic director should look in appearance and how a college athletic director (division I, II and III) should appear? Why or why not?
9. How would you reconcile the apparent conflict between being one's true self (being honest, even if messy) and putting on a false front by attempting to be something that one is not?
10. What would you recommend to the athletic director to do now, from this date onward?
11. What principles or guidelines might be appropriate in this case?
12. Comments . . .

RESPONSES FOR QUESTIONS FOR DISCUSSION

CASE #84

The Case of Problems Associated with Renting a Facility

The athletic director, Philip Weimer, was facing another financial crisis (were there any other kind?) in his role as first year athletic administrator for the brand new suburban high school. One of the boosters, Jeremy Michaels, had suggested the other night that the athletic department should rent out the athletic facilities, especially the field house, to outside groups like square dance organizations, social groups and youth organizations, etc.

"That way, you have a source of extra money that you can spend any way you want. There must be lots of dates on which the school doesn't use the field house or swimming pool or other indoor and outdoor facilities. Why don't you just develop some policies regarding rental of the facilities by outside groups, do a little advertising and publicity and start raking in the money. It would go a long way toward solving your financial crisis and also make you look smart in the eyes of the central administration and the booster club," added Mr. Michaels.

Proper crowd management and supervision makes for an enjoyable experience for fans and players alike. [Courtesy of Eastern Illinois University Sports Information]

After thinking about it for a week or so, Philip did just that. He went home one night and thought up some policies that seemed right at the moment and wrote them down and lo and behold the school had rental policies. The next day he announced to some contacts in the community that the athletic department was going to consider requests to rent out facilities to community groups. He sent a memo to the high school principal as well. Finally, the next week he made the formal announcement at the booster club's meeting and publicly thanked Mr. Michaels for his inspirational idea.

The following Saturday night was the first time that the gymnasium was rented to an outside group, a square dance organization sponsored by a local church. The AD made the arrangements over the phone with the minister of the church who was also in charge of the square dance organization. The group rented the gymnasium, two classrooms, rest rooms, locker rooms, use of the parking lot and the concession stand for $750 that evening. The minister said that he would bring the check Saturday and drop it off at the dance. The AD agreed and sat back in his chair thinking how smart he was to have thought of this super-duper fundraising idea.

However, disaster soon followed. When the athletic director arrived in school Monday morning he was faced with the head custodian who told him that there was severe physical damage (caused evidently by some children of the dancers who tagged along with their parents) to the tile ceilings of the hallway, broken sinks, cracked window panes to two doors, a broken coke dispenser, and clogged toilets. In all, the preliminary estimate of the damage was $4500. Later that morning the athletic director also learned that a young lady had injured herself by tripping over a rubber mat left in the locker room and was considering suing the AD and the school for negligence. And, finally, to top that, the check did not arrive the following week.

QUESTIONS FOR DISCUSSION

1. Summarize the essential elements of this situation, including each of the problems now faced by the athletic director.

2. Can the athletic director spend the income from the rental of facilities anyway he wants to? Elaborate.

3. Is the concept of renting out athletic facilities common among high schools? Among colleges at the division III level? At the division I level? Why or why not?

4. Did the athletic director go about the process of planning for the facility rental in the correct manner? Elaborate and provide alternative strategies.

5. Would a competent athletic director foreseen that such problems might occur? Explain in full.

6. If renting to community groups might be considered an appropriate move for a high school, what types of organizations might not be appropriate to rent to (specify), and why?

7. Should the athletic director sought permission (or input) from anyone before he implemented the practice of renting out facilities? Whose permission might he have sought? Why?

8. In what areas could the athletic director's superiors and outsiders now criticize the athletic director?

9. What suggestions would you make to the athletic director in terms of advertising, promoting and seeking outside groups who wanted to pay for renting athletic facilities?

10. Outline a sample policy statement (rules and regulations) that includes protection for the school in case there are problems (physical damage, personal injuries/accidents, etc.) as a result of renting the facility to outside groups.

11. What type of insurance situation should be in place for groups desiring to rent the facilities?

12. Should there have been a representative of the school in attendance while the outside group used the facility? Why or why not? Who?

13. What would you recommend to the AD in terms of hold harmless agreements? What are these agreements?

14. Should there be an advance and follow-up walk-through of the rented facilities? What about a damage deposit? What about requiring advance payment? Explain your rationale for each.

15. What should the athletic director do now that these disasters have cropped up? Be specific and provide a time line.

16. What should the athletic director have done differently in an effort to prevent each of the problems that did develop in this scenario?

17. What general administrative principles or managerial guidelines are applicable here?

18. Comments . . .

RESPONSES FOR QUESTIONS FOR DISCUSSION

Case #85

The Case of Fiscal Irresponsibility

The newly appointed athletic director, Lynn Rogers, knew she was in for a rough time when she took the post of AD. The president of the college was emphatic when he shared the fact that the athletic department was in a state of almost total disarray, especially in terms of finances and accountability.

"The previous AD had absolutely no control over things in the last few years of his tenure. In fact, the coaches (inmates) ran the department (insane asylum). Why, there was no financial control or accountability at all. The annual budget request that came up from the athletic department was always padded, usually significantly so. It ended up that our Vice president for Finances and I had to make the final decisions as to the actual needs of the athletic department. I am tired of being the substitute AD in respect to the budget decisions. Why am I making the cuts (and then getting the blame) when it should be the AD who makes the cuts in the individual budget requests submitted by the individual coaches, before the budget ever gets up to my office," moaned the president.

"You mean the athletic director merely sent up the budget requests for each sport exactly the way that individual coaches submitted them?" inquired Ms. Rogers.

"You bet that is what happened. The athletic director did not want to be unpopular with the coaches, especially the football and basketball coaches—the two flagship sports with the greatest booster support in town and across the state. Instead, when the Vice president (Tom Brown) and I had to cut the padded budget down to a reasonable figure it was Tom and I who got the blame from the coaches, the boosters and influential alumni," reiterated the president.

"Well, I certainly agree that it is the athletic director's responsibility to submit a reasonable budget request and to have gone through the individual budget requests submitted by individual coaches with a fine tooth comb. There should never be a padded budget or padded item submitted from the athletic director's office to the higher administration," Ms. Rogers submitted.

"Right you are," agreed the president. "If I am going to be making these decisions then, in effect, I am becoming the so-called super athletic director and I don't need an athletic director in that case," the president concluded.

Now sitting in her office before her first meeting of the athletic staff she was going over what she was going to share with the coaches. She was confident that her request for non-padded budget requests would be met with great resistance but she was determined to have each coach submit to her a realistic and non-padded budget request.

"It is either that or I will be the one to cut their stupid and exorbitant budget requests and then I will be especially ruthless with those coaches who dared to pad their budget requests," thought Lynn.

QUESTIONS FOR DISCUSSION

1. Summarize the essential elements of this situation, including each of the challenges now faced by the athletic director.
2. What does padding the budget request really mean? Describe and provide an example.
3. What is really wrong with individual coaches padding their budget requests?
4. Why should the athletic director be faced with being unpopular with the coaches by cutting their requests?
5. It is reasonable for the president to expect a non-padded budget request from the athletic program? Why or why not?
6. Is it appropriate that the president does not want to be blamed for cutting the athletic requests? Elaborate.
7. Is it normal for coaches to be angry or upset with athletic directors who don't agree with them as coaches, especially in terms of budgetary matters? Explain in detail.
8. What are some typical justifications that coaches use (to themselves) for the padding of their own budget requests that they submit to the athletic director?
9. How should the athletic director respond to the coaches' claim that if they did not pad their budget requests, that the higher administration would cut their requests anyway and that they would then end up with insufficient funds? Elaborate.
10. How would an athletic director and an athletic department gain the confidence of the higher administration that the budget that is to be submitted from the athletic arena is not padded and that all of the items in the request are actually needed?
11. Assume the role (role play) of the athletic director and indicate what you would share with the coaches in this first meeting in terms of getting them not to pad their requests that are submitted to the athletic director.
12. What steps might the athletic director take to double check and insure that each individual sport's budget that is forwarded to the central administration for final approval does not contain any padding or fat?
13. What is in it (what motivation) for the individual coaches *not to pad their requests*? What positive or negative consequences can accrue to the coaches who pad and who don't pad their requests?
14. What should the athletic director do (now and in the future) with coaches who continue to pad their budgets? Be specific.
15. Is this situation any different on the high school level? Why or why not?
16. What general administrative principles or managerial guidelines are applicable here?
17. Comments . . .

RESPONSES FOR QUESTIONS FOR DISCUSSION

_____

_____

_____

_____

_____

_____

_____

_____

_____

_____

_____

_____

_____

_____

_____

_____

_____

CASE #86

The Case of the Unsafe Practice Site

The athletic director, Stephen Stiles, received one of those phone calls that every AD fears, specifically, that an athlete had been injured at the pole vault landing pit during track practice that day. Mr. Stiles remembered just a few months earlier when he met with the head track coach and they discussed the matter of safety with the pole vault area.

Upon arriving at the practice site, he felt uneasy to see the ambulance already there and a young athlete being loaded onto a stretcher (gurney) by the attendants. Seeing the head coach (Joe Smackers) approach, he said: "Joe, what in the world happened? Fill me in on the details, please."

"Well, you know we discussed the need to upgrade the pit area and talked about insuring that we met the NFHS standards for the size of the pit area, the type of material used in creating the pit area, and the type of landing surface. We even decided to purchase and have installed all of the appropriate material."

"Well, what happened?" implored the AD.

"Stephen Combs, our sophomore track standout went out and tried the pole vault and on the very first try came down and crashed into the side of the pit area, an area where there were no protective material, and struck his head. I think he is seriously hurt. He was unconscious and I heard the ambulance attendant say that the youngster was unresponsive."

"How is it possible that he fell so far away from the center of the pit? My goodness, we decided to make the pit larger in accordance with the new standards of the NFHS and the NCAA. How could he have fallen so far out of the new projected landing area?"

"Well, that is just it. The new landing pit area was never put in. I requested the maintenance staff do it but you know how they are. They never do things on time and track practice came upon us so quickly, I never had time to really get on their backs. As a result, those incompetent idiots never made the change and here we are, practicing on last year's pit area. It is not my fault, blame those maintenance people, they never care about the kids."

QUESTIONS FOR DISCUSSION

1. What are the real main issues in this situation?
2. Whose responsibility is it to see that the pole vault pit area is safe for the youngsters? Justify your position.
3. Should the athletic director be held solely or partially responsible for something that a subordinate should have done or did do that should not have been done?

4. What about being totally, solely or partially responsible for what another person, one who is not directly responsible to the athletic director did or did not do (maintenance personnel)? Explain your position.

5. Why did the maintenance people fail to install the new pit material? Speculate?

6. What should the coach have done in terms of the maintenance staff and the use of the pit?

7. Did the track coach do anything wrong in this scenario? If so, explain in detail.

8. What responsibility does the athletic director assume in this situation as described? Be specific.

9. Who, if anyone, should the AD blame now that the injury has occurred?

10. What should the athletic director do now that the youngster is on the way to the hospital? Outline in detail the actions of the AD from this point on (for the next week or so). For example: what should be done in terms of the school principal; nurse; superintendent; parents; hospital; track coach; other coaches, etc.

11. Should this youngster who was injured even been allowed to try to pole vault? Why or why not?

12. What type of policy should have been in place that might have mitigated or prevented this situation? Be specific and state such policies.

13. What general administrative principles or managerial guidelines are applicable here?

14. Comments . . .

RESPONSES FOR QUESTIONS FOR DISCUSSION

_____

_____

_____

_____

_____

_____

_____

_____

CASE #87

The Case of the Upgrade to the Facility

The tennis courts were causing Jack Jock Flemmings, athletic director at Iroquois high school in Little Current, Florida, a real headache. In fact, the tennis courts, rather the condition of the courts, have become a source of real concern to him in recent weeks. Two factors combined for a situation that had quickly changed and had begun to put some real pressure on him as the athletic director. First, the overall condition of the courts have gradually deteriorated over the years until, today, they are obviously in a state of disrepair. And, second, the newest member of the school board, Big Daddy Big-Bucks, was an avid tennis player who was still an outstanding tennis player at age 50. Evidently, he had played tennis steadily ever since his graduation from college where he won the Ivy League championship his senior year.

"OK, so the board voted that we move the junior varsity tennis program up to varsity status in two years. Big deal. No one really cared about tennis until Mr. Big-Bucks came to town and got himself elected on the basis of upgrading the entire sports program as well as the academic status of the school. Do they (the board members) really know how bad the courts are? Why, I bet the courts will have to be totally replaced if we are really going to play top notch varsity tennis," concluded Flemmings.

The president of the school board called Mr. Flemmings the next morning and said: "Jack, we need to start moving on this tennis thing. You know how much the board has been influenced by Big Daddy Big-Bucks—now everyone seemingly wants a winning tennis program yesterday. But you and I know that our immediate problem is with the condition of the tennis courts. What I, what the board is asking you to accomplish is to do your homework and come back with a formal, written recommendation, an outline if you will, of what you want the board to consider in terms of what will be needed for a winning tennis program, facility upgrades included. I think we need this information by the next board meeting. Can you do this for me, Jack, for yourself, I might add?"

"Ah, why, sure, I guess so," replied the athletic director. "However, you know that I am not the resident expert on tennis facilities. Why, I never even played tennis. But, I will find and get the information for you, you can rest assured of that for sure."

"Great! I knew you would say "yes" and would be on board with our team," the board president indicated. "Why, I told Big Daddy Big-Bucks only this morning that you would have a top flight proposal ready to present at the next meeting. He is expecting it Jack, don't disappoint him or the board."

QUESTIONS FOR DISCUSSION

1. What circumstances got the athletic director into the predicament? Provide a complete summary.

2. How would you suggest the athletic director proceed from this point onward?

3. What are some factors that the athletic director should be cognizant of when writing specifications for the potential bidding process? What are some pitfalls in writing specifications for large and expensive (and complicated) facilities?

4. How much, in your area, would it cost to demolish six broken-down tennis courts and accompanying paraphernalia and to truck it away to the local landfill? Research it.

5. Should Mr. Flemmings seek out Big Daddy Big-Bucks? If so, when and how (under what circumstances)? If so, assume a role-playing stance as the athletic director and share what you would say to the board member.

6. How should the athletic director go about securing honest, appropriate and correct information and recommendations about costs and different methods of improvement, repair and/or replacement?

7. How should the athletic director insure that the information he obtains about the *present condition* of the courts is accurate and appropriate? What about the use of outside experts? Where can an athletic director go to obtain up-to-date information and data *on future tennis courts, their construction and* upkeep?

8. What criteria would one use to determine whether it would be wiser (and more cost effective) to (A) *keep old tennis courts* and to repair them or (B) to demolish and remove the courtsand *build brand new ones* (including accompanying paraphernalia).

9. What are some of the important elements that the athletic director should be aware of when evaluating or assessing tennis courts (or any outdoor facility, for that matter)?

10. What are some physical elements that the school board needs to consider when upgrading current courts or constructing new tennis courts that are to be used by the school as well as the community (night and day)? Be specific in your recommendations that would enhance the usage of the facilities both as a recreational and as a competitive site.

11. What type of upkeep do tennis courts need on a consistent basis? What needs to be done periodically to the courts and associated physical elements? Be specific.

12. Do some research and find out what six courts would cost in your area *and* what would be the estimated cost of annual maintenance.

13. Develop some sample policies, practices and procedures for these courts that would govern the management of the courts for both school and recreational (town) use. Actually list the policies, etc., and provide a justification or rationale for each.

14. What should be the form of the report (recommendations) that the athletic director has to make to the board? What should the athletic director use in verbally addressing the board? What about written or printed material?

15. What steps might the athletic director take in an effort to be prepared for any and all questions that might come from the board following his formal presentation? Be specific and outline a course of action.

16. List some general principles or guidelines that might be appropriate in this situation?

17. Comments . . .

RESPONSES FOR QUESTIONS FOR DISCUSSION

_____

_____

_____

_____

_____

_____

_____

_____

_____

_____

_____

_____

_____

_____

_____

Case #88

The Case of the Unkempt Facilities

The athletic director, Veronica Young, found herself the subject of criticism by the superintendent. It seems that the superintendent and the principal had both received complaints (some relayed from school board members) about the poor condition of some of the athletic facilities, especially the football stadium, the track and field site and the indoor pool.

The superintendent had stated: "Veronica, you have just got to be more on the ball with this facility thing. You know as well as I do that we cannot have the public going around complaining that the athletic facilities are in a state of disrepair, can we? You are the athletic director; it is your job to see that this kind of thing doesn't happen. I don't enjoy getting phone calls from tax payers, and especially from board members, complaining about your failure to do *your* job."

"How in the world does he expect me to do that?" thought Veronica. "Why, the director of plant management is in charge of the facilities and he never does his job. I keep calling over requests for repairs but nothing ever happens."

In meeting with the coaches later that week, the athletic director relayed the earlier conversation with the superintendent and asked for help and input from everyone in addressing this problem. "We need to address this as a cohesive group, people, or else we are all going to sink together. We must have neat and safe facilities. When members of the public start to complain about our unkempt facilities, things have really gone downhill. O.K., people, lets get to it. Any suggestions?"

"Well," said the women's field hockey coach, "we could start with the maintenance people and their boss. They are the ones who decide what is to be done and when and by whom. You, as athletic director, can only ask for things to be done, not demand. It is still up to plant management (maintenance) to actually make the final decision and to do the work."

"Yea, but when any of us ask for things to be done, the athletic director has to call over and practically beg for help," chimed in the softball coach.

"Should we develop a system of written requests so at least we have a record of what is being requested and when, as well as where, the work is or is not actually done?" added the baseball coach.

Questions for Discussion

1. Summarize the salient elements of this case.
2. Who is at fault in this situation? Explain your position.
3. What has the athletic director, evidently, failed to do in the past in terms of dealing with the upkeep of the athletic facilities and the maintenance department?

4. Was it a good move to share the conversation between the superintendent and the athletic director with the coaches or was this a sign of weakness? Why or why not?

5. Can the athletic director be held responsible for the upkeep of the athletic facilities when the plant management director does not report to the athletic director and doesn't have to do what the athletic director requests? Explain.

6. What might be some positive suggestions that could come out of this meeting (and any follow-up meeting) with the coaches? Elaborate.

7. What should the athletic director do in terms of the director of plant management, if anything? Provide a rationale for your response.

8. Why is the superintendent so angry? Be specific.

9. How might the athletic director have responded to the comments made by the superintendent? Provide examples.

10. What are the public relations consequences for the athletic director and the athletic department of having unkempt or unsafe facilities?

11. Explain the possible consequences (pros and cons) of *making all of the requests by phone* when dealing with facilities and facility management.

12. Provide some suggestions as to how the athletic director might deal with members of the general public, the parents, the school board and others in terms of the status of (neat, safe, uncluttered and organized) facilities.

13. Ideally, what should be the relationship between the athletic director and the director of plant management (maintenance) in terms of facility care, repair and maintenance? Ideally, to whom should the plant manager report to relative to athletic facilities? Justify your recommendations.

14. What are some of the key facilities and facility areas that athletic directors need to be especially concerned about in terms of mere appearance (not to mention safety)? Why.

15. Develop succinct policy statements (in detail) outlining how a high school athletic department should operate in terms of facility management.

16. What are the general principles or guidelines that are applicable in this case?

17. Comments . .

RESPONSES FOR QUESTIONS FOR DISCUSSION

_____

_____

_____

_____

_____

CASE #89

The Case of the Poorly Organized Inventory Process

The status of the equipment and supplies at Englewood High School in Scottsville, Washington was really in sad shape. It seemed that nobody (coaches, maintenance staff or the athletic director) really was 100% sure where all the equipment items were located, if they were even on hand within the school. No one was sure how this state of confusion came about but everyone agreed that it was an intolerable situation and something had to be done.

The athletic director, Monroe Scott, was really upset, upset with himself mainly for allowing this situation to develop to its present state. Actually, it wasn't all his fault since he inherited the situation some three years ago. However, he had not really done anything significant to correct the ever-deteriorating situation and the ever-gradual decline in the handling, storage and care of equipment and supplies that continued on his watch.

"I know that I bear some responsibility for this mess," he told the principal (Ray Hunt) one morning when they met to discuss the inventory/storage problem. "But, I am determined to do something about it," he added.

"Well, Monroe, I am glad to hear it because at last Tuesday's board meeting this topic came up when one of the parents complained to the board and the superintendent about the wasteful budgetary practices of your department due to the fact that no one seems to know what equipment and supplies are on hand. In fact, it was claimed that, in the past, the school had gone ahead and purchased items only to later find out that the very same item(s) had already been in the school. But, no one knew about it because the athletic inventory was so screwed up," concluded Mr. Hunt.

"OK. I admit I have a challenge. But I am up to it. In fact, I have a meeting on Friday with all of the coaches and another meeting on Monday with the maintenance people to begin to address this problem. Don't worry, I will handle it."

QUESTIONS FOR DISCUSSION

1. Outline the essential elements of this problematic situation from the school's perspective and from the viewpoint of the athletic director.
2. Just how much at fault is the athletic director in this situation, given the fact that he is relatively new to the job at Englewood High School?
3. Who else is at fault in this situation as outlined above? Be specific and justify your position.
4. Why has this problem progressed to this stage? Why did it take a complaint from the taxpayer at the school board for people to react?

5.   Is the athletic director approaching this problem in a professional and appropriate fashion? Why or why not?

6.   How should the athletic director proceed in the meeting with the coaches? What should the athletic director share with the coaches?

7.   How should the athletic director proceed in the meeting with the plant management/maintenance staff? What should the athletic director share with the coaches?

8.   How would you suggest setting up an inventory procedure for the high school athletic program? Be specific and explain how a well-managed and well-structured inventory/storage process works.

9.   What role should individual coaches play in the inventory/storage process?

10. What role should the maintenance staff play in the inventory/storage process?

11. How would you suggest equipment items and supplies be handed out to athletes at the beginning of the season and collected from athletes at the end of the season?

12. How do you keep track of who has what items? How do you keep track of who has handed in the items for washing/cleaning?

13. Create an inventory sheet or form (on a separate sheet of paper) that might be used to keep on-going accurate records of equipment and supplies.

14. Who should be given responsibility for maintaining inventory of each sport? Should the coaches of each sport? Should a different (neutral) person? What about someone from maintenance?

15. Who should be given the responsibility for insuring that equipment items are in a state of good repairs and for those items that need refurbishment that the items are repaired?

16. Cite some general administrative principles or guidelines that are applicable in this scenario?

17. Comments . . .

RESPONSES FOR QUESTIONS FOR DISCUSSION

_____

_____

_____

_____

_____

_____

_____

CASE #90

The Case of the Poorly Organized Game Promotion

The assistant athletic director, Gail Youngston, was so very proud of all of the efforts that she and her staff of student interns had put into the game promotion for yesterday's evening hockey game. The game was the second of the season and it involved the school's archrival, Roosterville State College. If only it had gone as planned, everything would have been just fine. She and the student helpers would have been heroes, no doubt. And she had been so proud when the athletic director had put her in charge of the home event (for the first time) since he was going to be out of town

Youth supporters are the future of sports programs.
[Courtesy of Purdue University Sports Information]

with the women's basketball team that had a tournament over the weekend.

However, not all went well. In fact, last night's promotional activity that she had scheduled to take place between the second and third period was an outright disaster, there was no point in denying that. Of course, her old college professor had always told her and the other students in his class that athletic administrators would be faced with problems, challenges and disasters—no matter how well one planned and worked. So, maybe she shouldn't feel so bad. Of course, the call this morning from the athletic director, Mr. Samuel Thompson, really scared the dickens out of her since he was so very curt when he said: "Gail, get up to my office the moment you are free and bring me up-to-date on this disaster of yours that took place at last night's hockey game while I was out of town."

"How was I suppose to know that the idiots in the stands would let loose with all 900 of the seat cushions that we gave away to the first 900 people through the turnstiles? I would love to get my hands around the throat of the idiot who threw first seat cushion onto the ice? People, why they are just like a herd of cattle. If one idiot throws a cushion, then the next person has to throw one, and the next and the next. Why it looked like it was raining black and gold cushions for about 5-10 seconds. Of course, it didn't help matters that one of the referees was hit in the eye with a seat cushion and had to leave for the hospital with a severe eye injury. And our stupid coach, what a jerk. Why did he have to face the crowd and wave his arms encouraging the fans to throw more seats? And, again in the morning paper, that stupid coach was quoted as saying: 'I thought that we finally got some real fan support with all of those flying seat cushions hitting the ice following that horrendous call by the official.' What was that stupid jerk thinking?" Gail said to herself as she trudged up the three flights of stairs to the AD's office.

Questions for Discussion

1. What really went wrong with the promotion? Summarize the goofs that occurred.
2. How could Gail have prevented this problem from occurring? Would announcements before the game been effective or would it just put ideas in the fan's minds?
3. With game promotions involving all types of give-aways how can athletic administrators continue to use this type of promotional activity without also having the items that are given away used as missiles and thrown onto the playing field/surface?
4. Is the athletic director especially angry because the problem occurred while he was out of town?
5. Is the AD still going to be held responsible by his superiors or can he rightfully blame the assistant in charge of the game? Can he blame the hockey coach? Speculate.
6. Whose fault is it that the hockey coach behaved like an idiot? How might his action been prevented?
7. Can Gail use the argument that problems will always happen in spite of the best laid plans? Will this position get her off the proverbial hook with her boss? Elaborate.
8. What should be Gail's explanation (to the athletic director) of why things went so badly? Why?
9. Should she blame (or partially blame) the student interns? Why or why not?
10. What type of damage control should the athletic department attempt to implement now, after the fact? Be specific.
11. Contemplate what the boss of the AD might say to the athletic director?
12. How might the athletic director respond to an inquiry by his boss? Be specific in providing an explanation of events and the culpability of those involved.
13. What other type of game promotion (between periods) might the assistant athletic director have implemented (that would not have resulted in such a disaster)? What might be the potential dangers that the administrator might want to be watchful for in this proposed promotional activity?
14. Cite some general administrative principles or concepts that are applicable in this type of situation?
15. Comments . . .

Responses for Questions for Discussion

_____

_____

_____

A Partial List of Suggested Publications, Journals and Magazines and Selected Journal Articles

SELECTED JOURNALS

Academic Athletic Journal
American School & University — Facilities, Purchasing and Business Administration
Annual of Applied Research in Coaching and Athletics
Athletic Business
Athletic Facilities and Purchasing Journal
Coach and Athletic Director
CoSida Digest
Cyber Journal of Sport Marketing
European Journal of Sport Management
IEG Sponsorship Report from the IEG International Events Groups
International Journal of Physical Education
International Journal of Sport
International Journal of Sport Management (IJSM)
International Review for the Sociology of Sport
Journal of the International Council of Health, Physical Education and Recreation (ICHPER)
Journal of Management Studies
Journal or Physical Education, Recreation and Dance JOPERD
Journal of the Philosophy of Sport
Journal of Revenue & Pricing Management (Athens Greece)
Journal of Sport Management
Journal of Sports Marketing & Sponsorship on Relationship Marketing
Journal of Sport Psychology
Leisure Studies
Mid-Atlantic Journal of Business — W. Paul Stillman School of Business, Seton Hall University
NIRSA — Journal of the National Intramural-Recreational Sports Association
Quest

Sociology of Sport Journal

Schole — a journal of leisure studies and recreation education

Sport Business Journal

Sport Journal — quarterly on-line, which is available free to the public
      http://www.thesportjournal.org

Sport Management Review

Sport Marketing Quarterly

Sports Marketing & Sponsorship

Sport Marketing Quarterly

Strategies

The Physical Educator

The Sport Psychologist

SELECTED JOURNAL ARTICLES AND BOOKS

Baker, J.A. & Collins M.S. (1995). *A bibliography of completed research on administration of pnysical education and athletics 1971-1982*. Champaign, Illinois: Stipes Publishing L. L. C.

Blanchard, Ken and Shula, Don. (1995). *Everyone's a coach*. Grand Rapids, Michigan: Zondervan Publishing House.

DeSensi, J. (1996). *Ethics in sport management.* Morgantown, West Virginia: Fitness Information Technologies.

Doughterty, N.J., Auxter, D., Goldberger, A.S., & Heinzmann, G.S. (1994). *Sport, physical activity, and the Law*. Champaign, Illinois: Human Kinetics.

Dougherty, N.J., Goldberger, A. S. & Carpenter, L. J. (2003). *Sport, physical activity, and the law* (2nd edition). Sagamore Publishing

Epstein, A. (2003). *Sports law*. Delmar Publishers

Event management for sport directors. (1996). American Sport Education Program. Champaign, Illinois: Human Kinetics Publishers.

Hernandez, R.A. (2003). *Managing sport organizations*. Champaign, Illinois: Human Kinetics Publishers.

Johnson, J.R. (1996). *Promotion for sport directors*. Champaign, Illinois: Human Kinetics Publishers.

Kestner, J. (1996). *Program evaluation for sport directors*. Champaign, Illinois: Human Kinetics Publishers.

Mullin, B.J., Hardy, S. & Sutton, W. (1993). *Sport marketing*. Champaign, Illinois: Human Kinetics Publishers.

Olson, J.R. (1996). *Facility and equipment management for sport directors.* Champaign, Illinois: Human Kinetics Publishers.

Parent and Education Title IX Team Project. (1996). Reston, VA.: NAGWS/AAHPERD.

Parkhouse, Bonnie L. (Ed.). (1991*). The management of sport: Its foundation and application.* St. Louis, Mo.: Mosby Year-Book and the National Association for Sport and Physical Education.

Parks, J.B. & Zanger, B.R.K. (1990). *Sport and fitness management — Career strategies and professional content.* Champaign, Illinois: Human Kinetics Publishers.

Parks, Janet B. & Zanger, Beverly, R.K. Editors. (1990). *Sport and fitness management — Career strategies and professional content.* Champaign, Illinois: Human Kinetics.

Patter, M.L. (1997). *Understanding research methods: An overview of the essentials.* Los Angeles, CA: Pyrczak Publishing.

Schneider, R.C. & Stier, W. F., Jr. (2000). Sport management curricular standards 2000 study — graduate level. *International Journal of Sport Management, 1*(2), 137-149.

Schneider, R.C., & Stier, W.F., Jr. (2003). A comparison of recommended educational experiences as perceived by athletic directors and principals. *North Carolina Journal of HPERD, 39*(1), 29-35.

Sawyer, T.H. (2003). *Facilities planning for health, fitness, physical activity, recreation, and sports: Concepts and applications* (10th edition). Sagamore Publishing.

Slack, T. (1997). *Understanding sport organizations: The application of organization theory.* Champaign, Illinois: Human Kinetics Publishers.

Sports law: Cases and materials (2000). Ohio: Anderson Publishers.

Stier, Jr., W.F. (1988). 2nd ed. *Policies, procedures and practices for intercollegiate athletics.* Published by State University of New York Press. Also published by Resources in Education. (ERIC), ED301558.

Stier, Jr., W.F. (1994). *Fundraising for sport and recreation.* (1994). Champaign, Illinois: Human Kinetics Publishers. Note: this book has also been translated into Chinese by Dr. Philip Cheng, Associate Professor, Department of Physical Education, National Taiwan Normal University, Taipei, Taiwan.

Stier, Jr., W.F. (1994). *Successful sport fund-raising.* Dubuque, Iowa: Wm. C. Brown & Benchmark.

Stier, Jr., W.F. (1997). *Sport management: Career planning and professional preparation.* Boston, MA: American Press.

Stier, Jr., W.F (1997). *Coaching modern basketball — Hints, strategies and tactics.* Boston, MA: Allyn & Bacon.

Stier, Jr., W.F. (1997). *More fantastic fundraisers for sport and recreation.* Champaign, Illinois: Human Kinetics Publishers.

Stier, Jr., William. Alternative career paths in physical education: Sport management. (1993, August). Monograph-ERIC Digest. ERIC [Educatonal Resources Information Center] CLearinghouse On Teaching and Teacher Education, American Association of Colleges for Teacher Education. Funded through the Office of Educational Research and Improvement, U.S. Department of Education. ERIC is the largest and most frequently used education database in the world.

Stier, Jr., W.F. (1998). Problem solving for coaches. Boston, MA: American Press.

Stier, Jr., W.F. (1998). 2nd ed. Coaching: Concepts and strategies. Boston, MA: American Press.

Stier, Jr. W.F. It's all in the planning. (1998, November). Athletic Management, X(6), 26, 28.

Stier, Jr. W.F. Fundraising — An essential competency for the sport manager in the 21st century. (1999). *The Mid-Atlantic Journal of Business,35*(2 & 3), 93-103.

Stier, Jr., W.F. (1999, July). *Resource manual and test bank for management of sport, recreation and fitness programs: Concepts and practices.* Boston, MA: Allyn & Bacon.

Stier, Jr., W.F. (1999, January). *Managing sport, recreation and fitness programs: Concepts and practices.* Boston, MA: Allyn & Bacon.

Stier, Jr. W.F. (2000, July). A fundraising and promotional primer for sport: Part two. *Applied Research in Coaching and Athletics Annual, 15,* 12-147.

Stier, W.F., Jr. The past, present and future of sport management. *PROCEEDINGS – Current Situations and New Directions for Sports Management: From the Perspectives of Cultural Differences.* The 2000 International Sport Management Congress, presented by the Korean National University of Physical Education, Seoul, Korea and the Korean National Physical Education Association.

Stier, W.F., Jr. Fund-raising and promotion secrets for the busy athletic director. *PROCEED-INGS — National Athletic Business Conference.* (2000). Wisconsin: Madison. Athletic Business.

Stier, Jr., W.F. (2000, February). *Fund raising made E-Z.* Deerfield Beach, Florida: E-Z Publishers.

Stier, W.F., Jr. (November, 2000). The new paradigm of sport marketing, promotions and fundraising in the 21st century. *PROCEEDINGS The 2000 Seoul International Sport Science Congress* — New Paradigms of Sport & Physical Education in the 21st Century, Seoul, Korea.

Stier, W.F., Jr., & Schneider, R. C. (2000). What high school principals expect of their athletics directors: A national investigation. *Journal of Physical Education, Recreation, and Dance, 71*(8), 45-49.

Stier, Jr. W.F. (2000, Summer). A fundraising and promotion primer for sport: Part one. *Applied Research in Coaching and Athletics Annual 2000, 15*, 219-242.

Stier, W.F., Jr. & Schneider, R. C. (2000). Sport management curricular standards 2000 study — Undergraduate level. *International Journal of Sport Management. 1*(1), 56-69.

Stier, W.F., Jr. (2003), *Marketing, fundraising and promotions for sport, recreation and fitness programs.* Boston, MA: American Press.

Stier, W.F., Jr. (2001, Summer). Essential skills, competencies and knowledge expected of athletic directors—By their principals. *International Sport Journal. 5*(2), 18-30.

Stier, W.F., Jr. (2001, Spring). Sport management internships — A double-edged sword. *The Clipboard, 2*(3), 5.

Stier, W.F., Jr. (2001). Current status of sport management and athletic (sport) administration programs in the 21ˢᵗ ventury. *International Journal of Sport Management, 2*(1), 66-79.

Stier, W.F., Jr. (2001). *The development of sport management. In The business of sport — Perspectives. Volume 3.* [chapter in a book published March 2001 by International Council of Sport Science and Physical Education (ICSSPE/CIEPSS) — Berlin, Germany].

Stier, W.F., Jr., & Schneider, R. (2002). Desirable qualities, attributes and characteristics of future interscholastic athletic directors—As recommended by high school athletic directors. (2002, Summer). *Applied Research in Coaching and Athletics Annual. 17*, 26-42.

Stier, W.F., Jr., (2002). Sport management internships — from theory to practice. *Strategies, 15*(4), 7-9.

Stier, W.F., Jr., & Schneider, R.C. (2003). Necessary personal qualities, attributes and characteristics for directing athletics: NCAA presidents' views. *Annual of Applied Research in Coaching and Athletics. 18* (194-211).

Stier, W.F., Jr., & Schneider, R.C. (2003). Recommended professional experiences and accomplishments for future athletic directors—A national survey of high school athletic directors. *Illinois Association of Health, Physical Education, Recreation and Dance Journal, 50,* 4-11.

Stumbo, N.J., & Folkerth, J.E. (2003). *Improving leisure services through marketing action.* Sagamore Publishing

Wolohan, J.T. and Mathes, S. (1996). *Title IX and sexual harassment of student athletes: A look back and to the future, 10,* 65-75.

APPENDIX B

Index

Accountable, 19
Administration by walking around
    (ABWA), 77, 355
Adversarial relationships, 57
Adversity, 104
Advisers, 97
American Red Cross, 24
Anticipation, 4
Antidotal information, 126
Appeal process, 49
Appearance, 223
Applying for a job, 393
Arbitrary decisions, 49
ARC move, 26
Art and Science, xviii, 5
Assertive (professional), 102
Assets, 79
Assumptions of risk, 16
Athletes, 92
Athletic administrator(s), 12
Athletic banquet, 433
Athletic director, 19, 467
Athletic participation, 52
Attitude, 12
Audience, 11
Authority, 80
Awards ceremony, 409

Backgrounds, 11
Benefits, xviii
Biases, 11
Blame, 46
Blaming others, 106
Blueprint, 38
Bluffing, 108
Boss (new), 285, 305, 327
Boycott, 153

Bridges (burning), 103
Budget process, 359

Calm, cool and collected (3Cs), 70, 71
Capricious decisions, 49
Career planning, 265
Carte blanche, 51
Case studies, xvii, 118, 121, 125
Case Study Tenets, xvii, 118
CEO, 44, 94
Challenges, xvi, 14
Change, 73
Change for change sake, 80
Change in administration, 101
Chapter Objectives, xvii
Cheerleaders, 429
Chicago Tribune, 25
Children of coaches, 397
Clients, 55
Coach, 195
Code of conduct, 141
College course work, 7
Collegial approach, 57, 58
Communication, 10
Communication skills, 9
Competent, 41
Competent administrators, 57
Competitive sports, 6
Complainer, 347
Complaints, 55
Compliments, 102
Compromise, 74
Concept, 26
Conceptual understanding, 7
Concession stand, 371
Conditioning, 185
Conferences, 7

Confidence, 70, 98
Confident, 70
Confidentiality, 49, 50, 51
Conflict of interest, 53
Confronting problems, 8
Conservative coach, 235
Consistency, 20
Constituencies, 8
Constituents, 55
Contests, 149
Control, 18
Controversial, 60
Controversy, 70
Corporate sponsorship, 437
Counterproductive, 57
Cover up, 60
Credibility, 25
Crisis management, 71, 269
Crisis mode, 13
Criticism, 56, 103, 108
Crossing the "T"s, 9, 81
Crowd control, 421
Custodian, 281
Customer, 53

Damage control, 35, 72
Data, 35, 78
Decision making, 20, 68, 257
Decisions, 15, 37, 59, 68, 79, 273
Decisive, 72
Delegation, 313
Demands of athletes, 189
Departmental handbook, 425
Differences of opinion, 12
Discretion, 49
Discrimination, 455
Dismissal from team, 133, 343
Disorganized, 219
Distraction(s), 13
Doing right things, 56
Doing things right, 56
Dotting the "I"s, 9, 81
Dress code, 173
Drug testing, 145
Due process, 48

Easy, 16
Effective, 9

Efficient, 9
Eligibility, 181
Embarrassment, 50, 92
Emotional, 69
Empathetic, 52
Employees, 94
End result(s), 42
Equipment, 44, 165
Error, 41
Ethics (ethical considerations), 58
Evaluations of coaches, 227, 405
Exceptions, 22
Excuses, 106
Exemplars, 125
Expectations, 83
Expectations of coaches, 227
Expedient, 58
Experience, 6
Experiences, 41
Extenuating circumstances, 40, 74

Facilities, 44, 165, 487, 491
Fact finding questions, 36
Facts, 35, 79
Faint of heart, 12
Family members, 97
Flexible, 74
Firing, 45, 94, 189
Firing line, 6, 75
Fiscal irresponsibility, 479
5Ps, 21, 83, 100
Following directions, 239
Forgetfulness, 289
French Fry Fiasco, 24
Fundamental principles, xvii
Fundraising, 293, 375, 437

Game promotion, 499
Game substituting, 149
Gathering facts, 35
General public, 8
Glass ceiling, 455
Global vision, xv
Goal(s), 8, 443
Grain of salt, 78
Group interaction, 125
Grudges, 57
Guide, 38

Handbook(s), 21, 84, 425
Hard person, 74
Harvard, 123
Hidden agendas, 75
Hindsight, 41
Hiring, 104
Honest, 59
Human behavior, 44
Humiliation, 92
Hurdles, 69

Image, 223
Impartiality, 20, 53, 70
Impolite, 261
Impropriety, 60
Inanimate objects, 44
Inconsiderate coach, 243
Indispensable, 301
Influence, 82
Influential people, 98
Information, 78
Injured athletes, 169
Integrity, 70
Interpersonal relationships, 8
Inventory process, 495

Job(s), 97, 463
Jump the chain of command, 98

Know it all, 76

Lack of resources, 47
Lazy, 12
Legal rights, 48
Legality, 47
Liberty Fund, 24
Listening rules, 10
Listening skills, 10
Living under the microscope, 215
Lone Ranger, 57, 59
Losing, 211
Loyalty, 99

Marriage, 331
Major changes, 72
Manuel, 83
MBA degree, 123
McDonald's Corporation, 24

Meal money (game contests), 161
Media, 26, 297
Mentor, 459
Message(s), 10
Messy athletic director, 471
Method of operation, 99
Missing equipment and supplies, 363
Mistakes, 39, 74, 107
Mitigating circumstances, 4
Moral implications, 59
Morally, 49

Negating, 4
Negative atmosphere, 351
Negative motivation, 231
Negotiate, 74
Newsletter, 309
News media, 26, 297
New organization, 79
New sports, 157
Nuisance, 4

Objective, 8, 53
Obstacles to communication, 11
Outcomes, 14
Outline, 38
Overreact, 70

Patron, 53
Part-time coach, 413
Partying coach, 339
Pass to play, 381
Patron, 53
Pay to play, 401
People business, 44
Perceptions, 12, 43, 46, 53, 60
Personally involved, 75
Persuasive, 11
Philanthropy, 25
Philosophies, xvi, 21
Pitfalls, 71
Plan of attack, 199
Plans, 19, 40
Playbook, 84
Policies, xvi, 21
Political climate(s), 39
Political ramifications, 36
Politically astute, 73

Potential problem, 24
Power, 15
Practices, xvi, 21
Predecessor, 107
Prejudices, 11
Pressure, 15, 18, 69
Prevent problems, 4, 17
Principles, xv
Priorities, xvi, 21
Privilege, 52
Proactive, 71
Problem situation, 107
Problem solver, 4
Problem solving by crisis, 13
Problem(s), xvi, 5, 95
Problematic situations, 60, 95, 124
Problems with athletes, 118, 131
Problems with coaches, 118, 119, 193
Problems with controversial issues, 118, 120, 317
Problems with other individuals, 118, 120, 255
Problems with policies, practices, procedures,
    Priorities and philosophies, 118, 120, 379
Problems with special situations, 118, 121, 441
Procedures, xvi, 21
Processes, 14, 23, 42
Production, 20
Professional opportunities, 7
Promotion, 323
Public, 14
Public scrutiny, 15
Publications, 503
Publicity director, 447
Publicly, 95
Purchase order, 247

Questions for Discussion, xvii, 121

Real world, 126
Reality, 43
Reality-based cases, 124
Reasonable amount of time, 35
Recognize problems, xv, 35
Records (keeping), 81
Recruitment for college, 177
Red Queen Syndrome, 77
Reduce impact, 4
Relationships, 92, 93, 102, 203
Remembering the past, 207

Rent-a-coach, 335, 405
Renting a facility, 475
Reoccurrence, 4, 42
Repertoire, xviii
Reprimand, 95
Resignation of a coach, 251
Resolve problems
Respect, 56, 77
Resources, 47
Responsibility, 15, 18
Results, 19, 20, 106
Risks, 14
Rude awakening(s), 54
Rule, 21
Rules of the game, 48

Save face, 50
Secretive, 60
Seeking help, 96
September 11th, 25
Sexual harassment, 319
Shoe purchases, 417
Solve problems, 17
SOPPs, 21
Sources of problems, xvi, 3
Spokesperson, 46
Staff, 93, 94
Strategic action plans (SAPs), xviii, 22, 34, 36,
    37, 38, 122,
Strategies, xv
Stress, 13
Superiors, supervisor, 98, 101, 305, 327
Survival strategies, xvii
Sympathetic, 52

Tactics, xvii
Talk is cheap, 40
Talk the talk and walk the walk, 46
Team approach, 57
Team building, 44
Teamwork, 44
Theory, 126
Thick skin, 56
Time, 13, 35
Time management, 22
Timeliness, 8, 22
Title IX, 157, 367
Tools, 79

TQM (Total Quality Management), 53
Transportation Policies, 169
Travel squad, 389
Truth, 22
Tunnel vision , xv

Unbiased, 53, 55
Unexpected, 69
Upgrading facilities, 487
Unkempt facilities, 491
Unsafe practice site, 483

Vacation policies, 385
Vacuum, 39
Verbally assaulted, 75
Violence, 137

World Trade Center, 24
Worse case scenario syndrome, 72
Would-be coach, 451